SPECIAL EDUCATION LAW

SPECIAL EDUCATION LAW

Laura F. Rothstein

Professor of Law
University of Houston

Longman
New York & London

Longman, 95 Church Street, White Plains, N.Y. 10601

Associated companies:
Longman Group Ltd., London
Longman Cheshire Pty., Melbourne
Longman Paul Pty., Auckland
Copp Clark Pitman, Toronto

Executive editor: Raymond T. O'Connell
Production editor: Carol Harwood
Cover design: Michael Jung
Production supervisor: Kathleen M. Ryan

Library of Congress Cataloging-in-Publication Data

Rothstein, Laura F.
    Special education law.

    Bibliography: p.
    Includes index.
    1. Special education—Law and legislation—
United States I. Title.
KF4210.R68 1988   344.73'0791   89-8170
ISBN 0-8013-0209-9   347.304791

ABCDEFGHIJ-ML-99 98 97 96 95 94 93 92 91 90

To My Parents,
Eric and Dorothy Friesen

Contents

Cases in Order of Appearance

Cases—Alphabetized

Preface

In 1975 Congress passed major legislation to facilitate the education of all handicapped children in the United States. The legislation was passed as a result of constitutionally based challenges to exclusion of handicapped children. The 1975 Education for All Handicapped Children Act, along with Section 504 of the Rehabilitation Act and other laws, has provided a framework for a highly specific set of legal requirements for the provision of special education.

These laws have been in existence for over a decade, and there has been an extensive body of judicial law interpreting the requirements under the special education statutes. Special education is one of the major issues with which school administrators and school attorneys must deal on a regular basis. The cost of providing special education is high, but the cost of not providing special education may be even higher. For the educational agency there is the potential loss of federal funding to state and local school systems. There may even be additional out-of-pocket financial liability when a school fails to comply with state and federal legal requirements. For the taxpayer, subsidizing an individual who is totally dependent on the government is a high cost. And for the handicapped individual, the *personal* cost is great.

It is becoming increasingly important for school administrators, including local superintendents, principals, special education directors, and psychologists, as well as regional and state administrators, to have familiarity with the legal requirements. Attorneys who represent schools and those who represent the parents of handicapped children also need to have an in depth understanding of the details of the laws that apply to children entitled to special education. It is also important for teachers, both regular classroom and special education teachers, to be aware of the laws that affect them.

The philosophy of this book is primarily one of prevention. The goal is to provide information that will enable policies to be developed and decisions to be made that comply with current legal requirements in order to avoid litigation to the maximum extent possible. Formal dispute resolution is costly and is not the best use of scarce education dollars. Of course, not all disputes or disagreements can be avoided, and the book discusses the procedures that are required should informal resolution or advance policy-making prove inadequate to address a problem. It is the hope of the author, however, that knowledge of the law can prevent many problems.

The text is designed to be used by both graduate students in education and by law students. It is the aim of the author that the materials should be usable by education students whose goal is administration, as well as by education students who are intending to be or who are classroom teachers, in both regular and special education. Law students who would find the materials of value are those who are interested in rights of the handicapped, school law generally, special education law in particular, or children's rights.

The format of the material is somewhat akin to textbooks used in law schools, with some modifications. The major judicial decisions, statutes, and regulations are presented as the primary resource material. Other decisions and related commentary are included as expansions on the major cases and legislative materials. Thought questions are included to highlight underlying policy issues, and problems are provided to have the student consider unresolved issues as well as practical and tactical considerations in addressing a specific problem. The goal is that the reader will consider not only whether current law is sound policy but also that the reader will be able to respond to specific problems that are likely to occur on a regular basis in our schools.

It is important to note that although the past decade has brought a substantial degree of clarification about many of the special education requirements that may have seemed ambiguous in 1975, many issues still remain unresolved. As to those issues, the various viewpoints are offered, and where appropriate, commentary provides an analysis of what seems to be required in certain types of cases.

I wish to thank those who assisted in writing this book: To Jan Cunningham, Regina Fisher, Colleen Scott, Sandra Jackson, and Juanita Alt for typing the manuscript, and to Michael Brady, Kay Lambert, Jan Sheldon, Linda Bluth, and Eric and Dorothy Friesen for reading and commenting on the manuscript, and to Alan York for his research assistance. My appreciation is also extended to Dean Robert L. Knauss, for providing institutional support for this project, and to Gail Sorenson for suggesting to me the need for a text on this topic.

Special thanks to Mark, Julia, and Lisa for their patience and support.

CHAPTER 1

History of Special Education Law

SPECIAL EDUCATION BEFORE THE 1970s

The development of educational philosophy toward handicapped children in schools occurred in several phases.[1] The first phase, in the late 1800s, was a philosophy of relieving stress on the teacher and other children by removing handicapped children to separate, special classes. This segregationist attitude continued in later years, but the underlying basis emphasized the need to avoid stress on the handicapped child. Eventually some educational programming was provided, first in the form of diluted academic training and later in the form of manual training. Again, the training was still segregated for the most part, and there was a continued concern about avoiding disruption in the classroom. Many students with handicaps were never sent to school.

By the mid-1900s an important shift had begun—the recognition of the worth and dignity of the person that led to the goal of teaching self-reliance. It was also at about this time that vocal leaders in education recognized that separation, or segregation, in the educational process was usually inherently negative. The education of children with other handicapping conditions, such as hearing and visual impairments, had a somewhat different history in terms of the types of training they received. There was a similarity historically, however, in the fact that education was usually provided in a segregated setting. The statements from congressional hearings included later in this chapter provide a first-hand perspective of the state of affairs at that time.

A CONSTITUTIONAL AND POLITICAL
FRAMEWORK FOR CHANGE

It was *Brown v. Board of Education*[2] that most forcefully stated the philosophy of integration. That decision was based on the federal constitutional principle of the fourteenth amendment, which provides that the states may not deprive anyone of "life, liberty, or property, without due process of law" nor deny anyone "equal protection of the laws."[3] While it has been consistently held by the Supreme Court that there is no federally protected right to education, nonetheless if the state undertakes to provide education (which all states do), a property interest is thereby created by the state. The *Brown* decision recognized that educating black children separately, even if done so in "equal" facilities, was inherently unequal because of the stigma attached to being educated separately and because of the deprivation of interaction with children of other backgrounds.

The concept of mainstreaming, or educating the handicapped child in the regular classroom as much as possible, paralleled the movement away from racial segregation and helped lead to the determination that separation of children was adverse. Congress made preliminary efforts to provide for special education by enacting grant programs in 1966 and 1970,[4] but these were primarily incentive programs with little in the way of specific guidelines and enforcement. Although mainly for personnel development, these programs attempted to address the issue of educating handicapped children in the regular school system.

By 1975 about three million handicapped children were not receiving appropriate programming in public schools. In addition, there were about another one million handicapped children who were excluded totally from public education. So, of the more than eight million handicapped children in the United States, more than half of them were receiving either inappropriate or no educational service.[5]

Financing was one reason that special education was inadequate; special education is costly and it is burdensome for local school districts to support it. By 1975, state education agencies had taken on a substantial role in special education, both by mandating special education and by allocating funds to help subsidize local school districts.[6]

By the 1970s special education could usually be described by a number of common practices. Identification and placement of handicapped children was haphazard, inconsistent, and generally inappropriate. Blacks, Hispanics, and some other groups were often stereotyped and disproportionately placed in special education programs. Parental involvement was generally discouraged. Special education placements were often made with the goal of avoiding disruption in the regular classroom. Both special educators and regular educators were competitors for resources, and the two groups did not work in a spirit of cooperation.[7]

The application of the principles set forth in the *Brown* decision to the education of handicapped children became a legal theory in more than 30 separately filed cases throughout the country. Two of these cases culminated in landmark de-

cisions in 1971 and 1972. In *Pennsylvania Association for Retarded Children (PARC) v. Pennsylvania*[8] and *Mills v. Board of Education,*[9] district courts approved consent decrees that enjoined states from denying education to mentally retarded and handicapped children without due process. The *Mills* consent decree went so far as to set out an elaborate framework for what that due process would entail. Both of these cases were based on constitutional theories of equal protection and due process under the fourteenth amendment and were the impetus for similar cases in a large number of other states.

As was previously noted, there is no federal constitutional right to education. It is only when the state undertakes to provide education that the fourteenth amendment comes into play. When states provide education, they must do so on equal terms, and they must not deny this state-granted right without due process.

In its evaluation of what is meant by equal terms, the Supreme Court has traditionally applied differing degrees of scrutiny in its examination of the practices of (different) governmental entities. If the individual affected by the practice is a member of a "suspect class" such as a racial minority, or if the right at issue is a "fundamental right" such as privacy, the practice will be strictly scrutinized (evaluated very carefully). Where the classification is not a specially protected class, or if the right is not an important one, the practice will usually be upheld if there is any rational basis for it. Individuals with handicaps have not been held to be members of a suspect class,[10] but education has been recognized as deserving of "special constitutional treatment," and an intermediate test of heightened scrutiny has been applied.[11] It is important to note that in assessing whether handicapped children are receiving equal protection in their educational programming, equal expenditures of money should not be the measure, although it is often difficult to determine exactly what constitutes equality.[12]

The due process clause of the fourteenth amendment requires procedures to be appropriate to the protected interest at stake. Obviously in a criminal proceeding, states must be extremely careful that the individual has received appropriate due process because incarceration is a serious deprivation of liberty. Education is recognized as an important property interest by states because without it, it is unlikely that a person can succeed in life. Education is important for handicapped individuals to live independently or semi-independently. For that reason the court in the *Mills* decision mandated that due process include procedures relating to the labelling, placement, and exclusionary stages of decision making. The procedures should include a right to a hearing (with representation, a record, an impartial hearing officer), a right to appeal, a right to have access to records, and written notice at all stages of the process.[13] The basic framework set out in *Mills* was incorporated into the Education for All Handicapped Children Act (EAHCA).

Because of potential confusion that might result from varying decisions in other jurisdictions and pressure from concerned states administrators about the cost of providing special education, Congress passed federal grant legislation to encourage states to adopt appropriate procedures for providing education to handicapped children. The civil rights movement and related activities provided a favorable political atmosphere for the enactment of strong legislation.

STATUTORY RESPONSES

The Education for All Handicapped Children Act

While the constitutional principles theoretically would mandate equal protection and due process for handicapped children in the public school setting without any statutory requirement at the federal level, Congress recognized that states might have difficulty implementing the constitutional requirement to provide education to handicapped children. And although most states already had statutes in place requiring the education of children with handicaps, there was a great deal of inconsistency in what states required, and many states did not have very strong programs of special education when *PARC* and *Mills* were decided.

Testimony and statements offered at congressional hearings on the subject of educational services for handicapped children during 1973 and 1974 indicated problems with the state of special education at that time. These statements indicated that, to a large extent, states that were acting in good faith and attempting to provide special education had serious problems of administration and financing. In other instances, parents had been successful in getting the school administration to implement a local program benefiting one or a few individuals, but this was a result of substantial effort and energy on the part of the parents. And perhaps most troubling was the fact that in some areas, significant numbers of children were still being excluded.

The following statements from those hearings illustrate more graphically some of these problems. The first statement indicates the most severe crisis, the child who is simply institutionalized and not given an education.

Statement of Dr. Oliver L. Hurley, Associate Professor of Special Education, University of Georgia, Athens (p. 657)[14]
Some years ago, during the course of a visit to the State institution for the mentally retarded, I encountered a little girl who was lying in a crib. Wondering why she was so confined while the other children were not, I began to play with her. I found that even though I could make eye contact with her, she was unable to follow me with her eyes for more than about 12 inches. I began to try to teach her. In about 15 minutes she could follow me about a quarter of the way around the bed. I was convinced then, and still am, that with a little work their child could have been taught some useful behavior and could have been gotten out of the crib. It seems safe to say that no one with any authority was concerned about the education of that little girl.

For me, this child, who showed some ability to learn, typified our reactions to these difficult cases—hide them away, exclude them, forget them. Such a prejudicial attitude toward those who are different must be changed. The "Education for All Handicapped Children Act" will help in this regard. Someone must assume responsibility for the education of such children. To me, the State education agencies are a logical choice. It seems antithetical to American philosophy, as I see it, that whether or not a handicapped child gets proper care and proper educational treatment depends on the fatness of that child's father's wallet.

The problem of different levels of services from state to state was raised by a parent of a hearing-impaired child.

Statement of Mrs. Gordon Huddleston, Orangeburg, S.C., Parent of a Severely Hard-of-Hearing Child (pp.796–799)
My husband and I are particularly interested in this bill because we have experienced education in four States for our hearing-impaired son, and in these four States we have found a vast difference in what is provided for him. Perhaps by telling my story, I can best illustrate to you some of these differences that we have experienced.

In 1950, our son David was born with a severe hearing impairment. We discovered this when David was 2 years of age. We were living in Parkersburg, W. Va., at the time, and because of limited medical facilities we were referred to Dr. Helmer Michelbust, at the Institute of Language Disorders at Northwestern University, in Evanston, Ill. Dr. Michelbust and his staff told us that David had a severe hearing impairment and was delayed in language, but with proper early education he could develop speech and lip reading ability, to function in society, and the emphasis was on early education. We were told that early ideology and language training was a must.

West Virginia did not have any facilities, but we were fortunate that we lived in an area where we could get to the speech and language clinic at Ohio University. So for 2 years David and I drove 100 miles a day for speech therapy. When David was 4, the educators at Ohio University told us that he was ready for academic training and should be placed in a school for hearing-impaired children, that because of the potential that he had shown during his period of work there they recommended that we definitely seek an oral deaf school placement for our son. There was such a school as part of the public school program in Columbus, Ohio, so at that time our family moved to Columbus, and at age 4 David entered the Alexander Graham Bell Oral School for Hearing-Impaired Children, as part of the public school program in Columbus.

He worked in a classroom with a trained teacher of the deaf, in a public school setting, with a maximum of eight students per class. After 2¾ years in this setting, we were told that David could integrate into the regular classroom in his own district: with supportive help, resource teachers, he could probably function very well. His teacher made use of audiovisual aids, and resource teachers were available to him. He was promoted to the second grade with a B-plus average.

At this time we were transferred to Wilmington, Del, with the Du Pont Co., and moved David there. There were facilities; there were resource teachers; there was also an oral school for hearing-impaired children at Newark, Del. David received from these resource teachers, in a regular classroom setting in Wilmington, one-to-one help in math, reading, and language. At the end of second grade, David was evaluated by the school psychologist and by a staff from the Margaret Sturk School for Hearing-Impaired Children, in Newark, Del. It was determined at that time that David was functioning very well in a normal classroom and it would be in his best interest to continue in a regular classroom setting. This is where he could reach his potential, with supportive help. He completed third grade, had a B average, and we were told that he was on his way, and with supportive help he should be able to continue in a normal classroom setting with normal children.

Meanwhile, we were faced with two transfers from the company and felt compelled to turn them down. My husband was then transferred into the international department with Du Pont and was going to be faced with a lot of travel. This concerned us, this being away from home and the possibility of more transfers, and a job opportunity came along in South Carolina that would be a permanent job for us, so we felt that we must think in terms of finding a permanent location for our family. But before we would go for the job interview we came to South Carolina first and had an interview with the superintendent of schools in Orangeburg district, with the school psychologist, and with the director of curriculum there. We told them of David's problems and his needs thus far in his education. Yes, they explained, they did have reading teachers, they did have a speech therapist, and they did have a school psychologist for the district.

Services Not Available in South Carolina
We moved, and we started the school year, and David entered Sheridan Elementary School in Orangeburg, in the fourth grade. We were dismayed to find that he was not able to have a reading teacher help him. He was placed for one-half hour a week in a group session speech therapy with children who did not have a similar defect to his. There were no resource teachers. We sought counseling from the school psychologist: he was very sympathetic. But they explained to us that because of their caseload they just were not able to take him into therapy; consequently, we would have to go it on our own.

Being concerned, I volunteered as a parent to work at school 4 days a week in David's science and math classes to help him come through the year. He did come through. He was on an individual math program. We came through the year, and at the end of the year we tested out 4.9. He had made progress in this area. However, his language and reading teacher was not able to give him the benefit from extra help, and David started downhill. He became frustrated. He started falling behind. His behavior became disruptive. And I might add that he had two teachers, and when he was working in the area of math and areas where he could still compete, his behavior was fine. When he entered the reading and the language area, his behavior became a problem.

The Child Should Adapt
Rather than find help for him, he was given such tasks, as punishment, to write 500—not 50 or 100—500 times a night, "I will sit in my seat and I will behave."

We again sought help from the school psychologist, but again were told that they would really like to help but the caseloads were just so heavy that it was just impossible to give him the help that he needed. . . .

Our son has been evaluated at the Institute for Language Disorders at Northwestern University; Ohio State University; Mid-American Hearing Association, headed by Dr. George Shambaugh, in Chicago; and Margaret Sturk School for

Hearing-Impaired Children. All have felt that David had potential and emphasized that he would be able to take his place in a hearing society, and with proper resource teachers in education would not be a burden to society, in that someday, if he were allowed to reach his potential, he could take his place and function in society and would not have to have residential placement or wind up in a correctional institution. He could be a self-supporting member of this society.

I am here today because we have experienced vast differences in education in the different States that we have been in. Quite honestly, we have seriously considered leaving the State of South Carolina, but my husband likes his work, and we very, very much like this State. We would like to remain here. In addition to that, we have met other parents facing the same problems in Orangeburg. If we leave, that's not going to help them a bit. But hopefully this bill will help others, and all across the country, not just in certain States.

Other parents noted that even when appropriate programming was provided, parents often were required to provide transportation in order to obtain the programming for the child.

Statement of Mrs. Mary Ellen Ward, Avon Park, Fla., Member of the Ridge Area Association for Retarded Children and the Florida and National Associations for Retarded Children (pp. 812–813)
I'd like to describe a particular case, and this is of a multihandicapped girl now 10 years old, severely crippled by cerebral palsy, mentally retarded, and with very limited speech. She was enrolled in our Association-sponsored Division of Retardation funded developmental training program at the age of 4, when she was beginning to roll and crawl on the floor. Before she moved to another county last July she had learned to walk with crutches and braces, to feed herself; she'd been toilet trained and was learning to swim and to perform some self-care chores. She, with her family, moved to another Florida county in order to maintain the father's employment status. Beginning 10 days after the move, the mother started investigating, as carefully as her abilities would permit, the educational opportunities for Jerri.

The parents completed a number of applications, submitted to tests and examination, met appointments for interviews, and paid for medical and psychological exams. Eight months after first making application, 10-year-old Jerri, who had been in a training program for 5½ years in our county, was accepted in a program for 2 hours daily, provided the mother transport Jerri a distance of 7 miles and remain as her babysitter while Jerri attends this particular school. At the end of the first week the mother reported Jerri's instructions were coming from her, and at last hearing there is still no program for Jerri.

This happened in 1973 in one of the highest-ranked States in terms of percentages of handicapped persons served. I think it demonstrates the need for further statewide help in designing, funding, evaluating, and accounting for local services for the handicapped. It emphasizes the need to provide services for the low-functioning handicapped, who may never qualify for a job but who certainly need to know skills of self-help and self-care.

The problems of funding in poor states, the need for funding to support construction of physical facilities, and a program to support training of qualified personnel were also noted.

Statement of Dan Delong, Executive Director, South Dakota Association for Retarded Children (p. 1296)
We have been fortunate in South Dakota to have successfully passed mandatory special education legislation, which requires the provision of appropriate educational opportunities to all exceptional children from birth to 21 years. Since the passage of that bill in 1972, rapid progress has been made in the development of public school programs for handicapped children, but still it has not been enough. DHEW estimates indicate that only 24.8% of our handicapped children are receiving appropriate educational services. We feel that the estimate may be too high and that the actual figure is closer to 20%. Leading special education experts in our state estimate that more than 5,000 handicapped children will exit from our school systems during the next four years almost totally lacking in skills which will allow them to move into competitive employment areas or successful adjustment to community living.

As an advocate group, we are in the business of making ideals become realities. We recognize that it is ideal that all handicapped children receive a free public education, and in our efforts to make that a reality, we have had to face some very harsh realities about education in a rural state with large impoverished areas.

Statement of Edward Kirsch, Parent of a Retarded Child (p. 1550)
[T]he ratio as I understand it in speech therapy is approximately three full-time or two full-time speech therapists and one part-time speech therapist for the needs of 737 children, and this is rather a ridiculous ratio. These people are really only involved with trainable children so it's hardly likely the children will get much speech therapy. Then again there are the facilities the speech therapists have to share. In one instance there is a speech therapy room sharing space with a piano tuner and a music class. It's hard to imagine anybody can accomplish anything in a situation like that.

One of our biggest concerns is the lack of funds to provide facilities for these children because presently a plan the school board has in mind is to move these children, all 562 of them, to an 88-year-old building on the north side of Pittsburgh in the Manchester area. It's certainly not adequate for the needs of these children in view of the fact that some of them are multiply handicapped and blind and have many other physical handicaps. To put these children in a four-story building seems ridiculous, but there doesn't seem to be any place else for them to go because there are no funds available for new construction. . . .

Many of the parents complain that the children that are teenagers and don't have many more years to spend in the system, and that they are very much concerned because their children have received very minimal vocational and occupational training and shortly they will be out of the system. Where will they go to from there? Many of them were 15 years old when the consent agreement came down so they maybe only have 3 more years left and agewise they will have to be removed from the system and put into supportive programs outside of the right to education program.

Statement of Carl Wass, Pennsylvania Mental Health, Inc. (p. 1556)
There are many school districts we find throughout the State who leave it to the intermediate unit to provide services for the handicapped child. And the intermediate units sometimes are not providing these services and when they do we find that the classes that provide services for the handicapped are either overcrowded, as was suggested in the case of Pittsburgh, or that the personnel, the teaching personnel, is not equipped to handle the particular problem. The end result is that many of these children who have an identifiable handicap are not getting the kind of education that is contemplated by the Department of Education or by the consent order. I think on the grass roots level competent personnel are needed.

Perhaps of unique interest were statements from a variety of individuals from Pennsylvania, a state under a consent decree to implement the *PARC* decision. Many of the comments illustrated the frustration of wanting to carry out the intent and spirit of the order, but needing supportive funding to do so. The following is one of many comments from Pennsylvania that indicate the gaps left by the consent agreement.

Statement of William H. Wolfinger, Director Special Education Services, Hamburg State School, Pennsylvania (pp. 1538–1539)
We are now at a point of having had over a year and a half of time go by with certainly many accomplishments, but also much remaining to be done.

First, this act, in my opinion, will be a stimulus for our state legislature to look at the total problem of education for all handicapped children since the consent agreement was limited to only the mentally retarded.

Second, it soon became apparent in our implementation of programs for the mentally retarded that much more money was needed for staff, equipment, and physical facilities.

Third, perhaps from such a review by our legislature will emerge the potential for providing a better balance of programs for the handicapped, one that will provide these children with the same program advantages afforded the so-called "normal" child.

Fourth, perhaps a year-round, twelve-month school can also emerge since this is so important for handicapped children; 220 days of school instead of the customary 180. . . .

Much remains to be done and without adequate financing most of our needs at each of the state schools will remain unanswered.

Most pressing is the need for adequate physical facilities in which to conduct the educational programs and the related services that are so critical in order to reach the total needs of the child. Buildings are desperately needed that are equipped for the handling of the physically handicapped, since most of the severely and profoundly retarded children found in institutions are also inflicted with severe multiple handicaps. Handicapped children should not be compelled to attend classes or individual sessions in crowded or substandard facilities.

In response to these concerns, as an initial stopgap measure, Congress in

1974 passed an interim funding bill that required states, as a condition of receiving federal funds, to adopt "goal/s/ of providing full educational opportunities to all handicapped children."[15] The interim bill was adopted to give Congress a year to study the issue more carefully, and the following year Congress passed the Education for All Handicapped Children Act of 1975,[16] which became effective in 1977. There was significant congressional concern about the cost of the legislation. The result of that concern is that the EAHCA is not intended to fund the costs of special education fully, but is intended as a subsidization to state and local educational agencies.

The EAHCA is technically an amendment to the 1970 Education of the Handicapped Act (EHA),[17] which had provided for grants to states to provide special education. The EAHCA amends Part B of the EHA, and is significant because it provides the important elements of procedural safeguards, integration, and nondiscriminatory testing and evaluation materials and procedures.

The EAHCA is basically a grant statute that creates individual rights. A state can receive federal funding to support payment for handicapped children ages 3 through 21 based on a formula of average per-pupil expenditures, if the state develops a plan of providing for *all* handicapped children in the state a "free, appropriate public education which emphasizes special education and related services designed to meet their unique needs."[18]

The Act specifies the general parameters of the procedural safeguards required of the recipients, and the details of these requirements were eventually developed in the regulations finalized in 1977.[19] The basic underlying principles of the EAHCA should be noted here, however.

- *All* handicapped children must be given education.[20]
- It must be provided in the *least restrictive appropriate* placement.[21]
- Education is to be *individualized* and *appropriate* to the child's unique needs.[22]
- It is to be provided FREE.[23]
- *Procedural protections* are required to ensure that the substantive requirements are met.[24]

Controversy over what these terms mean has resulted in a multitude of cases, and there are now hundreds of reported judicial decisions relating to these issues.

The EAHCA is often referred to by its Public Law number, 94–142, or as the EHA. Although it is acceptable to use any of these designations, the use of EAHCA is incorporated throughout this text primarily because it is the most significant portion of the EHA.

State Statutes

Initially every state except New Mexico elected to receive federal grant support under the EAHCA. The *PARC* and *Mills* decisions and similar actions in other states had arguably required the states to implement much of what was being required under the EAHCA even for states not electing to apply for the federal support. In addition, Section 504 of the Rehabilitation Act of 1973[25] may also have been statutory authority for the states to provide education in a nondiscriminatory manner to handicapped children. Perhaps because of this, New Mexico eventually also elected to apply for EAHCA funding.

The EAHCA and its regulations set out minimum requirements for states to be eligible. Those states with statutes and regulations already in place before enactment of the EAHCA sometimes had difficulty adjusting to the new law, and those without any policy in place had the task of developing one. Occasionally, conflicts still arise between state and federal mandates.

Section 504 of the Rehabilitation Act

Even before passage of the EAHCA, Congress passed the Rehabilitation Act of 1973, which includes Section 504. That section requires that

> No otherwise qualified individual with handicaps . . . shall solely by reason of his handicap, be excluded from the participation in, be denied the benefits of, or be subjected to discrimination under any program or activity receiving Federal financial assistance.[26]

Even before the EAHCA, which granted federal financial assistance to states specifically for the purpose of providing special education, states had received a great deal of funding from the federal government to support other educational programs. Although Section 504 did not grant funds to the states to provide education for children with handicaps, the law made it illegal for any programs receiving federal funding to discriminate against an individual on the basis of handicap.

Although it might appear that the EAHCA is not necessary because Section 504 already provides protection, it is important to recognize several factors that make the EAHCA essential to the provision of special education. First, Section 504 only refers to nondiscrimination, and the EAHCA contemplates that a substantial amount of subsidization will take place to ensure that handicapped children not only receive educational services but also benefit from this education. While Section 504 case law has indicated that some reasonable accommodation must be provided to meet the nondiscrimination standard, the level of accommodation being provided in public education under the EAHCA goes beyond what is required in other contexts. Second, while Section 504 was passed in 1973, before the 1975 EAHCA, the regulations under Section 504 were not finalized until 1978, and there was no detailed framework for the schools to follow. Finally, because of the fact that the Section 504 regulations were finalized after the EAHCA regulations, they are much less detailed, and in fact incorporate by reference the EAHCA regulations. Should the EAHCA be repealed or deregulated (as was attempted in the early 1980s), Section 504 would provide much less protection both in terms of substantive requirements and procedural safeguards. The fact that Section 504 is not a funding statute provides an additional problem with it as a source of ensuring educational services.

Summary of Special Education Legal Developments

1954   *Brown v. Board of Education:* Supreme Court holds that separate but equal is not equal for purposes of education in a case involving racial segregation.

1966   Title VI added to Elementary and Secondary Education Act: Established the Bureau of Education for the Handicapped to provide leadership in special education programming.

1970   Title VI repealed, and the Education of the Handicapped Act passed: Part B provides for grants to states to encourage special education programming.

1971/72   *PARC* and *Mills* decisions (and numerous similar cases in other states) set the stage for a constitutional right to special education because states provide education.

1973   Section 504 of the Rehabilitation Act passed: Discrimination prohibited on basis of handicap by recipients of federal financial assistance.

1974   Amendments to Elementary and Secondary Education Act provided basic elements of what would be the EAHCA, but without a timetable.

1975   EAHCA passed (Pub. L. 94–142): Timetable established for implementing the funding of states that provide a framework of special education and due process protection for children with handicaps.

SUMMARY

The right to education for children with handicaps did not become a comprehensive program until 1975 with passage of the Education for All Handicapped Children Act (EAHCA). Before 1975 some states provided some educational programming to some children with certain handicaps. Federal law before 1975 provided incentive funding to those states that provided special education.

The 1975 amendment to the federal incentive programs was the real guarantee of a comprehensive and consistent program for providing education to children with handicaps. The 1975 EAHCA included the important requirements that appropriate education must be provided to all children with handicaps in the least restrictive appropriate setting at no cost, and detailed procedural safeguards for parents to enforce these rights.

Although the EAHCA does not mandate that states comply with its requirements unless they seek funding under the EAHCA, states need the additional federal funding. They also recognize that public educational agencies are subject to the 1973 Rehabilitation Act prohibiting discrimination on the basis of handicap as well as constitutional equal protection and due process requirements. For these reasons, all states have elected to accept funding under the EAHCA.

QUESTIONS AND PROBLEMS

1. Sometimes choices about using scarce resources must be made. If the choice is between providing for special education or providing for upgrading the teaching of the "average" student, which choice is best? Why? Who should make these choices?

2. Is there a potential conflict between requiring special education in the regular classroom and providing appropriate education that is individualized? Without adequate support staff, a handicapped student will often not be able to survive in a so-called regular class. That student may be better off spending part of the day in a special grouping. How can the stigmatization be avoided, or is it simply impossible to do so?

NOTES

1. These phases are described in more detail in M.L. HUTT & R.G. GIBBY, THE MENTALLY RETARDED CHILD, 386–91 (1958).
2. 347 U.S. 483 (1954).
3. U.S. CONST. amend. XIV.
4. Pub. L. No. 89–750, § 161, 80 Stat. 1204; Pub. L. No. 91–230, 84 Stat. 175, Part B.
5. *See* 20 U.S.C. § 1401(b)(1)–(5). *See also* Lynn, *The Emerging System for Educating Handicapped Children,* 2 POLICY STUD. REV. 21–35 (1983).
6. Lynn, *Emerging System* at 28–34.
7. *Id.* at 32–34. For mention of other practices, *see also* H.R. TURNBULL, FREE APPROPRIATE PUBLIC EDUCATION, THE LAW AND CHILDREN WITH ABILITIES 13–17 (1986).
8. 334 F. Supp. 1257 (E.D. Pa. 1971) 343 F. Supp. 279 (E.D. Pa. 1972).
9. 348 F. Supp. 866 (D.D.C. 1972).
10. City of Cleburne v. Cleburne Living Center, 473 U.S. 432 (1985).
11. Plyler v. Doe, 457 U.S. 202 (1982).
12. For a more in-depth discussion of these issues, see L. ROTHSTEIN, RIGHTS OF PHYSICALLY HANDICAPPED PERSONS, § 2.02–2.07 [hereinafter cited as RPHP]. *See also,* Barlett, *The Role of Cost in Educational Decisionmaking for the Handicapped Child,* 48 LAW & CONTEMP. PROBS. 7 (1985).
13. 348 F. Supp. at 878–83. *See also* RPHP at § 2.07.
14. To Provide Financial Assistance to the States for Improved Educational Services for Handicapped Children: Hearings on S. 6 Before the Subcomm. on the Handicapped of the Senate Comm. on Labor and Public Welfare, 93rd Cong., 1st Sess. May 14, 1973, Oct. 19, 1973, and March 18, 1974) [hereinafter referred to by witness and page number].
15. Pub. L. No. 93–380, 88 Stat. 579, 583 (1974). The first major effort to provide special education at the federal level had occurred in 1966 when Title VI of the Elementary and Secondary Education Act, Pub. L. No. 98–750 (1966) was passed. Title VI provided a single administrative body to coordinate efforts, namely the Bureau of Education for the Handicapped (BEH). Title VI was replaced in 1970 by a separate act, the Education of the Handicapped Act (EHA), Pub. L. No. 91–230 (1970). Part B of the EHA authorized grants to states to assist in providing special education.
16. 20 U.S.C. §§ 1401 *et. seq.*
17. Pub. L. No. 91–230 (1970).

18. 20 U.S.C. § 1401(c). For a discussion of the legislative history, *see* R. WEINER P.L. 94–142, IMPACT ON THE SCHOOLS ch. 1 (1985). *See also* RPHP § 2.12.
19. 34 C.F.R. §§ 300.1–.754. *See also* R. WEINER, *supra* note 18, at ch. 2. Portions of these regulations are found at Appendix D.
20. See Chapter 5.
21. See Chapter 8.
22. See Chapter 7.
23. See Chapter 13.
24. See Chapters 14, 15.
25. See the following section.
26. 29 U.S.C. § 794.

CHAPTER 2

The Legal System and How It Works

STATE AND FEDERAL LAWS

The United States Constitution and State Constitutions

The primary and basic source of law in the United States is the Constitution. Federal statutes passed by Congress must be based on some provision of the Constitution. State constitutions and statutes may go beyond what is provided in the federal law, as long as there is no conflict between them and as long as state laws do not address areas reserved to the federal government, such as providing for the national defense.

The Constitution of the United States, because it is a general framework, does not specifically answer every question of law, and it has been subject to substantial interpretation over the past two centuries. The Constitution provides for the establishment of legislative, executive, and judicial powers of the United States, as well as procedures for modifying the Constitution. In addition to the articles of the Constitution, there are 26 amendments to the Constitution. Of major importance to special education are the constitutional provisions that provide for spending money to protect the general welfare[1] (which is the basis for the Education for All Handicapped Children Act [EAHCA][2] and Section 504 of the Rehabilitation Act[3]) and the fourteenth amendment providing that no states shall "deprive any person of life, liberty, or property, without due process of law . . . nor deny . . . equal protection of the laws."[4] It should be noted that there is no constitutional provision requiring that the federal government provide education. Under the tenth amendment to the Constitution, "powers not delegated to the United States by the Constitution, nor prohibited by it to the States, are reserved to the States. . . ."[5] All states have, by virtue of that authority, provided for public education, either by state constitution or by state statute or both. States are, there-fore, required under the due process and equal protection clauses of the four-teenth amendment to provide education on an equal basis and to provide due process before denying equivalent educational programming. As the following chapters demonstrate, however, it is not always clear what it means to be "equal," and it is not always easy to determine what "process" is due.

In addition, the fourteenth amendment applies only to states or state agents acting within state authority. Where an individual teacher or other educator is acting without a specified state policy to spell out whether the particular act is per-missible or not, it is not always clear whether the individual is acting within state authority, in order to meet the "state action" element of the fourteenth amend-ment. For example, if an administrator refuses to return phone calls of a parent of a handicapped child, and as a result, the appropriate programming of the child is substantially delayed, it is unclear whether the administrator's acts would be deemed to be within the authority of the state.

Statutes

The Constitution provides that Congress shall have the power to "make all Laws . . . necessary and proper for carrying into Execution the foregoing Powers."[6] Pursuant to that authority, Congress has enacted an enormous body of laws that cover everything from civil rights in the workplace to aviation safety laws.

The federal statutes of relevance to special education are the EAHCA and Section 504 of the Rehabilitation Act. These were both passed pursuant to the constitutional provisions that authorize the expenditure of money to protect the general welfare. The EAHCA authorizes the expenditure of federal funds to subsi-dize special education provided by the individual states. Section 504 of the Reha-bilitation Act requires that programs receiving federal financial assistance must not discriminate on the basis of handicap.

Most statutes of relevance to education generally are state statutes rather than federal statutes. Although education is highly regulated indirectly by fed-eral programs, such as Head Start and other funding programs, education is for the most part a state function, with some functions delegated to local school districts. All states have as part of their overall educational program a plan for providing education to handicapped students within the state. By having a plan that complies with the guidelines set forth in the EAHCA, all states qualify for federal funding to assist in providing that education to students with handicaps.

Regulations and Guidelines

Statutes are usually passed as a general framework of policy relating to a particular issue. Congress and state legislatures generally delegate to administrative agencies the task of developing detailed regulations pursuant to federal and state statutes.

These regulations must be within the authority of the statute. Federal regulations and some state regulations are finalized only after an opportunity for notice and public comment. If a regulation is developed within the boundaries of the statute, it has the weight of law.

In addition to regulations, administrative agencies often develop guidelines, which suggest how the laws administered by the relevant agency should be interpreted. While these do not have the weight of law, they are often given a great deal of deference by both policymakers and courts.

Special education is an area in which elaborate sets of regulations exist at both the federal and state level. At the federal level, the EAHCA regulations spell out in considerable detail the procedures and programming that must be provided to children with handicaps in order for states to receive federal funding.[7] States may go beyond what is required in the EAHCA regulations as long as their regulations are not inconsistent with the federal requirements. For example, some states have broadened the definition of which children are entitled to special education, and thus may include gifted children in their special education programming. States also often regulate areas such as bus transportation, pupil/teacher ratios, and other issues that are really more appropriate for state regulation.

Case Law

Case law is the law developed in the courts. Historically it was a means of establishing law before there was a great deal of written statutory law. Judges would render opinions that incorporated custom. This early law was known as common law. Most judicially rendered law today is opinion not about custom, but interprets a constitutional provision or statute as it applies to a particular set of facts.

Courts are limited to rendering opinions about the specific facts in the cases before them. Pronouncements of a broader nature are not prohibited, but they do not have the force of law. Broader pronouncements are known as *dicta,* and they provide guidance to potential litigants about their chances of success should they decide to seek a remedy in the courts.

In this country, there is a fairly universal acceptance of the concept of *stare decisis,* which means that courts are bound to render decisions consistent with previous decisions in the same jurisdiction and with decisions of higher courts over that jurisdiction. If a court reaches a result different from a previous decision, it must usually justify the decision by explaining why the set of facts before it is different, or why circumstances have changed, or why the previous decision was wrong. So that judicial law can be known to the public, most judicial opinions at the federal level, and a significant portion of opinions within state judicial systems, are published. These published opinions are available in law libraries, and part of one's legal education includes training in how to find relevant court opinions as well as how to research statutes and regulations.

THE JUDICIAL SYSTEM

To understand which court opinions on the relevant subject matter apply to a specific case, it is necessary to understand the court system in the United States.[8]

In the United States there are really 51 court systems: the federal court system, and a court system in each of the 50 states. Each system has the power to decide both criminal cases and civil cases, but the jurisdiction of the federal courts is limited by the Constitution. Article III, which defines the judicial power of the federal courts, says that this power extends only to cases "arising under this Constitution [and] the Laws of the United States."[9] This limitation on the types of cases that can be decided by courts of the United States is the most important limitation for those who deal with legal issues in education. Often referred to as "federal question jurisdiction," it means that cases concerning the fourteenth amendment's equal protection provision or cases involving sex discrimination in education (which is prohibited by federal law) can be decided by federal courts. On the other hand, a case involving alleged defamation cannot be decided by a federal court, but would generally have to be tried in a state court because it is based on state law only. State courts, in addition to dealing with a variety of criminal and civil matters, also have the power to decide cases concerning issues of federal statutory and constitutional law. Because many legal problems in education involve federal questions (either constitutional or statutory), litigants in such cases have a choice as to which court system (federal or state) they will initially choose. A case filed in a state court can reach the U.S. Supreme Court if a controversy still exists after it has been heard and decided by the highest state court. Figure 2.1 shows the alternative paths of a judicial controversy.

The federal judicial system and most state judicial systems are three-tiered. They have a relatively large number of trial courts, where the facts are determined and where the law is applied to the particular facts; a smaller number of intermediate appellate courts, which review the way the law has been applied to the facts; and one final court of appeals, which is the highest court of the particular jurisdiction. The names of these courts vary from state to state; they are often called superior court, court of appeals, and supreme court, respectively; but this is not always true, so care should be taken in determining whether one is reading a case from a trial court or from the highest court of a state. In New York State, for example, the lowest trial court of general jurisdiction is the Supreme Court, whereas the state's highest court is the Court of Appeals. In the federal system, the nearly 100 trial courts are called United States District Courts, the 13 courts of appeals are called the United States Courts of Appeals, and the highest court is officially called the United States Supreme Court.

Judicial controversies generally move from the trial court level to the intermediate appellate court level and, finally, to the highest court of the jurisdiction. Additionally, a case can move from the highest court of a state to the U.S. Supreme Court, if the losing party submits a request to the Supreme Court to consider the case. This request usually comes in the form of a "petition for certiorari," which the U.S. Supreme Court can either accept or reject. After careful consideration, a vote is taken by the nine justices; if four vote in favor of considering the case, the justices will issue a "writ of certiorari" asking that the case be sent to the Court. This often occurs when the various federal courts of appeals are in conflict over a particular issue.

When reading one of the many cases decided by the various state and federal courts, an important point to consider is whether or not the particular decision of the court (often called the court's "holding") is binding in your state or region. Decisions of the Supreme Court are binding everywhere, but the decisions of the lower federal courts are binding only in their respective territories. All federal courts of appeals (except for the one in Washington, D.C., and one dealing with special patent and copyright issues) cover more than one state, and there is more than one federal district court in most states. A map of the jurisdictions covered by the federal courts of appeals is contained in Appendix A. The opinions of state courts are binding only in the state where they are decided. However, decisions from courts other than the one deciding the case may be used as precedent; although not binding, these decisions are often considered persuasive in other jurisdictions.

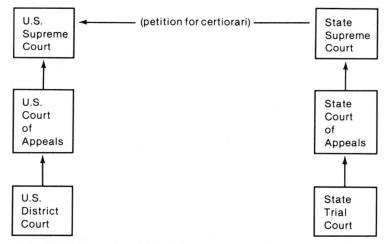

Figure 2.1. Alternative paths of a judicial controversy. (Source: L. FISCHER and G.P. SORENSON, SCHOOL LAW FOR COUNSELORS, PSYCHOLOGISTS, AND SOCIAL WORKERS (1985). Reprinted by permission of Longman, Inc.)

REGULATORY DECISION MAKING

Congress sometimes delegates to an administrative body the function of deciding disputes or determining whether a statute has been violated. The reason is often one of efficiency and quality of decision making. It is costly and time-consuming to litigate disputes in court. Theoretically, a resolution before an administrative hearing officer is quicker and less expensive, although this does not always prove to be true in practice. In addition, in some cases an administrative decision-maker may have a particular area of expertise that makes decision making better than it might be by a judge in court.

Special education is one of the areas in which Congress has delegated dispute resolution and other decision making to administrators. Where parents believe that appropriate special education is not being provided, the EAHCA sets up a detailed framework providing an opportunity for an impartial hearing, with a right of review by the state educational agency, and a subsequent right of review in state or federal court. In addition, anyone believing that the school has violated Section 504 of the Rehabilitation Act may complain to the federal Department of Education, which may then investigate and possibly hold a hearing to determine if a violation has occurred. In this forum the complaining party is not a party in the hearing. In other words, it is not really a hearing to provide a remedy to the individual complainant, but to determine whether a violation has occurred and whether corrective action, such as withholding future federal financial assistance, is an appropriate remedy. Because this administrative decision making does not really resolve the problem for the individual complainant, many individuals choose to go directly to court to seek relief. As Chapter 14 indicates, it is not entirely clear whether it is permissible to do that, and as Chapters 3 and 15 illustrate, even if it is permissible to claim a violation of Section 504 in court, most claims involving special education must be decided under the EAHCA anyway, and the parents must first seek relief through the impartial hearing process mentioned above.

RELATIONSHIP OF CONSTITUTIONAL LAW, STATUTORY LAW, REGULATORY LAW, AND CASE LAW IN THE DEVELOPMENT OF SPECIAL EDUCATION LAWS

It is interesting to note that laws are not developed by the various agents (Congress, administrators, judges) in the system in a vacuum. Often laws are made by one agent as a response to developments in other arenas. And state and federal law is frequently interactive in this process. The development of special education law is an excellent example of this metamorphosis.

While many states had laws providing for some education for at least some types of handicapped children before 1971, the real watershed year for special education law was 1971. In that year, and a year later, two judicial opinions interpreted the fourteenth amendment to the United States Constitution to require that, because the District of Columbia and the Commonwealth of Pennsylvania provided education to children within their jurisdictions, it was a denial of due process and equal protection to exclude handicapped children from the educational system.[10] As a result of these judicial opinions rendered by federal courts, and the fact that a number of similar lawsuits were awaiting final decision throughout the United States, Congress decided that in the interest of consistency, as well as to assist states in what appeared to be constitutionally mandated education of handicapped students to some degree, a federal program of subsidization should be developed.[11]

The program that resulted from this was the EAHCA, passed in 1975. It provided for granting funds to states that developed educational plans ensuring that education would be provided to all handicapped children of appropriate age, at no cost to the parent with nonhandicapped children to the maximum extent appropriate, and with procedural safeguards in place.

The statute itself set the general framework, but a great deal of detail was needed to clarify what was meant by the various provisions relating to procedural safeguards. The Department of Health, Education, and Welfare (now separated into the Department of Education and the Department of Health and Human Services) developed an elaborate set of regulations to flesh out these details. These regulations became effective in 1977 after extensive public comment.

As of now, all states have elected to seek funding support under the EAHCA, and as a result, they have all developed state statutes and regulations incorporating the requirements of the EAHCA, and usually providing for additional requirements relating to special education.

Even with detailed statutory and regulatory requirements, a number of issues became the subject of debate. These issues included matters such as whether states were required only to provide the same number of school days to handicapped students that they provided to nonhandicapped students, whether residential placements must be paid for entirely by the state and under what circumstances, and whether services such as catheterization must be provided at no charge. Several issues reached the level of the Supreme Court, which then issued its interpretation of the law. When Congress disagrees with the Court's interpretation, Congress can rewrite or pass new legislation. One Supreme Court case that prompted Congress to amend the EAHCA to clarify its intent was the 1984 case of *Smith v. Robinson*.[12] In that case the Supreme Court held, among other things, that under the EAHCA, as it was then written, parents could not recover attorneys' fees. Congress subsequently passed the Handicapped Children's Protection Act (HCPA)[13] in 1986 to allow for attorneys' fees in certain circumstances under the EAHCA. Already there has been a substantial amount of litigation concerning situations in which those attorneys fees can be awarded.[14] It is possible that Congress may decide to clarify the HCPA as a result of this litigation or that the Department of Education may promulgate regulations for the same reason. It is likely that the interaction among the various agents in the development of law will continue for some time because the interpretation of the EAHCA continues to evolve.

SUMMARY

Legal requirements applicable to education of handicapped children are currently found primarily in a federal statute (EAHCA) and its regulations. The development of these requirements was a result of the dynamic workings of our legal system. The U.S. Constitution (through the fourteenth amendment equal protection and due process requirements) was interpreted by federal courts (in *PARC* and *Mills*). These courts set out a general framework for what the Constitution requires of states in providing special education. The general framework of the decisions was then the basis for the passage of a federal statute (the EAHCA) and the detailed regulations developed pursuant to it.

Although the EAHCA and its regulations now are the primary source of law for special education, numerous judicial interpretations of the EAHCA are essential additional reference points. The Supreme Court has issued several opinions clarifying certain issues but leaving others unresolved. An enormous body of case law at lower court levels continues to provide additional and sometimes conflicting interpretations of the EAHCA. Statutory amendments (such as the HCPA) have been passed in response to judicial decisions and recognized gaps in the statute.

With this expanding body of statutory, regulatory, and judicial law it might seem that answers to most questions about what is required of schools in providing special education would by now be found within existing law. As the following chapters illustrate, however, many questions remain unanswered, and it is likely that the development of law on these issues will continue for some time.

QUESTIONS AND PROBLEMS

1. Why doesn't Congress develop all the details of the EAHCA and other statutes, rather than leaving that to administrative agencies?
2. Is it positive policy to enact a statute that may be intentionally somewhat vague on certain points?
3. Which is the fastest and most efficient way to develop law—through the court system or the legislative process? What are the advantages and disadvantages of each?

NOTES

1. *See* U.S. CONST. art. I, § 8, cl. 1.
2. 20 U.S.C. §§ 1400 *et seq.* (1982).
3. 29 U.S.C. § 794 (1982).
4. *See* U.S. CONST. amend. XIV.
5. *See* U.S. CONST. art. X.
6. *See* U.S. CONST. art. I, § 8, cl. 18.
7. *See* 34 C.F.R. §§ 300.1–.754 (1987). Regulations under Section 504.
8. The following four paragraphs and the chart are from L. FISCHER and G.P. SORENSON, SCHOOL LAW FOR COUNSELORS, PSYCHOLOGISTS, AND SOCIAL WORKERS (1985) (included with permission).
9. U.S. CONST. art. III, § 2, cl. 1.
10. This is a somewhat simplified statement of the holdings in Pennsylvania Association

for Retarded Children v. Pennsylvania, 334 F. Supp. 1257 (E.D. Pa. 1971); 343 F. Supp. 279 (E.D. Pa. 1972) and Mills v. Board of Education, 345 F. Supp. 886 (D.D.C. 1972).
11. The history of these developments is discussed more fully in Chapter 1.
12. 468 U.S. 992 (1984).
13. 20 U.S.C. § 1415(e)(4).
14. *See* L. ROTHSTEIN, RIGHTS OF PHYSICALLY HANDICAPPED PERSONS § 2.41 (1988 cumulative supplement).

CHAPTER 3

Statutory Provisions:
A General Overview

The material in this book focuses primarily on the requirements of the Education for All Handicapped Children Act (EAHCA).[1] Before looking in detail at what the EAHCA requires, it is important to have an overall picture not only of the EAHCA but also the other statutory provisions that relate to the education of students with handicaps. These provisions include Section 504 of the Rehabilitation Act[2] (basically a nondiscrimination statute), the EAHCA (which provides a detailed framework for delivery and procedural protections), state laws (which usually fill in some of the gaps and supplement the federal EAHCA), and a variety of other laws that relate to student records, confidentiality issues, and even tortious conduct. Having a broad overview of all of these laws will be important for placing the EAHCA in context.

SECTION 504 OF THE REHABILITATION ACT

The most comprehensive handicapped rights statute other than the EAHCA is the Rehabilitation Act, specifically Section 504. The 1973 Rehabilitation Act was actually an amendment to a much older law providing for vocational rehabilitation—the focus of the older law being solely on employment.[3] The 1973 Act provided, among other things, that recipients of federal financial assistance, such as schools, should not discriminate on the basis of handicap. It provided that

> No otherwise qualified individual with handicaps . . . shall solely by reason of his handicap, be excluded from the participation in, be denied the benefits of, or be subjected to discrimination under any program or activity receiving Federal financial assistance.[4]

This requirement is significant because it reaches not only employment, where the recipient has federal grants or other assistance, but also institutions such as welfare providers, hospitals, federally supported transportation providers, and, of course, public schools.

Most early litigation under the Rehabilitation Act focused on procedural and jurisdictional issues, such as whether the recipient actually received federal financial assistance, whether there was a private right of action, and whether one must exhaust administrative remedies before going to court.[5] More recent judicial opinion has addressed substantive issues such as whether the particular person is within the protected class, whether discrimination has actually occurred, and whether reasonable accommodations are required.[6]

Who Is Protected under Section 504?

To be entitled to protection under Section 504, an individual must meet the definition of a handicapped person. That definition is as follows:

> any person who (i) has a physical or mental impairment which substantially limits one or more of such person's major life activities, (ii) has a record of such an impairment, or (iii) is regarded as having such an impairment.[7]

Major life activities include

> caring for one's self, performing manual tasks, walking, seeing, hearing, speaking, breathing, learning and working.[8]

Simply being handicapped does not lead to success in a lawsuit claiming that the individual has been discriminated against. The individual must also be "otherwise qualified." That has been interpreted to mean that the individual must be someone "who is able to meet all of a program's requirements in spite of his handicap."[9] For example, in the employment setting, a hearing-impaired employee must be able to carry out the essential requirements of the job. Although the recipient need not make substantial modifications or fundamental alterations to the program, the recipient must still make reasonable accommodation.[10]

What Programs Are Covered?

Recipients under Section 504 are those who receive funds, personnel services, and interests in property, whether received directly or through another recipient.[11] In *Grove City College v. Bell,*[12] the Supreme Court addressed the question of whether Title IX[13] (a sex discrimination statute similar to Section 504) applies to an entire college when the college receives only indirect federal financial assistance by having students with federally subsidized loans attend the college. The Court held that only the program that receives the federal financial assistance is subject to Title IX. A similar analysis was subsequently applied to Section 504. After several years of congressional efforts, in 1987 Congress passed the Civil Rights Restoration Act, which amended Section 504 of the Rehabilitation Act by providing that a program or activity means *all* of the operations of a local or state educational agency.[14] The undecided issue then is the retroactive application of this statute.

The issue of program specificity has not been addressed to a great extent in a public education context, probably because public education is so permeated with federal funding. One of the few cases to address the issue of program specificity is *Gallagher v. Pontiac School District,*[15] in which a deaf and mentally retarded student sought a remedy for a claimed denial of an appropriate education. The Sixth Circuit Court of Appeals held that because the student had not sought to participate in a specific program receiving federal financial assistance that he was not covered by Section 504. This is a rather narrow reading of the holding in the *Grove City* case, and similar rulings are unlikely since the passage of the Civil Rights Restoration Act. It should be pointed out that a Supreme Court decision, *School Board of Nassau County v. Arline,*[16] applied Section 504 to a handicapped teacher without requiring her to show that she was seeking to participate in a specific program receiving federal funds. The program in that case was deemed to be the entire school system.[17]

Enforcement

Anyone with a grievance against a recipient of federal financial assistance can file a complaint with the Department of Education within 180 days of the adverse action.[18] After investigation by the Department of Education, if informal resolution does not address the complaint satisfactorily, the Department may hold a hearing.[19] The individual who complained to the funding agency is not a party to the hearing and does not receive an individual remedy, although that person will be given notice of the hearing.[20]

If a violation of Section 504 is found, the agency issues an appropriate order, which would normally be termination of federal funds. Following the *Grove City*[21] holding, the termination would only apply to the program subject to the discrimination claim. The recipient may also be barred from receiving federal financial assistance in the discriminating program in the future.[22] As a practical matter this is unlikely to happen. Decisions by administrative agencies are subject to judicial review.[23]

For the student claiming discrimination, it will be of little comfort to know that the school has been terminated from receiving federal funds. What the student may want is reimbursement for counseling or some other monetary remedy. This is usually not available through administrative procedures. The question then arises whether the individual may bring an action directly in court to obtain an individual remedy.

While the clear majority of federal circuit courts have decided that there is a private right of action under Section 504,[24] the Supreme Court has not yet directly ruled on this question although it has addressed several Section 504 claims.[25]

The standard for implying a right of action is established in *Cort v. Ash.*[26] The standard has four prongs that must be satisfied. They are:

1. Is the claimant a member of the class to be benefited by the statute?
2. Is there an explicit or implicit legislative intent to indicate whether there should be a private right of action?
3. Is it consistent with legislative intent to allow a private right of action?
4. Is the cause of action one that should traditionally be brought under state law?

Most commentators and judges who have applied this test to Section 504 have found that the standard has been met.

A related question is whether a party must exhaust administrative remedies before bringing an action in court. The weight of authority on this matter is not quite as strong as on the matter of whether there is a private right of action at all. Most authorities, however, indicate that because administrative remedies do not provide relief to the individual and because of the general ineffectiveness of administrative procedures, exhaustion of administrative remedies is not required in Section 504 cases.

Assuming that the individual does have a private right of action, the more difficult questions are what the burden of proof is in these cases and what remedies are available to the individual who is successful in proving a Section 504 discrimination claim. Where the individual can prove that he or she is an otherwise qualified handicapped individual within Section 504, and that benefits were denied to the individual, the general rule seems to be that the burden then shifts to the recipient to demonstrate either that the individual is not qualified or that the denial was for some reason other than the handicap.[27]

Remedies

The normal remedy when an administrative agency finds a violation of Section 504 is the termination of federal assistance. The individual who has been discriminated against is usually more interested in a remedy that will redress the specific injury. One remedy that may benefit the individual is an injunction. Courts have generally found that injunctive relief is available under Section 504 in spite of the fact that there is no specific provision for it in the Act.[28]

There is less consistency relating to monetary relief in the form of damages as a remedy under Section 504.[29] This would provide compensation for out-of-pocket expenses, prospective expenses, or recovery such as lost potential earnings. There is no question that damages are available if the action is brought under Section 1983 of the Civil Rights Act[30] for a violation of Section 504. Section 1983 permits individuals deprived of the rights, privileges, or immunities of the Constitution or federal laws to bring action in courts and also to recover damages.[31] It is not yet well settled whether Section 1983 may be used to remedy Section 504 violations, although there is some precedent allowing it.[32]

The remedy where there is the most clarity is that of attorney's fees. The Rehabilitation Act has a specific provision allowing attorneys' fees for individuals who are successful in Section 504 actions.[33] Individuals who are successful in Section 1983 actions are also entitled to attorneys' fees.[34]

In the first years after the passage of the EAHCA and Section 504 of the Rehabilitation Act, it was unclear whether an individual could seek redress under both statutes and/or use Section 1983 of the Civil Rights Act as the basis for bringing an equal protection claim.[35] The following case resolved this issue to a significant extent.

SMITH V. ROBINSON

468 U.S. 992 (1984)
Justice BLACKMUN delivered the opinion of the Court.

This case presents questions regarding the award of attorney's fees in a proceeding to secure a "free appropriate public education" for a handicapped child....

We turn to petitioners' claim that they were entitled to fees under sec. 505 of the Rehabilitation Act, because they asserted a substantial claim for relief under sec. 504 of that Act.

Much of our analysis of petitioners' equal protection claim is applicable here. The [Education for All Handicapped Children Act (EHA)] is a comprehensive scheme designed by Congress as the most effective way to protect the right of a handicapped child to a free appropriate public education. We concluded above that in enacting the EHA, Congress was aware of, and intended to accommodate, the claims of handicapped children that the Equal Protection Clause require that they be ensured access to public education. We also concluded that Congress did not intend to have the EHA scheme circumvented by resort to the more general provisions of sec. 1983.

Section 504 and the EHA are different substantive statutes. While the EHA guarantees a right to a free appropriate public education, sec. 504 simply prevents discrimination on the basis of handicap. But while the EHA is limited to handicapped children seeking access to public education, sec. 504 protects handicapped persons of all ages from discrimination in a variety of programs and activities receiving federal financial assistance.

Because both statutes are built around fundamental notions of equal access to state programs and facilities, their substantive requirements, as applied to the right of a handicapped child to a public education, have been interpreted to be strikingly similar. In regulations promulgated pursuant to sec. 504, the Secretary of Education has interpreted sec. 504 as requiring a recipient of federal funds that operates a public elementary or secondary education program to provide a free appropriate public education to each qualified handicapped person in the recipient's jurisdiction. The Secretary declined to require the exact EHA procedures, because those procedures might be inappropriate for some recipients not subject to the EHA, but indicated that compliance with EHA procedures would satisfy sec. 104.36.

On the other hand, although both statutes begin with an equal protection premise that handicapped children must be given access to public education, it does not follow that the affirmative requirements imposed by the two statutes are the same. The significant difference between the two, as applied to special education claims, is that the substantive and procedural rights assumed to be guaranteed by both statutes are specifically required only by the EHA. . . .

In *Southeastern Community College v. Davis,* the Court emphasized that sec. 504 does not require affirmative action on behalf of handicapped persons, but only the absence of discrimination against those persons. In light of *Davis,* courts construing sec. 504 as applied to the educational needs of handicapped children have expressed confusion about the extent to which sec. 504 requires special services necessary to make public education accessible to handicapped children.

In the EHA, on the other hand, Congress specified the affirmative obligations imposed on States to ensure that equal access to a public education is not an empty guarantee, but offers some benefit to a handicapped child. Thus, the statute specifically requires "such . . . supportive services . . . as may be required to assist a handicapped child to benefit from special education," including, if the public facilities are inadequate for the needs of the child, "instruction in hospitals and institutions."

There is no suggestion that sec. 504 adds anything to petitioners' substantive right to a free appropriate public education. The only elements added by sec. 504 are the possibility of circumventing EHA administrative procedures and going straight to court with a sec. 504 claim, the possibility of a damages award in cases where no such award is available under the EHA, and attorney's fees. As discussed above, Congress' intent to place on local and state educational agencies the responsibility for determining the most appropriate education plan for a handicapped child is clear. To the extent sec. 504 otherwise would allow a plaintiff to circumvent that state procedure, we are satisfied that the remedy conflicts with Congress' intent in the EHA. The Act appears to represent Congress' judgment that the best way to ensure a free appropriate public education for handicapped children is to clarify and make enforceable the rights of those children while at the same time endeavoring to relieve the financial burden imposed on the agencies responsible to guarantee those rights. Where sec. 504 adds nothing to the substantive rights of a handicapped child, we cannot believe that Congress intended to have the careful balance struck in the EHA upset by reliance on sec. 504 for otherwise unavailable damages or for an award of attorney's fees.

We emphasize the narrowness of our holding. We hold only that where, as here, whatever remedy might be provided under sec. 504 is provided with more clarity and precision under the EHA, a plaintiff may not circumvent or enlarge on the remedies available under the EHA by resort to sec. 504.

Defenses

There are a number of defenses to a Section 504 action. As was pointed out by the *Smith v. Robinson* decision, there will be few situations in the future where Section 504 will be applicable to a special education case. For that reason these defenses will not be discussed in detail. They should, however, be mentioned.

One defense that is no longer relevant for cases arising since 1986 is the defense of immunity. The eleventh amendment to the Constitution[36] prohibits actions that are not based on constitutional violations, against states or state agencies. There are two exceptions to this rule: (1) where Congress has specifically abrogated immunity and (2) where the state has expressly waived immunity. The

Supreme Court in 1985, in *Atascadero State Hospital v. Scanlon,*[37] held that states and state agencies were immune from suits under Section 504 of the Rehabilitation Act because neither exception applied. As a result of that decision Congress amended the Rehabilitation Act to specify that states are not immune from Section 504.[38]

Other defenses under Section 504 include cost, and safety or health risks. The defense of cost could arise if the defendant claimed that it would be unduly burdensome to provide reasonable accommodation to allow participation to handicapped persons in a program. This is an issue that has not frequently been raised in Section 504 cases involving special education so there is little case law to provide guidance. The health issue has begun to be addressed, as it relates to children with infectious diseases, and it will be discussed more fully in Chapter 5. The safety issue arises most frequently in cases involving the participation of handicapped students in contact sports.

THE EDUCATION FOR ALL HANDICAPPED CHILDREN ACT—P.L. 94–142

As we pointed out in Chapter 1, EAHCA was founded on constitutional principles of equal protection and due process. While there is no direct constitutional right to education or special education, states that provide education to citizens of their states must do so on an equal basis. Any denial of this state-created right requires due process.

States could choose to comply with these equal protection and due process requirements by setting up a program of special education without following the federal requirements of the EAHCA, as long as the special education program meets the constitutional standards of equal protection and due process.

Congress has recognized, however, that the additional costs of special education can be burdensome, and that as a policy matter it makes sense to encourage some degree of consistency among the various states. To that end, Congress passed the EAHCA, often referred to as P.L. 94–142. The EAHCA is a funding statute that creates substantive rights. Under the EAHCA the federal government will provide supportive funding to those states that provide special education within the framework of federally developed guidelines. An exploration of many of these guidelines is the major substance of this book, but it is useful to have an overview of what those guidelines are before examining the requirements in depth.

The Funding Mechanism

The EAHCA is not intended to cover the entire cost of special education. The assumption after the *PARC* and *Mills* decisions and numerous other similar actions throughout the country is that states are obligated to provide special education anyway. Appropriations under EAHCA assist states in providing what they must provide even without the EAHCA.

To qualify for federal funds, the state educational agency is required to submit an annual program plan setting out how it intends to provide education to handicapped children within the state. A detailed framework of information must be provided in this annual program plan.[39] Details of the plans include what services will be provided (including a comprehensive system of personnel development) and what procedural safeguards will be in place to ensure that programming is being provided. The services must include not only the education itself but also a system for identifying, evaluating, and locating children in need of special education.[40] States must also set up a system for allocating the funding to the local educational providers.

The amount of funding that states may receive if they comply with the EAHCA guidelines is based on the number of handicapped children in the state. This number is then multiplied by an average per-pupil amount. States often set out a similar formula for local educational entities to be reimbursed from state funds. There is also a cap on the number of pupils in each state that will be funded by federal sources through the EAHCA. The maximum number of children served may be no more than 12% of the total number of children ages 5 to 17 within each state. There is an additional maximum set for learning-disabled children; no more than 2% of those students identified may be funded through the federal program. It should also be noted that the funding mechanism is designed to provide support primarily at the local level where it is most needed. For that reason the formula requires that 75% of the federal funding is to be passed through by the state to the local educational agencies.[41]

The formula funding has created a number of problems. One problem, of course, is simply the complexities of counting the handicapped children. Another major problem is the fact that the subsidy is based on an average cost of educating a handicapped pupil (based on national figures). The cost of educating children who have severe disabilities is much higher than educating mildly handicapped children. A local educational agency, for example, that has two or three residential placements within its locality will use up its entire special education budget very quickly, when compared to an area that has less incidence of severe handicapping conditions. Another problem concerns definitions. Many disputes erupt over the appropriate definition of certain handicaps, particularly learning disability. Depending on what definition is used, one locality may have a much larger number of handicapped children than another. In addition, the cap on the number of children who may be served by federal funding is itself a disincentive to identify all children with handicaps.

The Substance of Special Education

One of the major principles of the EAHCA is that the education is to be provided to *all* children who meet the age eligibility requirements.[42] This is based on the idea that all children are capable of benefiting from education. This in turn requires a definition of "education" as incorporating more than the three R's. Education under the EAHCA would seem to include basic self-help skills such as feeding, toilet training, and vocational training. Those children who meet the age eligibility requirements are those aged 6 through 18. In addition, states that provide education to children between ages 3 and 5 and ages 19 and 21 must also provide special education on an equal basis. A 1986 amendment to the EAHCA provides for additional incentive grants for infants and toddlers.

A second major principle of the EAHCA is what is commonly known as the mainstreaming mandate. This comes about as a result of the requirement that education is to be provided in the *least restrictive appropriate* placement.[43] One of the early fears of educators was that the EAHCA mainstreaming mandate meant that all handicapped children, regardless of the severity of handicap, were to be "dumped" into the regular classroom without support. While there are certainly instances of inappropriate placements of severely handicapped children into the regular classroom, the EAHCA requires that the child be placed in the least restrictive *appropriate* setting. While the goal is to move the child to less restrictive settings, for some children full time in the regular classroom may never be an appropriate placement. The theory underlying the mainstreaming goal includes the "separate is not equal" principle of *Brown v. Board of Education.*[44] Segregated placements are inherently stigmatizing. In addition, for many children, interaction with nonhandicapped peers is an essential component of role-modeling and appropriate social development. It is important to emphasize that the EAHCA does *not* require placement in the *best* placement, only the least restrictive appropriate placement. While states may choose to make the *best* placement a part of special education, it is not required under federal law.

A third major principle of the EAHCA is that education is to be *individualized* and *appropriate* to the child's needs.[45] The EAHCA requires that once a child is identified as being handicapped, an individualized educational program (IEP) must be developed with the involvement of several educators and parent(s). This would preclude a practice such as simply photocopying and using the same educational program plan for all visually impaired children aged 10. The principle requires an individual assessment of the specific needs and abilities of the particular child and the development of not only the educational placement but also of a plan to assess whether the goals are being met. It is important to note that the goals set forth in these plans are not contracts between the parents and the educational agency, and that schools are not to be held liable simply because certain goals have not been met.

The final substantive principle of the EAHCA is that education is to be provided *free.*[46] This basically means that all of the child's *educational* needs are to be provided at no cost to the parents, regardless of their ability to pay. Disputes have arisen about whether certain kinds of expenses were really medical rather than educational, and whether expensive residential placements must be paid for by the educational agency. More recently, disagreements have arisen among various public social service agencies as to whose budget must bear the costs of certain placements. These issues are discussed in greater detail in subsequent chapters. It should be noted, however, that even if a parent is financially well off, if the placement is deemed to be the appropriate placement, the educational costs are to be paid by the school. There are those who might argue that, as a policy, this does not make sense, and that at least for some expenses there should be a sliding scale. For the time being, however, Congress has decided otherwise.

Procedural Safeguards under the EAHCA

Congress recognized that for the substantive requirements to be carried out, procedural protections would need to be in place. These protections are in place at all stages of the educational process, including identification, evaluation, placement decision making, and implementation. Parents have the right to challenge a decision as well as withdraw consent at any stage of the process.[47]

The specific procedural protections include a right to notice of a proposed decision about a child entitled to special education, as well as notice of all of the procedural and substantive protections available. If a special education placement is being proposed, it is to be developed at a meeting that includes the parents. The individualized educational program (IEP) can then be challenged at a hearing. The hearing must be impartial, the parents are entitled to be represented at the hearing, and there is a right both to a record of the hearing and to written findings of fact and decisions. There is also a right of review with the state educational agency and an ultimate right to seek review in the courts. There has been litigation over circumstances that might permit the parents to seek redress directly in court, and this issue is discussed more fully in subsequent chapters. Other procedural issues in dispute have revolved around such things as whether the hearing officer is impartial or when can a child be removed from the classroom pending a resolution of the dispute. A recently resolved issue is whether one can use Section 504 of the Rehabilitation Act to seek relief, or whether one is limited to using the procedures of the EAHCA. The Supreme Court in *Smith v. Robinson*[48] held that where the EAHCA provides relief, that statute, and not Section 504, must be the basis for seeking redress. What remains under dispute, however, are questions about situations in which Section 504 might still be available.

One procedural issue that has recently been clarified through congressional amendment is that right to attorneys' fees. As a result of the litigation and decision in *Smith v. Robinson,* Congress amended the EAHCA to clarify that parents who are successful may recover attorney's fees and costs. This amendment has resulted in a flurry of litigation involving issues such as whether the fees are available in administrative proceedings as well as in court litigation, whether the provision is retroactive in certain respects, and what expenses and fees are considered permissible under the statute.

There are some who criticize the EAHCA procedures as really only providing protection to aggressive middle-class parents. Others argue that the procedures are cumbersome and an inefficient use of educational resources. But there are many who believe that the existence of these procedures has been an important and essential component of ensuring that the goals of the EAHCA have been substantially complied with.

STATE EDUCATION STATUTES

Although education is primarily state controlled, special education, in practice, has become federally controlled by the EAHCA. Although states are not required to follow the EAHCA requirements, they must do so if they wish to receive federal funding for special education. The federal budgetary support for special education is of extreme importance. It should be emphasized also that states may well be required to comply with many of the substantive and procedural requirements of the EAHCA, in any case, as a result of the *PARC* and *Mills* decisions. All states have elected to develop annual program plans to be eligible for federal funding under the EAHCA.

For those states providing special education even before the EAHCA, it was necessary for them to adapt their existing state educational programs to fit the requirements of the EAHCA. States that did not have special education programs in place were required to develop them.

Virtually all states have adopted as a basic framework the federal regulations. Many have expanded on these regulations and have provided more detailed or additional requirements for special education programming. To the extent that these do not conflict with federal requirements and to the extent these meet the federal minimums, they are permissible.

There are a number of areas in which state statutes are likely to expand on the federal special education requirements. For example, states may elect to provide special education to children outside the age mandates of the EAHCA. States may include other categories of children entitled to special education—such as gifted students. As long as the procedures are consistent with the EAHCA, states may allow for additional procedural safeguards, such as having a panel of hearing officers, rather than just one. In addition, states set out their own specific requirements relating to matters such as teacher certification, age-span requirements in the classroom, teacher-pupil ratios, and maximum time for transportation.

The funding mechanism is another area in which states have some flexibility. States are required to distribute at least 75% of the federal allocation to local and intermediate educational agencies. States may, however, choose to distribute more than the 75% directly to the local and intermediate units. Of the funding retained at the state level, states are limited in the amount that is to be used for administrative costs. States may, however, choose to use less than this amount for administrative costs. The intent of the funding formula is to ensure that funding goes directly to educational services as much as possible. The way that states choose to allocate funding within these federal guidelines can have a significant effect on local educational budgets. For example, if certain types of expensive programs are provided directly by the state budget, this can be of substantial benefit to a local educational agency with a small budget.

One area in which there has been some recent difficulty involving state policies relates to the deinstitutionalization movement. In a significant number of states, litigation under state constitutions, mental health and mental retardation laws, and other statutes have resulted in a policy of moving institutionalized individuals (both children and adults) into the local community. For those children who are eligible for public education, there are often disputes over which agency has responsibility for funding the child's placement needs. State health and human service agencies have sometimes tried to shift fiscal responsibility for these placements and certain services to state educational agencies. While there have been some recent efforts to establish interagency cooperation in a number of states, this is an area in need of greater clarity of policy.

It should be noted that states are given a substantial degree of deference in the choice of educational programming to be provided within the framework. The role of the federal government is not intended to be one that mandates how states are told to educate a deaf child, for example. This point was emphasized in the first Supreme Court case to decide an EAHCA issue, *Board of Education v. Rowley.*[49]

OTHER RELEVANT LAWS

When a parent or school is concerned about the requirements for educating a child with a handicap, the primary laws will be the EAHCA, state education laws, and to a lesser extent Section 504 of the Rehabilitation Act. There are a number of other federal and state laws of which the professional involved in special education law should be generally aware.

Student Records Laws

The Family Educational Rights and Privacy Act (FERPA)[50] is more commonly known as the Buckley Amendment. It is intended to provide protections in two major areas—access and accuracy. It requires that schools subject to FERPA, which includes public schools, must permit parents and students over 18 to have access to their records in certain circumstances, and it provides for protections against unauthorized disclosure of school records. By having access to the records, the student can ascertain whether the information in the records is accurate and complete. FERPA provides mechanisms for making appropriate changes and corrections.

In addition to FERPA, most states have a variety of state record laws. These may have additional protections and may provide for additional rights and remedies where violations have occurred. State confidentiality requirements and related laws are particularly important in cases involving children with AIDS or other communicable diseases. It can be critical to know when certain information must be reported to public health officials, and to whom it is permissible to disclose information about the condition of a child. Many states are in the process of revising their state confidentiality and communicable disease laws because of these concerns.

State Health Laws

State laws relating to communicable diseases can be of importance in the special education context. Where a child has a communicable disease that may be viewed as one posing a risk to others, but where that same child is potentially considered to be "handicapped" within the EAHCA or Section 504, there is the potential for tension between the various laws. This is an area where the need for policy revision has become apparent, but until a clear-cut national policy is established, or until a statewide policy is established in the state where the child is attending school, it is important to at least recognize that there may be conflicting policies.

In addition to communicable disease laws, there are state mental health/ mental retardation statutes. These laws usually involve the provision of services to individuals who are mentally ill or mentally retarded. A child with a severe emotional disturbance or autism, who might have simply been institutionalized 20 years ago, will now be entitled to at least the educational component of a placement under state special education laws. There is considerable tension between agencies in many states, and the laws themselves do not always clearly delineate the agency having the primary administrative and/or fiscal responsibility for the services needed by the child.

Tort and Contract Law

In addition to the major laws noted previously, there are a number of instances where issues of tort and/or contract law may become relevant. While this is not a major area of concern, it is an area where a brief general overview is appropriate.

Tort law includes a variety of potential actions that could arise relating to special education. These could include defamation, libel, slander, or invasion of privacy, where information about a child is improperly or inaccurately conveyed by school officials to others who are not authorized to receive the information.

The tort issue most likely to arise, however, is negligence—or special education malpractice. As will be discussed in more depth in Chapter 16, while there is currently little judicial acceptance of the malpractice theory in special education cases, there is something of a change in judicial attitude in recent years. Related to the negligence issue is a breach-of-contract issue. The question that is raised in some circumstances is whether the failure to accomplish the goals of an IEP constitutes a breach of contract. As a general rule, such a theory will not be accepted by the courts, but it is important to be aware that it maybe raised.

SUMMARY

Section 504 of the Rehabilitation Act prohibits recipients of federal financial assistance (such as educational agencies) from discriminating on the basis of handicap. This provides some protection for the student who has a handicap. Section 504, however, does not contain a basis for the additional support services and major accommodations necessary in many cases for appropriate provision of special education. Neither does it contain a clear procedural framework to enforce educational rights.

The EAHCA does provide these missing elements. It goes beyond a mere nondiscrimination mandate and requires special education and related services to be provided to all children with handicaps in the least restrictive appropriate setting at no cost. Perhaps the most important feature of the EAHCA is its elaborate set of procedural protections including notice and an opportunity to have a disagreement resolved by an impartial decision-maker.

Because of the detailed requirements of the EAHCA, the Supreme Court has held that Congress intended the EAHCA to be the exclusive avenue through which special education claims were to be addressed—at least where the substantive rights of the child are protected through the EAHCA. The *Smith v. Robinson* decision left open the question of what circumstances remain to justify reliance on other avenues of redress.

What remedies are available remains an unresolved issue under both the EAHCA and Section 504. The Supreme Court has yet to clarify this issue, and lower courts have reached a variety of conclusions about the question of damages and other remedies in special education cases.

While Section 504 and the EAHCA provide the federal statutory framework, state special education statutes and regulations incorporate the EAHCA mandates and frequently expand on various issues. In addition, state health, tort, and contract laws and federal and state law relating to privacy for students must also be reference points in evaluating legal requirements affecting students with handicaps. While it is important to recognize state law requirements, the wide variance from state to state makes an indepth examination of these laws impossible in this text.

QUESTIONS AND PROBLEMS

1. With the Rehabilitation Act providing protection against discrimination on the basis of handicap, why is the EAHCA necessary?
2. What problems are there with the EAHCA funding formula?
3. Would the EAHCA be a viable statute without the procedural protections? Why or why not?
4. What do state education statutes relating to special education add to the EAHCA? Why doesn't the EAHCA cover these issues?

5. As a practical matter, how can an administrator keep up on all of the legal requirements affecting special education?

NOTES

1. 20 U.S.C. §§ 1401 *et. seq.*
2. 29 U.S.C. § 794.
3. *See* 1973 U.S. CODE CONG. & AD. NEWS 2076.
4. 29 U.S.C. § 794. Other provisions of the Rehabilitation Act prohibit discrimination by federal employers and federal contractors.
5. *See generally* L. ROTHSTEIN, RIGHTS OF PHYSICALLY HANDICAPPED PERSONS (RPHP) (1984) and cumulative supplements.
6. *Id.*
7. 29 U.S.C. § 706(7)(B).
8. 34 C.F.R. § 104.3(j)(2)(ii).
9. Southeastern Community College v. Davis, 442 U.S. 397 (1979).
10. *Id.*
11. 34 C.F.R. § 104.3(f) & (h).
12. 465 U.S. 555 (1984).
13. 20 U.S.C. § 1681(a).
14. Pub. L. No. 100–259.
15. 807 F.2d 75 (6th Cir. 1986).
16. 107 S. Ct. 1123 (1987).
17. 772 F.2d 759, 763 (11th Cir. 1985).
18. The address is U.S. Department of Education, Office for Civil Rights, 400 Maryland Avenue, S.W., Washington D.C. 20202. The procedures are those used for implementation of Title VI of the Civil Rights Act. See 34 C.F.R. §§ 100.6–.10 and 600.1–131.
19. 34 C.F.R. § 100.9. The agency may also refer the matter to the Department of Justice.
20. *Id.* at § 100.9(a).
21. 465 U.S. 555 (1984).
22. 34 C.F.R. § 100.10(f).
23. *Id.* at § 100.11.
24. *See* RPHP § 3.18.
25. Southeastern Community College v. Davis, 442 U.S. 397 (1979); Camenisch v. University of Texas, 451 U.S. 390 (1981); Bowen v. American Hospital Association, 106 S.Ct. 2101 (1986); United States Department of Transportation v. Paralyzed Veterans of America, 106 S.Ct. 2705 (1986); County of Los Angeles v. Kling, 106 S.Ct. 300 (1985); Consolidated Rail Corporation v. Darrone, 464 U.S. 624 (1984); Atascadero State Hospital v. Scanlon, 105 S.Ct. 3142 (1985); and School Board of Nassau County v. Arline, 107 S.Ct. 1123 (1987).
26. 422 U.S. 66 (1975).
27. *See* RPHP § 3.20.
28. *Id.* at § 3.25.
29. *Id.* at § 3.26.
30. 42 U.S.C. § 1983. *See* RPHP § 3.21.
31. *See* RPHP § 2.36.
32. *Id.*

33. *Id.*
34. 42 U.S.C. § 1988 (the Civil Rights Attorney's Fees Awards Act of 1976). *See* H.B. NEWBERG ATTORNEY FEE AWARDS § 12.04 (1986).
35. *See* RPHP §§ 2.32, 2.35, 2.36.
36. U.S. CONST. amend. XI.
37. 473 U.S. 234 (1985).
38. Pub. L. No. 99–506, 100 Stat. 1807 (1986), 29 U.S.C. § 701.
39. 34 C.F.R. Subpart B.
40. 34 C.F.R. § 300.128.
41. 20 U.S.C. § 1411(a)(5)(i) & § 1411(c)(1)(B).
42. See Chapter 5.
43. See Chapter 8.
44. 347 U.S. 483 (1954).
45. See Chapter 7.
46. See Chapter 13.
47. See Chapter 14.
48. 468 U.S. 992 (1984).
49. 458 U.S. 176 (1982).
50. 20 U.S.C. § 1232(g).

CHAPTER 4

The People

Before examining in detail the substantive and procedural requirements and the remedies available under the laws relating to special education, it is useful to have a sense of the various individuals who are involved in these issues. These include the children themselves, their parents, the educators, and advocates. The following sections describe the major characteristics of these people.

THE STUDENTS

Categorization

The EAHCA defines a handicapped child as one who is

> mentally retarded, hard of hearing, deaf, speech impaired, visually handicapped, seriously emotionally disturbed, orthopedically impaired, or other health impaired . . . or with specific learning disabilities, who by reason/ of the handicap/ require/s/ special education and related services.[1]

Approximately 12% of the school-age population fit this definition. It should be emphasized that the child must not only fit one of the categories listed in the statute, but must also require special education and/or related services because of the handicap. About 25% of school-age children need significant assistance to benefit from standard education, but only about half of these fit the EAHCA label.[2]

There are a number of problems with the categorization system used for providing special education services under the EAHCA. One problem is that the labels attached to these children do not always accurately reflect the characteristics of the children. Additional problems include the stigmatization that results from labelling and the fact that once a child is labelled, it is unlikely that the label for that child will ever be changed. A further problem is that attaching a label to a child may well result in a self-fulfilling prophecy.

Of most concern in terms of educational planning is that the labels do not really address the appropriate means of providing instruction and training for teachers. These concerns have resulted in the recommendation by a number of professionals that the classification of children be noncategorical.[3] These recommendations have been implemented in many states. For example, Texas and California train and certify special educators noncategorically. While this has been achieved positively in a variety of programs throughout the country, unless and until the funding formula for the EAHCA is changed, it is still necessary for funding purposes to categorize children according to their labels.

While some of the legal issues relating to labelling will be discussed more fully in Chapter 6, a few general points should be noted here. Within the categories set out by the EAHCA definition of a handicapped child, a wide degree of difference exists among children. The educational needs of children within these categories is correspondingly widely disparate. And even children with the same functional level may have differing educational needs because of differences in the type of home environment and other factors. It should, therefore, be apparent that attaching a label to a child provides only the most general information about that child. It is one of the reasons that individualized educational programming is required for handicapped children under the EAHCA. Placement and services should not be based on the child's label.

Gaps in Coverage

One group not covered by the EAHCA is the gifted and talented child. Although the EAHCA does not provide coverage for this group of children, many states provide special educational programming for gifted children.

Two other categories of children should be mentioned that are not really comprehensively covered by the EAHCA. The first is the chronically ill child, the child with an illness such as cancer or diabetes who may be frequently absent from school for treatment or because of illness. It is not always clear that this child is "other health impaired [requiring] special education and related services" by reason of the handicap. Where the child is frequently absent and needs a program of home-bound instruction, the child may fit the definition. Even more problematic is the child with AIDS or another infectious disease. In many cases the child with AIDS does not meet the definition of "handicapped" for purposes of the EAHCA, although the child is probably handicapped under Section 504 of the Rehabilitation Act. This can be important if the child is seeking to take advantage of the procedural safeguards available under the EAHCA that are not available under Section 504. The safeguards include the right to remain in the current placement, an impartial determination as to the appropriate placement, and other due process protections.

The second category to be noted is the "slow learner." This is a child who falls through the cracks between special and regular education. Unless the child is defined as learning disabled or mentally retarded, the child is not entitled to the individualization and special attention accorded to the handicapped child under the EAHCA. Because regular education is geared primarily to the average student, the slow learner is left with little attention in the education program. Because there is so much disagreement among professionals about the definition of learning disabled, there is a substantial amount of misclassification. Some children who are really slow learners have been classified as learning disabled and have been provided with special education services, and others who are actually learning disabled have not been provided with special education because they have been misidentified.[4]

There is yet a third category of children that is problematic—children who are socially maladjusted. There is a substantial controversy over the question about whether to separate or even identify socially maladjusted children from those who meet the definition of emotionally disturbed. Separating out this group of students would mean that they would not be entitled to the EAHCA protections. Unlike slow learners, who may be able to receive some extra help through Chapter 1 funding, for educationally deprived children, the socially maladjusted child would have no safety net of services.[5]

In sum, most children entitled to special education are more different from each other than they are alike. They are more like other children in the school system than they are different. But for most of them their differences require some accommodation if they are to benefit from the educational system.

It is also important to note that most attention to special students has occurred on the elementary school level. This is reflected in programming and teacher training. There has, however, been an increasing recognition of the importance of early education and the transition at the secondary level to the workplace. This recognition is reflected in federal policy changes providing for early childhood and infant programs under the EAHCA and in an increasing emphasis on vocational training for special education students.[6]

THE PARENTS

Who Are "Parents"?

When determining the special education placement of an individual entitled to services under the EAHCA, the individual who will usually be consenting to the evaluation, placement, or other decision is the parent. Children under the age of 18 are generally presumed legally incompetent to consent to most decisions made on their behalf, although the preferences of the child may be a consideration.

For purposes of the EAHCA, whenever reference is made to decision making or involvement by the parent, the term is intended to include not only the actual parent, but also could include a grandparent, stepparent, a surrogate parent appointed by the court or a social service agency, or a court-appointed guardian.[7] The intent is that the person who is legally responsible for the child shall be the party responsible for making special education decisions. In instances where the child is a ward of the state, a surrogate parent would have to be appointed or some other arrangement would have to be made because the term does not include the state itself in the role of parent.

Given the divorce rate in the United States, it is not unusual for a child to have parents who do not live in the same household. Where one parent has legal custody, ordinarily that parent will have the authority to make decisions about special education placement and will be the party to whom notice of special education decisions is to be sent. Problems can arise, however, where divorced parents have joint legal custody of a child. Must the school send both parents copies of all general school notices, or only notices about special education matters? While there is not a great deal of litigation in this area, it is an issue that arises from time to time. One of the few cases to address this issue indicates that while it is unreasonably burdensome to send copies of routine announcements about school activities to both parents with legal custody, they are probably both entitled to access to school records.[8] It is probably also advisable to send both parents notices about testing, placement, etc., that relate to the individual child.

The Role of Parents

Parents are an essential component to the effectiveness of the EAHCA. Only by requiring that parents be apprised of their rights and informed of the procedures available is the attainment of the EAHCA goals possible. Parental participation requirements include mandatory notification of parents at various stages of the process and mandates ensuring that the opportunity for parental participation is available.[9]

In addition to the role of representing the interests of their own individual children, parents have a role in special education policy-making, as well. The EAHCA provides for parental involvement in state advisory panels on special education,[10] and some local educational agencies have found that having a local advisory panel is helpful.

Although there is probably a general consensus about the significance of the parental role in carrying out the requirements of the EAHCA, there are those who would argue, however, that not all handicapped children are benefiting from the EAHCA because they do not all have strong parental advocates. The argument would be that the aggressive middle-class parent who is not intimidated by the educational or legal system will take advantage of the procedural and substantive protections available, and the child whose parents may be less well educated is less likely to benefit. Middle-class parents are more likely to be aware of both the availability and benefits of special education. While the same may be true of wealthy parents, they are more likely to pay for a private placement in order to have the "best" educational programming rather than seeking to have the public education system provide the special education to the child. While it is difficult to trace whether it is in fact true that handicapped children in lower income/less well educated families are being less well served, this may well be the case. If this is so, it may be that additional policy changes should be made. In any case, it seems undeniable that the parents play a significant role in carrying out the requirements of the EAHCA.

A number of situations arise in which the interest of the parent conflicts with that of the child. Many parents seek very restrictive placements out of fear that their children may become lost in the mainstream or because they do not want to be bothered with the responsibility of the child. While the fear is reasonable and the unwanted burden is understandable, the goal should be to ensure that the needed services are in place in the least restrictive appropriate setting. For the attorney who has been consulted by the parent, it can be difficult because the attorney must decide whether the client is the parent or the child. It may be important for the attorney to discuss this possibility at the outset. It is also important to recognize that the school district's obligation is to ensure appropriate education *regardless* of parental wishes. Schools often give in to parents even when the child's best interest is not served.

THE EDUCATORS

Teachers

The primary contact person for the handicapped child is, of course, the teacher. This includes both the regular classroom teacher and the special education teacher. It also includes teachers of special subjects such as art, physical education, vocational education, and music.

For many regular classroom teachers, the implementation of the EAHCA brought a great deal of stress. They feared that masses of handicapped children would be "dumped" into the regular classroom. Regular education teachers (as well as teachers in general) had already been faced with increasing professional demands at the same time that financial and professional rewards were diminishing. This new pressure was not welcomed. Most of these teachers had received their degrees and teaching certificates before special education was mandatory and had little exposure to the requirements of being a teacher in a "mainstream" classroom. The added requirements of recordkeeping were often viewed as an unnecessary burden. Another concern was the lack of role clarification. Regular teachers who had been teaching for some time questioned why they should consult with a young, newly trained special education teacher. There was additional anxiety because a number of requirements were initially unclear, and it was difficult to learn all of the requirements even if they were clear. For example, if a regular education teacher wanted to place the child in a speech therapy or other remedial program, the teacher could no longer simply do this. Notice to parents of the plan and an opportunity for them to be involved in the decision was now required.

In spite of the initial negative reaction to the EAHCA, teachers have come to accept the mainstreaming requirement as a fact of life in public education, and there is improvement in the amount of support provided to the regular classroom in the form of consultation with special educators, teaching assistants, volunteers, etc. In addition, many teachers are more likely to complete their teacher education programs with more exposure to special education issues and educational methodology for handicapped children. Some states now require exposure to special education for all teachers. Teachers are also more likely to have access to inservice training relating to special education issues, to compensate for knowledge they did not get while acquiring their teaching degrees.

Although the attitude and preparation of the regular education teacher has improved since 1975, it is important to recognize that there are still some serious obstacles for the regular classroom teacher. The initial funding promises and plans of the EAHCA have not been entirely fulfilled by the federal government, and there remain significant problems of understaffing in the regular classroom. For example, where placement for a mildly mentally retarded child may be appropriate in the regular classroom, to the extent that the child may need additional support for certain aspects of the educational program, there may not be funding to provide the teacher's assistant in the classroom. In addition, there is a need for coordination and cooperation between the regular classroom teacher and the special education teacher. These two groups need to know how to communicate needs, problems, and solutions to each other. Another concern is that the regular education teacher may need more in the way of training relating to identification of handicapping conditions, behavior management, and direct instruction methods for students who do not learn from the usual teaching strategy. Teacher education programs, state certification requirements, and local hiring practices should require regular education teachers to have these skills. While there have been a number of positive improvements in these areas, the need to improve regular education teacher preparation for providing education programming in the regular classroom is ongoing and in serious need of attention. In addition to providing training and support services, increasing the financial compensation of educators will be an essential component if future efforts are to be successful.

One of the needs of the special education professional is being able to work with the regular educators in developing an appropriate program that maintains the child in the least restrictive setting. Historically, many special education teacher training programs were developed to match definitional categories, and this continues in many programs today. For example, teacher training programs for learning-disabled children exist separately from teacher training programs for behavior-disorder children. But the interrelationship of the various special education teacher preparation programs was minimal.[11] While there have been improvements in this area, it is important that this trend continue.

A major concern for both the regular classroom and the special education program is teacher shortages. There continues to be a shortage of teachers adequately trained to provide education to special students. While the EAHCA requires program personnel development for states receiving funding, the low pay and high demands of teaching in general (and special education teaching in particular) continue to keep special education understaffed. This is even more problematic in rural and inner-city areas.[12]

One of the ironies of the EAHCA is that often the teacher of specialized subjects—such as art—is the least likely to have teacher preparation to address the needs of the special student, but is the most likely to have the child mainstreamed into the class. It is not unlikely for a child to be placed in a segregated special education class for most of the academic-type subjects, but to be placed with his or her age-appropriate peers for music or art. It is this teacher who particularly needs training in behavior management, in communicating with the regular and special education teacher, and in teaching methodology. It is important that teacher certification and teacher training programs recognize this needed training in preparing teachers of special subjects. Perhaps the most important teachers for handicapped learners are the vocational education teachers. There is an increasing awareness today that high school students, who are chronologically at the end of the public education service system, need to be provided with skills that will enable them to be productive members of society. The recognition of the importance of this transition has resulted in recent attention to the fact that our public school systems are not adequately staffed with appropriately trained vocational teachers.[13]

Administrators

The most important administrator in providing special education is probably the local director of special education. It is that person who has the responsibility for ensuring that local schools are adequately staffed with appropriately trained personnel and for overseeing the development and implementation of the individualized educational programs for each child in the local school district. The special education director must also develop the data necessary for obtaining funding from the state educational agency. The special education director must plan systematic steps to transition students between regular and special education. It is essential that special education directors be able to communicate with the local principal and local board of education to ensure that appropriate policies are made and carried out. It is also important that the school principal be supportive of and knowledgeable about special education. This is a key factor to the successful implementation of the EAHCA.

At the state level, administrators responsible for special education must develop the program plans for federal and state funding, ensure appropriate funding to the local school districts, and have teacher certification requirements that ensure adequate teacher preparation. It is becoming increasingly important that state administrators be able to coordinate and cooperate with other social service agencies, as certain types of placements fall under the responsibility of several agencies. Not only will it be necessary to coordinate the appropriate services to be provided but it will also be necessary to establish which budget will fund those programs.

In many states, particularly states with large populations, an intermediate level of regional administration has been developed. Regional activities often include development of in-service programs and cooperative plans for providing certain services among local education agencies within the regions.

Other Personnel

Providing special education involves a variety of other individuals within the educational system. These include school psychologists, guidance counselors, school nurses, therapists, bus drivers, teachers' aides, and clerical staff. Virtually all of these individuals will at some point have contact with the special student, and all should have training appropriate to respond to those contacts.

A number of other individuals are likely to be directly or indirectly involved in the special education placement. These include physicians and social workers. It is increasingly important that these people be able to communicate with those responsible for developing education plans for special students.[14]

ADVOCATES

Passage of the EAHCA was in large part due to the concerted efforts of advocacy groups in bringing litigation and lobbying for legislation that has affected children with handicaps. The role of advocates continues to be a vital part of the implementation of special education law. Advocates are not only necessary to pressure for implementation, but in many cases they can be valuable resources of information.

There are currently an enormous number of advocacy, consumer, and voluntary health organizations at the national, state, and local level.[15] Many of these organizations focus on advocacy on behalf of one particular group, such as the National Association of the Deaf. The value of these organizations in advocacy is demonstrated by the fact that the Pennsylvania Association for Retarded Citizens was the plaintiff in the landmark *PARC* case, which, along with *Mills,* set the stage for passage of the EAHCA.

In many areas of the country, at the local level, there are lay advocate organizations that are helpful in advising parents on how to accomplish the goal of obtaining appropriate special education for their children. These groups can suggest strategies for working with school systems and can even help to prepare parents for due process hearings. In some cases they may actually represent the parents in these proceedings.

The passage of the Handicapped Children's Protection Act (HCPA) in 1986,[16] an amendment to the EAHCA, was an important step in ensuring effective advocacy. Before that point it was unclear whether parents could be reimbursed for attorneys' fees and costs incurred in disputes involving special education placements and other decisions. The HCPA clarifies that these fees are available to prevailing parties in appropriate circumstances.[17] While there are still some areas of confusion about what the HCPA requires in certain instances, it would seem that the availability of attorneys' fees has made this an area of law that is more attractive to the practicing attorney, and as a result it should follow that an increase in advocacy will occur. Parents may have difficulty, however, in finding an attorney willing to wait for payment until resolution of the dispute.

An important point for advocates to keep in mind is that resolution of special education disputes involves parties who must maintain an ongoing close relationship. After the dispute is resolved the child may often be placed in a setting where the educator has had an adversarial and perhaps defensive attitude toward the parent(s). It is important that both anger and frustration resulting from resolving disagreements do not adversely affect the child's education. In recognition of this, it should be emphasized that negotiation and other alternative dispute resolution should be used as much as possible when appropriate.

In addition to representation in particular disputes, advocacy is important for general policy changes or development. Advisory councils are mandatory at the state level[18] and also used at the local level. These are important opportunities for advocacy. These councils include parents and other advocates who play an important role in recommending practices and policies to state and local school boards.

SUMMARY

Participants in special education include the students, the parents, the educators (teachers, administrators, and others), and advocates.

The students are a varied group that includes individuals with orthopedic, sensory, mental, emotional, and health impairments. The wide diversity of types and degrees of impairments under the EAHCA makes individualization in providing special education an essential component of the Act.

There are numerous unsettled controversies about whether labelling should be done at all and whether certain definitional labels (such as learning disability) are appropriately defined or applied. Gifted and talented students and those with certain health impairments are not really protected by the EAHCA, although Section 504 may provide some relief to the latter group and some states protect students in the former. The slow learner, however, seems not to be specially protected by the EAHCA, Section 504, or state law.

The parents in special education situations have important rights and an essential role. Their rights include a right to a hearing and an opportunity to challenge the school's proposal decisions. With that right comes an important role— that of being a participant at almost all stages of the development of an appropriate program and deciding on an appropriate placement for the child. These rights and roles are unique to special education. In no other aspect of public education do parents have such an important role and such significant rights.

Educators have enormous burdens and obligations as a result of special education legal requirements. These expensive and stressful demands too frequently overburden understaffed, underpaid, and undertrained educational personnel. The issues to be resolved at a policy level include how to fund educational agencies at an appropriate level to meet these demands. Within the legal framework of the EAHCA the issue is related more to accountability—for personnel development and for conduct toward and programming for the student.

Advocates had a strong role in the initial passage of the EAHCA. Initially, lay advocates were probably the primary force in the enforcement of special education mandates, but the 1986 attorneys' fees amendment to the EAHCA has set the stage for an increased advocacy role for practicing attorneys. Whether this is positive or not remains to be seen.

QUESTIONS AND PROBLEMS

1. If teacher preparation for special education teachers is categorical, and if this is not a desirable way to train teachers, how can this be changed?
2. As a policy matter what should be done about the slow learner, the socially maladjusted student, the chronically ill child, the child with an infectious disease? Should gifted and talented students be included in the children protected under the EAHCA? Why or why not?
3. As a policy matter, how can the EAHCA be designed to ensure that it is not only middle-income, well-educated parents who take advantage of the requirements relating to special education?
4. As a policy matter, should schools be required to give notice under the EAHCA to both parents if they are divorced? Should it matter whether the parents have joint legal custody or not? What administrative burdens might result if both parents must be given notice, etc.?
5. How can educational systems ensure that the teachers are adequately trained? Should regular education teachers be required to take courses in special education? What requirements can be imposed on teachers who already have been certified and who have a teacher contract in existence?
6. Who should be liable if teachers are not adequately trained and a physical or education injury occurs as a result?
7. Is the availability of attorneys' fees and the resultant increase in litigation positive or negative in carrying out the goals of the EAHCA?
8. Where should the funding for special education come from?

NOTES

1. 20 U.S.C. § 140(1). For a detailed discussion of the history, definition, prevalence, causes, characteristics, and education programming applications, *see* EXCEPTIONAL CHILDREN AND YOUTH (N.G. HARING & L. McCORMICK eds. 4th ed. 1979). While most of the individuals entitled to special education are children, because age eligibility can extend to individuals over 18, it is not always appropriate to refer to the individuals protected by the EAHCA as children. For purposes of this book the terms will be used interchangeably as most appropriate.

2. M.C. Reynolds & J.W. Birch, Teaching Exceptional Children in All America's Schools 1–29 (rev. ed. 1982).
3. Brady, Conroy, & Langford, *Current Issues and Practices Affecting the Development of Noncategorical Programs for Students and Teachers,* 7(1) Teacher Education & Special Education 20–21 (1985).
4. *Id.*
5. Zasel, *Inclusion of Socially Maladjusted Children and Youth in the Legal Definition of the Behaviorally Disordered Population,* Behavior Disorders 213 (1986).
6. Exceptional Children and Youth, *supra* note 1 at *ch.1.*
7. 34 C.F.R. § 300.10.
8. Fay v. South Colonie Central School District, 802 F.2d 21 (2d Cir. 1986).
9. 34 C.F.R. § 300.345. *See also* H.R. Turnbull, Free Appropriate Public Education: The Law and Children with Disabilities, Ch. 8 (1986).
10. 34 C.F.R. § 300.651.
11. *See* Brady, *supra* note 3, at 22–23.
12. *See* Exceptional Children and Youth, *supra* note 1 at 495–503 for a discussion of the personnel issue in general.
13. *Id.* at 36–37.
14. *Id.*
15. For a listing of these organizations and their services, see Directory of National Information Sources on Handicapping Conditions and Related Services, U.S. Department of Education Office of Special Education and Rehabilitation Services (June 1986), available from the U.S. Government Printing Office, Washington, D.C. 20402. *See also* L. Rothstein, Rights of Physically Handicapped Persons (1984) at Appendix C.
16. 20 U.S.C. § 1415(e)(4).
17. This is discussed in detail in Chapter 18.
18. 20 U.S.C. § 1413(a)(12).

CHAPTER 5

Who Is Protected?

CONSTITUTIONALLY BASED CASES

Under the fourteenth amendment to the United States Constitution, states may not deprive their citizens of "equal protection of the laws." In determining whether a state has complied with the equal protection clause of the fourteenth amendment, the courts have traditionally applied different levels of scrutiny depending on the type of case involved. Two major factors are at issue in deciding what level of scrutiny to apply. One is whether the person claiming a denial of equal protection is a member of a class of individuals who are or should be entitled to special consideration. The other is the importance of the right at issue.

Classification of Handicapped Individuals

The following opinion demonstrates the level of scrutiny that is to be applied to mentally retarded individuals. The decision did not involve the educational setting but it is instructive in evaluating potential constitutional claims involving handicapped individuals. The fact-setting of the case involved the city council's denial of a special use permit to operate a group home. The applicant for the permit wanted to operate a group home for 13 mentally retarded men and women with constant staff supervision. The reason for the city's denial included negative attitudes and fears of nearby property owners, concern that residents would be harassed by junior high students from a nearby school, the location of the home on the flood plain, and concern that a group home would result in crowded conditions. In deciding what level of scrutiny to apply in evaluating whether the denial was constitutional, the Supreme Court examined the classification of the group affected.

CITY OF CLEBURNE V. CLEBURNE LIVING CENTER

473 U.S. 432 (1985)
Justice WHITE delivered the opinion of the Court.

The Equal Protection Clause of the Fourteenth Amendment commands that no State shall "deny to any person within its jurisdiction the equal protection of the laws," which is essentially a direction that all persons similarly situated should be treated alike. Section 5 of the Amendment empowers Congress to enforce this mandate, but absent controlling congressional direction, the courts have themselves devised standards for determining the validity of state legislation or other official action that is challenged as denying equal protection. The general rule is that legislation is presumed to be valid and will be sustained if the classification drawn by the statute is rationally related to a legitimate state interest. . . .

When social or economic legislation is at issue, the Equal Protection Clause allows the states wide latitude, and the Constitution presumes that even improvident decisions will eventually be rectified by the democratic processes.

The general rule gives way, however, when a statute classifies by race, alienage or national origin. These factors are so seldom relevant to the achievement of any legitimate state interest that laws grounded in such considerations are deemed to reflect prejudice and antipathy—a view that those in the burdened class are not as worthy or deserving as others. For these reasons and because such discrimination is unlikely to be soon rectified by legislative means, these laws are subjected to strict scrutiny and will be sustained only if they are suitably tailored to serve a compelling state interest. Similar oversight by the courts is due when state laws impinge on personal rights protected by the Constitution. Legislative classification based on gender also call for a heightened standard of review. . . .

A gender classification fails unless it is substantially related to a sufficiently important governmental interest. Because illegitimacy is beyond the individual's control and bears "no relation to the individual's ability to participate in and contribute to society," official discriminations resting on that characteristic are also subject to somewhat heightened review. Restrictions "will survive equal protection scrutiny to the extent they are substantially related to a legitimate state interest."

A gender classification fails unless it is substantially related to a sufficiently important governmental interest. Because illegitimacy is beyond the individual's control and bears "no relation to the individual's ability to participate in and contribute to society," official discriminations resting on that characteristic are also subject to somewhat heightened review. Restrictions "will survive equal protection scrutiny to the extent they are substantially related to a legitimate state interest."

We have declined, however, to extend heightened review to differential treatment based on age. The lesson is that where individuals in the group affected by a law have distinguishing characteristics relevant to interest the state has the authority to implement, the courts have been very reluctant to closely scrutinize legislative choices as to whether, how and to what extent those interests should be pursued. In such cases, the Equal Protection Clause requires only a rational means to serve a legitimate end.

Against this background, we conclude for several reasons that the Court of Appeals erred in holding mental retardation a quasi-suspect classification calling for a more exacting standard of judicial review than is normally accorded economic and social legislation. First, it is undeniable, and it is not argued otherwise here, that those who are mentally retarded have a reduced ability to cope with and function in the everyday world. Nor are they all cut from the same patterns: as the testimony in this record indicates, they range from those whose disability is not immediately evident to those who must be constantly cared for. They are thus different, immutably so, in relevant respect, and the states' interest in dealing with and providing for them is plainly a legitimate one. How this large and diversified group is to be treated under the law is a difficult and often a technical matter, very much a task for legislators guided by qualified professionals and not by the perhaps ill informed opinions of the judiciary. Heightened scrutiny inevitably involves substantive judgments about legislative decisions, and we doubt that the predicate for such judicial oversight is present where the classification deals with mental retardation.

Second, the distinctive legislative response, both national and state, to the plight of those who are mentally retarded demonstrates not only that they have unique problems, but also that the lawmakers have been addressing their difficulties in a manner that belies a continuing antipathy or prejudice and a corresponding need for more intrusive oversight by the judiciary. . . .

Such legislation thus singling out the retarded for special treatment reflects the real and undeniable differences between the retarded and others. That a civilized and decent society expects and approves such legislation indicates that governmental consideration of those differences in the vast majority of situations is not only legitimate but desirable. . . . Especially given the wide variation in the abilities and needs of the retarded themselves, governmental bodies must have a certain amount of flexibility and freedom from judicial oversight in shaping and limiting their remedial efforts.

Third, the legislative response, which could hardly have occurred and survived without public support, negates any claim that the mentally retarded are politically powerless in the sense that they have no ability to attract the attention of lawmakers. Any minority can be said to be powerless to assert direct control over the legislature, but if that were a criterion for higher level scrutiny by the courts, much economic and social legislation would now be suspect.

Fourth, if the large and amorphous class of the mentally retarded were deemed quasi-suspect for the reasons given by the Court of Appeals, it would be difficult to find a principled way to distinguish a variety of other groups who have perhaps immutable disabilities setting them off from others, who cannot themselves mandate the desired legislative responses, and who can claim some degree of prejudice from at least part of the public at large. One need mention in this respect only the aging, the disabled, the mentally ill, and the infirm. We are reluctant to set out on that course, and we decline to do so.

Doubtless, there have been and there will continue to be instances of discrimination against the retarded that are in fact invidious, and that are properly subject to judicial correction under constitutional norms. But the appropriate method of reaching such instances is not to create a new quasi-suspect classification and subject all governmental action based on that classification to more searching evaluation. Rather, we should look to the likelihood that governmental action premised on a particular classification is valid as a general matter, not merely to the specifics of the case before us. Because mental retardation is a characteristic that the government may legitimately take into account in a wide range of decisions, and because both state and federal governments have recently committed themselves to assisting the retarded, we will not presume that any given legislative action, even one that disadvantages retarded individuals, is rooted in considerations that the Constitution will not tolerate.

Our refusal to recognize the retarded as a quasi-suspect class does not leave them entirely unprotected from invidious discrimination. To withstand equal protection review, legislation that distinguishes between the mentally retarded and others must be rationally related to a legitimate governmental purpose. This standard, we believe, affords government the latitude necessary both to pursue policies designed to assist the retarded in realizing their full potential, and to freely and efficiently engage in activities that burden the retarded in what is essentially an incidental manner. The State may not rely on a classification whose relationship to an asserted goal is so attenuated as to render the distinction arbitrary or irrational. Furthermore, some objectives—such as "the bare. . .desire to harm a politically unpopular group"—are not legitimate state interest. Beyond that, the mentally retarded, like others, have and retain their substantive constitutional rights in addition to the right to be treated equally by the law.

We turn to the issue of the validity of the zoning ordinance insofar as it requires special use permits for homes for the mentally retarded. . . .

Requiring the permit in this case appears to us to rest on an irrational prejudice against the mentally retarded, including those who would occupy the Featherston facility and who would live under the closely supervised and highly regulated conditions expressly provided for by state and federal law. [The denial of the permit was invalid].

The *Cleburne* case demonstrates that mentally retarded individuals specifically, and handicapped individuals generally, will not be given any heightened level of scrutiny, because they are neither a suspect nor a quasi-suspect class. It is important to note, however, that the Supreme Court emphasized that irrational prejudice could not be the basis for unequal treatment. This standard will be important in assessing the exclusion of children with AIDS, because it is well documented that the fear of being infected with AIDS through the types of casual contacts that occur in the education setting is irrational.

Heightened Scrutiny for Education

The *Cleburne* case examined the classification of handicapped individuals and concluded that their status does not give them any special protection. As the following case excerpt demonstrates, however, special education cases will be examined with special scrutiny, not because handicapped children are involved, but because education is considered to be a right entitled to "special constitutional sensitivity." The case involved whether undocumented alien children residing in the United States were entitled to public education.

PLYLER V. DOE

457 U.S. 202 (1982)
Public education is not a "right" granted to individuals by the Constitution. But neither is it merely some governmental "benefit" indistinguishable from other forms of social welfare legislation. Both the importance of education in maintaining our basic institutions, and the lasting impact of its deprivation on the life of the child, mark the distinction. . . .

We have recognized "the public schools as a most vital civic institution for the preservation of the democratic system of government," and as the primary vehicle for transmitting "the values on which our society rests." . . .

[H]istoric "perceptions of the public schools as inculcating fundamental values necessary to the maintenance of a democratic political system have been confirmed by the observations of social scientists." In addition, education provides the basic tools by which individuals might lead economically productive lives to the benefit of us all. In sum, education has a fundamental role in maintaining the fabric of our society. We cannot ignore the significant social costs borne by our Nation when select groups are denied the means to absorb the values and skills upon which our social order rests. In addition to the pivotal role of education in sustaining our political and cultural heritage, denial of education to some isolated group of children poses an affront to one of the goals of the Equal Protection Clause: the abolition of governmental barriers presenting unreasonable obstacles to advancement on the basis of individual merit. Paradoxically, by depriving the children of any disfavored group of an education, we foreclose the means by which that group might raise the level of esteem in which it is held by the majority. But more directly, "education prepares individuals to be self-reliant and self-sufficient participants in society." Illiteracy is an enduring disability. The inability to read and write will handicap the individual deprived of a basic education each and every day of his life. The inestimable toll of that deprivation on the social economic, intellectual, and psychological well-being of the individual achievement make it most difficult to reconcile the cost or the principle of a status-based denial of basic education with the framework of equality embodied in the Equal Protection Clause. . . .

In these days, it is doubtful that any child may reasonably be expected to succeed in life if he is denied the opportunity of an education. Such an opportunity, where the state has undertaken to provide it, is a right which must be made available to all on equal terms. . . .

If the State is to deny a discrete group of innocent children the free public education that it offers to other children residing within its borders, that denial must be justified by a showing that it furthers some substantial state interest. No such showing was made here.

As the preceding two opinions demonstrate, it would seem that constitutionally based cases involving unequal treatment in the education system are going to incorporate a "heightened equal protection" test, which will probably result in a very close examination of the state's treatment of handicapped children. The judicial opinion in the *PARC* case, issued before either *Plyler* or *Cleburne,* similarly indicated that exclusions of retarded children are unlikely to be rationally based.[1]

Inasmuch as a constitutionally based challenge to unequal treatment or denial of education without due process would seem to be likely to succeed for children with handicaps, why then are all special education cases not brought alleging constitutional violations? In answering this question, it should be noted first that some *are* brought alleging constitutional violation. The two major reasons, however, that more are not constitutionally based are that constitutional cases are cumbersome and complex to litigate, and that the *Smith v. Robinson*[2] decision established that most special education claims must be brought under the EAHCA. (See Chapter 3 for an excerpt of the opinion in that case.) While that excerpt focuses solely on the preemption of special education by the EAHCA as related to Section 504 of the Rehabilitation Act, the Supreme Court also concluded in that case "Where the [EAHCA] is available to a handicapped child . . . [it] is the exclusive avenue through which the child and his parents or guardian can pursue their [equal protection claim]."[3] In most cases, the EAHCA will provide an adequate basis for redress.

CASES UNDER THE EAHCA

What Is a Handicap?

The EAHCA defines a handicapped child as one who is

> mentally retarded, hard of hearing, deaf, speech impaired, visually handicapped, seriously emotionally disturbed, orthopedically impaired, or other health impaired . . . or with specific learning disabilities, who by reason [of the handicap] require[s] special education and related services.[4]

Chapter 4 mentioned briefly some of the problems of labelling. Chapter 6 will address these problems in greater detail. This section will focus on some of the problems and issues that arise under the definition of "handicapped child" under the EAHCA.

It should first be noted that a handicapped child who needs only related services but not special education is apparently not covered under the EAHCA. For example, a child who is able to participate fully in the regular classroom, but who is orthopedically impaired and needs assistance in moving from class to class or who needs special transportation to and from school, is not protected by the EAHCA. Similarly, a child with spina bifida who is mentally and physically able to participate in the regular academic program, but who requires intermittent catheterization, is not handicapped within the Act. Failure to provide needed services to these children, however, is probably a violation of the Section 504 requirement to provide reasonable accommodation.

One of the more unusual cases involving a handicapping condition that required related services was *Espino v. Besteiro.*[5] In that case the boy had a condition that made it impossible for him to regulate his body temperature. Although his condition was unusual, the EAHCA provided protection, and it was held that the school was required to air-condition the entire classroom in order that his handicapping condition could be accommodated and the boy could have maximum classroom interaction with his classmates.

Another interesting decision involved a 13-year-old intellectually gifted girl who had anorexia nervosa. The court concluded that this physical condition resulted from underlying emotional disturbance, and that she was classified as emotionally disturbed and handicapped within the EAHCA.[6]

The problem of children with chronic and infectious diseases and whether they are handicapped under the EAHCA is demonstrated by the following decision. The case involved a six-year-old boy with hemophilia who had gotten AIDS through a blood transfusion. When the school board decided to exclude him pursuant to their policy on children with chronic communicable diseases (adopted to respond to his situation), it became necessary to resolve whether his mother was required to pursue EAHCA remedies in challenging the exclusion. The following excerpt illuminates the problem.

DOE V. BELLEVILLE PUBLIC SCHOOL DISTRICT

672 F. Supp. 342 (S.D. Ill. 1987)
The plaintiff . . . contends that he is not "handicapped," as that term is statutorily defined in EAHCA, and thus is not afforded a remedy by that Act. Consequently, plaintiff argues that he is not required to exhaust his administrative remedies because his claim does not arise under EAHCA, but rather under the Rehabilitation Act.

Because defendants' argument relies on the applicability of EAHCA to the plaintiff, the court must determine if plaintiff's diagnosis of AIDS brings him within the statutory definition of a handicapped individual. EAHCA defines "handicapped children" as children who are:

> mentally retarded, hard of hearing, deaf, speech or language impaired, visually handicapped, seriously emotionally disturbed, orthopedically impaired, *or other health impaired children,* or children with specific learning disabilities, *who by reason thereof require special education and related services.*

20 U.S.C. § 1401(a)(1) [Emphasis added.]
In this case the parties agree that the only category into which Johnny fits is that of "other health impaired children." That phrase is defined as children who have:

> [l]imited strength, vitality or alertness due to chronic or acute health problems such as a heart condition, tuberculosis, rheumatic fever, nephritis, asthma, sickle-cell anemia, *hemophilia,* epilepsy, lead poisoning, leukemia, or diabetes, *which adversely affect a child's educational performance.*

34 C.F.R. § 300.5(b)(7) [Emphasis added.]
In applying these definitions to the plaintiff, the Court concludes that three tests must be met before the provisions of EAHCA can be made to apply in this case: 1) there must be limited strength, vitality, or alertness due to chronic or acute health problems, 2) which adversely affects a child's educational performance, and 3) which requires special education and related services. Here, the record reveals virtually no evidence that plaintiff suffers from limited strength, vitality, or alertness. Furthermore, given such evidence as is in the record of Johnny's limited strength, there is virtually no evidence that this limitation has adversely affected his educational performance.

The Court also finds it noteworthy that, while the defendants assert that Johnny's hemophilia brings him within the statutory definition of "other health impaired children," the health impairment they are apparently concerned with is Johnny's AIDS virus. AIDS is not listed as an example of an acute or chronic health problem in the statute. Furthermore, the United States Department of Education, directly addressing the applicability of EAHCA to AIDS victims, has opined that a child with AIDS might be considered "handicapped" under EAHCA, depending upon his or her condition.

More significantly, the Department's opinion concludes that a child with AIDS is not considered to be "handicapped," as the term is defined in the EAHCA, unless he or she needs special education. With respect to the availability of special education programs for children with AIDS, the opinion states:

> Children with AIDS could be eligible for special education programs under the category of 'other health impaired,' if they have chronic or acute health problems which adversely affect their educational performance.

Based on the Department of Education's opinions and the tenor of the statutory language, the Court concludes that EAHCA would apply to AIDS victims only if their physical condition is such that it adversely affects their educational performance; i.e., their ability to learn and to do the required classroom work. There is no such showing at the present time, and it seems clear that the only reason for the Board's determination that Johnny needs "special education" is the fact that he has a contagious disease—AIDS. In the Court's opinion, given the facts of this case as they now exist, the provisions of EAHCA would not apply to the plaintiff at this time.

The decision in this case denied the defendant's motion to dismiss the claim for failure to exhaust administrative remedies because the claim was proper under the Rehabilitation Act, and exhaustion is not required under that Act.

Age Eligibility

To be eligible for federal funding under the EAHCA, states are to provide special education to *all* handicapped persons aged 3 through 21.[7] But for those aged 3, 4, 5, 18, 19, 20, and 21, education need only be provided in certain situations. One such situation is where education is provided to *all* children in a particular age and disability category.[8] For example, if blind children are required by state law or a court order to be provided preschool education (ages 3 to 5), then *all* blind children in that age range would be covered under the EAHCA in that state. Other situations in which special education must be provided to 3- to 5-year-olds and 18- to 21-year-olds is where education is provided generally to a population within the age range. In those cases a proportionate number of handicapped children must be given the same opportunity. For example, if a local educational agency makes optional kindergarten available to all five-year-olds in the school district a proportionate number of handicapped five-year-olds must have the opportunity to participate in special education in that school district.[9] Where 50% of the children with a particular handicapping condition are provided education by an educational agency, all children with that condition are entitled to education under the EAHCA.[10] Thus, if a local school district provides education to 50% or more of the deaf five-year-olds in the district, it must make education available to all deaf five-year-olds in the district if they want it.

In addition to these mandatory requirements, the EAHCA has recently added some incentive programs for preschool-age children and infants and toddlers. These programs recognize the importance and benefit of providing early intervention, but policies on this have just been formulated and there is little case law. These are discussed more fully later in this chapter.

At this point it should be noted that problems can arise at the other end of the spectrum. What happens if the individual was eligible for public education before the EAHCA was enacted? The following case addresses this issue.

GALLAGHER V. PONTIAC SCHOOL DISTRICT

807 F.2d 75 (6th Cir. 1986)
This case presents the unfortunate and sad circumstance of young man, Dennis Gallagher, who is deaf and mentally handicapped. . . .

Gallagher cannot speak and can communicate only through a very limited use of sign language. He was born on January 13, 1954. [He was enrolled in public education from 1973–1979. From 1977–1979 he was enrolled in a special education program]. At no time was he ever excluded from attending any of defendants' schools or from participating in their special education programs. It is also important to note that Gallagher was never enrolled in a program that received federal financial assistance. . . .

In this case the primary dispute regarding the EAHCA concerns the date the act went into effect. Plaintiff claims the act became effective in 1975; defendants contend it did not become effective until 1977. . . .

Because we find that the requirement to have a free appropriate public education available did not become effective until 1977, defendants were not required to provide a free "appropriate" public education for any handicapped children before October 1, 1977.

Dennis Gallagher was enrolled in the Oakland County Intermediate School District only through the academic year 1975–76. The EAHCA was not in effect until after he left the Oakland schools. He was enrolled in the Farmington School District only in the academic year 1976–77. The EAHCA became effective in October 1977, four months after Gallagher left Farmington. When he entered the Pontiac School District program in the fall of 1977, he was 23 years old. The EAHCA requires an appropriate public education only for handicapped children between the ages of 3 and 21. Gallagher thus does not have a valid claim under the EAHCA, because the act did not require any of the defendants to provide an appropriate education to Gallagher at the time he was enrolled in their special education programs.

The *Gallagher* decision demonstrates the problem with the individual who was over age before the EAHCA became effective. There are additional problems with students who have reached the age of 18, but who have not graduated, or who have been given a diploma even though they do not actually meet the competency requirements for graduation. State policies differ substantially in their treatment of these individuals. In some states once the individual has been given a diploma, the individual is no longer eligible for public education. Some states even prohibit educational agencies from providing public education once the student has graduated, basing this on state constitutional or state statutory provisions. In these states it may violate state policy to provide compensatory education even in cases where it is determined that the state had not provided appropriate education to the student before he or she graduated. Other states are more permissive about providing education beyond the receipt of a diploma. There is a developing body of state administrative decisions and judicial decisions on this issue, and thus far the federal special education policymakers have not overridden state policies that conclude state responsibility at graduation.[11]

CASES UNDER SECTION 504—
BROADER COVERAGE

Section 504 of the Rehabilitation Act of 1973 provides that "no otherwise qualified individual with handicaps . . . shall solely by reason of his handicap, be excluded from the participation in, be denied the benefits of, or be subjected to discrimination under any program or activity receiving Federal financial assistance."[12]

While *Smith v. Robinson*[13] makes it unlikely that most cases involving handicapped children will be brought alleging a violation of Section 504, there will be cases in which Section 504 is relevant. For example, in *Wolff v. South Colonie Central School District,*[14] a girl who wanted to participate in a school-sponsored trip to Spain was denied participation because her limb deficiency would make it too difficult for her to keep up with many of the activities involved in the trip. The case was decided under Section 504, and it was held that the exclusion was permissible because she was not "otherwise qualified." Because there will be occasional cases that do not involve EAHCA issues, it is important to examine the coverage of Section 504.

Under the Rehabilitation Act, a handicapped person is one who "has a physical or mental impairment which substantially limits one or more major life activities [which includes learning], has a record of such an impairment, or is regarded as having such an impairment."[15] The student with an orthopedic impairment who requires neither special education nor related services is probably one of the most frequent cases where a student would fall under Section 504, but perhaps not the EAHCA coverage. There will be other instances where the student is covered under both statutes. Where policy clarification is becoming increasingly important is in those instances where the student has an infectious disease such as AIDS or hepatitis B. The Supreme Court addressed whether an individual with such a disease is "handicapped" under the Rehabilitation Act in a 1987 decision.

SCHOOL BOARD OF NASSAU COUNTY V. ARLINE

107 S.Ct. 1123 (1987)
Justice BRENNAN delivered the opinion of the Court.

Section 504 of the Rehabilitation Act of 1973 prohibits a federally funded state program from discriminating against a handicapped individual solely by reason of his or her handicap. This case presents the questions whether a person afflicted with tuberculosis, a contagious disease, may be considered a "handicapped individual" within the meaning of § 504 of the Act, and, if so, whether such an individual is "otherwise qualified" to teach elementary school. . . .

In determining whether a particular individual is handicapped as defined by the Act, the regulations promulgated by the Department of Health and Human Services are of significant assistance. As we have previously recognized, these regulations were drafted with the oversight and approval of Congress.

The regulations are particularly significant here because they define two critical terms used in the statutory definition of handicapped individual. "Physical impairment" is defined as follows:

> [A]ny physiological disorder or condition, cosmetic disfigurement, or anatomical loss affecting one or more of the following body systems: neurological; musculoskeletal; special sense organs; respiratory, including speech organs; cardiovascular; reproductive, digestive, genito-urinary; hemic and lymphatic; skin; and endocrine. 45 CFR § 84.-3(j)(2)(i)(1985).

In addition, the regulations define "major life activities" as:

> . . . functions such as caring for one's self, performing manual tasks, walking, seeing, hearing, speaking, breathing, learning, and working. § 84.3(j)(2)(ii).

Within this statutory and regulatory framework, then, we must consider whether Arline can be considered a handicapped individual. According to the testimony of Dr. McEuen, Arline suffered tuberculosis "in an acute form in such a degree that it affected her respiratory system," and was hospitalized for this condition. . . . Thus, Arline's hospitalization for tuberculosis in 1957 suffices to establish that she has a "record of . . . impairment" within the meaning of 29 U.S.C. § 706(7(B)(ii), and is therefore a handicapped individual.

Petitioners concede that a contagious disease may constitute a handicapping condition to the extent that it leaves a person with "diminished physical or mental capabilities," and concede that Arline's hospitalization for tuberculosis in 1957 demonstrates that she has a record of a physical impairment. Petitioners maintain, however, Arline's record of impairment is irrelevant in this case, since the School Board dismissed Arline not because of her diminished physical capabilities, but because of the threat that her relapses of tuberculosis posed to the health of others.

We do not agree with petitioners that, in defining a handicapped individual under § 504, the contagious effects of a disease can be meaningfully distinguished from the disease's physical effects on a claimant in a case such as this. Arline's contagiousness and her physical impairment each resulted from the same underlying condition, tuberculosis. It would be unfair to allow an employer to seize upon the distinction between the effects of a disease on others and the effects of a disease on a patient and use that distinction to justify discriminatory treatment.*

Nothing in the legislative history of § 504 suggests that Congress intended such a re-

---

* The United States argues that it is possible for a person to be simply a carrier of a disease, that is, to be capable of spreading a disease without having a "physical impairment" or suffering from any other symptoms associated with the disease. The United States contends that this is true in the case of some carriers of the Acquired Immune Deficiency Syndrome (AIDS) virus. From this premise the United States concludes that discrimination solely on the basis of contagiousness is never discrimination on the basis of a handicap. The argument is misplaced in this case, because the handicap here, tuberculosis, gave rise both to a physical impairment *and* to contagiousness. This case does not present, and we therefore do not reach, the questions whether a carrier of a contagious disease such as AIDS could be considered to have a physical impairment, or whether such a person could be considered, solely on the basis of contagiousness, a handicapped person as defined by the Act.

sult. That history demonstrates that Congress was as concerned about the effect of an impairment on others as it was about its effect on the individual. Congress extended coverage, in 29 U.S.C. § 706(7)(B)(iii), to those individuals who are simply "regarded as having" a physical or mental impairment. The Senate Report provides us an example of a person who would be covered under this subsection as a person with some kind of visible physical impairment which in fact does not substantially limit that person's functioning." Such an impairment might not diminish a person's physical or mental capabilities, but could nevertheless substantially limit that person's ability to work as a result of the negative reactions of others to the impairment.

Allowing discrimination based on the contagious effects of a physical impairment would be inconsistent with the basic purpose of § 504, which is to ensure that handicapped individuals are not denied jobs or other benefits because of the prejudiced attitudes or the ignorance of others. By amending the definition of "handicapped individual" to include not only those who are actually physically impaired, but also those who are regarded as impaired and who, as a result, are substantially limited in a major life activity. Congress acknowledged that society's accumulated myths and fears about disability and disease are as handicapping as are the physical limitations that flow from actual impairment. Few aspects of a handicap give rise to the same level of public fear and misapprehension as contagiousness. Even those who suffer or have recovered from such noninfectious diseases as epilepsy or cancer have faced discrimination based on the irrational fear that they might be contagious. The Act is carefully structured to replace such reflexive reactions to actual or perceived handicaps with actions based on reasoned and medically sound judgments: the definition of "handicapped individual" is broad, but only those individuals who are both handicapped *and* otherwise qualified are eligible for relief. The fact that *some* persons who have contagious diseases may pose a serious health threat to others under certain circumstances does not justify excluding from the coverage of the Act *all* persons with actual or perceived contagious diseases. Such exclusion would mean that those accused of being contagious would never have the opportunity to have their condition evaluated in light of medical evidence and a determination made as to whether they were "otherwise qualified." Rather, they would be vulnerable to discrimination on the basis of mythology— precisely the type of injury Congress sought to prevent. We conclude that the fact that a person with a record of a physical impairment that is also a contagious disease does not suffice to remove that person from coverage under § 504. . . .

We hold that a person suffering from the contagious disease of tuberculosis can be a handicapped person with in the meaning of the § 504 of the Rehabilitation Act of 1973, and that respondent Arline is such a person. We remand the case to the District Court to determine whether Arline is otherwise qualified for her position.

In examining this decision, it should be noted that the Supreme Court specifically stated in a footnote that it was not deciding whether someone with AIDS was protected under the Rehabilitation Act. A number of subsequent decisions indicated the general judicial consensus that AIDS is a handicap under the Rehabilitation Act, and Congress amended the Rehabilitation Act in 1987 to protect individuals with infectious diseases. The amendment is as follows:

For the purposes of sections 503 and 504, as such sections relate to employment, such term does not include an individual who has a currently contagious disease or infection and who, by reason of such disease or infection, would constitute a direct threat to the health or safety of other individuals or who, by reason of the currently contagious disease or infection, is unable to perform the duties of the job.[16]

While this amendment would seem to apply only to employment, most commentors would find it also applicable to other areas, such as education.

   While in all likelihood future judicial decisions will hold that AIDS is a handicap under Section 504, a determination that an individual fits the definition of handicap is only the first step toward challenging a discriminatory practice. The definition specifies that the individual must be "otherwise qualified." The first Supreme Court case to address any issue under Section 504 dealt with this requirement. In *Southeastern Community College v. Davis,*[17] the Court found that a nursing student with a hearing impairment was not otherwise qualified to participate in the nurse-training program because she could not meet the program's requirements *"in spite of"* her handicap. Recipients of federal financial assistance are not obligated to make substantial modifications or fundamental alterations to the program to accommodate the handicap. They are, however, required to make reasonable accommodations where these do not pose an undue hardship on the program.[18] It should be noted that the Supreme Court in *Arline*, while finding tuberculosis to be a handicap, remanded the case for a determination as to whether the plaintiff was otherwise qualified. The Court indicated that issues such as the duration and severity of the condition and the probability of whether the disease would be transmitted required a factual determination in order to decide whether she was "otherwise qualified." The Court noted that:

> A person who poses a significant risk of communicating an infectious disease to others in the workplace will not be otherwise qualified . . . if reasonable accommodation will not eliminate that risk.[19]

The Court further stated that a determination of that risk should be based on "reasonable medical judgments given the state of medical knowledge, about. . .the nature. . .duration. . .and severity of the risk. . . and . . .the probabilities the disease will be transmitted and will cause varying degrees of harm."[20] Two years after the Supreme Court decision, the district court found Gene Arline not to be a risk and to be otherwise qualified.

   Applying this standard, the presumption should be that as a general rule a child with AIDS is otherwise qualified because the weight of medical knowledge is that AIDS is not casually transmitted. This presumption may be rebutted in specific cases, such as where because of a child's behavior (biting) or manifestation of symptoms (open sores, oozing lesions that cannot be covered, etc.) there is a risk of communicating the disease. Also, if the child with AIDS is at a point where the immune system is so depressed that exposure to ordinary childhood infections, such as colds and chicken pox, would pose a serious danger to that individual child, it may be that child is not otherwise qualified to attend regular school. And in either case, where the child is at risk or poses a risk, in most cases the child would at least be "otherwise qualified" for homebound instruction, unless the child is simply too ill to do schoolwork. In response to the concern about children with infectious diseases in schools, the Centers for Disease Control (CDC) developed and published Guidelines in August 1985. The Guidelines apply to children who are positive for the AIDS virus, as well as those with AIDS related complex (ARC) or clinical AIDS.

The Guidelines are premised on the fact that current medical evidence indicates that "casual person-to-person contact as would occur among schoolchildren appears to pose no risk." The lack of information about younger children and neurologically handicapped children lacking control of body secretions is noted as a caveat to this premise. This group is perhaps in need of different treatment both in terms of the risk of transmission of AIDS to other children and the risk to the child with AIDS.

The CDC recommendations provide the following:[21]

- Case-by-case decision making regarding participation
- Decision making by a team (including child's physician, public health personnel, child's parent or guardian, and personnel involved in proposed educational program, such as the classroom teacher)
- Presumption of inclusion for *most* children
- A more restricted environment for preschool and neurologically impaired children until further study of transmission in these settings is done
- Precautions in handling child's bodily fluids
- Routine procedures for handling bodily fluids of *all* children
- Continuing monitoring of the child's hygienic practices and appropriate responses to any changes
- Children in risk groups (such as those born to mothers with AIDS) might be considered for being tested for AIDS in order to avoid giving vaccinations that might be dangerous and to monitor behavior and exposure to infections
- No mandatory screening as a condition of enrollment
- Educational personnel should respect right to privacy and maintain confidentiality as much as possible
- Provide education to parents, children, and educators about AIDS and how it is transmitted

While some states and local educational agencies have already adopted procedures for dealing with children who have infectious diseases there is a need for a more comprehensive federal policy. Such a policy should address the following issues:[22]

- the need to amend the definition of "handicapped individual to include children with AIDS under the EAHCA
- the need for an expedited decision-making process for children with AIDS because of their shortened life span
- the importance of having EAHCA impartial hearing officers make decisions about inclusion of children with AIDS because of the political pressure on school board members and other local administrators

- the importance of ensuring that confidential issues are addressed more specifically in the EAHCA regarding children with AIDS and other infectious diseases
- ensuring that the individualized placement program provides for ongoing monitoring of changing conditions of the child
- personnel development to include mandatory training about AIDS and its transmission and appropriate safety and hygiene practices

SPECIAL SITUATIONS

Gifted Students

The following case illustrates the current status of education for gifted children under the EAHCA.

ROE V. COMMONWEALTH

638 F. Supp. 929 (E.D. Pa. 1986)
Plaintiff, a student in the Bensalem Township School District, raises various statutory and constitutional challenges to her exclusion from gifted education. . . .

The extent to which Pennsylvania chooses to apply the same [as the EAHCA] procedural protections to its determinations regarding the placement of students in gifted and handicapped educational programs is within constitutional limitation. Plaintiff alleges that gifted education is the preferred educational placement, and therefore that defendants violated her rights by placing her in regular education classes without prior notice and an opportunity to be heard. Second, she alleges that when she initiated due process proceedings to determine her eligibility for gifted education, the procedures employed by defendants were constitutionally defective.

A threshold issue in any due process inquiry is whether the plaintiff was deprived of a constitutionally protected interest. Plaintiff argues that because gifted education is the preferred educational assignment, she has both a property and a liberty interest in being placed in gifted education. I disagree.

Property interests are not created by the Constitution, but by independent sources, such as state law. As to placement in gifted education, Pennsylvania law provides as follows:

> Persons shall be assigned to a program for the gifted when they have an IQ of 130 or higher. A limited number of persons with IQ scores lower than 130 may be admitted to gifted programs when other educational criteria in the profile of the person strongly indicate gifted ability. . . .

Assuming, without deciding, that this regulation creates a property interest in gifted education for students with IQs of 130 or higher, it does not confer such an interest upon plaintiff, as she does not allege that her IQ falls within the specified range. To have a property interest in a benefit, a person must have "more than an abstract need or desire for it. . . . He must . . . have a legitimate claim of entitlement to it." Neither the provision in the regulation that select students with IQs under 130 may be admitted to gifted programs, nor, if such is the case, the fact that gifted education is the preferred educational assignment, creates in plaintiff a legitimate claim of entitlement to it. Therefore, I conclude that plaintiff does not have a property interest in being placed in gifted education. [The court also denied that a liberty interest had been denied]. . . .

Count III of plaintiff's complaint alleges four equal protection and substantive due process violation. Summarized briefly, plaintiff challenges the use of IQ scores to define mental giftedness, the fact that students with IQs of 130 or higher are placed in educational programs purportedly designed to maximize their potential, while students with IQs under 130 are not entitled to be placed in such programs, and the fact that only exceptional students, i.e., those deemed gifted or handicapped, are legally entitled to be placed in the least restrictive educational environment. . . .

Plaintiff's claims must be evaluated under the rational relation standard. Under this standard, the proper inquiry is whether the regulations challenged by plaintiff are "so underelated to the achievement of any combination of legitimate purposes" that one can only conclude that defendants, in promulgating the challenged regulation, acted irrationally. . . .

Plaintiff's argument that the creation by defendants of the gifted student classification is irrational in light of the enabling legislation is not convincing as either a logical or a factual matter. The enabling legislation requires the Board of Education to prescribe standards for the education of all exceptional children, and defines exceptional children as those who "deviate from the average . . . to such an extent that they require special educational facilities or services." I fail to see how it could be irrational for the Board of Education to conclude that children with high IQs "deviate from the average" and thus come within the purview of the enabling legislation. Moreover, since the creation of the gifted student classification by the Board of Education, the legislature has placed its imprimatur upon the provision of special education to gifted children.

Children in Private Schools

This section focuses on the availability of special education services to the child whose parents have chosen to place the child in a private school, not for purposes of receiving special education, but as a choice for the child's regular education. The issue that arises is to what extent is special education programming to be available to the child. The issue can become more complex when the private school involved is a sectarian school, because of first amendment issues of separation of church and state. The issue is not unlike the issue of whether public educational agencies may provide books and supplies and transportation to children who attend private schools.

The regulations under the EAHCA require that state and local educational agencies must ensure that special education and related services are provided to children attending private school.[23] This probably means that when a parent whose child is in a private school requests the public educational agency to provide special education and related services, these must be provided. This, of course, can present a number of administrative and logistical problems for the public agency. Should an itinerant teacher be sent to the private school? Should the student be required to go to the public school site to obtain the education?

Who is required to pay for the transportation in such cases? This issue is discussed more fully in Chapter 11.

Incarcerated Juveniles

Another issue that arises relating to eligibility is how special education is to be provided to incarcerated juveniles. It has been suggested that in many cases juveniles have gotten in trouble because of problems relating to their handicapping conditions. How to prevent that from occurring is perhaps one of the underlying goals of the EAHCA. But once the individual is in a juvenile detention facility or otherwise incarcerated, the individual is technically still entitled to special education if he or she is eligible otherwise. The logistics of providing special education in detention facilities are quite difficult in many instances, and this is a topic that is receiving increasing attention. In addition, many learning-disabled and emotionally disturbed children have never been identified and are therefore not receiving services. The transient nature of this population is a further obstacle to satisfactory implementation of the EAHCA.

Children with Learning Disabilities

Children with learning disabilities present unique problems under the EAHCA, primarily because there is substantial disagreement about which children fit into the definition, and also because there is disagreement about what kind of services should be provided. The definition for learning disability under the EAHCA is

> a disorder in one or more of the basic psychological processes involved in understanding or in using language, spoken or written, which may manifest itself in an imperfect ability to listen, think, speak, read, write, spell, or to do mathematical calculation. The term does not include children who have learning problems which are primarily the result of visual, hearing, or motor handicaps, of mental retardation of emotional disturbance, or of environmental, cultural, or economic disadvantage."[24]

The numbers of children being identified as learning disabled increase every year, now totalling over one million children. The reasons for what is probably overidentification of children as learning disabled include overburdened regular education teachers, improperly trained personnel, and, to a lesser extent, federal reimbursement for identifying a child as learning disabled. In addition, the fact that professionals are just finding out about learning disabilities makes overidentification likely. More positive reasons for the increase in numbers include greater public awareness, improved assessment methods, reevaluation of minority placement where children had been identified as mentally retarded, and the less stigmatizing label of learning disability versus mental retardation.[25] Whatever the reasons, the numbers of learning-disabled students are increasing, and this is an area where there is likely to be dispute about whether a child really meets the definition.

Preschool Children

The value to the learning process of early intervention is generally recognized by experts in child development. This is particularly true for handicapped children. The earlier they are provided with developmental programming, the better able to benefit from public education they will be. It is also generally recognized that while it is costly to provide early educational programs, in the long run there is a significant cost savings to the public. The child who is provided early programming will be less likely to require substantial public support after public educational programming has been completed.

In recognition of this, Congress in 1986 amended the EAHCA to provide for special education benefits for children up to the age of five. Title I of P.L. 99–457 provides that states should make available to handicapped infants and toddlers a statewide, comprehensive, coordinated, multidisciplinary interagency program of early intervention.[26] This program is to be available to children from birth to age two. A similar grant program is provided for under Title II of the amendments, which applies to handicapped children ages three to five.[27] The financial incentives are particularly strong for the program for Title II, in terms of additional federal support to be made available to states electing to take advantage of the program.

These are basically two distinct programs. The first program is included in Part B of the EAHCA and allows for additional grant support to states who provide programming to handicapped children aged three to five inclusive. To be eligible for this additional funding, the state must provide special education and related services using the EAHCA procedural and substantive protections. This does not repeal the requirements described above. Rather, it is a supplementary grant statute for those states wanting to provide special education to the entire population within that age range.

The second program is part of the Education for the Handicapped Act, and is not included within Part B of the EAHCA, but rather is an additional part of the EHA, Part G. Part G provides additional grant support to states that establish early intervention programs for handicapped infants and toddlers. The protected group is defined as individuals from birth to age two inclusive, who need early intervention services because of developmental delays or who have a diagnosed physical or mental condition that has a high probability of resulting in developmental delay. The importance of noting that this program is distinct from the preschool amendments for three- to five-year-olds is that the funding for this program does not necessarily go to the state educational agency. Instead, *any* state agency establishing a State Interagency Coordinating Council meeting specified requirements would be eligible to obtain the grant support. The council is to be made up of several designated individuals representing parents, providers of early intervention services, the state legislature, and agency personnel. The function of the agency is primarily one of coordinating early intervention services.

Neither program is mandatory, but the benefits of early intervention should be a strong incentive to implementation of the programs. These amendments are too recent to have developed any case law, but they will undoubtedly be a source of dispute once they become more widely adopted and implemented.

"Uneducable" Children

The EAHCA has as one of its principles the concept of "zero reject." This is found in the requirement that states are to provide education to *all* handicapped children. In spite of this seemingly clear mandate, a few courts have adopted a position that at least some children are uneducable.[28] The following is a somewhat troubling decision on this point. While it may well be that this decision will not withstand federal circuit court review, until the Supreme Court addresses the issue, other lower courts may follow this line of reasoning.

TIMOTHY W. V. ROCHESTER SCHOOL DISTRICT

1987–88 EHLR DEC. 559:480 (D.N.H. 1988)

I. Background

Timothy was born on December 8, 1975 at Frisbie Memorial Hospital in Rochester, New Hampshire, two months premature. His mother, Cindy, was fifteen years old at the time. He weighed four pounds at birth. Shortly after birth, he was transferred to Mary Hitchcock Hospital in Hanover, New Hampshire, for respiratory difficulties. While at Mary Hitchcock, he suffered intracranial bleeding, hydrocephalus (fluid on the brain), and seizures. He was discharged from Mary Hitchcock after three months, during which time a ventriculoperitoneal shunt was installed to drain excess cranial fluid. By this time, he was diagnosed as suffering from severe developmental retardation, with suspected hearing and vision deficits.

Tim's physical and apparent mental development was dishearteningly slow. He attended the Rochester Child Development Center during the 1979–80 school year, receiving occupational and physical therapy. On February 19, 1980 the school district's pupil evaluation team attempted to determine whether Tim qualified as educationally handicapped under EAHCA. In arriving at a determination, the evaluation team apparently reviewed the plethora of medical evaluations and documented history of Tim. The team also considered the report and observations of therapists as well as instructors. On March 7, 1980 the Rochester School District Placement Committee determined that Tim did not qualify for District sponsored education under EAHCA or R.S.A. 186-C, due to Tim's inability to benefit from special education.

Soon after this determination, Tim began receiving care from the New Hampshire Department of Health and Welfare pursuant to the Social Security Disabled Children's Program. Tim's involvement in this program resulted in the development of an Individualized Service Plan (ISP) which included medical care, physical therapy, tactile stimulation, feeding therapy, and respite care.

In June of 1983, the defendant's evaluation team reassessed Tim's situation concerning qualification for special education pursuant to EAHCA. The evaluation team failed to reach a decision on this issue, and deferred determination pending the acquisition of additional evaluations by neurologists. The School District allegedly sought permission of Tim's mother, in order to perform the neurological evaluation. . . .

[In its hearing on the issue of whether Tim qualified for special education under the EAHCA] the Hearing Officer ruled that Tim qualified for special education under the apposite special education laws. The Hearings Officer held that the special education laws entitle all handicapped children, regardless of the severity of the handicap, to special education. The officer further ruled that inquiry as to whether a child might benefit from special education is no longer relevant.

The defendant . . . appealed the decision of the hearings officer to this Court. The defendant asserts that the legal conclusion arrived at by the administrative officer was clearly erroneous and that since this legal conclusion precluded any factual determinations concerning the plaintiff, the issue is appropriate for summary disposition.

This appeal presents several issues for the court's consideration. The court must initially determine the correctness of the Administrative Officer's decision concerning the eligibility for special education of all handicapped children, regardless of the ability of a child to benefit from the education. Specifically, the court must decide whether the rights and opportunities propounded by EAHCA provide special education services for all handicapped children, notwithstanding the inability of a child to benefit from all education. . . .

Despite the language of EAHCA, the defendants contend that Congress' intent in passing the Act was to provide special education for those handicapped children who could benefit from such education. The defendants claim it was not the intent of Congress to provide special education to those children who cannot benefit from that education.

The parties cite a wide variety of authorities in support of their respective positions. These authorities range from Supreme Court rulings to decisions of administrative officers, to law review articles.

There appears to be a split of opinion as to whether EAHCA was intended to mandate that special education be provided to handicapped children regardless of whether or not a child could benefit from the education. For the following reasons, this court concludes that no such mandate was intended by the Act and that an initial determination as to the ability of a handicapped child to benefit from education is requisite.

It is certainly true that the Act provides special public education to all handicapped children, regardless of the severity of the handicap. Does this mean that if a child suffers from a handicap of such severity that the child is incapable of cognitive learning, that child is to be the subject of attempted education? This court will not support such a proposition.

Both parties allude to *Hendrick Hudson Dist. Bd. of Ed. v. Rowley*, 458 U.S. 176 (1982). . . .

In deciding the issue of "free appropriate public education" under the Act, the Court held that this phrase requires "educational instruction specially designed to meet the unique needs of the handicapped child, supported by such services as are necessary to permit the child to 'benefit' from the instruction."

It logically follows that a handicapped child who cannot "benefit" from special education, or who does not have learning capacity was not intended to receive special education under the EAHCA. Surely, Congress would not legislate futility!

As previously mentioned, this interpretation of EAHCA is not unique, since there exists a number of contrasting decisions concerning the necessity of a potential bene-fit to exist as a precondition to a child's entitlement to special education under the Act. The case of *Parks v. Pavkovic* 753 F.2d 1397 (7th Cir. 1985) is germane to this ac-tion in two respects. The case describes a series of hypothetical situations involving the EAHCA, and it also provides an interpretation of *Rowley,* concerning the very issue confronting this court.

In analyzing the special education requirements of EAHCA in light of the potential types of handicaps with which a school district may be faced, the court identified three hypothetical situations, representing the minimum, the maximum, and the mean handicapped child situation which could confront a school district. *Id.* The en-tire analysis is noteworthy; however, it is the hypothetical addressing of the maximum handicap which is of import to this action.

> In our second hypothetical case, the child is in a coma, and is institution-alized because he cannot be cared for at home. We understand the plaintiffs to be conceding . . . that since the child would be completely uneducable in his condition—since he could not benefit from special education no matter how expensive—his living expenses in the institution would not be charge-able to the state under the Act. They would not be expenses of or related to education, made pursuant to the "individualized education program" that the law requires the state to create for each handicapped child.

It is clear that implicit in *Parks'* interpretation of *Rowley* is the necessity of a child to possess an ability to benefit or be capable of benefitting from special education, prior to qualifying for such education under EACHA. . . .

Although other authority exists for concluding that a handicapped child must nec-essarily be capable of benefitting from education in order to qualify for special educa-tion under EAHCA, these cases merely serve to reiterate the same theme.

The court is not aware of those decisions which interpret EAHCA literally, requir-ing states participating in the EAHCA grant to provide special education to handi-capped students regardless of their capacity to benefit from the education.

Therefore this court concludes that under EAHCA, an initial determination as to a child's ability to benefit from special education must be made in order for a handi-capped child to qualify for education under the Act. This determination is necessary to close that gap which is not explicit in the Act, and which involves those rare (and the court emphasizes rare) cases where a child is afflicted by such extreme handicap(s) that the child is not capable of benefitting from special education.

SUMMARY

Students with handicaps who seek to challenge practices and policies of public ed-ucational agencies will find their rights affected by the theory under which they bring action.

A constitutionally based case offers students with handicaps protection from school policies and practices by applying a standard of heightened scrutiny—that is, the school must show that its action furthers some substantial state interest.

This standard is applied, not because handicapped individuals fall into a specially protected class, but because education is deemed to be such an important interest.

Federal statutes offer more specific and special treatment for students with handicaps. The EAHCA is categorical in its definitional coverage and requires not only that the individual have one or more of the listed disabilities, but must also require special education and related services because of the disability. The student must also be within the specified age range. While it might seem that the law is fairly specific in defining who is covered, a number of questions remain subject to varied judicial interpretations. These questions include who is actually learning disabled, whether chronically ill children or those with contagious diseases (such as AIDS) fit within the definition, and whether students who are still age eligible, but who have received a high school diploma, are covered.

The Rehabilitation Act's definition is much broader—covering not only those with substantial impairments, but also those who have a record of or are perceived to have an impairment. In the *Arline* case, this statute was interpreted to apply to an individual with a contagious disease. Following that decision, Congress amended the Rehabilitation Act definition of a person with a handicap to protect an individual with a contagious disease as long as that person does not pose a risk to others and is able to carry out the requirements of the program. While this amendment focuses on employment, it seems to clarify or restate what is already required to participate in any federally funded program. The individual must be otherwise qualified. Posing a risk to others or being too ill to participate would mean that the student is not otherwise qualified and therefore not protected.

Despite the fact that the Constitution, the EAHCA and the Rehabilitation Act offer varying degrees of protection depending on how an individual is defined within that coverage, there are still a number of unresolved questions regarding eligibility. The student with AIDS is probably covered under the Rehabilitation Act, but is probably not covered under the EAHCA in most instances. Exclusion of such a student would probably be judicially examined, applying heightened constitutional scrutiny because of the importance of education. The urgency of resolving such cases quickly, however, does not seem to be well addressed in current theories of legal recourse. This may be an area where legislative amendment is needed.

Other special situations relating to who is protected include the issue of gifted students. The EAHCA does not provide protection for this group, but many state laws do. The issue then is whether the criteria for selection of these students and the application of these criteria are valid. As a general rule, courts give a great deal of deference to educational agencies in their implementation of such programs.

Children with handicaps who are in private schools are eligible for special education through the public educational agency. The same is true for incarcerated juveniles. With both groups, however, there are logistical problems of identifying the children and providing the education to students who are geographically separate from the public school program.

A recognition of the value of early intervention and education services for young children has led to the development of additional incentive grant programs for children to the age of five. While states are not required to provide these programs to be eligible for general EAHCA funding, there is a clear recognition of the value of these programs and the importance of having federal subsidization of state efforts to provide preschool programming. As these programs become implemented throughout the country it is probable that courts will be required to address several unresolved issues including the application of the mainstreaming requirements to this age group. State and federal administrative agencies will need to address what is perhaps the more difficult issue of how to ensure interagency cooperation among various public social service agencies.

One other group of children has received special attention by courts and administrators, namely "uneducable" children. While the zero-reject principle of the EAHCA would seem to prevent the exclusion of any child with a handicap from public education, there are educational agencies that have done so on the basis that the child is uneducable and cannot benefit from education. Although not many courts accept such a position, the question does raise an important general policy question, namely whether educational agencies should be the parties responsible for providing certain expensive quasi-custodial, quasi-medical services to severely handicapped children. Those who would argue that they should would probably agree, however, that additional funding or better interagency funding responsibility is required if educational agencies are to carry this burden.

QUESTIONS AND PROBLEMS

1. Keeping in mind the age eligibility criteria of the EAHCA, should a 19-year-old neurologically impaired individual who has not yet graduated from high school be permitted to be on the basketball team, when ordinarily the age criteria limits participation to students age 18 or under?

2. What would be the probable outcome for Dennis Gallagher *(Gallagher v. Pontiac School District)* under Section 504 or a constitutional theory?

3. Marjorie is an 18-year-old hearing-impaired individual whose parents have been disputing during the past three years whether the school has been providing an appropriate education. Marjorie is bright, and has earned a C average in spite of not receiving appropriate programming. She has done well enough to pass the graduation competency tests. The school now concedes that it did not provide entirely appropriate programming over the past three or four years, but the programming was not grossly inadequate. Now that Marjorie has qualified for graduation, the school claims that if she accepts the diploma, she is no longer eligible for public education. Who would win if the parents litigated this issue? What would be the theory? What remedy?

4. Suppose Marjorie (problem 3) were 16 instead of 18, and were a junior in high school, and wanted to drop out. In most states there is no mandatory public school attendance after age 16. If Marjorie is receiving a special education program and wants to drop out, and her parents are agreeable to allowing her to do so, is there any obligation on the school system to keep Marjorie in school?

5. In 1980, Ted was found to be emotionally disturbed and was placed in a public school junior high program. He was to be provided psychological counseling, parent consultation, and academic monitoring. In 1984, Ted was found by the local court to be a juvenile delinquent. The court placed him in a juvenile delinquent center, and subsequently a special school for juvenile delinquents. Who is required to pay for the placement, the school district or the town?

6. Is a state-established experimental program for gifted children, for which eligibility is based on having a certain IQ and subsequent selection based on lottery, likely to be upheld? This would mean that only some children identified as gifted would receive special programming.

7. If a state has a program for gifted children based only on IQ score, doesn't this eliminate children who are musically or otherwise talented? Could this have disparate impact racially?

8. With reference to the requirement that special education be provided to children in private schools, what obligation does the school have if the public and private schools are not in close geographic proximity? Who is required to pay additional costs of transportation if these are incurred, that is, the cost of transporting the child to an educational center or the cost of sending a public school teacher to the private school?

9. As a policy matter, how should the dispute about the definition of learning disability be resolved? At the federal level, state level, local level? Through what process, hearings by educational administrative agencies, litigation, amendment to statutes?

10. With reference to children with AIDS, if the school requested an opinion from a private physician as to the risk of a child with AIDS to other children in the classroom, and that physician determined there would be a reasonable risk (although opinions of other physicians in the area were otherwise), should the court defer to the medical judgment of private physicians on which the school has relied in excluding the child? (Refer back to *Arline* in this chapter.)

11. The concern about privacy for a child with AIDS and the need for school employees to know that a child has AIDS so that appropriate precautions can be taken are both legitimate concerns. How can these concerns be reconciled?

12. Should the EAHCA be amended to address issues relating to children with AIDS and other contagious diseases? If so, how? Or should this be left to the state or local educational agency?

13. Does the amendment to Section 504 really establish that children with AIDS are protected under the Act?

14. Because preschool is not mandatory in most states, how can the mainstreaming goals of the EAHCA be accomplished for children under five?

15. Assuming that the court in *Timothy W.* went too far, when, if ever, can a child be denied an education under the EAHCA?

NOTES

1. Pennsylvania Association for Retarded Children v. Commonwealth of Pennsylvania, 343 F. Supp. 279 (E.D. Pa. 1972).
2. 468 U.S. 992 (1984).

3. 468 U.S. at 1013.

4. 20 U.S.C. § 1401(a)(1).

5. 520 F. Supp. 905 (S.D. Tex. 1981).

6. Antkowiak v. Ambach, 638 F. Supp. 1564, 1577, 1579 (W.D.N.Y. 1986). Pending a final decision in the case, the court also ordered that Lara Antkowiak be placed in the Devereaux Treatment Center at no cost to her parents, an extremely expensive private treatment center.

7. 34 C.F.R. § 300.300(a).

8. *Id.* at § 300.300(b)(1).

9. *Id.* at § 300.300(b)(2).

10. *Id.* at § 300.300(b)(3).

11. *See generally,* RPHP § 2.13.

12. 29 U.S.C. § 794.

13. 468 U.S. 992 (1984). See Chapter 3 for excerpts from the opinion.

14. 534 F. Supp. 758 (N.D.N.Y. 1982). *See also* RPHP § 2.11.

15. 29 U.S.C. § 706(7)(B).

16. 29 U.S.C. § 706(7)(8), amended Pub. L. No. 100–259 (1987). *See also* Chalk v. United States District Court, 840 F.2d 701 (9th Cir. 1987) (teacher with AIDS was handicapped, and was also otherwise qualified under Section 504 and posed no significant risk to students in the classroom); Doe v. Belleville Pub. School Dist., 672 F. Supp. 342 (S.D. Ill. 1987) (child with AIDS not covered under EAHCA; is covered under § 504); Thomas v. Atascadero Unified School Dist., 662 F. Supp. 375 (C.D. Cal. 1987) (children with AIDS are handicapped under Section 504); Ray v. School Dist., 666 F. Supp. 1524 (M.D. Fla. 1987).

17. 442 U.S. 397 (1979).

18. *Id.* at 407, 413.

19. 107 S.Ct. at 1131, n. 16.

20. 107 S. Ct. at 1131, quoting Brief for American Medical Association.

21. Centers for Disease Control Recommendations for the Education and Foster Case of AIDS-Infected Children (August 1985) (hereinafter cited as CDC Guidelines). Current information on AIDS issues can be obtained from the Center for Disease Control, Atlanta, Georgia.

22. For a detailed discussion of these issues, see Rothstein, *Children with AIDS: A Need for a Clear Policy and Procedure for Public Education,* 12 Nova L. Rev. 1259(1988).

23. 34 C.F.R. § 300.450–.452.

24. *Id.* at § 300.5(b)(9).

25. *See* R. Weiner, P.L. 94–142, Impact on the Schools Ch. 7 (1985).

26. 20 U.S.C. §§ 1471–1485.

27. 20 U.S.C. §§ 1419. *See also* R. Weiner & J. Koppelman, From Birth to 5: Serving the Youngest Handicapped Children (1987).

28. *See* Rothstein, *Educational Rights of Severely and Profoundly Handicapped Children,* 61 Neb. L. Rev. 586 (1982).

CHAPTER 6

Identification and Evaluation

Before a child can receive special education or related services under the EAHCA, the child must be identified as being handicapped within the EAHCA. This chapter focuses on the specific problems of identification and evaluation in terms of when an evaluation can and should be done, when parental consent must be obtained, what happens if consent is refused, and what occurs if there is disagreement about the evaluation or other identification procedures. The chapter also notes limitations of assessment instruments.

For children with some handicapping conditions, such as orthopedic impairment or blindness, identification will have occurred long before the child enters public school. The parent or family physician will have identified the problem. In some cases, the child may already be receiving early educational programming. For many others, however, it will not be until the child enters the educational system that a problem will be noticed. A child having a hearing deficit or a learning disability or with certain behavior problems may have functioned fairly well until the demands of reading, arithmetic, or simply remaining in the seat were placed upon the child by the school system. A difficulty may be noticed when the school does a sweep-screening of all children for vision or hearing. Or it may be noticed simply through observation by the regular classroom teacher.[1]

TYPES OF ASSESSMENTS

There are a number of types of assessment relevant to the eligibility for educational services for handicapped students.[2] These assessments purport to measure physical and mental impairment, emotional and behavioral impairment, achievement levels, competency, perceptual ability, and intelligence quotients. Before addressing the legal issues surrounding identification and evaluation, it is important to have at least a general sense of the types of assessments involved in the educational setting, and to be aware of some of the problems about the validity and reliability of the testing instruments.

Group Assessment

One of the most common types of tests that occurs in schools is sweep-screening of all children for hearing and vision problems. Ordinarily, these are very quick and routine screening programs, where any deviation from normal performance results in a referral or recommendation that the child be further assessed either by a school evaluator or by the family's personal physician. Other types of sweep-screenings that commonly occur in many schools include testing of basic fine motor skills (the ability to manipulate small objects, for example), gross motor skills (such as the ability to throw a ball or jump on one foot), and basic perceptual motor skills (such as drawing a triangle). Often kindergarten-age children are screened for basic cognitive development by testing the ability to recognize common objects and common words. If a problem is identified in one of these areas at this level, additional testing may be recommended and parental consent must be obtained for individualized testing. Achievement tests are also examples of sweep-screening for academics. Very low scores on these may be the basis for further special education eligibility testing.

Not only are schools *permitted* to do this type of sweep-screening of groups of students, but to some extent they are *required* to do so under the EAHCA. State and local educational agencies are required to proactively develop policies and procedures for the identification, location, and evaluation of all handicapped children in the state or local school district.[3] As a practical matter it would be difficult, if not impossible, to carry this out without using sweep-screening.

Beyond the sweep-screening, there are a number of group testing mechanisms that are used every day in the school setting. Periodic standardized achievement tests are common in most states. These are less likely to identify a handicapping condition, however, unless they are used in conjunction with other assessment instruments. For example, unless there is a comparison between achievement and ability, it may not be known that the student is actually intellectually gifted, but has a learning disability that makes it difficult to fill in standardized computer-scored test grid sheets.

Group testing also occurs every day at the classroom level. Whenever a class is given a chapter review math test or spelling test, the student's competency is being measured at the same time as the entire group. To at least some extent, the performance of other members of the class will be a determining factor in the student's competency. For example, if a teacher gives a test on geography to the fifth-grade class, asking class members to name the capitals of all the states, the average performance of the entire class will probably be a factor in the teacher's assessment of what is a competent level of performance. A child who has just moved to the United States from a foreign country, and who has not been exposed to information about state capitals, however, might do poorly on that particular examination, but might be quite intelligent. This example illustrates the importance of understanding what is being measured and what is not being measured in any particular situation.

Individual Assessment

Whenever a sweep-screening or a personal observation or other factor signals the need for individual assessment of a child's educational needs, a variety of individualized assessments may result. The purpose of sweep-screening is to provide a quick and efficient means to obtain data to determine whether to refer the student for indepth comprehensive assessment. The purpose of individual assessment is quite different. It is to determine eligibility for special education services.

Individual medical or health assessments might be performed by a physician or other qualified professional. These could take the form of a general physical examination or a specialized examination of hearing, vision, or other ability. For children with potential academic problems it is possible that some type of standardized educational performance measure might be given. This instrument must be a validated test with identifiable norms and a measure of reliability. These tests are typically administered by psychologists or other educational diagnosticians. State law determines who is qualified to administer them. The type of tests vary, but they typically include individual measures for IQ (purportedly measuring intelligence in relation to age), achievement (measuring performance), and ability (purportedly measuring potential). In addition, specialty tests may be administered for a particular behavioral function, such as speech.

OBTAINING CONSENT TO AN EVALUATION

Although the teacher may believe that the child should receive a special education service, such as speech therapy, the service cannot be provided without a preplacement evaluation.[4] Before an evaluation, other than a sweep-screening, can be done, the parent must consent to the evaluation. Written notice must be provided about the proposed action, the evaluation procedure to be used, and the procedural safeguards available under the EAHCA.[5] The notice must be understandable to the parent, and therefore must be in the parent's native language or other mode of communication used by the parent. To ensure that the request is understood by the parent, written evidence, usually a signature, must be obtained by the educational agency. The importance of these requirements is noted in the following excerpt from a judicial decision.

QUACKENBUSH V. JOHNSON CITY SCHOOL DISTRICT

716 F.2d 141, 147–48 (2d Cir. 1983), cert. denied, 465 U.S. 1071 (1984)
Jason was placed in a regular kindergarten class in the defendant district in September 1978, although the district then knew or should have known that he was a handi-

capped child in need of special educational services. Plaintiff Quackenbush, Jason's mother, took no action at that time because district employees told her to wait until the following year. However, during the following year Jason repeated kindergarten, again in a regular classroom setting.

Concerned about her son's lack of progress in the second year, Quackenbush had Jason evaluated by a psychologist who recommended that he be classified as learning disabled. A copy of the psychologist's evaluation was sent to the district's COH [Committee on the Handicapped] in April 1980. In June 1980 Quackenbush requested that Jason be reviewed by the COH. Immediately thereafter, defendant Rowlind [a school district employee] came to Quackenbush's home with a "parental permission form" which Quackenbush filled in. On instructions of defendant Rowlind, Quackenbush left blank the area to be checked with respect to giving permission to conduct an evaluation of Jason. Rowlind took the form.

Although the complaint does not allege what action the school district took on plaintiff's request for special services, we infer that the district took no action whatsoever from that time forward. We also infer from the allegations that the district took no action on the request because Rowlind, without plaintiff's authority, put a check mark on the form in the box indicating that she denied the district permission to conduct an evaluation of Jason. Plaintiff alleges that Rowlind altered the form "for the sole purpose of denying [Jason] the special education he is entitled to." She further alleges that he acted pursuant to a policy of the defendant school district to refuse special education to handicapped children for financial reasons. As a result Jason was denied the special education to which he was entitled, suffered damages to his intellect, emotional capacity, and personality, and was impeded in acquiring necessary training. In addition, plaintiff alleges that she moved to a different school district to get the services Jason needed and that she herself suffered emotional distress. . . .

It is unthinkable that Congress would have intended that a plaintiff such as Quackenbush, who as the case presented itself sought for two years to have the school district provide services, made a direct request for evaluation, and was deprived of that request by school district forgery, should be left without any remedy. Particularly in a statutory scheme such as the EHA where great emphasis is placed upon procedural safeguards, we must assume that Congress intended some kind of relief when, through school district policy or misconduct of school officials or both, a handicapped child is deprived of the procedural safeguards guaranteed by sec. 1415. Assuming, then, that Congress intended a remedy here, the question remains whether that remedy, which all parties to this appeal assume to exist, is to be implied in sec. 1415(e)(2), or whether it is to be found in sec. 1983, which guarantees a citizen relief from state deprivations of federally granted rights.

Section 1983 is a general remedial statute aimed at preventing lawlessness by state and local governments. Defendants' deliberate interference with procedural safeguards guaranteed by Congress for the purpose of depriving Jason of special educational services necessary to provide him with free appropriate public education would constitute the deprivation of a right guaranteed under federal law within the meaning of sec. 1983. . . .

We express no opinion on what damages, if any, plaintiff might be entitled to recover should she prove her allegations. We find it fitting, however, that defendants should be required to respond in damages for those injuries caused by their conduct which deprived plaintiffs of access to the administration system and procedural safeguards guaranteed to them by Congress.

It is probable that if either the parent or the educational agency requests an evaluation, the evaluation will be done or arranged by the school. There may be cases, however, where the parent refuses to consent to the evaluation, or where the school refuses to conduct the evaluation. If the disagreement cannot be resolved informally, *either* party may initiate due process procedures under the EAHCA.[6] Disagreement may also arise after an evaluation has been made. If the parents do not accept the results of the school's evaluation, they may want to have an independent evaluation as part of the eligibility decision. There is no question as to the right of the parent to have an independent evaluation done by a qualified examiner and to have the evaluation used in making the decision as to the child's placement.[7] The difficulty is in determining who must pay for the cost of the evaluation. For some types of expensive evaluations, this can be an important issue. Before looking at the question of who pays for evaluations, it should also be noted that evaluations and communications with parents are to be in the the native language or other appropriate mode of communication.[8] Of perhaps more importance is the requirement that no single criterion should be used in assessing the child.[9]

PAYMENT FOR EVALUATIONS

When the school conducts, requests, or arranges for the evaluation, it is paid for at public expense. Problems can arise even in this situation, where the evaluation cost is beyond what the school may have originally contemplated, as illustrated by the following case:

SEALS V. LOFTIS

614 F. Supp. 302 (E.D. Tenn. 1985)
[Travis Seals has special education needs relating to a seizure disorder, visual difficulty, and learning disabilities. He began elementary school at one school, and was later transferred to another school to better meet his needs. It was noted at the time of his transfer that his behavior had changed and his school performance had deteriorated. The multidisciplinary team met and recommended to his parents that Travis be evaluated by a pediatrician because they did not want to do anything that would affect his education without a recent medical evaluation.]

Acting on the recommendation of the Department's M Team, Travis' parents brought him to Dr. Richard E. Poehlein, a pediatrician of their own choice. Dr. Poehlein referred Travis to Dr. Lawrence T. Ch'ien for a neurological evaluation. Upon completion of this evaluation, Dr. Ch'ien, along with Dr. Poehlein, referred Travis to Dr. William M. Hillner, a psychologist, for a psychological evaluation. While the M Team had not specifically requested the neurological and psychological evaluations, it is quite clear that Dr. Poehlein felt that both of those evaluations were necessary to help him ascertain the source of Travis' difficulties. It is also clear that the Department became aware of the evaluations by Drs. Ch'ien and Hillner, and made some use of a written report by Dr. Hillner in ascertaining Travis' special education needs. The neurological and psychological evaluations did not result in any changes in

Travis' individualized education plan, but might have resulted in changes had the evaluations reached different conclusions.

When a dispute arose over whether the Department or Travis' parents were to pay for the evaluations done by Drs. Ch'ien and Hillner, a "due process" hearing was convened before a hearing officer. The hearing officer concluded that the Department "pay the amount which is in excess of the cost borne by the Seals' insurance for Travis' medical and neurological evaluation." [The total cost of evaluations was close to $450, some of which had been paid for by the Seals' insurance company. This had not affected their insurance premium payments, but had reduced their lifetime maximum benefit for psychological services.]

The Seals elected to bring this action pursuant to 20 U.S.C. sec. 1415(e)(2), seeking *inter alia* reimbursement of the insurance proceeds paid by the Seals' insurer to Drs. Ch'ien and Hillner. The Seals contend that the hearing officer erroneously required them to use their insurance coverage to pay for the evaluations done by Drs. Ch'ien and Hillner. The Department contends that the hearing officer decided the insurance question properly, but erred in requiring the Department to pay the rest of the cost of these evaluations. This Court has . . . received the records of the administrative proceedings and has heard additional evidence at the request of the parties.

The questions which must be decided here are:

(1) Whether the evaluations by Drs. Ch'ien and Hillner are within the scope of aid which is to be provided the Seals pursuant to the EAHCA, and, if so,
(2) Whether the Seals can be required in this case to utilize the proceeds of their medical insurance to pay for the evaluations of Drs. Ch'ien and Hillner.

It is apparent that these services were requested and required by the Department to assist Travis, in the words of 20 U.S.C. sec. 1401(17), "to benefit from special education." As such, they must be furnished to Travis by the Department pursuant to the EAHCA. . . .

There is little specific guidance from the EAHCA on this insurance reimbursement issue. On the one hand, the EAHCA requires the furnishing of a *free* appropriate public education to handicapped children. On the other hand, the United States Department of Education has promulgated a rather cryptic regulation which is found at 34 C.F.R. sec. 300.301(b) which provides:

> Nothing in this part relieves an insurer or similar third party from an otherwise valid obligation to provide or to pay for services provided to a handicapped child.

The above regulation, being directed only at the obligations of insurers, does not deal directly with whether the Seals may be required to use their medical insurance for the services of Drs. Ch'ien and Hillner. Because of EAHCA's emphasis upon a *free* appropriate public education, this Court concludes that parents of a handicapped child cannot be required to utilize their private medical insurance benefits where the utilization of those benefits would cause them to incur a financial cost. Any other conclusion would be inconsistent with the concept of a free appropriate public education which underlies the EAHCA.

This Court further holds that the Seals in this case did incur a cost with respect to the insurance payment to Dr. Hillner in that the payment reduced the lifetime benefits available to them under their policy. Defendants must therefore reimburse the Seals in the amount of Ninety Nine and 70/100 Dollars ($99.70). [This is the amount by which the lifetime maximum benefit would be reduced.]

Since the Seals' insurance payment to Dr. Ch'ien did not result in a "cost" to the Seals, the decision of the hearing officer, to the extent that it requires the Seals to use their insurance for this purpose, is affirmed. [This amount did not affect the Seals' insurance benefits or premiums in any way.]

Payment for independent evaluations is somewhat more problematic than payment for evaluations conducted or requested by the school. As noted previously, the parent has a right to have an independent evaluation done and considered in the placement decision. The educational agency may not agree that an additional or independent evaluation is necessary to make the placement decision and may, therefore, be unwilling to pay the additional cost of such an evaluation. If the school believes its evaluation to be appropriate, a hearing may be held to determine the appropriateness of the school's evaluation and the right to have an independent evaluation paid for at public expense.[10] The educational resources involved in holding a hearing may serve as a deterrent to the school trying to obstruct reasonable requests from the parent. This leverage has the potential of being abused by parents who know that the cost and disruption of a hearing serve to coerce the school into simply agreeing to pay for an independent evaluation. On the other hand, the parent may not be fully informed about due process rights, or may be intimidated by the educational procedures, and may be reluctant to undergo all that is involved in a hearing. Independent evaluations that are requested by a hearing officer at any point, however, are clearly to be paid for at public expense.[11]

PROTECTION AGAINST DISCRIMINATION

As noted previously, "no single procedure is used as the sole criterion for determining an appropriate educational program. . . . [12] In addition, it is essential that the testing procedures have been validated for their intended purpose.[13] While there has been much criticism of certain types of testing procedures in general, there has been specific criticism about the disproportionate placement of some children in special education classes.

LARRY P. V. RILES

793 F.2d 969 (9th Cir. 1984)
In the mid-60's California created programs for several categories of students with educational problems. The "educable mentally retarded" (EMR) program was for schoolchildren of retarded intellectual development who are considered incapable of being educated through the regular educational program, but who could benefit from special educational facilities to make them economically useful and socially adjusted. The "trainable mentally retarded" (TMR) category was for children with more severe retardation than educable mentally retarded. In addition, there were two categories

for students who, with help, could be returned to a regular school program. These were the programs for "culturally disadvantaged minors," children with cultural or economic disadvantages, but with potential for successfully completing a regular educational program; and for "educationally handicapped minors" (EH), students with marked learning or behavioral disorders, capable of returning to a regular school program but who cannot presently benefit from the regular program.

The EMR classes are for children who are considered "*incapable* for learning in the regular classes," and the EMR curriculum "is not designed to help students learn the skills necessary to return to the regular instructional program." The EMR classes are designed only to teach social adjustment and economic usefulness.

The [EMR] classes are conceived of as "deadend classes," and a misplacement in EMR causes a stigma and irreparable injury to the student.

From 1968 until trial in 1977, black children have been significantly over-represented in EMR classes. For example, in 1968–69, black children were about 9% of the state school population, yet accounted for 27% of the EMR population.

[In 1975 the state placed a moratorium on IQ testing, pending the outcome of the *Riles* case.]

. . . Since the moratorium on IQ testing in 1975, the total percentage of black children in EMR classes has not changed substantially. The district court, however, examined the data concerning *new* EMR placements, which were made without IQ tests, and found that uncontradicted expert testimony showed that the four percent drop in the placement of black children into EMR classes is not likely to have occurred by chance. . . .

The court found that "the tests were never designed to eliminate cultural biases against black children; it was assumed in effect that black children were less 'intelligent' than whites . . . . The tests were standardized and developed on an all-white population, and naturally their scientific validity is questionable for culturally different groups." Since the 1920's it has been generally known that black persons perform less well than white persons on the standardized intelligence tests. IQ tests had been standardized so that they yielded no bias because of sex. For example, when sample tests yielded different scores for boys and girls, the testing experts assumed such differences were unacceptable and modified the tests so that the curve in the standardization sample for boys and girls was identical. No such modifications on racial grounds has ever been tried by the testing companies. The district court noted that "the experts have from the beginning been willing to tolerate or even encourage tests that portray minorities, especially blacks, as intellectually inferior."

The district court analyzed and rejected the defendants' arguments advanced at trial that would explain the test score differences, which theorized that the lower scores for blacks were the result of actual, relevant differences between black and white children. The first argument is the genetic argument, which states that natural selection has resulted in black persons having a "gene pool" with lower intelligence than whites. The district court found the assumptions underlying the genetic argument highly suspect, and in any event that the defendants "were unwilling to admit any reliance on [this theory] for policy-making purposes."

The second theory is the socioeconomic argument, which theorizes that because of blacks' lower socioeconomic status, they are at a greater risk for all kinds of diseases due to malnutrition and poor medical attention. The district court found that the facts did not support this theory, since it did not explain why more severe mental retardation, *e.g.* that consistent with placement into classes for the trainable mentally retarded children, does not occur in greater proportions among blacks and poorer sections of the population.

The district court found that the appellants failed to show that the IQ tests were validated for blacks with respect to the characteristics consistent with EMR classes, *i.e.,* that the defendants failed to establish that the IQ tests were accurate predictors that black elementary schoolchildren who scored less than 70 were indeed mentally retarded.

The district court found that alternatives to IQ testing for EMR placement have been in effect since the state moratorium on IQ testing in 1975. These procedures, in which schools take more in time and care with their assessments for EMR classification and rely more on observational data, are less discriminatory than under the IQ centered standard. . . .

The gravamen of appellees' complaint is not against the use of IQ tests in general, but that the *particular* tests selected by the State Board of Education were culturally or racially biased. . . .

[T]he Education For All Handicapped Children Act specifically requires that tests and evaluation procedures be free of racial and cultural bias. Both the EAHCA and the Rehabilitation Act require that the tests used for evaluation be validated for the specific purpose for which they are used, and that placement not be based upon a single criterion but on a variety of sources. . . .

Appellant argues that the IQ tests were validated for the specific purposes for which they are used. Appellant analogizes to Title VII cases, for the proposition that tests that are valid predictors of future performance can be utilized even if they have a discriminatory impact. There are two problems with appellant's proposition. First, the employment context is quite different from the educational situation. As the district court stated, "[i]f tests can predict that a person is going to be a poor employee, the employer can legitimately deny that person a job, but if tests suggest that a young child is probably going to be a poor student, the school cannot on that basis alone deny that child the opportunity to improve and develop the academic skills necessary to success in our society." Assigning a student to an EMR class denies that child the opportunity to develop the necessary academic skills, since EMR classes do not teach academic subjects and are essentially a dead-end academic track. Second, and more important, the question for predictive validity in schools is not whether the standardized intelligence tests predict future school performance generally, as appellant argues, but whether the tests predict specifically that black elementary schoolchildren (as opposed to white elementary schoolchildren) who score at or below 70 on the IQ tests are mentally retarded and incapable of learning the regular school curriculum. In this case, the appellant would have to have shown that the tests are a proven tool to determine which students have characteristics consistent with EMR status and placement in EMR classes, *i.e.,* "whose mental capabilities make it impossible for them to profit from the regular educational programs" even with remedial instruction. The regulations place the burden of showing such validation on the defendants.

The district court found that defendants failed to show that the tests were validated for placing black students with scores of 70 or less in EMR classes. The district court noted that very few studies had examined the difference of IQ predictability for black as compared to white populations, and that those studies which had examined this problem found the tests much less valid for blacks than for whites. Further, the district court found that, even assuming the tests were validated for placement of white schoolchildren in EMR classes, such validation for blacks had been generally assumed but not established. For example, the tests had been adjusted to eliminate differences in the average scores between the sexes, but such adjustment was never made to adjust the scores to be equal for black and white children. They found that the reason for this was a basic assumption of a lower level of intelligence in blacks than in whites. The fact that early test developers indeed made this assumption is borne out by the literature and testimony at trial. In addition, no studies have been made, either by the defendants or the testing companies, to investigate the reasons for the one standard deviation difference in test scores between the races or to determine whether test redesign could eliminate any bias. There was expert testimony that a much larger percentage of black than white children had been misplaced in EMR classes. Based on the evidence in the record, the district court finding that the appellant had not established validation of the test is not clearly erroneous.

The district court also found that the appellant did not utilize the variety of information required by statute and regulation to make EMR placements, but relied primarily on the IQ test. This finding also is not clearly erroneous. Testimony showed that school records lacked sufficient evidence of educational history, adaptive behavior, social and cultural background or health history for these factors to have been utilized in placement.

Since the appellant has not shown that these findings are clearly erroneous, we affirm the district court's holding that the defendants violated the provisions of the Rehabilitation Act and the Education For All Handicapped Children Act (1) by not insuring that the tests were validated for the specific purpose for which they are used, and (2) by not using the variety of statutorily mandated evaluation tools.

The following is a much condensed opinion from the *PASE* case. The case covered 52 pages in the official reporter, and includes a detailed discussion of the various versions of IQ tests. These portions are omitted, but review of the full opinion on these points is useful for those interested in greater detail on these points.

PARENTS IN ACTION ON SPECIAL EDUCATION (PASE) V. HANNON

506 F. Supp. 831 (N.D. Ill. 1980)
This case presents the question whether standard intelligence tests administered by the Chicago Board of Education are culturally biased against black children. The action is brought on behalf of all black children who have been or will be placed in special classes for the educable mentally handicapped ("EMH") in the Chicago school system. The defendants are the Chicago Board of Education and its officers responsible for administration of the relevant programs. The named plaintiffs are two black children who were placed in EMH classes after achieving low scores on standard intelligence test. . . .

Three and 7/10 percent of all black students enrolled in the system are in EMH, whereas only 1.3 percent of the white students are in EMH. . . .

[Lengthy discussion of intelligence tests and their validity and bias according to various experts is omitted].

The Assessment Process
Defendants' system for the identification and placement of mentally handicapped children, which is spelled out in manuals and printed regulations, involves several lev-

els of investigation. It is important to understand that an IQ test is not the first level, nor is an IQ score the catalyst for the assessment process. The first level of investigation is the classroom. Unless the child is having difficulty with his studies in the classroom, the question of EMH placement will never arise and there is no occasion for an IQ test. Individually administered IQ tests of the kind involved in this case have never been given routinely in the Chicago school system, and the former practice of giving group-administered general intelligence tests to all students was discontinued some years ago.

If the classroom teacher has reason to believe the child has an educational handicap, the matter is taken up with the school principal. The teacher prepares a written report concerning the child, using the prescribed form. The principal then convenes a screening conference. The participants are the principal, the classroom teacher, a parent of the child and any other appropriate persons.

The screening committee makes a recommendation to the principal as to whether a case study should be requested for the child. If the principal determines on the basis of this recommendation that a case study is warranted, the matter is referred to the Special Education Bureau for the development of an appropriate case study program.

Various professional personnel then determine what areas of evaluation are appropriate for the child. On the basis of this determination, the child is examined by persons in the appropriate disciplines. This may involve a medical examination, a psychiatric examination, a psychological assessment or reference to a social worker or a speech therapist.

When the case study evaluation has been completed, the principal convenes a multidisciplinary staff conference. The members of this staff include a representative of the special education program, all of the professionals who evaluated the child, the school principal, and parents of the child. The purpose of this multidisciplinary staff meeting is to determine whether the child should be placed in a special education program, and if so, what program it should be. The report of the staff conference is in writing. Each participant must sign it and indicate whether he or she concurs in the recommendation.

No child can be placed in an EMH class unless the placement is recommended by a psychologist who has evaluated the child. While the conference can decline an EMH placement recommended by the psychologist, it cannot make such a placement without the psychologist's recommendation.

If either the child or his parents on the one hand or the school officials on the other are dissatisifed with the decision, they may request further hearings on the matter. Placement of the child is stayed pending the hearing, which is conducted by an impartial hearing officer assigned from another school district by the State Department of Education. Ultimately, the matter is subject to administrative review in the courts of Illinois.

The evaluation and placement process is not carried out hastily. There are more children in need of placement than there are available seats in the EMH classrooms. Sometimes the decision is against placement even though the parent desires it. A motive for unnecessary placement is nonexistent, since the cost to the local system of administering the program far exceeds the state and federal aid received for it. The total cost of the Chicago special education program exceeds by 50 million dollars per year the state and federal funds received to support it. . . .

In the circumstances of this case, where defendants have shown that IQ scores are only one factor which enters into the EMH assessment and that a low IQ score frequently does not result in such placement, I believe the burden of showing an absence of racial bias in the tests does not rest on the defendants. . . .

It is unfortunately true that, despite what I believe are sincere efforts on the part of the defendants to avoid erroneous placements, some children are placed in EMH classes who should not be there. Small but significant numbers of EMH students are constantly being moved out of EMH classes back into the regular curriculum. Some of these transfers are due to the fact that the child has progressed in the EMH class and is ready for a greater challenge. In other instances, however, the child is transferred because it is belatedly discovered that he should not have been there in the first place.

These erroneous placements have not been shown to be due to racial bias in the IQ tests. The situations of the two named plaintiffs illustrate this failure of proof. These two black children, Barbara B. and Angela J., were each evaluated as being mentally retarded and were transferred out of their regular classes to EMH classes. Each child was evaluated by a school psychologist and achieved a low score on one of the WISC tests or the Stanford-Binet. . . .

The Larry P. Case

This is not a case of first impression. The exact issue of racial bias in the WISC, WISC-R and Stanford-Binet tests has been decided by Judge Robert F. Peckham of the United States District Court for the Northern District of California in the case of [*Larry P. v. Riles* (1984)].

Plaintiffs rely upon that decision heavily, since Judge Peckham held that the tests are culturally biased against black children. Judge Peckham heard a number of the same witnesses who testified here. He found their testimony persuasive. Judge Peckham's lengthy and scholarly opinion is largely devoted to the question of what legal consequences flow from a finding of racial bias in the tests. There is relatively little analysis of the threshold question of whether tests bias in fact exists, and Judge Peckham even remarked that the cultural bias of the tests ". . . is hardly disputed in this litigation . . . " I find reference to specific test items on only one page of the opinion. . . .

As is by now obvious, the witnesses and the arguments which persuaded Judge Peckham had not persuaded me. Moreover, I believe the issue in the case cannot properly be analyzed without a detailed examination of the items on the tests. It is clear that this was not undertaken in the *Larry P.* case.

Conclusion

I have found one item on the Stanford-Binet and a total of eight items on the WISC and WISC-R to be culturally biased against black children, or at least sufficiently suspect that their use is in my view inappropriate. These few items do not render the tests unfair and would not significantly affect the score of an individual taking the tests. The evidence fails to show that any additional test items are racially or culturally unfair or suspect.

I believe and today hold that the WISC, WISC-R and Stanford-Binet tests, when used in conjunction with the statutorily mandated ["other criteria] for determining an appropriate educational program for a child" (20 U.S.C. § 1412(2)(D)(5), do not discriminate against black children in the Chicago public schools. Defendants are complying with that statutory mandate.

Intelligent administration of the IQ tests by qualified psychologists, followed by the evaluation procedures defendants use, should rarely result in the misassessment of a child of normal intelligence as one who is mentally retarded. There is no evidence in this record that such misassessments as do occur are the result of racial bias in test items or in any other aspect of the assessment process currently in use in the Chicago public school system.

The *Larry P.* and the *PASE* decisions have been the two lead cases involving the use of IQ tests and their implications for racial and cultural bias. In a case alleging that the use of achievement tests for special education placement had a disproportionate impact on black children, the court held that while relief was not available under the Rehabilitation Act, EAHCA procedures could be applied.[14] In another decision the court approved guidelines for placement to avoid disproportionate racial impact, and included a requirement that the students be observed in the classroom to note any personality clashes between the regular classroom teacher and the student that may have resulted in the recommendation for removal.[15]

REEVALUATION

Once the child has started to receive an individualized education program, it is important to ensure that the program remains appropriate for the child. To accomplish that goal, the EAHCA requires that the child's program be reviewed at least annually,[16] and that the child be reevaluated at least every three years or more frequently if warranted or requested.[17] When reevaluation is done to comply with EAHCA requirements, parental consent is not required, although state law often requires consent for any testing.[18]

The necessity of the periodic reevaluation is illustrated in the case of *Hoffman v. Board of Education.*[19] In that case a kindergarten-age boy was tested by a psychologist and was placed in a class for mentally retarded children. Although the psychologist recommended reevaluation within two years, the boy was never retested for intelligence until 12 years later. When he was retested, in 1969, it was determined that he was not mentally retarded and had been inappropriately placed for 12 years. In recognition of the disastrous consequences of such a wrongful placement, the trial court awarded the parents $750,000 to compensate for the boy's lost earnings. Although that decision was eventually overruled at the appellate court level because of New York State judicial deference to educational decision making, it is arguable that this failure to retest could today be the basis for liability because the EAHCA clearly establishes a requirement that such children be periodically reevaluated.[20]

MINIMUM COMPETENCY TESTING AND HANDICAPPED CHILDREN

In the last decade the move by education administrators toward excellence has resulted in requiring minimum competency testing in many states before a high school diploma can be awarded. These requirements have been challenged in a number of cases. The decisions in those cases establish that as a general rule, as long as there has been adequate notice that the tests would be required, and if the tests actually cover material in the curriculum, these tests will be permissible under the due process and equal protection clauses of the Constitution.[21] The application of minimum competency requirements to handicapped children has been addressed by the courts and has been held to be valid.[22] In recognition of the importance of having tangible evidence of achievement, some states and local school districts have adopted programs of providing special certificates of achievement or attendance to acknowledge the accomplishments or attendance of students who have not achieved the minimum competency requirements necessary to obtain a diploma. The flip side of this effort, however, has been to award a diploma in spite of the failure to meet minimum competency requirements. Schools in some local areas do this as a way of "getting rid of" difficult students. By awarding the diploma, the school is supposedly absolved from any further responsibility for the education of the students. The obligations of schools in these cases is not well settled.

EVALUATION PROCEDURES AND LIMITATIONS

The EAHCA specifies a number of points about evaluation procedures. These requirements include testing in the child's native language or appropriate mode of communication unless infeasible, using validated testing materials, administration of tests by trained personnel, evaluating specific needs not just general IQ, selecting and administration of tests to reflect aptitude or achievement accurately, using more than one criterion for decision making, evaluation by a multidisciplinary team, and assessment in all areas related to the suspected disability.[23]

An example of why some of these requirements are necessary can be illustrated by considering a child with cerebral palsy who is given the WISC-R, a commonly used IQ test. The test includes 12 different types of verbal and performance tests. Several of the items on the test are timed. The child with limited motor skills and slow speech would have difficulty with many of the performance tests requiring manipulation of objects and would have difficulty in many cases with items that require speed to perform. The child with cerebral palsy, however, may very well have high intelligence, but the use of this particular testing instrument could inaccurately seem to indicate that the child was mentally retarded.

It should be emphasized that the evaluation is to be made by a multidisciplinary team or group of individuals. This group should include at least one teacher or other specialist who is knowledgeable about the specific disability. It is also important that the child be assessed in all areas related to the suspected disability. These might include health, vision, hearing, social and emotional status, general intelligence, academic performance, communicative status, and motor abilities.[24]

Additional procedures are necessary for children with learning disabilities.[25] These procedures include additional team members, specific criteria relating to this disability, and a requirement that observation be an evaluation procedure. The additional team members are to be the child's teacher or a qualified educator and a person qualified to conduct individual diagnostic examinations of children. Criteria for determining that a child has a learning disability are that the child does not achieve commensurate with his or her age and ability levels and that there is a severe discrepancy between achievement and intellectual ability in one or more of several specified areas such as basic reading skill or mathematics. If the discrepancy is primarily a result of another handicapping condition (such as vision or mental retardation) or sociological disadvantage, the child may not be identified as learning disabled.[26] The written report that is to result from the team's evaluation is to be certified by each team member. Dissenting views are to be submitted separately by a team member who does not agree with the conclusions of the other members of the team.[27]

Testing and evaluation are necessary. It is necessary to identify children who have special needs and to identify what type of programming is appropriate. Under the EAHCA it is necessary to classify children in order to obtain funding. It is also necessary to test and evaluate in order to assess whether programming being provided is working. The EAHCA requirements that testing be individualized and the case law and statutory requirements that testing be nondiscriminatory have raised a number of concerns. These include the appropriateness of using IQ tests for special education placement, the amount of time and effort required in the evaluation process, the volume of paperwork required for proper documentation of evaluations, and questions about whether certain groups of children (behaviorally disordered/emotionally disturbed, learning disabled, and mildly mentally retarded) are being appropriately identified.[28]

It is important to be aware that all testing instruments have limitations and problems. These problems relate to how a test is administered, to whom it is administered, how it is interpreted, what decisions are made because of it, and what its original purpose is. Seemingly objective tests that are supposedly administered uniformly are subject to misuse. For example, a child's ability to perform on a standard achievement test or an IQ test may be affected by the time of day it is given (because the child may be tired or hungry), by the temperature of the room, by noise distractions, or by a variety of other external conditions. The attitude of the test administrator may subtly affect the outcome of tests such as an IQ test. Although test administrators are trained to avoid bias in the test administration, many instances arise in which the patience or general attitude of the administrator could have an effect on the performance. A valid and reliable test, effective when used for screening, would be inappropriate for determining eligibility. In sum, testing instruments are not perfect, and there is an ongoing effort to improve the assessment process. Schools do, however, need to rely on the instruments currently available to appropriately identify students, determine eligibility, and evaluate progress. It is important that those advocating for appropriate placement of special education children be aware of the limitations of the tests. It is also important to recognize the dilemma of labelling under current policy requirements to do so—the child may need a label to qualify for services, but the label may result in a stigma or in lower expectations of the child that may have adverse consequences in the long run.

SUMMARY

Before a child can receive special education or related services, the child must first be identified as having a handicapping condition, and an assessment of the particular needs of that child based on the condition must be made. Because of the stigma that can occur through labelling and also because of the importance of parental participation, the EAHCA requires that parental notice and consent occur before an individual evaluation can be made. The regulations are quite specific as to the form of the notice to ensure that it is actually provided. What is not clear from the statute or regulations is what consequences there are if the educational agency does not comply with notice and consent requirements of the EAHCA. Noncompliance with these requirements is clearly a violation of the EAHCA, but whether a violation can be the basis for a recovery of damages is not well settled.

When the educational agency provides appropriate notice and requests permission to evaluate, it is clear that parents may refuse. A disagreement on whether to evaluate may be resolved through an administrative hearing under the EAHCA. Where permission to evaluate has been granted, but the parents disagree with the results of the evaluation, it is also clear that they may have an independent evaluation done. Results of an independent evaluation must be considered in making programmatic and placement decisions.

Issues of payment for evaluations are less clearly resolved. Parents may recover the cost of the independent evaluation if they are successful in challenging the appropriateness of the school's evaluation at a due process hearing. It has been suggested that the cost of a due process hearing in effect forces schools to agree to pay for the independent evaluation to avoid the cost and disruption of a hearing. Such a suggestion could be countered, however, by noting that widespread abuse is unlikely because the parents must still incur the cost of legal representation if they are unsuccessful.

The use of certain testing procedures, such as IQ tests, has been challenged in several major court cases in which it has been claimed that these procedures discriminate on the basis of race. While these cases have reached differing results in terms of upholding the validity of IQ tests, there is clarity on the requirement that such tests should never be the sole criterion for making a placement decision. The EAHCA is specific in that regard, and judicial attention to this issue is consistent on that point. Inherent in the EAHCA policy is a recognition that no assessment procedure is perfect and that evaluation by a number of different individuals using different types of evaluation instruments is essential for a reasonably accurate assessment of needs and abilities.

Flaws in testing instruments and the fact that a child's abilities and performance can change over time (and in fact should change with appropriate programming) is foundation for the EAHCA's mandate that a child placed in a special education program should be reevaluated at least every three years and the program reviewed at least annually. Failure to comply with that requirement can have disastrous results if a child is permitted to remain in an inappropriate program over an extended period of time. An unresolved issue is whether the educational agency should be accountable for violating this requirement.

The EAHCA does not directly address minimum competency testing, the testing that is used to determine whether students are eligible to receive a high school diploma. Several court cases have addressed the question as to whether such requirements illegally discriminate against students with handicaps. Courts have been generally consistent in holding that such requirements are reasonable as long as students have adequate notice of these requirements.

QUESTIONS AND PROBLEMS

1. The court left open the question of what damages, if any, would be recoverable in the *Quackenbush* case. What damages or other remedy would compensate Jason and his mother for the denial of procedural safeguards in this case? What action should be taken with respect to Rowlind, assuming that any monetary recovery is collected from the school system, rather than Rowlind as an individual?

2. In *Seals v. Loftis,* how might the school have avoided this type of referral evaluation expense or at least controlled the referral to some extent?

3. In *Larry P. v. Riles,* might the court have been more likely to uphold even the validity of IQ tests had the tests been a less significant component in the placement decision?

4. Who has the burden of proving the validity or invalidity of tests used for placing a child in an educational program?

5. Can the *Larry P.* and *PASE* decisions be reconciled? Should a Director of Special Education advise evaluators not to use IQ tests for eligibility determinations?

6. In the *PASE* decision, the court notes that because of the high cost of EMH placement, the "motive for unnecessary placement is nonexistent." While the local educational agency's motive for unnecessary placement may not exist, isn't it possible that the classroom teacher may have a motive to refer out children who are disruptive?

7. As a policy matter, can we reconcile the need to identify and place with the avoidance of the stigmatizing effect of certain placements?

NOTES

1. Under EAHCA regulations relating to personnel development, it is reasonable to expect that educators have the ability to spot certain handicapping conditions, and administrators should ensure that educators in direct contact with students have appropriate training to do so. *See* 34 C.F.R. §§ 300.380–.387.
2. J. Salvia & J. Ysseldike, Assessment in Special and Remedial Education (1981).
3. 34 C.F.R. §§ 300.128 & 300.220.
4. 34 C.F.R. § 300.531.

5. 34 C.F.R. § 300.505.

6. 34 C.F.R. § 300.506. These procedures are discussed more fully in Chapter 14.

7. 34 C.F.R. § 300.503.

8. 34 C.F.R. § 300.532(a).

9. 34 C.F.R. § 300.532(d).

10. 34 C.F.R. § 300.503(b). *See* Chapter 14 for hearing procedures.

11. 34 C.F.R. § 300.503(d).

12. 34 C.F.R. § 300.532(d).

13. 34 C.F.R. § 300.532(a)(2).

14. Georgia State Conference of Branches of NAACP v. Georgia, 775 F.2d 1403 (11th Cir. 1985).

15. Lora v. Board of Education, 587 F. Supp. 1572 (E.D.N.Y. 1984).

16. 34 C.F.R. § 300.343(d).

17. 34 C.F.R. § 300.534.

18. Carroll v. Capalbo, 563 F. Supp. 1053 (D.R.I. 1983).

19. 49 N.Y.2d 121, 400 N.E.2d 317, N.Y.S.2d 376 (1979).

20. Rothstein, *Accountability for Professional Misconduct in Providing Education to Handicapped Children,* 14 J.L. & ED. 349 (1985).

21. Debra P. v. Turlington, 730 F.2d 1405 (11th Cir. 1984). *See also* L. FISCHER & G. SORENSON, SCHOOL LAW FOR COUNSELORS, PSYCHOLOGISTS AND SOCIAL WORKERS 111–17 (1985).

22. Brookhart v. Illinois State Board of Education, 697 F.2d 179, 182 (7th Cir. 1983).

23. 34 C.F.R. § 300.532.

24. 34 C.F.R. § 300.532(e).

25. 34 C.F.R. § 300.504–.543.

26. 34 C.F.R. § 300.541(b).

27. 34 C.F.R. § 300.543(c).

28. These issues are raised and discussed in H.R. TURNBULL, FREE APPROPRIATE PUBLIC EDUCATION: THE LAW AND CHILDREN WITH DISABILITIES 98–102 (1986).

CHAPTER 7

Appropriate Education

THE *ROWLEY* STANDARD

In order to qualify for federal support under the EAHCA the state must have a policy "that assures all handicapped children the right to a free *appropriate* public education"[1] (emphasis added). The development of a program of appropriate special education and related services occurs through the vehicle of the individualized education program (IEP).[2] This program is a written statement of a child's present education performance, the annual goals to be achieved (including short-term instructional objectives), a statement of specific services to be performed, dates for initiation and duration of services, and criteria, procedures, and schedules for evaluating whether the objectives are being achieved.[3]

The IEP is developed at a meeting in which the following people are present: the public agency representative (other than the teacher) who is to provide or supervise the provision of special education, the child's teacher, the parents, and the child, if appropriate. Other individuals may be included at the discretion of either the parent or the agency. If the child has been evaluated for the first time, the evaluator or someone qualified to address the evaluation is also to be present.[4]

It is this program that is to be individual to the needs of the specific child and it is to be appropriate for that child. The term "appropriate" is, of course, a term that is very subjective. Neither the statute nor the regulations are particularly helpful in defining the term further. The first Supreme Court case to address any issue of the EAHCA was concerned with precisely what the term "appropriate" means.

BOARD OF EDUCATION V. ROWLEY

458 U.S. 176 (1982)
Justice REHNQUIST delivered the opinion of the Court.

This case presents a question of statutory interpretation. . . .

I

The Education of the Handicapped Act provides federal money to assist state and local agencies in educating handicapped children, and conditions such funding upon a State's compliance with extensive goals and procedures. . . .

In order to qualify for federal financial assistance under the Act, a State must demonstrate that it "has in effect a policy that assures all handicapped children the right to a free appropriate public education." That policy must be reflected in a state plan submitted to and approved by the Secretary of Education, which describes in detail the goals, programs, and timetables under which the State intends to educate handicapped children within its borders. States receiving money under the Act must provide education to the handicapped by priority, first "to handicapped children who are not receiving an education" and second "to handicapped children . . . with the most severe handicaps who are receiving an inadequate education," and "to the maximum extent appropriate" must educate handicapped children "with children who are not handicapped.". . .

The "free appropriate public education" required by the Act is tailored to the unique needs of the handicapped child by means of an "individualized educational program" (IEP). . . .

In addition to the state plan and the IEP already described, the Act imposes extensive procedural requirements upon States receiving federal funds under its provisions. . . .

Thus, although the Act leaves to the States the primary responsibility for developing and executing education programs for handicapped children, it imposes significant requirements to be followed in the discharge of that responsibility. . . .

II

This case arose in connection with the education of Amy Rowley, a deaf student at the Furnace Woods School in the Henrick Hudson Central School District, Peekskill, N.Y. Amy has minimal residual hearing and is an excellent lipreader. During the year before she began attending Furnace Woods, a meeting between her parents and school administrators resulted in a decision to place her in a regular kindergarten class in order to determine what supplemental services would be necessary to her education. Several members of the school administration prepared for Amy's arrival by attending a course in sign-language interpretation, and a teletype machine was installed in the principal's office to facilitate communication with her parents who are also deaf. At the end of the trial period it was determined that Amy should remain in the kindergarten class, but that she should be provided with an FM hearing aid which would amplify words spoken into a wireless receiver by the teacher or fellow students during certain classroom activities. Amy successfully completed her kindergarten year.

As required by the Act, an IEP was prepared for Amy during the fall of her first-grade year. The IEP provided that Amy should be educated in a regular classroom at Furnace Woods, should continue to use the FM hearing aid, and should receive instruction from a tutor for the deaf for one hour each day and from a speech therapist for three hours each week. The Rowleys agreed with parts of the IEP, but insisted that Amy also be provided a qualified sign-language interpreter in all her academic classes in lieu of the assistance proposed in other parts of the IEP. Such an interpreter had been placed in Amy's kindergarten class for a 2-week experimental period, but the interpreter had reported that Amy did not need his services at that time. The school administrators likewise concluded that Amy did not need such an interpreter in her first-grade classroom. They reached this conclusion after consulting the school district's Committee on the Handicapped, which had received expert evidence from Amy's teacher and other persons familiar with her academic and social progress, and visited a class for the deaf.

When their request for an interpreter was denied, the Rowleys demanded and received a hearing before an independent examiner. After receiving evidence from both sides, the examiner agreed with the administrators' determination that an interpreter was not necessary because "Amy was achieving educationally, academically, and socially" without such assistance. The examiner's decision was affirmed on appeal by the New York Commissioner of Education on the basis of substantial evidence in the record. Pursuant to the Act's provision for judicial review, the Rowleys then brought an action in the United States District Court for the Southern District of New York, claiming that the administrators' denial of the sign-language interpreter constituted a denial of the "free appropriate public education" guaranteed by the Act.

The District Court found that Amy "is a remarkably well-adjusted child" who interacts and communicates well with her classmates and has "developed an extraordinary rapport" with her teachers. It also found that "she performs better than the average child in her class and is advancing easily from grade to grade," but "that she understands considerably less of what goes on in class than she could if she were not deaf" and thus "is not learning as much, or performing as well academically, as she would without her handicap." This disparity between Amy's achievement and her potential led the court to decide that she was not receiving a "free appropriate public education," which the court defined as "an opportunity to achieve [her] full potential commensurate with the opportunity provided to other children." According to the District Court, such a standard "requires that the potential of the handicapped child be measured and compared to his or her performance, and that the resulting differential or 'shortfall' be compared to the shortfall experienced by nonhandicapped children." The District Court's definition arose from its assumption that the responsibility for "giv[ing] content to the requirement of an 'appropriate education'" had "been left entirely to the [federal] courts and the hearing officers."

A divided panel of the United States Court of Appeals for the Second Circuit affirmed. . . .

III

A

This is the first case in which this Court has been called upon to interpret any provision of the Act. "[T]he Act itself does not define 'appropriate education,'" but leaves "to the courts and the hearing officers" the responsibility of "giv[ing] content to the requirement of an 'appropriate education.'"

We are loath to conclude that Congress failed to offer any assistance in defining the meaning of the principal substantive phrase used in the Act. It is beyond dispute that, contrary to the conclusions of the courts below, the Act does expressly define "free appropriate public education":

> The term 'free appropriate public education' means *special education* and *related services* which (A) have been provided at public expense, under public supervision and direction, and without charge, (B) meet the standards of the State educational agency, (C) include an appropriate preschool, elementary, or secondary school education in the State involved, and (D) are provided in conformity with the individualized education program required under section 1414(a)(5) of this title.

"Special education," as referred to in this definition, means "specially designed instruction, at no cost to parents or guardians, to meet the unique needs of a handicapped child, including classroom instruction, instruction in physical education, home instruction, and instruction in hospitals and institutions." "Related services" are defined as "transportation, and such developmental, corrective, and other supportive services . . . as may be required to assist a handicapped child to benefit from special education."

According to the definitions contained in the Act, a "free appropriate public education" consists of educational instruction specifically designed to meet the unique needs of the handicapped child, supported by such services as are necessary to permit the child "to benefit" from the instruction. Almost as a checklist for adequacy under the Act, the definition also requires that such instruction and services be provided at public expense and under public supervision, meet the State's educational standards, approximate the grade levels used in the State's regular education, and comport with the child's IEP. Thus, if personalized instruction is being provided with sufficient supportive services to permit the child to benefit from the instruction, and the other items on the definitional checklist are satisfied, the child is receiving a "free appropriate public education" as defined by the Act. . . .

When . . . express statutory findings and priorities are read together with the Act's extensive procedural requirements and its definition of "free appropriate public education," the face of the statute evinces a congressional intent to bring previously excluded handicapped children into the public education systems of the States and to require the States to adopt *procedures* which would result in individualized consideration of and instruction for each child.

Noticeably absent from the language of the statute is any substantive standard prescribing the level of education to be accorded handicapped children. Certainly the language of the statute contains no requirement like the one imposed by the lower courts—that States maximize the potential of handicapped children "commensurate with the opportunity provided to other children."

B

(i)

. . . By passing the Act, Congress sought primarily to make public education available to handicapped children. But in seeking to provide such access to public education, Congress did not impose upon the States any greater substantive educational standard than would be necessary to make such access meaningful. . . .

Thus, the intent of the Act was more to open the door of public education to handicapped children on appropriate terms than to guarantee any particular level of education once inside. . . .

Mills and *PARC* both held that handicapped children must be given *access* to an adequate, publicly supported education. Neither case purports to require any particular substantive level of education. That the Act imposes no clear obligation upon recipient States beyond the requirement that children receive some form of specialized education is perhaps best demonstrated by the fact that Congress, in explaining the need for the Act, equated an "appropriate education" to the receipt of some specialized educational services.

(ii)

Respondents contend that "the goal of the Act is to provide each handicapped child with an equal educational opportunity." We think, however, that the requirement that a State provide specialized educational services to handicapped children generates no additional requirement that the services so provided be sufficient to maximize each child's potential "commensurate with the opportunity provided other children."

The educational opportunities provided by our public school systems undoubtedly differ from student to student, depending upon a myriad of factors that might affect a particular student's ability to assimilate information presented in the classroom. The requirement that States provide "equal" educational opportunities would thus seem to present an entirely unworkable standard requiring impossible measurements and comparisons. Similarly, furnishing handicapped children with only such services as are available to nonhandicapped children would in all probability fall short of the statutory requirement of "free appropriate public education"; to require, on the other hand, the furnishing of every special service necessary to maximize each handicapped child's potential is, we think, further than Congress intended to go. Thus to speak in terms of "equal services" in one instance gives less than what is required by the Act and in another instance more. The theme of the Act is "free appropriate public education," a phrase which is too complex to be captured by the word "equal" whether one is speaking of opportunities of services.

The legislative conception of the requirements of equal protection was undoubtedly informed by the two District Court decisions referred to above. But cases such as *Mills* and *PARC* held simply that handicapped children may not be excluded entirely from public education. In *Mills,* the District Court said:

> If sufficient funds are not available to finance all of the services and programs that are needed and desirable in the system then the available funds must be expended equitably in such a manner that no child is entirely excluded from a publicly supported education consistent with his needs and ability to benefit therefrom.

The *PARC* court used similar language, saying "[i]t is the commonwealth's obligation to place each mentally retarded child in a free, public program of education and training appropriate to the child's capacity. . . ." The right of access to free public education enunciated by these cases is significantly different from any notion of absolute equality of opportunity regardless of capacity. To the extent that Congress might have looked further than these cases which are mentioned in the legislative history, at the time of enactment of the Act this Court had held at least twice that the Equal Protection Clause of the Fourteenth Amendment does not require States to expend equal financial resources on the education of each child. . . .

Assuming that the Act was designed to fill the need identified in the House Report—that is, to provide a "basic floor of opportunity" consistent with equal protection—neither the Act nor its history persuasively demonstrates that Congress thought that equal protection required anything more than equal access. Therefore, Congress' desire to provide specialized educational services, even in furtherance of "equality," cannot be read as imposing any particular substantive educational standard upon the States. . . .

(iii)
It would do little good for Congress to spend millions of dollars in providing access to a public education only to have the handicapped child receive no benefit from that education. The statutory definition of "free appropriate public education," in addition to requiring that States provide each child with "specially designed instruction," expressly requires that provision of "such . . . supportive services . . . as may be required to assist a handicapped child *to benefit* from special education." We therefore conclude that the "basic floor of opportunity" provided by the Act consists of access to specialized instruction and related services which are individually designed to provide educational benefit to the handicapped child.

The determination of when handicapped children are receiving sufficient educational benefits to satisfy the requirements of the Act presents a more difficult problem. The Act requires participating States to educate a wide spectrum of handicapped children, from the marginally hearing-impaired to the profoundly retarded and palsied. It is clear that the benefits obtainable to children at one end of the spectrum will differ dramatically from those obtainable by children at the other end, with infinite variations in between. One child may have little difficulty competing successfully in an academic setting with nonhandicapped children while another child may encounter great difficulty in acquiring even the most basic of self-maintenance skills. We do not attempt today to establish any one test for determining the adequacy of educational benefits conferred upon all children covered by the Act. Because in this case we are presented with a handicapped child who is receiving substantial specialized instruction and related services, and who is performing above average in the regular classrooms of a public school system, we confine our analysis to that situation.

The Act requires participating States to educate handicapped children with nonhandicapped children whenever possible. When that "mainstreaming" preference of the Act has been met and a child is being educated in the regular classrooms of public school system, the system itself monitors the educational progress of the child. Regular examinations are administered, grades are awarded, and yearly advancement to higher grade levels is permitted for those children who attain an adequate knowledge of the course material. The grading and advancement system thus constitutes an important factor in determining educational benefit. Children who graduate from our public school systems are considered by our society to have been "educated" at least to the grade level they have completed, and access to an "education" for handicapped children is precisely what Congress sought to provide in the Act.[*]

---

[*] We do not hold today that every handicapped child who is advancing from grade to grade in a regular public school system is automatically receiving a "free appropriate public education." In this case, however, we find Amy's academic progress, when considered with the special services and professional consideration accorded by the Furnace Woods school administrators, to be dispositive.

C

When the language of the Act and its legislative history are considered together, the requirements imposed by Congress become tolerably clear. Insofar as a State is required to provide a handicapped child with a "free appropriate public education," we hold that it satisfied this requirement by providing personalized instruction with sufficient support services to permit the child to benefit educationally from that instruction. Such instruction and services must be provided at public expense, must meet the State's educational standards, must approximate the grade levels used in the State's regular education, and must comport with the child's IEP. In addition, the IEP, and therefore the personalized instruction, should be formulated in accordance with the requirements of the Act and, if the child is being educated in the regular classrooms of the public education system, should be reasonably calculated to enable the child to achieve passing marks and advance from grade to grade.

The provision that a reviewing court base its decision on the "preponderance of the evidence" is by no means an invitation to the courts to substitute their own notions of sound educational policy for those of the school authorities which they review. The very importance which Congress has attached to compliance with certain procedures in the preparation of an IEP would be frustrated if a court were permitted simply to set state decisions at nought. . . .

Therefore, a court's inquiry in suits brought under sec. 1415(3)(2) is twofold. First, has the State complied with the procedures set forth in the Act? And second, is the individualized educational program developed through the Act's procedures reasonably calculated to enable the child to receive educational benefits? If these requirements are met, the State has complied with the obligations imposed by Congress and the courts can require no more.

B

In assuring that the requirements of the Act have been met, courts must be careful to avoid imposing their view of preferable educational methods upon States. The primary responsibility for formulating the education to be accorded a handicapped child, for choosing the educational method most suitable to the child's needs, was left by the Act to state and local educational agencies in cooperation with the parents or guardian of the child. . . .

We previously have cautioned that courts lack the "specialized knowledge and experience" necessary to resolve "persistent and difficult questions of educational policy." We think that Congress shared that view when it passed the Act. As already demonstrated, Congress' intention was not that the Act displace the primacy of States in the field of education, but that States receive funds to assist them in extending their educational systems to the handicapped. Therefore, once a court determines that the requirements of the Act have been met, questions of methodology are for resolution by the States.

V

Entrusting a child's education to state and local agencies does not leave the child without protection. Congress sought to protect individual children by providing for parental involvement in the development of state plans and policies, and in the formulation of the child's individual educational program.

As this very case demonstrates, parents and guardians will not lack ardor in seeking to ensure that handicapped children receive all of the benefits to which they are entitled by the Act. [The Act does not require the provision of a sign language interpreter in this case.]. . . .

Dissent (Justices White, Brennan, and Marshall)
The majority opinion announces a different substantive standard, that "Congress did not impose upon the States any greater substantive educational standard than would be necessary to make such access meaningful." While "meaningful" is no more enlightening then "appropriate," the Court purports to clarify itself. Because Amy was provided with *some* specialized instruction from which she obtained *some* benefit and because she passed from grade to grade, she was receiving a meaningful and therefore appropriate education.

This falls far short of what the Act intended. The Act details as specifically as possible the kind of specialized education each handicapped child must receive. It would apparently satisfy the Court's standard of "access to specialized instruction and related services which are individually designed to provide educational benefit to the handicapped child," for a deaf child such as Amy to be given a teacher with a loud voice, for she would benefit from that service. The Act requires more. It defines "special education" to mean "specifically designed instruction, at no cost to parents or guardians, to *meet the unique needs* of a handicapped child. . . ." Providing a teacher with a loud voice would not meet Amy's needs and would not satisfy the Act. The basic floor of opportunity is instead, as the courts below recognized, intended to eliminate the effects of the handicap, at least to the extent that the child will be given an equal opportunity to learn if that is reasonably possible. Amy Rowley, without a sign-language interpreter, comprehends less than half of what is said in the classroom—less than half of what normal children comprehend. This is hardly an equal opportunity to learn, even if Amy makes passing grades.

Although the EAHCA does not require a "potential maximization" standard, some states have done so. This is demonstrated in *Barwacz v. Michigan Department of Education*[5] in which the court addressed the validity of Michigan's state statute that requires educational agencies to "provide special education programs and services designed to develop the maximum potential of each handicapped person." The educational agency had argued that because Michigan's statute was enacted before the 1975 EAHCA, the later standard as interpreted by *Rowley* was the correct standard. The court did not accept that argument and held that the potential maximization standard should apply. The court further noted, however, that the higher standard still does not require that the best possible education be provided. These standards, which go beyond what the Act requires, have been upheld as being valid.

One case applied the *Rowley* determination of appropriateness to emphasize that in the choice of education content significant deference would be given to the school. In that case, *Rettig v. Kent City School District*,[6] the parents of a severely handicapped teenage boy requested summer classes, continuous occupational therapy, and an hour of extracurricular activity each week. The court remanded the case to the lower court on the issue of extracurricular activity, but held that as to the other requests, it was not up to the courts to "choose between competing educational theories and impose that selection upon the school system," because courts lack the expertise to do so. This degree of deference to educational decision-makers is not universal. In *Beasley v. School Board,*[7] the court reviewed an individual education plan for a 15-year-old boy with a learning disability. The program was basically a continuation of a reading program that had not benefited Darren Beasley. He had remained a nonreader after almost five years in the school's program. The court noted that neither the best education nor the maximization of potential was required, but it noted the following in finding the educational program not appropriate within the EAHCA:

> The evidence of the . . . 1983–84 school year . . . coupled with the evidence in the whole record, established that Darren in fact could learn to read, and consequently was not benefiting from the continued program in the Campbell County schools. [A] reading disability, and particularly one that can be overcome, warrants special efforts within the formal educational process. In that context, while he remained a non-reader, the fact that Darren was able to progress in other areas of his education by artificial support, such as oral instructions and examinations is not persuasive. . . . Darren remained a non-reader in the Campbell County school system. The 1984–85 proposed education plan was essentially a continuation of that which had not benefited Darren in the past to overcome his disability. His ability to learn to read in a proper program was demonstrated by his experience [for one year in a private program] which offered a program not available within the [public school system].

EXTENDED SERVICES

In a line of cases that arose around the time that *Rowley* was being decided, parents challenged state policies of providing only 180 days of school to handicapped children because that was being provided to nonhandicapped children. The courts have consistently struck down such policies as being inconsistent with the requirement that education be individualized and appropriate. The following is one of the more recent decisions.

ALAMO HEIGHTS INDEPENDENT SCHOOL DISTRICT V. STATE BOARD OF EDUCATION

790 F.2d 1153 (5th Cir. 1986)

I

Steven G. was born July 30, 1972. He lives with his mother, Beverly G., within the boundaries of the Alamo Heights Independent School District. Steven suffers from cerebral dysplasia or hyperplasia, which is an abnormal development of the brain. Steven's hands and face are deformed. He has an unusual laxity in his joints, an uncoordinated gaze, a significant lack of muscle tone, and can walk only with assistance. He has been diagnosed as severely mentally retarded, has frequent tantrums, and cannot communicate by oral expression, although he does communicate by means of pointing to pictures and symbols on a "communication board." Because of Steven's mental and physical handicaps, he is not, in education terminology, considered "educable," but rather is "trainable," that is, he can be taught to communicate with others and to take care of his physical needs. [From 1975 to 1977 he was in a year-round program, and later had other programming. In spring of 1980, summer programming was requested by Mrs. G., but none was provided. When it was denied again the following summer, Mrs. G. pursued legal challenges.]

II

The School District argues that it has a legal duty to provide summer placement only if a handicapped child will suffer "severe regression in cognitive skills gained and disciplines learned" due to an interruption of programming. . . .

Thus, the issue presented is whether this particular child, Steven G., is entitled under the Act to have structured summer programming included in his IEP.

Pursuant to the provisions of the EAHCA, the School District is required to provide Steven with a "free appropriate public education." That mandate includes "the requirement that the education to which access is provided be sufficient to confer some educational benefit upon the handicapped child." [Citing *Rowley.*] "The basic substantive standard under the Act, then, is that each IEP must be formulated to provide some educational benefit to the child," in accordance with "the unique needs" of that child. The some-educational-benefit standard does not mean that the requirements of the Act are satisfied so long as a handicapped child's progress , absent summer services, is not brought "to a virtual standstill." Rather, if a child will experience severe or substantial regression during the summer months in the absence of a summer program, the handicapped child may be entitled to year-round services. This issue is whether the benefits accrued to the child during the regular school year will be significantly jeopardized if he is not provided an educational program during the summer months. This is, of course, a general standard, but it must be applied to the individual by the ARD Committee in the same way that juries apply other general legal standards such as negligence reasonableness. . . .

In *Tatro v. Texas,* Judge Gee, writing for the court, stated that the EAHCA has "placed primary responsibility for formulating handicapped children's education in the hands of state and local school agencies in cooperation with each child's parents." In deference to this statutory scheme and the reliance it places on the expertise of local education authorities, we stated in *Tatro* that the Act creates a "presumption in favor of the education placement established by [a child's] IEP," and "the party attacking its terms should bear the burden of showing why the educational setting established by the IEP is not appropriate." . . .

The testimony concerning Steven's particular regression-recoupment tendencies was directly conflicting: The School District's employees and consultants were unanimous that they observed no significant regression, while the doctors, therapists, and former teachers who testified on behalf of Steven all agreed that Steven required a continuous structured program in order to prevent significant regression. The record thus clearly supports, although it does not compel, the district court's assessment of the facts presented—"that Steven G. would suffer at least substantial regression without continuous, structured programming."

The district court carefully phrased its conclusion and, while it did not explicitly state that the educational program offered by the School District did not meet the "some educational benefit" standard of *Rowley,* the district court showed that it was aware of that decision and its judgment is therefore tantamount to such a conclusion. Hence, we hold that the district court applied the appropriate standard to the factual determinations supported by the record. The general injunctive relief granted by the court was appropriate to ensure that Steven receives the summer programming to which he is entitled under the Act.

The *Alamo Heights* decision is one of several decisions invalidating policies of denying summer programming. The landmark case on that issue was *Battle v. Commonwealth.*[8] That case was a class action in which the policy was struck down, but the individual complaints were remanded for case-by-case determination. The fact that post-*Rowley* decisions, such as *Alamo Heights,* have reached similar results emphasizes that the standard of appropriateness will sometimes acquire programming beyond the basic time frame of regular educational programming.

SUMMARY

One of the major underlying principles of the EAHCA is that special education and related services granted to students with handicaps must be appropriate. The term "appropriate," however, is highly subjective and evades precise definition. The Supreme Court made an attempt to define the term in its 1982 opinion in *Board of Education v. Rowley.* In that case the Court held that a child was being provided an appropriate special education if the child was receiving personalized instruction with sufficient supportive services to permit the child to benefit from the instruction. In addition, the educational agency must have provided the program at public expense, must approximate the child's age-appropriate grade level, and the IEP must be complied with. The EAHCA due process procedures must also be complied with. The Court was correct in anticipating that this standard would not always be easily applied to all situations. Numerous judicial opinions since the *Rowley* decision have continued to address these issues.

While the EAHCA does not require that the child's potential be maximized in order for the child to be viewed as receiving an appropriate education, it is within an individual state's discretion to adopt this or any other higher standard that is consistent with the EAHCA. The Supreme Court's opinion in *Rowley* also indicated that substantial deference to the educational agency would be given in determining whether the child's program is appropriate. While it would seem that a substantial number of subsequent judicial opinions have deferred to the educational agency's programmatic recommendations, it is noteworthy that this deference has not been absolute.

Of the issues that have come under question within the requirement of appropriateness, one is the application and existence of policies that make no allowance for the individual needs of the child. Policies of providing only 180 days of school per year, for example, have consistently been struck down as invalid because of this reasoning. Similar policies, such as providing only a certain number of hours of education per day, are likely to meet similar attack with equivalent results in the courts. The fact that such a policy is struck down, however, does not mean that every child with a handicap who is affected by such policies is automatically eligible for the extended-year or extended-day programming. Entitlement to such programs is to be determined on an individual basis.

QUESTIONS AND PROBLEMS

1. What standard did the lower courts in *Rowley* apply?
2. What standard did the Supreme Court apply?
3. Will the *Rowley* standard work when applied to other types of cases, i.e., when a severely retarded student is not placed in the regular program?
4. Did the fact that Amy Rowley was bright actually work to her detriment? What would happen if a child needed the interpreter to pass from grade to grade?
5. What happens if a child needs a particular service for which funds are not available?
6. Once a school develops an individualized education program, what role is left for the courts?
7. What standard of review are the courts to apply?
8. What is the burden of proof?
9. How likely is it that the educational agency's decision will be overridden by the courts?
10. What is the concern of the dissent?
11. The Court indicated that protection for the child was available by virtue of the procedural safeguards, and the fact that parents do "not lack ardor in seeking to ensure that handicapped children receive all the benefits [of the Act]." This assumes that all parents are aware of their rights and have the means to pursue them. How valid is that assumption?
12. Alison is five and autistic. The evaluations done by the parents' evaluators indicate that Alison requires a full-day program in order to benefit from an educational program. In the state where Alison resides, public kindergarten is currently provided, but only for half a day. Must the school provide a full-day program to Alison?

NOTES

1. 20 U.S.C. § 1412(1). See L. ROTHSTEIN, RIGHTS OF PHYSICALLY HANDICAPPED PERSONS, § 2.17 (1984) and cumulative supplements.
2. 34 C.F.R. § 300.343.
3. 34 C.F.R. § 300.346.
4. 34 C.F.R. § 300.344.
5. 674 F. Supp. 1296, 1303–1306 (W.D. Mich. 1987). Other states with higher standards include New Jersey (Geis v. Board of Education, 774 F.2d 575 (3d Cir. 1985) and Massachusetts (David D. v. Dartmouth School Committee, 775 F.2d 411 (1st Cir. 1985).
6. 720 F.2d 463, 466 (6th Cir. 1984).
7. 367 S.E. 2d 738, 742 (Va. App. 1988).
8. 629 F.2d 269 (3d Cir. 1980), *cert. denied,* 449 U.S. 1109 (1981).

CHAPTER 8

Mainstreaming and Integration

EAHCA FOUNDATIONS

Statute and Regulations

One of the primary principles of the Education for all Handicapped Children Act is the concept of educating handicapped children along with nonhandicapped children to the maximum extent appropriate. While this is often referred to as *mainstreaming,* the term is not found anywhere in the statutory or regulatory language under the EAHCA. The statute provides that

> to the maximum extent appropriate, handicapped children, including children in public or private institutions or other care facilities, [should be] educated with children who are not handicapped, and that separate schooling, or other removal of handicapped children from the regular educational environment [should] occur only when the nature or severity of the handicap is such that education in regular classes with the use of supplementary aids and services cannot be achieved satisfactorily. . . .[1]

It is in the regulations, rather than the statute, however, that the concept of least restrictive environment is provided for. The regulations allow for a "continuum of alternative placements" and that "in selecting the least restrictive environment, consideration [should be] given to any potential harmful effect on the child or on the quality of services which he or she needs."[2] The goal of providing education to handicapped children in the regular classroom does not discount the requirement to individualize a child's program and to respond to situations where the child is disruptive in the regular classroom.[3]

In the early years after the EAHCA was passed, some educators mistakenly thought that the Act requires all handicapped children to be placed in the regular classroom, and they expressed anxiety over such a mandate. It should be emphasized that least restrictive placement must also be *appropriate*. For some children, a more restrictive placement may be necessary.

Philosophy behind Least Restrictive Environment

The philosophy of placing students in a setting that is as "normal" as possible, where education takes place along with nonhandicapped peers, is based on several principles. One principle is that, as a general philosophy, separation in education is inherently stigmatizing. Another concern is that once a child is placed in a separate special education setting, the self-fulfilling prophecy occurs—for example, the child will only be expected to perform at a particular level, and the expectations will generally be borne out by the child's performance. Another principle, which is discussed in both of the cases included in this chapter, is the value of peer interaction for both handicapped and nonhandicapped children.[4]

It should be emphasized that, while the concept of least restrictive environment is one of the major principles of the EAHCA, it is not the *sole* consideration. That education be individualized and appropriate are other major considerations. It is clear that the EAHCA incorporates the idea that in some situations separation may be necessary to ensure that the education is appropriate. The EAHCA, however, can be viewed as requiring a presumption of nonseparation— for example, that as much as possible the education should be provided in the regular classroom environment with necessary supplementary aids and services. The following case demonstrates to some extent the debate that still occurs at a judicial level.

RONCKER V. WALTER

700 F.2d 1058 (6th Cir. 1983)
... The plaintiff's son, Neill Roncker, is nine years old and is severely mentally retarded. He is classified as Trainable Mentally Retarded (TMR), a category of children with an IQ of below 50. Less severely retarded students are classified as Educable Mentally Retarded (EMR) and are generally educated in special classes within the regular public schools.

There is no dispute that Neill is severely retarded and has a mental age of two to three with regard to most functions. Neill also suffers from seizures but they are not convulsive and he takes medication to control them. No evidence indicated that Neill is dangerous to others but he does require almost constant supervision because of his inability to recognize dangerous situations.

In 1976, Neill was evaluated and recommended for the Arlitt Child Development Center. It was believed that he would benefit from contact with non-handicapped children. In the spring of 1979, a conference was held to evaluate Neill's Individual Education Plan (IEP) as required by the Act. Present at the conference were Neill's parents, school psychologists, and a member of the Hamilton County Board of Mental Retardation. After evaluating Neill, the school district decided to place him in a county school. Since these county schools were exclusively for mentally retarded children, Neill would have received no contact with non-handicapped children. . . .

While the dispute over placement continued, Neill began attending a class for the severely mentally retarded at Pleasant Ridge Elementary School in September 1979. Pleasant Ridge is a regular public school which serves both handicapped and non-handicapped children. Neill's contact with non-handicapped children at Pleasant Ridge is limited to lunch, gym and recess. Neill has remained at Pleasant Ridge during the pendency of this action. . . .

The Act does not require mainstreaming in every case but its requirement that mainstreaming be provided to the maximum extent appropriate indicated a very strong congressional preference. The proper inquiry is whether a proposed placement is appropriate under the Act. In some cases, a placement which may be considered better for academic reasons may not be appropriate because of the failure to provide for mainstreaming. The perception that a segregated institution is academically superior for a handicapped child may reflect no more than a basic disagreement with the mainstreaming concept. Such a disagreement is not, of course, any basis for not following the Act's mandate. In a case where the segregated facility is considered superior, the court should determine whether the services which make that placement superior could be feasibly provided in a non-segregated setting. If they can, the placement in the segregated school would be inappropriate under the Act. Framing the issue in this manner accords the proper respect for the strong preference in favor of mainstreaming while still realizing the possibility that some handicapped children simply must be educated in segregated facilities either because the handicapped child would not benefit from mainstreaming, because any marginal benefits received from mainstreaming are far outweighed by the benefits gained from services which could not feasibly be provided in the non-segregated setting. Cost is a proper factor to consider since excessive spending on one handicapped child deprives other handicapped children. Cost is no defense, however, if the school district has failed to use its funds to provide a proper continuum of alternative placements for handicapped children. The provision of such alternative placements benefits all handicapped children.

In the present case, the district court must determine whether Neill's educational, physical or emotional needs require some service which could not feasibly be provided in a class for handicapped children within a regular school or in the type of split program advocated by the State Board of Education. Although Neill's progress, or lack thereof, at Pleasant Ridge is a relevant factor in determining the maximum appropriate extent to which he can be mainstreamed, it is not dispositive since the district court must determine whether Neill could have been provided with additional services, such as those provided at the county schools, which would have improved his performance at Pleasant Ridge. . . .

Dissent

. . . Congress has expressed a clear preference for educating handicapped children in the regular classrooms of the public schools. Handicapped children should be removed from regular classes only when their education cannot be achieved satisfactorily with the use of supplementary aids and services. Despite this preference for "mainstreaming," however, the statute clearly contemplates that there will be some separate schools and schooling. Section 1412(5) does not require that class for the severely mentally retarded, such as Neill Roncker, whose only interaction with non-handicapped children is to observe them, be located in the regular elementary school. Rather, this section is directed to the handicapped child who can spend some time in the regular classroom if given special aids or assistance.

Other than costs, the District Court in the present case has fully considered whether Neill Roncker could be educated in a self-contained handicapped classroom in a regular school. The severity of Neill's handicap is such that even with supplementary aids and services, the District Court found that Neill cannot achieve a satisfactory education or indeed any education in a regular class.

The appellant has nevertheless argued that if Neill must be educated in a 169 program, that program must be provided within the "regular school environment" even if the only benefit from such placement is to avoid the stigma of attending a special school. Because the 169 program requires children of chronological age with roughly the same developmental ability to be placed together, a classroom for each age could not be located at each regular school. However, the classrooms for one age could be at one school and those for another at a different school. The children could probably be bused to assemblies. Special gym teachers, physical and occupational therapists and special remedial teachers could go from school to school. Appellant argues that this is required unless the children could learn "zero" in such environment.

The appellant's arguments essentially represent one of two competing educational theories presented by this case. The first is that a program with all of the components of the 169 program can only be fully implemented in a separate school. This program alone, it is argued, is appropriate for severely handicapped children such as Neill Roncker who cannot benefit from any regular classroom experience. The second theory is that all handicapped children (except those who can be in the regular classroom) must be placed in special classrooms located in regular elementary schools, unless a child would get zero benefit from a classroom so situated. . . .

Section 1412(5), far from unambiguously requiring that school districts place severely handicapped children in the regular school environment even if they cannot be satisfactorily educated in that environment, requires only that handicapped children be "mainstreamed" to the maximum extent appropriate. For those more severely retarded children, such as Neill Roncker, who are unable to be satisfactorily educated in any respect in a regular classroom, the statute does not prohibit the school district from making the judgment as to where their classrooms should be located.

Continuum of Placements

The EAHCA regulations provide for a "continuum of alternate placements" to be available.[5] Within the educational community there has been developed a "cascade system" of placement alternatives that places the regular classroom as the least restrictive placement and the ideal goal, and hospital placement as the most restrictive placement. Between these two extremes are the following placements: regular classroom with special education consultant, regular classroom with itinerant teachers, regular classroom with use of resource room for part of the time, part-time special class, full-time special class, special day school, and residential school.

While some children may never be placed in the regular classroom for academic work, the philosophy of least restrictive environment is to place the child in a setting that is the least restrictive placement *appropriate* to the child's needs and that will not cause undue disruption to other children.

It is essential that educators and parents be conscious of the fluid nature of placements. It may be necessary for a particular child to be placed in a full-time special class for the first part of a school year, or even for an entire school year, but at least annually the placement must be reviewed and a less restrictive one considered. It may well be that the child's appropriate placement is to continue in the full-time special class for most of the school day. It is important to note that the goal of moving to a less restrictive point on the continuum is the goal of the mainstreaming mandate. Therefore, the behaviors or needs that are necessitating the segregated placement should be targeted for remediation on the IEP.

In examining compliance with mainstreaming principles, there are several contexts in which the issue arises. If the child is placed in the regular classroom, to what extent should the child be placed with age-appropriate peers? To what extent should there be true interaction with peers in the regular classroom? Is it always possible to provide supportive services within the regular classroom or is temporary removal from the regular classroom better in some cases? If the separate resource room or separate special education class is located within the regular public school facility, where must it be placed? How can appropriate interaction for separately placed children occur for at least some activities? Does the child have a right to be placed in a neighborhood school? And finally, when are completely separate facilities appropriate?

The following sections address some of these issues.

THE CLASSROOM

The Importance of Peer Interaction

The following case involves an unusual factual setting, and it demonstrates the importance of peer interaction and the problems of cost that can arise in meeting the mainstreaming mandate.

ESPINO V. BESTEIRO

520 F. Supp. 905 (S.D. Tex. 1981)
This action was brought by Raul Espino, Jr., a seven-year-old multi-handicapped child who cannot adequately regulate his body temperature, by and through his parents, seeking declaratory and injunctive relief and damages for the alleged failure of Defendants to provide him with an education in the "least restrictive environment appropriate to his individual needs." It is alleged that the failure of Defendants to provide Raul with a fully air-conditioned classroom wherein he can interact fully with his peers, and their decision instead to provide him with an air-conditioned plexiglass cubicle within a regular non air-conditioned classroom, violate the Education for All Handicapped Children Act of 1975. . . .

Raul had suffered a broken spine at the age of 11 months, which had resulted in quadriplegia and damage to his nervous system preventing proper body temperature regulation. Raul needed to be in an environment where the temperature was between sixty-eight and seventy-eight degrees Fahrenheit. Raul attends school in Brownsville, Texas, and during the warmer months of the year, air-conditioned classrooms are necessary. Raul attended kindergarten in an air-conditioned classroom.

During first grade Raul was placed in a regular first grade classroom within a portable five-foot-by-five-foot plexiglass cubicle with an air-conditioning unit. Raul's grades during first grade were exceptional and he had very positive peer interaction during that time. The cost of air-conditioning the entire classroom was about $5,700 per year. The school district had $250,000 earmarked for special education. It was when Raul was to enter second grade that his parents challenged the cubicle solution and requested that his entire classroom be air-conditioned. . . .

The "mainstreaming" provisions of the EAHCA, as set out previously, require that a handicapped child be educated with his non-handicapped peers "to the maximum extent appropriate" and that any removal from the regular education environment occurs only when the nature of the handicap is such that education in regular classes with the use of supplementary aids "cannot be achieved satisfactorily." In the case at bar, it is undisputed that air-conditioning is a supplementary aid or "related service" which Raul Espino, Jr. needs in order to be able to attend school during the hotter months of the year. There is no evidence to suggest that a fully air-conditioned environment would be inappropriate for Raul's educational needs. There is also no evidence which suggests that a regular classroom at Egly Elementary cannot be satisfactorily modified to provide such an environment. In this set of circumstances it seems self-evident that the decision to provide air-conditioning for Raul in a plexiglass cubicle, and therefore at times segregate him from his non-handicapped classmates, is prima facie a violation of the mainstreaming provisions of the EAHCA.

Assuming that Raul's placement in the cubicle is not to the "maximum extent appropriate," the analysis then must focus on whether it is a reasonably appropriate accommodation in that it provides for Raul's special needs "to the maximum extent practicable" and consistent with the mainstreaming provisions of the Act. One court has suggested that the important personal needs of an individual handicapped child must be balanced against the realities of limited funding in reaching a reasonable accommodation. At least one commentator has recognized that "appropriate" cannot mean the best possible education a school can provide if given access to unlimited funds, but that the EAHCA contemplates a standard between the best education and merely opening the doors of a regular classroom to those capable of learning without special assistance. Defendants in this case have not made a serious contention that maintaining a fully air-conditioned environment for Raul is prohibited by the financial condition of the [Brownesville Independence School District] BISD. The evidence presented suggests that the cost of air-conditioning a classroom would be minimal in relation to the amount of federal funds received by BISD and BISD's total budget. Balancing the important needs of Raul Espino, Jr. for an air-conditioned environment within which he can be effectively mainstreamed and interact fully with non-handicapped students, against the cost of BISD of providing him with such an environment, it cannot be said that the provision of an air-conditioned cubicle, with its concomitant isolative effect on Raul when it is being used, represents a reasonable accommodation resulting from the fiscal impracticability of providing air-conditioning for him to the maximum extent appropriate.

Realizing that the concept of "practicability" is not necessarily limited to monetary consideration, this court must analyze the other reasons advanced for the existence of the cubicle to determine whether it presents a reasonably appropriate accommodation. Superintendent Besteiro felt that a fully air-conditioned classroom for Raul's class might open "Pandora's box" in that parents of children in non-air-conditioned classrooms and the children's teachers would complain of unequal treatment in that one teacher and Raul's classmates would receive the benefits of air-conditioning during the hot months of the school year. Yet, Mr. Besteiro testified that he had received no official requests seeking air-conditioning for students other than Raul. A purely theoretical risk of parental or teacher complaints is probably insufficient to offset the countervailing needs of Raul Espino, Jr. for an education with his peers "to the maximum extent appropriate" and does not substantially justify segregation from his classmates in the cubicle. . . .

Dr. Schraer feels that Raul's sterling performance in the first grade proves that he is being provided with an appropriate education. While there is no question that Raul's grades establish that he is receiving an "adequate" education, this does not necessarily mean that he is receiving an "appropriate" education. One court has held that an "appropriate" education is one which lies between the extremes of a merely adequate education (i.e., one that is substantial enough to facilitate a child's progress from grade to grade) and one which enables a handicapped child to achieve his or her full potential. . . .

It is apparent that Raul misses out on a great deal of class interaction and group participation while he is confined to the cubicle. This is of particular significance in Raul's case since the ARD committee which decided to mainstream Raul felt that the Moody facility was "too restrictive" to meet his "intellectual and social needs." Full social interaction is an important part of today's educational curriculum and is even more vital to a child like Raul who necessarily suffers a certain degree of isolation as a result of his handicap. While it is true that Raul's scholarship is superb and he displays no psychological damage as a result of his semi-isolation in the cubicle, he derives no education benefits from it. Under the circumstances it is doubtful that Raul is being provided an opportunity for maximization of his social interaction skills commensurate with that provided to other students in his class. Raul's excellent academic performance and his ability to get along with his classmates attest to his courage and tenacity, and he should not be penalized for the fruits of his own efforts. For these reasons this Court feels that the placement of Raul in the cubicle may deprive him of a full educational opportunity and may not be in conformity with his IEP as originally espoused in the ARD committee's original report. If this indeed is the case, Raul is not being provided with an "appropriate" education under the EAHCA.

Age Appropriateness as a Mandate

The court in *Besteiro* recognized the importance of peer interaction for both intellectual and social needs. The court in *Roncker* noted that children should be placed with other children of roughly the same chronological age and developmental ability. While these two courts recognized these factors as part of an "appropriate" placement, neither the EAHCA nor its implementing regulations specifically states anything about chronological age placement.[6]

Some states have recognized the importance, however, of chronological age placement and have adopted specific age-span requirements for classrooms. For example, a state regulation might provide that students in a separate class for mentally retarded children be no more than four years apart in age. This would prevent the placement of a 13-year-old with children who are 6 or 7. State age-span requirements can also relate to placements within the regular classroom.

Whether state regulations require it or not, there is support in education literature for the philosophy of age-appropriate placements. The underlying principle is that education involves not only academic development, but also social development.[7] Students need to have experience with age peers to encourage modeling of age-appropriate behavior.

Thus, while there is substantial support among educators for age-appropriate placements, and the Supreme Court in *Board of Education v. Rowley*[8] notes that an appropriate placement must "approximate the grade levels used in the State's regular education," there is little guidance at the federal statutory or regulatory level as to the parameters of age-appropriate placement requirements.

Location of Classrooms

The principle of mainstreaming and its underlying philosophy of social interaction can be used as a basis to support the importance of locating separate special education in the "mainstream" of the school facility itself. In addition, the stigmatizing effect of separate placements should be avoided by encouraging close proximity of special education classrooms to regular classrooms rather than "clustering" them in separate wings or portions of the building.

Unfortunately, in some schools the separate special education classes and resource rooms are located in trailers, basements, or other locations not physically proximate to the regular education program. While neither the EAHCA nor its regulations make any specific statement about where within a facility a special education program should be placed, it is certainly questionable whether the intent and spirit of the least restrictive environment mandate has been met when the physical location of special education isolates handicapped students from non-handicapped students. Unless regular classes are located in trailers or basements on an equivalent basis, it is probable that these placements violate section 504 of the Rehabilitation Act.

There is little discussion of this issue in judicial decisions, but administrators would do well to give careful thought to this issue when deciding where to locate special education classrooms within a public school facility.

THE LOCAL SCHOOL

The EAHCA does not create an absolute right to be placed in the neighborhood school, but it does require, in its regulations, that the handicapped student should be placed "as close as possible to . . . home."[9] The child is to be "educated in the school which he or she would attend if not handicapped" unless the IEP provides otherwise.[10]

The local neighborhood school goal must be balanced with the requirement that education be appropriate and individualized. The regulations are unclear on what "as close as possible" means. Must support services such as therapy or a resource room be provided at every local school site? Or is it permissible to place a child in a reasonably proximate school that is not the child's neighborhood school but that provides a particular support service necessary for the child to benefit from the education program?

Regulations under Section 504 of the Rehabilitation Act do not require that every existing facility be made barrier free, and they recognize compliance if the program is accessible when viewed in its entirety.[11] This could be interpreted as permitting placement of an orthopedically impaired student in a barrier-free building that is not the child's neighborhood school. There is some case authority for requiring delivery of therapy or programming in the neighborhood school, but it is not a well-settled issue. It would seem, then, that a similar analysis could be applied to other programs. It could be argued, by analogy, that a child could be placed in other than the neighborhood school in order to have access to certain types of therapy or other special educational programming.

The mainstreaming principle supports education with nonhandicapped peers. If that can be achieved by providing the education at other than the neighborhood school, it would seem at least that part of the principle would be satisfied by providing education in a reasonably close regular school. It is, of course, desirable to provide the education to the child in the neighborhood school, if possible. By doing so, this provides the child to be educated with children who are neighbors and with whom the child may have interaction outside the classroom. It also avoids the concern about having a child spend an undue amount of time being transported to and from home. But it may be unduly expensive and in some cases impossible to provide every support service and program in every local neighborhood school.

Urban areas provide greater opportunity than do rural areas for creative arrangements. For example, one school site could be made barrier free to serve several closely surrounding local school site populations. A similar plan could be applied for children needing physical therapy or speech therapy or several local neighborhood schools could be served by having a particular type of program available at one of them. An argument could be made that such placements are for administrative convenience rather than to address the individual needs of the children. It is important in setting up consortium-type arrangements that there are not so many placements of special education students at one site that the result is a "special education school." There is no specific federal statutory guidance of what percentage of the student population should be nonhandicapped. Many special education advocates take the position that the percentage of handicapped students in a school should be no more than what occurs in natural proportions in the community. The avoidance of "ghetto-izing" special education students, however, is an important consideration for school district planners.

Another relevant factor in deciding to place a child in a regular school other than the child's neighborhood school is the time the child will spend in transit. Although the school will most probably be required to provide transportation in such cases, lengthy trips should be avoided. Depending on the age and handicap of the child, long bus rides can have serious detrimental effects on students. In addition, time spent in transit cannot be counted as instructional time and cannot be used to reduce the length of the school day. Where possible, it may be better to have certain services or programming provided by itinerant personnel. For the student with certain types of related service needs, such as suctioning, it is not an alternative.

While it is certainly an ideal goal that all children (particularly those in elementary school) attend the neighborhood school, there are sometimes countervailing policies. Busing children to other than the neighborhood school has been used to achieve the policy of racial desegregation. For handicapped students, the ability to provide appropriate programming efficiently is another important social policy. But when transporting handicapped students to distant schools for the sake of efficient delivery of special education services has a significantly adverse effect on the student or is done solely for administrative convenience, it is possible that the placement is not going to be viewed as "appropriate."

SEPARATE FACILITIES

For some students, temporary placement in a residential institution or hospital is necessary in order to benefit from education. Chapter 10 addresses issues of residential placements in greater detail. It should be noted here, however, that any placement in a separate facility is viewed as restrictive, and such placements should only be made when absolutely necessary.

The past decade brought a movement in both directions for residential placements. The EAHCA and other federal and state laws provide the basis for moving mentally retarded students back into the local communities and into the local schools. The movement in the other direction came from parents of students whose problems were alcohol or drug related. Because of the heavy emotional demands such students place on their families, parents frequently prefer residential placement for their disturbed or disruptive children. The high costs of these placements, however, often cause schools to avoid approving them.

Another population about which there is dispute over separate facilities is deaf students. A significant diversity of opinion exists over whether deaf students should be educated in special schools or centers or whether education in the regular school is desirable.

The following case illustrates one judicial response to that debate.

LACHMAN V. ILLINOIS STATE BOARD OF EDUCATION

852 F.2d 290 (7th Cir. 1988)
Benjamin Lachman is a profoundly deaf seven-year-old child who resides within the district boundaries of the east Maine, Illinois School District No. 63 ("the school dis-

trict"). The school district is a member of the Maine Township Special Education Program ("MSTEP") and through MSTEP contracts with Northern Suburban Special Education District to provide services for its hearing-impaired students through a Regional Hearing Impaired Program ("RHIP"). Since the time Benjamin became eligible for participation in the RHIP pre-school program, in September, 1984, his parents and the school district have disagreed as to the manner in which his education should be facilitated. That disagreement eventually led the Lachmans to initiate this private cause of action [under] the Education for All Handicapped Children Act.

I

The Lachmans believe that Benjamin can best be educated at a neighborhood school near his home, in a regular classroom with the assistance of a full-time cued speech instructor.* In contrast, the school district has consistently proposed that all or at least half of Benjamin's school day be spent in a RHIP self-contained classroom with other hearing-impared children. Those self-contained classrooms are located in schools outside Benjamin's neighborhood. The placements advocated by the school district have all incorporated components providing that, to varying degrees, Benjamin would be integrated into classes and activities with the non-hearing-impaired children in the regular classrooms at those schools. The course of education recommended by the school district centers on the use of the total communication approach to educating hearing-impaired children, which relies primarily upon sign language as a means of communication. The school district has proposed only interim utilization of the cued speech approach, to the extent necessary to effectively transition Benjamin into the total communication-based program. . . .

At its core the complaint alleges that the IEP proposed by the RHIP and the school district, and approved by the Illinois State Board of Education, fails to provide Benjamin with a free appropriate public education as required by § 612(1) of the EAHCA.**

[This is an appeal from the dismissal of the parents' complaint.]

It is well established that in reviewing the outcomes reached through the §§1415(b) and (c) administrative appeals procedure, a district court is to make an independent decision as to whether the requirements of the Act have been satisfied. That decision is to be based on a preponderance of the evidence, giving due weight to the results of those state administrative proceedings. The district court's determination that the IEP proposed for Benjamin by the school district constituted a free appropriate public

---

* Cued speech is a technique for aiding hearing-impaired persons to understand spoken language. It is used in conjunction with speech (lip) reading and employs eight hand shapes held in four positions close to the mouth to clarify phonetic ambiguities.

** [The IEP] proposed that Benjamin be placed at Forest View School in a self-contained total communication hearing-impaired program at the primary level. An FM auditory training unit would be provided. Benjamin would be mainstreamed with an interpreter in social studies, science, gym and art. He would receive reading and math in the self-contained classroom at an early second grade level. He would receive interpreter services. He would participate in a pilot project in the areas of speech development and introduction of new vocabulary. Cued speech would also be utilized to assist Benjamin in the transition to signed English. Forest View is an integrated K-5 school with 317 students, thirty-five of whom are hearing-impaired.

education as required by the EAHCA is founded on its application of the relevant provisions of the Act to the facts attendant to Benjamin's circumstance. We review the determination of that mixed question of law and fact *de novo.* . . .

III

Examination of the district court opinion reveals that it considered the focal point of the disagreement between the Lachmans and the school district to be a question of whether Benjamin's education can best be facilitated by utilization of the cued speech technique or the total communication concept. The Lachmans dispute that inference by the district court. They perceive that the outcome-determinative question in this case is whether the challenged IEP fails to satisfy the Act's § 612(5) requirement that "to the maximum extent appropriate" Benjamin, as a handicapped child, be "educated with children who are not handicapped," and that he be removed from the regular classroom environment and placed in a special class only to the extent that "the nature or severity of [his] handicap is such that education in regular classes with the use of supplementary aids and services cannot be achieved satisfactorily." 20 U.S.C. § 1412(5)(B).

In *Rowley,* the Supreme Court was not directly confronted with a claim that the § 1412(5)(B) mainstreaming goal had not been satisfied. In that opinion, the Court made only a passing reference to the "preference" for mainstreaming handicapped children reflected in § 612(5)(B) of the Act. *Rowley,* 458 U.S. at 202–03, 102 S.Ct. at 3049. Thus, the Lachmans claim that the district court erred because, in applying the *Rowley* test for satisfaction of the Act's general (§ 612(1)) requirement that Benjamin be provided a free appropriate public education, it failed to adequately address the issues raised by the § 1412(5)(B) preference for mainstreaming handicapped children.

The district court opinion is carefully drawn and fully addresses the components of the *Rowley* test for compliance with the general, overriding requirement of the EAHCA, imposed by § 1412(1), that Benjamin Lachman be provided with a free appropriate public education. However, because it believed the real point of contention between the Lachmans and the school district to be a disagreement as to which of two communication methodologies should be used to facilitate Benjamin's early primary education, the district court engaged in a prototypal *Rowley* analysis, devoting only one paragraph to the issue of mainstreaming. That paragraph concludes with the observation that under the proposed IEP "Benjamin will be completely mainstreamed in a short period of time."

Rowley makes clear that "once a court determines that the requirements of the Act have been met, questions of methodology are for resolution by the State." The mainstreaming preference articulated in § 1412(5)(B) is one of the "requirements of the Act" referred to in the above excerpt from *Rowley.* Because the parties' disagreement as to the extent to which Benjamin is to be mainstreamed is inexorably intertwined with their disagreement as to the choice between the cued speech and total communication methodologies, we must first ascertain which of those issues, if any, predominates here.

In order to divine the true crux of the dispute that prompted the present cause of action, we must establish the nature of the mainstreaming obligation created by § 1412(5)(B) and clarify the relationship of that statutory language to the general § 1412(1) requirement that handicapped children be provided with a free appropriate public education. Several post-*Rowley* decisions by the U.S. Courts of Appeals for the

Sixth, Eighth and Ninth Circuits, as well as a small number of reported district court opinions, have addressed this topic. . . .

[I]t is clear that the courts considering this issue have determined that the Act's mainstreaming preference is to be given effect only when it is clear that the education of the particular handicapped child can be achieved satisfactorily in the type of mainstream environment sought by the challengers to the IEP proposed for that child. . . .

We are convinced that appellants' effort to characterize the sole, true issue in this case as whether the proposed IEP satisfies the § 1412(5)(B) mainstreaming preference is misdirected. Undoubtedly, this case does present a valid question of whether the IEP proposed by the school district and affirmed by the Illinois State Board of Education would result in Benjamin being mainstreamed to the "maximum extent appropriate" as contemplated by § 1412(5)(B). However, on careful examination, it becomes apparent that a determination of whether the IEP proposed for Benjamin provides for mainstreaming to the maximum extent appropriate can be made only within the context of the methodology employed to facilitate his education.

The degree to which a challenged IEP satisfies the mainstreaming goal of the EAHCA simply cannot be evaluated in the abstract. Rather, that laudable policy objective must be weighed in tandem with the Act's principal goal of ensuring that the public schools provide handicapped children with a free appropriate education. A major part of the task of local and state officials in fashioning what they believe to be an effective program for the education of a handicapped child is the selection of the methodology or methodologies that will be employed. "The primary responsibility for formulating the education to be accorded a handicapped child, *and for choosing the education method most suitable to the child's needs,* was left by the Act to state and local education agencies in cooperation with the parents or guardians of the child."

The Lachmans' contention that their son can be fully mainstreamed rests squarely on their belief in, and preference for, the cued speech technique. They do not maintain that the fully-mainstreamed placement they seek would be possible without the use of cued speech and the utilization of a cued speech instructor working at Benjamin's side, full-time, in the classroom. Further, appellants do not claim that Benjamin could be mainstreamed in any greater extent than called for in the proposed IEP, if the total communication methodology is utilized. The reasons relied on by the school district for refusing to place Benjamin in a regular classroom full-time focus on its lack of confidence in the cued speech technique as a means of facilitating immediate, full mainstreaming in Benjamin's case. Instead, the school district believes that the total communication concept is the most appropriate way to facilitate Benjamin's early primary education and it has selected that methodology for his IEP.

On the facts of this case, it is clear that the § 1412(5)(B) issue of mainstreaming is subsumed by the parties' disagreement as to methodology. In the absence of the parties' difference of opinion as to that question of educational methodology, there would be no disagreement between them as to the extent of mainstreaming that could presently be achieved for Benjamin. Given the nature of the disagreement between the parties and the concomitant thrust of the Lachmans' cause of action, we can only conclude that the district court did not err when it framed its substantive analysis in a manner closely tracking the *Rowley* opinion, without expressly addressing the § 1412(5)(B) mainstreaming issue.

IV

We have determined that the core, dispositive issue in the controversy that underlies this cause of action is one centering on a disagreement between appellant parents and appellee school district as to the most appropriate method whereby the education of the parents' handicapped child is to be facilitated. . . .

Rowley and its progeny leave no doubt that parents, no matter how well-motivated, do not have a right under the EAHCA to compel a school district to provide a specific program or employ a specific methodology in providing for the education of their handicapped child. . . .

It is clear that the IEP proposed by the school district is based upon an accepted, proven methodology for facilitating the early primary education of profoundly hearing-impaired children. Further, nothing in the record indicates that the proposed IEP does not provide that Benjamin will be educated in a regular classroom environment to the maximum extent appropriate as required by § 612(5)(B) of the Act. Given these findings, we conclude that the proposed IEP will provide Benjamin Lachman with a free appropriate public education as required by § 612(1) of the Act. Accordingly, the judgment of the district court is AFFIRMED.

It is important to note that a decision about whether to mainstream is to be based on the individual needs, abilities, and other factors for that student. Several judicial decisions have addressed factual situations involving deaf students and mainstreaming, and these decisions have reached a variety of results in terms of the appropriate placement.[12]

In all cases, the decision about separate facilities should be based on an individualized determination about what is appropriate *for that student.* The least restrictive environment mandate establishes a presumption that separate placement is inappropriate, and the party wanting a more restrictive placement has the burden of justifying it.

To the extent that a separate facility is permitted as being temporarily necessary for the child's educational needs, it should be noted that the "facility and the services and activities provided therein are comparable to the other facilities, services, and activities of the program."[13]

OTHER ISSUES

Nonacademic Programming

The EAHCA is very clear that not only should the academic portion of the program be provided in the least restrictive setting possible but also that nonacademic and extracurricular services and activities be nonrestrictive. These activities include meals, recess periods, sports, and student organizations.[14] For some children, whose "academic" placement is very restrictive—i.e., placement in a separate class within the regular school setting—the interaction in nonacademic programming such as the physical education class may be the only opportunity to benefit from the experience of age-peer interaction. Not only should it be stressed that mainstreaming is a requirement for such activities, but it will be important that the staff and faculty who are responsible for these activities have appropriate training in working with handicapped children.[15]

Of all the issues that arise in the context of sports and athletics, one is the potential risk to the child. For some activities, the concern for risk may have to be addressed by providing more supervisory personnel. There are, however, certain activities, such as contact sports, where the risk cannot be alleviated by greater supervision. According to the weight of judicial opinion, a student who is blind in one eye or who has one kidney may be legally excluded from certain contact sports. The courts have generally recognized that students under the age of majority cannot appreciate the risk in such cases, and cannot waive liability.[16]

For students with minimal disabilities or disabilities that do not qualify the youngster as a handicapped student under the EAHCA, protection against discrimination will be provided only under Section 504 of the Rehabilitation Act rather than the EAHCA. These students would not have available the detailed procedural safeguards available under the EAHCA. Section 504, however, would require that reasonable accommodation be provided to those students who were otherwise qualified for the activity. One interesting case related to this issue involved a high school student with a limb deficiency that significantly impaired her walking ability. She was prevented from participating in a trip to Spain by the school because she could not do the walking required for the trip. The court upheld the exclusion and found that because the student was not otherwise qualified, there was no violation of Section 504.[17]

The Interests of Nonhandicapped Students

The interest of the handicapped student in being exposed to age-appropriate peers occasionally is at odds with the interest of nonhandicapped students in being able to be provided education. Where the handicapped student is so disruptive that the education of the other students is significantly impaired, removal from the regular classroom is permitted.[18] The handicapped student must still be provided education, but not in the regular classroom setting.[19] The issues that will be subject to dispute, of course, are whether the disruption is "significant" and whether support personnel or different modifications might not prevent the disruption.

In addition, a child whose health condition poses a risk of contagion to other children may be removed without violating either the EAHCA or Section 504. The issue in such cases will be whether there actually is a risk.

The issue of disruption will be discussed more fully in Chapter 14, and the issue of health risks has already been addressed in Chapter 5. It should be noted that consideration for the nonhandicapped student should not be overridden by the least restrictive environment mandate for the handicapped.

Cost as an Issue

The issue of cost is addressed more fully in Chapter 13, but it is of interest to note at this point, however, that at least one court has recognized cost as a relevant factor in a decision involving mainstreaming. In assessing whether a school is required to place a severely mentally retarded elementary-aged boy in a regular elementary school, the court in the following case considered cost. The district court analysis was accepted by the Eighth Circuit in its holding.

A.W. V. NORTHWEST R-1 SCHOOL DISTRICT

813 F.2d 158 (8th Cir. 1987)
In light of the minimal benefit A.W. would receive from placement in House Springs, the Court finds that the placement is not feasible. The specific difficulty with placement at the House Springs School is that there is no teacher who is certified to teach severely retarded children like A.W. The addition of a teacher is not an acceptable solution here since the evidence before the Court shows that the funds available are limited so that placing a teacher at House Springs for the benefit of a few students at best, and possibly only A.W., would directly reduce the educational benefits provided to other handicapped students by increasing the number of students taught by a single teacher at [State School No. 2]. The Court finds that although the plaintiff presented evidence that A.W. might benefit from exposure to nonhandicapped peers, this possible benefit is insufficient to justify a reduction in unquestioned benefits to other handicapped children which would result from an inequitable expenditure of the finite funds available. . . .

It is consistent with the Supreme Court's conclusion in *Rowley* that the Act does not require states to provide each handicapped child with the best *possible* education at public expense, and the Court's recognition that available financial resources must be equitably distributed among all handicapped children. . . .

We decline to construe the Act in the manner A.W. urges. To do so would tie the hands of local and state educational authorities who must balance the reality of limited public funds against the exceptional needs of handicapped children. To do so would also encourage the federal courts to ignore the Supreme Court's admonition that "[t]he primary responsibility for formulating the education to be accorded a handicapped child, and for choosing the education method most suitable to the child's needs, was left by the Act to state and local educational agencies in cooperation with the parents or guardian of the child." *Rowley,* 458 U.S. at 207. We hold that the district court did not err in considering whether A.W. would benefit from placement in House Springs or in considering the cost to Northwest R-1 of such a placement.

At least one other circuit considered state finances in addressing a mainstreaming issue, and at least three other circuits have considered cost as a factor in placement decisions in general.[20]

SUMMARY

One of the underlying principles of the EAHCA is that the education of children with handicaps is to be provided to the maximum extent appropriate along with children who are not handicapped. Judicial interpretation of this principle has added the element of age appropiateness as an element of this requirement.

The goal of "mainstreaming," or the provision of education in the least restrictive environment, does not require that every child be educated in the regular classroom. The statute and regulations specifically contemplate that more restrictive placements may be necessary, and that the schools should provide a continuum of alternative placements to meet these situations.

The general principle of mainstreaming is based on a recognition of the stigma of separate placement and the benefit of peer modeling. Courts have looked to these factors in addressing issues of mainstreaming within the classroom itself, the location of the classrooms within the school building, the right to attend the local school, placement in totally separate facilities, and participation in extracurricular activities. They have reached a variety of conclusions in applying these factors to such issues. In these cases courts have also had occasion to consider the interests of the nonhandicapped students and cost considerations as additional factors to weigh in determining whether a particular placement is too restrictive. It has generally been recognized as appropriate for courts to take these factors into account.

QUESTIONS AND PROBLEMS

1. Should a severely mentally retarded child such as Neill Roncker who could interact in a regular gym or music class be required to be mainstreamed into a regular school setting?

2. The court in the *Besteiro* decision issued a temporary injunction requiring that an air-conditioned classroom be provided. It is likely from the language in the opinion that this would be the result if the plaintiffs were seeking a permanent injunction. The court did not, however, address several other issues. Should the school be required to air-condition the entire school building, so that Raul could attend music, art, and other classes?

3. *Besteiro* was decided before the *Rowley* Supreme Court decision clarifying the meaning of "appropriate." Would the fact that Raul was making straight A's change this court's decision as to whether Raul was receiving an appropriate education in the separate cubicle?

4. The 1986 amendments to the EAHCA provide for incentive programs to allow programming for handicapped children from birth to age five. Most states do not have preschool programming available to all children within the state. As a practical matter, can the goal of mainstreaming be accomplished in the preschool setting without requiring states to establish preschool programs for nonhandicapped children on a broad scale? Is the mainstreaming philosophy important for preschool children?

5. What obligation does the school have to protect the mainstreamed handicapped child from undue testing by other students?

6. If peer interaction is deemed to be essential in a particular case, how can that be accomplished if the child also needs year-round programming? In other words, how will peer interaction occur during the summer months?

7. If public school buildings are used for nonschool-sponsored programs, such as Brownies and Girl Scouts, is it permissible to have separate Scout troops for children who are mentally retarded? Does this violate the EAHCA, or is there a constitutional violation at issue?

8. If a state requires that eligibility for certain extracurricular activities be based on maintaining a particular grade point average, is there any problem with such a policy for handicapped students? Should it make a difference if the eligibility requirements apply only to major sports, rather than all extracurricular activities such as the Glee Club?

9. In 1985, the Department of Education considered, but ultimately rejected, a policy that would require that a placement in a regular program be tried before a more restrictive placement could be attempted. Would this be a good policy? Why or why not?

NOTES

1. 20 U.S.C. § 1412(5)(B); 34 C.F.R. § 300.551. *See also* L. ROTHSTEIN, RIGHTS OF PHYSI-CALLY HANDICAPPED PERSONS ch. 2 (1984) and cumulative supplements.
2. 45 C.F.R. §§ 300.551 and 300.552(d).
3. Comment following 45 C.F.R. § 300.552. The issue of removal for disciplinary reasons is discussed more fully in Chapter 14.
4. These issues are discussed in much greater detail in H.R. TURNBULL III, FREE APPROPRI-ATE PUBLIC EDUCATION, THE LAW AND CHILDREN WITH DISABILITIES ch. 6 (1986).
5. 34 C.F.R. § 300.551. *See also,* Reynolds, *A Framework for Considering Some Issues in Special Education,* 28 EXCEPTIONAL CHILDREN 367–70 (1962).
6. For a discussion of this issue, *see* Comment, *Age Appropriateness as a Factor in Educational Placement Decisions,* 40 L. & CONT. PROB. 93 (1985).
7. This principle is supported in Brown v. Board of Education, 347 U.S. 483 (1954).
8. 458 U.S. 176, 189 (1982).
9. 34 C.F.R. § 300.552(a)(3).
10. *Id.* § 300.552(c).
11. 34 C.F.R. § 104.22(a). It should be emphasized, however, that new construction should be accessible within the standards set by the American National Standards Institute. *Id.* at § 104.23.
12. 34 C.F.R. § 104.34(c).
13. *See* Visco v. School Dist., 684 F. Supp. 1310 (W.D. Pa. 1988) (placing two deaf children in a school for the hearing impaired was appropriate because the mother was also deaf and unable to assist in developing aural skills); Lachman v. Illinois State Board of Education, 852 F.2d 290 (7th Cir. 1988) (appropriate to place profoundly hearing-impaired child in self-contained classroom for half a day); Barwacz v. Michigan Department of Education, 674 F. Supp. 1296 (W.D. Mich. 1987) (deaf student was appropriately mainstreamed).
14. 34 C.F.R. § 300.306 & § 300.553.
15. 34 C.F.R. § 300.383.
16. *See generally* L. ROTHSTEIN, RIGHTS OF PHYSICALLY HANDICAPPED PERSONS §§ 2.17 & 3.11 (1984).
17. Wolff v. South Colonie Cent. School Dist., 534 F. Supp. 758 (N.D.N.Y. 1982).
18. Comment following 34 C.F.R. § 300.552.

19. This is by virtue of the requirement that *all* handicapped children be provided education. 34 C.F.R. § 300.1(a).
20. Tokarcik v. Forest Hills School Dist., 665 F.2d 443, 458 (3d Cir. 1981) (mainstreaming did not affect state finances); Department of Education v. Katherine D., 727 F.2d 809, 813–14 (9th Cir. 1983); Age v. Bullitt County Public Schools, 673 F.2d 141, 145 (6th Cir. 1982); Doe v. Anrig, 692 F.2d 800, 806–07 (1st Cir. 1982).

CHAPTER 9

Related Services

Related services are part of the free appropriate public education that must be provided to all handicapped children within the state in order for the state to be eligible for funding under the EAHCA. The child must need the services to benefit from special education. The statute defines related services as

> transportation, and such . . . other supportive services (including speech pathology and audiology, psychological services, physical and occupational therapy, recreation, and medical and counseling services, except that such medical services shall be for diagnostic and evaluation purposes only) as may be required to assist a handicapped child to benefit from special education, and includes the early identification and assessment of handicapping conditions in children.[1]

One issue that frequently becomes a point of contention about some related services is the extent to which the provision of such services impedes the goal of mainstreaming. For example, certain services such as physical therapy or health-related services may be administratively easier to provide in a setting that is more restrictive. Cost and availability of personnel will often determine administrative decisions. It is not easy in some cases to balance the mandate to have appropriate programming and appropriate related services with the mainstreaming goal. Legal guidance on this issue is found in case law interpretation rather than directly in the statute or regulation.

Another problem that arises in the related service context is the problem of public agency and other provider responsibility. Many of the related services required by the EAHCA are services that were provided by other agencies before passage of the EAHCA. Services such as residential placements for severely emotionally disturbed children or certain kinds of therapy may have been forthcoming from state agencies such as departments of health and human services and departments of welfare. Other health-related services were provided or at least paid for by family health insurance agencies.

The EAHCA, however, makes the state education agency the primary supervisor for the provision of related services that are required for the child to benefit from special education. State educational agencies must have the general supervisory role for coordinating service delivery by other agencies,[2] but the EAHCA provides no real means to mandate that other agencies provide certain services. The EAHCA states that it is not to be viewed as limiting "the responsibility of [other] agencies . . . from providing or paying for some or all of the costs of a free appropriate public education. . . ."[3] The EAHCA requires the adoption of interagency agreements including a mechanism for resolving interagency disputes.[4]

Not only do the state education agencies often lack the authority but they also lack the funding to provide all of the services they are now responsible for. A number of states have developed workable plans for interagency cooperation and systems for funding. Some of these plans have developed through agency-initiated agreements; others by state legislative mandate.[5] Where good interagency cooperation does not exist, agencies sometimes compete to provide certain types of inexpensive services and yet try to refuse responsibility for expensive services, particularly residential placements.[6] The following sections address some of the related services where legal questions arise.

TRANSPORTATION

The issue of transportation is important because of the cost involved. Transportation includes getting to and from school and getting around the facility.[7] In being responsible for transportation, schools must also provide specialized equipment if it is needed.[8] The school may be required to purchase special lift equipment for a bus or other special equipment such as a van to ensure that the student can get to and from school and to benefit from school once the student is there. Many states supplement the EAHCA-mandated transportation requirements. State regulations usually include matters such as maximum amount of time in transit and location of bus stops. Readers should consider the following problems as they relate to the issue of transportation.

A number of legal questions are raised in providing transportation. Many of these are not directly answered by the EAHCA or its regulations, nor are they answered in judicial interpretation. These issues have often been debated at the administrative hearing level, however.

When Must Transportation Be Provided?

If a child needs transportation in order to benefit from special education, the service must be made available. It has been suggested that a child who needs no special education would not qualify for related services, but if that were the case, a child who only needs catheterization (but no special education) to benefit from education would be denied the service on that basis. It is not clear what the EAHCA responsibility is in a situation where a school district provides no one with transportation service, but a child cannot get to school without a special vehicle. Where the school does provide transportation to other children, the failure to provide a special lift or other method to transport the student in a wheelchair might be viewed as discriminatory and thus violating Section 504 of the Rehabilitation Act. It is not clear, however, whether the reasonable accommodation requirement of Section 504 would mandate the purchase of expensive equipment.

What if the child lives within a certain range where transportation is normally not provided? For example, what if a school district only normally provides transportation to children outside of a four-mile radius of a school? Must the school provide transportation? The answer is probably yes if the transportation is needed to enable the child to attend school.

What about the child in a residential setting? Must the school provide transportation for the child to visit home and for parental visits to the placement site? Case law indicates that where parental visits are essential for developing interpersonal family relationships, the transportation cost of these visits must be compensated.[9]

What Is the Extent of Transportation Service?

The specific requirements relating to the location of bus stops, the time in transit, and the degree of assistance required are not specifically covered by federal law. Many state and local agencies have adopted and implemented regulations and guidelines on these matters. Whether there are regulatory guidelines or not, limits can and should be specified in the IEP.

Unusual instances of liability can result when appropriate safety measures relating to bus stops are not taken. In one case the school was sued by the driver of a car for emotional trauma when she struck and killed a four-year-old deaf child. The bus driver had not taken proper care to ensure the child reached safety. The school board was held liable.[10] Negligent selection of transportation personnel can also be the basis of liability, in cases where the schools are not protected by the immunity defense.[11]

One question not clearly answered by the EAHCA is whether, when transportation is provided, it must be door to door, and if so what is meant by door to door. If a child is unable to get to the regular bus stop, door-to-door transport is probably required.[12] One national expert on special education transportation suggests that door to door means curbside.[13] For children living in high-rise apartments, it means that parents have the responsibility of getting the child to the curbside location and meeting the child at the end of the day. To require the driver to take a child to the door of a 16-floor apartment is probably outside what is contemplated by the EAHCA. This would mean the driver would leave other children unattended, or the school would have to provide additional personnel to assist.

Although the EAHCA may not mandate such service, state or local regulations or the IEP may do so. The *Hurry v. Jones* decision in the next section offers two views of this issue.

Excessive time in transit can be damaging to a student's level of energy, ability to concentrate, and so forth. For that reason it is important in developing an IEP to take this into account, and to designate the amount of time to be spent on the bus.

Parent-Provided Transportation

Where the parent is providing transportation as a matter of preference, and the school has made available appropriate transportation services, the school need not reimburse the parents. Because special education and related services are to be provided at no cost to the child's family, the school is required to reimburse parents for transportation costs necessitated by the school's failure to provide appropriate transportation or where the parents and school agree to parent-provided transportation in lieu of school-provided service.[14] As the following decision demonstrates, the parents' recovery may not necessarily be limited to out-of-pocket expenses.

HURRY V. JONES

734 F.2d 879 (1st Cir. 1984)
Defendants/appellants, who are school and transportation officials in Providence, appeal from a decision . . . awarding damages to George Hurry, a physically and mentally handicapped minor, and to his parents. The district court found that appellants' failure to provide George with door-to-door transportation to and from school violated both the Education for All Handicapped Children Act of 1975 (EAHCA) and the Rehabilitation Act of 1973. The court awarded $14,546.00 under the EAHCA and $5,000.00 under section 504 of the Rehabilitation Act; appellants challenge both awards.

George Hurry (George) suffers from cerebral palsy and a degree of mental retardation, and is confined to a wheelchair by spastic quadriplegia. He has attended various special education programs in the Providence area. Until January 1976 the City of Providence provided him with door-to-door bus transportation to and from school. By January of 1976, however, George had reached a weight of 160 pounds, and the bus drivers deemed it unsafe to continue to carry him up and down the steep concrete steps that led from his front door to the street. Mr. and Mrs. Hurry began to transport George to and from school in their van.

Starting in June 1976 Mr. Hurry held a position that required him to work until 5:15 p.m. each day. Because Mrs. Hurry could not lift George from the van and carry him up the steps without her husband's aid, he had to wait in the car for several hours each day until Mr. Hurry left work. He frequently missed school when the weather was too hot or too cold to permit him to wait in the van. In December of 1977, Mr. and Mrs. Hurry stopped transporting him to school; George did not attend school again until the fall of 1979.

The Hurrys discussed their transportation problem with the Providence School Department, but the parties were unable to reach a satisfactory solution. Plans to construct a permanent wheelchair ramp at the Hurrys' home failed when the Mayor's office refused to provide public funding for the project unless multiple liens on the property were discharged. The Hurrys refused the School Department's offer of home instruction for George because they believed that this instruction would not provide their son with the "least restrictive environment" available. In September of 1978 the Rhode Island Protection and Advocacy System (RIPAS) requested that the Providence School Department conduct a hearing on the Hurrys' problem. When the School Department did not respond to the request within the statutory time limit, RIPAS contacted the State Commissioner of Education on November 7, 1978, to request a hearing. This second request likewise failed to produce the statutorily required hearing, and RIPAS filed this action in the Hurrys' behalf on December 19, 1978. By October 29, 1979, the parties had agreed on an Individual Educational Program for George that provided him with transportation to and from school and obviated the need for injunctive relief.* RIPAS withdrew from the action at this point, but the Hurrys pursued claims for damages for the period during which George attended school only if they were able to transport him and for the period during which he did not attend school at all.

The Hurrys based their claims for damages on the EAHCA, the Rehabilitation Act, the Developmentally Disabled Assistance and Bill of Rights Act, 42 U.S.C. § 1983, the Fifth and Fourteenth Amendments of the United States Constitution, Article 12 of the Constitution of Rhode Island, and R.I. Gen. Laws § 16-24-4. The court found, and the parties do not dispute, that further pursuit of administrative remedies would have been futile, and that the action was properly before the court. The court found that the Hurrys could not recover damages under the Developmentally Disabled Assistance and Bill of Rights Act, and that they had failed to make out their claims under the federal and state constitution, § 1983, and the state statutory provision. The Hurrys do not contest these conclusions. The court did award damages under the EAHCA and the Rehabilitation Act, and defendants challenge these awards on appeal.

I. Damages Under the Education for All Handicapped Children Act
The EAHCA provides that a state receiving federal assistance for education of the handicapped must assure "all handicapped children the right to a free appropriate public education." The Act further provides that parties aggrieved by decisions affecting a handicapped child's education may bring a civil action in state or federal court, and that the court hearing such an action may grant "such relief as the court determines is appropriate."

A number of courts have interpreted the relief provision of the EAHCA as being limited to injunctive remedies, and have held that damages are not recoverable under the Act absent exceptional circumstances.

At the time the district court reached its decision, this circuit subscribed to the . . .

---

* The initial solution was for the school bus to pick George up at his home before his father left for work so that Mr. Hurry could carry him down the steps, and to transport George to another school in the afternoon where he could wait in comfort until his father left work and took him home. Ultimately, Mrs. Hurry's mother purchased an adjoining property with a sloping driveway, and the Hurrys were able to wheel George out the back door of their house and down the driveway to meet the school bus.

Appellants argue that the Hurrys had a duty to "mitigate damages" by helping to engineer an appropriate solution to the problem at an earlier date. We note that this theory is doubtful at best; but since it was never raised before the district court, we decline to address it on appeal.

view that reimbursement is available to parties aggrieved by violations of the EAHCA only in exceptional circumstances. We have since adopted a more expansive view of reimbursement under the EAHCA, allowing reimbursement of interim educational and related expenses even when the "exceptional circumstances" . . . are not present. Under this approach, it is clear that the district court correctly found that the Hurrys are entitled to reimbursement under the EAHCA for the interim transportation services they provided until the parties agreed on an appropriate Individual Educational Program for George. . . .

The district court made three separate damage awards to the Hurrys under the EAHCA. First, it reimbursed Mr. and Mrs. Hurry $1,150.00 for the out-of-pocket expense of driving George to school. It calculated this expense by multiplying the 92 school weeks in 1976 and 1977 during which the School Department failed to supply transportation by Mr. Hurry's $12.50 estimate of the weekly cost he incurred in transporting George himself. The parties did not contest this portion of the award, so we have no need to address it on appeal. Second, the court awarded the Hurrys $4,600.00 for their contributed services in driving George to and from school. It arrived at this figure by compensating the Hurrys at a rate of $10.00 per day for the 92 five-day school weeks during which the Hurrys transported George themselves. Third, the court awarded George $8,796.00 for the period from January 1978 until June 1979 during which he did not attend school at all. This award represented "the amount Defendants were not required to expend" on George's education, an amount the court calculated by multiplying the average per pupil cost for special education during the relevant period by the number of months George was absent. Appellants did not challenge the district court's method of computing damages; instead, they contend that the award to the Hurrys for contributed services and the award to George were improper.

The award of $4,600.00 for Mr. and Mrs. Hurry's contributed services in driving George to school requires us to determine whether the reimbursement available under the EAHCA is limited to out-of-pocket expenses, or whether it may also include compensation for the expenditure of time and effort. We see no reason why the latter type of expense should not be reimbursed, except for the possibility that, when reimbursement is given for the monetary equivalent of time and effort, excessive payments might be made. To the extent that this could occur, the distinction between "reimbursement" and "damages" would be blurred. Here, however, we are considering the district court's award of $10.00 per day for two daily round trips of ten to fifteen miles, taking several hours of the Hurrys' time. This is obviously a barebones figure, well within any reasonable estimate of fair reimbursement. Moreover, it cannot be argued that the service in question—transporting George to and from school—called for any special skill or training that the Hurrys lacked.

It is clear that if the Hurrys had hired a private agency to drive George to and from school, this expense would have been reimbursable under the EAHCA, just as the expense of placing George in a private school would have been reimbursable had the School Department wrongfully declined to provide him with an appropriate public education. The fact that the Hurrys performed the service themselves rather than hiring someone else to perform it should not bar them from recovering the reasonable value of their time and effort.

The $4,600.00 award to the Hurrys also requires us to consider whether they waived their right to reimbursement by engaging in "self-help" rather than seeking court approval for the action that gave rise to their claim for reimbursement. In this case, the Hurrys . . . undertook to transport the child to the school where the School Department had placed him. Under these circumstances, we do not believe that the Hurrys' self-help should bar their recovery. We affirm the award of $4,600.00. [The court went on to deny compensation for the time George was not in school and to deny recovery under the Rehabilitation Act.]

DISSENT

I concur in those portions of the opinion that deny recovery, but cannot in the part ordering reimbursement for transportation. I am sorry to dissent over what, in dollars and cents, is not a large matter, but I feel I must because, with great respect, I believe the court, in declining to face a dispositive issue, is being basically unfair. Both to demonstrate the unfairness, and the consequence to defendants, I first consider the merits, viz., that in spite of a regulation calling for transportation of handicapped children from and to their street-level front door, defendants have been charged with additional burdens due to the fact that plaintiffs' front door was twelve damaged steps above the street.

The district court found,

> Bus drivers for the school department would carry George from the front door of his home down approximately twelve steps to the street level and into the bus. By January of 1976, however, George had gained weight and was so heavy (160 lbs.) that the bus drivers would no longer carry him. In addition to the child being overweight, the concrete steps were steep and cracked in some places, making it somewhat unsafe for anyone to attempt to carry George down to the street.

According to defendants' witness's uncontradicted testimony,

> The stairs were extremely steep. The stairs were broken and uneven in places . . . [The] regulations said street level . . . [The supervisor] came back to me and said nobody will accept the liability of carrying George Hurry, with all his problems, who also has an obesity problem, for fear they might fall and there might be some legal ramification.

The underlying statute, Education for All Handicapped Children Act (EAHCA), 20 U.S.C. §§ 1413(a)(4)(B) and 1401(17), required furnishing, simply, "transportation." The Rhode Island regulation, which the court quoted, and considered, spelt this out, one with respect to transportation generally ("door to door") and one specifically with regard to assistance, manifestly defining what was meant by "door."

> 1.0. Responsibility—All handicapped children who need special transportation as a related service and as determined by the evaluation process and described in the I.E.P. shall be provided such service. It shall include free transportation to and from the home (door to door, if necessary) to the educational program in which he/she is enrolled. . . .
>
> 2.0. Transportation Needs of Handicapped Children.
>
> 2.1.2. A minimum of one aide assigned to each bus. Such aide, in addition to providing general care and supervision of all handicapped children on such bus, shall also provide assistance (from street level entrance of dwelling) to such children lacking the mobility to leave the home and board trans-

portation vehicles, and shall further assist such children in debarking the vehicle and entering the school. . . ."

The district court found these regulations "clear," and that, in failing to arrange for George's reaching the street level, defendants "ignored their obvious duty." I find them clear, but just the reverse. In my opinion "street level" means exactly what it says, and the court, although recognizing, ante, that the door was above the street level, excised from the regulation, without even discussion, precisely what had caused all the difficulties.

My brethren feel that because defendants did not attack it, the district court's interpretation is the law of the case. Before reaching that question, I must first consider whether the ruling was wrong. I believe it plainly so. If anything seems clear, it is that there is a difference in kind between a street level entrance from which, if need be, a physically handicapped child may be taken in a wheelchair, or otherwise safely guided by the bus attendant, and the door twelve dangerous steps up, requiring a special attendant, or possibly two, and the risk of a substantial claim for negligence if anything goes wrong. . . .

Disciplinary Problems

What happens when a child's behavior is such that if the child were not handicapped, the child would be suspended from riding the bus? That is, can a special education student ever be suspended from transportation services? Case law suggests that if the behavior relates to the handicapping condition, complete withdrawal of service is not permitted. There is an exception for short-term emergency situations. And in such emergency situations, a prompt meeting of the IEP Committee should address the issue and make appropriate recommendations. The issue of discipline in all contexts is discussed more fully in Chapter 14.

PSYCHOLOGICAL SERVICES AND COUNSELING

"Psychological services" and "counseling" are specifically included in the EAHCA as related services.[15] Counseling about hearing loss, as well as speech and language disorders for both the child and the family, is within the related service mandate.[16] Providing information to parents about child development is also required.[17] Specific psychological services to be provided also include assessing the child and using the information to develop an appropriate learning program as well as a program of counseling if needed.[18] Individual and family counseling are also contemplated under the heading of "social work services" that would be included as related services.[19]

Because of the expense involved in providing some counseling services, a number of cases have addressed the issue of counseling. The general result in those cases is that where the service is so related to the educational program that it is necessary if the student is to benefit from education, the service must be provided at the school's expense.[20] This issue will be discussed in more detail in Chapter 10 on residential placements. In the following case, the court addresses the issue of whether the parents may be compensated for counseling services performed by a psychiatrist.

MAX M. V. ILLINOIS STATE BOARD OF EDUCATION

629 F. Supp. 1504 (N.D. Ill. 1986)
The plaintiffs are Max M., a handicapped child within the meaning of the EAHCA, and his parents. The parties named as defendants are [various educational agencies and administrators].

Max M. attended New Trier West, a public high school in Northfield, Illinois, from 1977 to 1981. Because of his disorganization, difficulty in writing, and anxiety, his academic performance was poor. In January of Max's freshman year, Max was referred to New Trier's Department of Special Education for evaluation. Max was examined by New Trier's consultant, Dr. Traisman, who later issued a written report recommending long-term "intensive psychotherapy" for Max. Although the parents and Dr. Traisman believed that Max should be seen by a male therapist, no male therapists were provided by New Trier for Max during his freshman year.

New Trier recommended to Max' parents that he be placed in two special education classes for the remainder of his freshman year, but the Ms rejected this recommendation as too drastic. Instead, a compromise was reached allowing Max to spend one hour a day in a resource room where a student is allowed to work individually with a teacher on a particular subject. Shortly thereafter, New Trier again proposed that Max be enrolled in a special education math class, and this time the parents agreed. Max' first semester freshman grades in his major subject were four Ds. After a special education component was implemented during Max' second semester, Max received three Cs and one D in his major subjects.

During the summer following his freshman year, Max attended summer school at New Trier. The Ms met with representatives of New Trier that summer to discuss Max, and the Ms formally requested that their son receive psychotherapy from Frank Brull, a New Trier social worker.* Also during that summer, Max saw a private psychotherapist, Dr. Burg, for four sessions.

New Trier developed an Individual Education Program (IEP) for Max to commence in September of his sophomore year. The IEP included one special education class, attendance in the resource room three days a week, and four standard courses in which Max was to be mainstreamed with the general student body. This IEP was shown to the Ms sometime in late November. Although the IEP did not so state, Max was also offered psychotherapy twice a week by New Trier social worker, Frank Brull. Max, however, failed to attend his therapy sessions with Mr. Brull on a regular basis. By the end of his sophomore year, Max' academic and social behavior had shown serious deterioration. Max received a D in the class he took during the summer between his freshman and sophomore year and received three Cs and two Fs in his first semester sophomore year. During his second semester, Max received three Ds and one F.

On May 30, 1979, New Trier recommended that Max attend the Central Campus Learning Center (CCLC), New Trier's off-campus facility designed for emotionally

---

* Qualified social workers are among the personnel authorized to administer psychotherapy as a related service under the EAHCA. 34 C.F.R. § 300.13(b)(2) 1983.

disturbed or behavior disordered students. In the CCLC a core teacher is assigned to each student and acts as instructor in most if not all the classes in which the student is enrolled. Students at the CCLC have no unsupervised time. Between 1979 and 1981, the maximum number of students attending CCLC at any one time was forty, and the average class size was eight.

On July 6, 1979 Max began receiving psychotherapy from Dr. Robert Rosenfeld, a psychiatrist. Aside from providing psychotherapy for Max, the Ms relied on Dr. Rosenfeld for input for Max' junior year placement. In that regard Rosenfeld first met with New Trier personnel on August 6, 1979 to discuss the proposed CCLC placement for Max' junior year. Rosenfeld informed the Ms that the CCLC placement could not be made without their knowledge and permission. Although Rosenfeld and the Ms discussed the possibility of a residential placement for Max, they all agreed not to pursue this option.

New Trier called a second meeting on August 20, 1979 to discuss Max' junior year placement. In addition to Dr. Rosenfeld, Dr. Wolter, New Trier's Director of Special Education, as well as the Ms, were in attendance. At this meeting, the CCLC placement for Max' junior year was approved by the parties. Rosenfeld felt the CCLC placement was a reasonable next step in addressing some of the problems Max had experienced in the larger setting of New Trier West. The Ms were informed by Dr. Wolter that if the CCLC placement did not work out, a due process hearing could occur.

A specific Individualized Education Plan (IEP) was prepared for Max naming Judy Knox as Max' core instructor. Knox observed that when Max first arrived at the CCLC, he seemed afraid to socialize with the other students, but as the year progressed he became much more socially interactive with his fellow classmates. At the end of his first semester at CCLC, Max received one A, two Bs, and one C. At the end of his second semester, Max received three As and one B. Max' scholastic improvement was a result of certain modifications in the regular CCLC program which enabled Max to succeed academically despite his insistence on not performing written work. Max was held accountable for work that he did not perform. The Ms received several low scholarship notices during his junior year explaining that Max was not completing his assigned work. Max' classroom behavior also showed improvement by the end of his junior year.

Aside from the educational component of Max' IEP, Max received group therapy at CCLC. Although family therapy sessions were to be provided by New Trier for the Ms, time conflicts with scheduling eventually led to a mutual agreement to discontinue the sessions. During Max' junior year, Dr. Rosenfeld was also providing private psychotherapy for Max at the Ms' expense. From July of 1979 to January of 1980, Rosenfeld saw Max twice a week. Thereafter he saw Max once a week. This reduction in sessions per week was due to the Ms' financial constraints.

Rosenfeld discussed Max' senior year placement with the Ms and a decision was reached allowing Max to continue at CCLC. Max' senior year IEP was discussed with the Ms in a conference on October 20, 1980 with New Trier. Ms. Knox noticed that Max began to socialize and interact more successfully with his classmates during his senior year. However, Max began to experience problems academically. During his first semester senior year, Max received one C, two Ds, and two Fs. Second semester senior year, Max received two Cs and three Ds. Although Ms. Knox felt that Max met the minimal expectations that she had for him in every class, she agreed that Max had many of the same problems at the end of his senior year as at the beginning of his junior year. Max' weakening academic performance was reflected to the Ms through a series of low scholarship notices. The notices universally cited Max' lack of preparation and failure to complete assigned work.

By the end of Max' senior year he had earned more than the required amount of credits to graduate and was ranked 455 out of 546 students in the senior class. On May 15, 1981, the Ms filed a request for a due process hearing. Because of financial considerations, the Ms decided to discontinue Max' psychotherapy from Dr. Rosenfeld on June 16, 1981 and concentrate their resources on the due process hearing. The Ms expended a total of $8,855 for Max' private psychiatric care while he attended New Trier and CCLC.

Max graduated on June 11, 1981. Both Max and his parents rejected the idea of continuing at CCLC during the pendency of the due process hearing. Instead, the Ms wanted a different special education program combining advanced academic work, vocational training, and therapy. No such special education program was offered by New Trier. In September of 1982, the Ms enrolled Max at Brehm Preparatory School, a residential facility for learning disabled and behavior disordered children. After several months of attendance at Brehm, Max developed acute psychiatric problems and was hospitalized at Hartgrove Hospital. Max was discharged to the Ridgeview Shelter Care Facility in Evanston, Illinois, on October 10, 1983, and received outpatient psychotherapy from Dr. Gary Phillips, a clinical psychologist. The Ms spend between $16,000 and $17,000 to place Max at Brehm and incurred approximately $3,500 in fees from Dr. Phillips.

Meanwhile, on October 13, 1981, Dr. Robert Monks conducted the due process hearing requested by the Ms. On October 16, 1981, Dr. Monks issued a decision revoking Max' graduation and ordering that services be continued and that an appropriate IEP be prepared. New Trier promptly appealed the Monks' decision and on February 12, 1982, the Illinois State Board of Education (ISBE) issued an Administrative Order reversing the hearing officer's decision. Both the hearing officer's opinion and the ISBE's Administrative Order found that Max had been denied an appropriate education with related services because New Trier failed to provide Max with the intensive psychotherapy recommended by the school district's psychologist, Dr. Thraisman. The ISBE order reversing the hearing officer's decision to revoke Max' diploma and continue services was based on an alleged pleading defect on the part of the Ms.

On October 26, 1982, the Ms filed their complaint in this Court. Although the Ms' initial complaint challenged the ISBE order on various federal and state statutory and constitutional provisions, this Court's four prior decisions limited the Ms' complaint to two basic claims under the EAHCA: (1) reimbursement from Local Defendants of the $8,855 expended by the Ms for Max' psychiatric treatment while attending New Trier; and (2) compensatory remedial educational services from all defendants to compensate Max for the alleged deprivation of EAHCA benefits while he attended New Trier and an injunction revoking Max' diploma to reestablish his eligibility under the EAHCA. [The lengthy opinion in this case covered a number of issues. Only the portion relating to the related services is included.]

Although the EAHCA is interpreted to include psychotherapy as a related service school districts must provide, limitations exist on required medical services. Specifically, services provided by a licensed physician are limited to diagnosis and evaluation. Due to the Local Defendants' failure to apprise the Ms of their rights under the EAHCA and provide Max with the psychotherapy he was identified as entitled to receive, this Court ruled that the Ms' uninformed selection of a psychiatrist would not bar their claim for reimbursement.

The EAHCA's limitation on physician provided services was held to reflect a conscious effort on the part of Congress to limit costs by requiring a school district to provide only the minimum level of health care personnel recognized as legally and professionally competent to perform an EAHCA required service. Since many of the enumerated "related services" under the EAHCA could be provided by a physician or nonphysician, this Court reasoned that Congress intended to limit the nature of the services required rather than the personnel who provided the service. In that line of reasoning this Court held that where a school district failed to provide services required under the EAHCA and failed to properly inform the deprived EAHCA recipients of their right to seek review, the school district would be liable to reimburse the deprived recipients for the cost of privately obtained required services, even if a physician provided the services. Reimbursement for these physician rendered related services were subject to certain limitations. Specifically, the school district could be held liable for no more than the cost of the service as provided by the minimum level health care provider recognized as competent to perform the related service. The liability of the school district in such a case would be computed from the amount that such qualified personnel would normally and reasonably charge for the EAHCA services obtained privately by the deprived party. Thus, if the deprived party is not fully reimbursed, then the portion of the cost the deprived party must incur is the cost of exercising the freedom to select a special care provider. . . .

Max M. III [592 F. Supp. 437 (N.D. Ill. 1984) represented an effort to reconcile the EAHCA's requirement that each child receive an appropriate and free public education including related services with the EAHCA's limitations on expenditures for medical services. To abandon the limitation on reimbursement for physician rendered related services in Max M. III would require this Court to completely ignore the clear language of the statute which limits medical services to diagnosis and evaluation. *Burlington* simply cannot be read to encompass the question of physician administered related services decided in Max M. III. Thus, the Ms' motion for reconsideration as to the reimbursement limitation imposed in Max M. III is denied.

HEALTH SERVICES

One of the early cases decided by the Supreme Court under the EAHCA related to health services. The service at issue was catheterization, and the question was whether it was a medical service *not* required under the EAHCA or whether it was a related health service.

IRVING INDEPENDENT SCHOOL DISTRICT V. TATRO

468 U.S. 883 (1984)
Chief Justice BURGER delivered the opinion of the Court.

We granted certiorari to determine whether the Education of the Handicapped Act or the Rehabilitation Act of 1973 requires a school district to provide a handicapped child with clean intermittent catheterization during school hours.

I

Amber Tatro is an 8-year-old girl born with a defect known as spina bifida. As a result, she suffers from orthopedic and speech impairments and a neurogenic bladder, which prevents her from emptying her bladder voluntarily. Consequently, she must be catheterized every three or four hours to avoid injury to her kidneys. In accordance with accepted medical practice, clean intermittent catheterization (CIC), a procedure involving the insertion of a catheter into the urethra to drain the bladder, has been prescribed. The procedure is a simple one that may be performed in a few minutes by a layperson with less than an hour's training. Amber's parents, babysitter, and teenage brother are all qualified to administer CIC, and Amber soon will be able to perform this procedure herself.

In 1979 petitioner Irving Independent School District agreed to provide special education for Amber, who was then three and one-half years old. In consultation with her parents, who are respondents here, petitioner developed an individualized education program for Amber under the requirements of the Education for All Handicapped Children Act of 1975. The individualized education program provided that Amber would attend early childhood development classes and receive special services such as physical and occupational therapy. That program, however, made no provision for school personnel to administer CIC.

Respondents unsuccessfully pursued administrative remedies to secure CIC services for Amber during school hours. In October 1979 respondents brought the present action in District Court against petitioner, the State Board of Education, and others. They sought an injunction ordering petition to provide Amber with CIC and sought damages and attorney's fees. . . .

[Lower court proceedings omitted.]

II

This case poses two separate issues. The first is whether the Education of the Handicapped Act requires petitioner to provide CIC services to Amber. The second is whether Section 504 of the Rehabilitation Act creates such an obligation. We first turn to the claim presented under the Education of the Handicapped Act.

States receiving funds under the Act are obliged to satisfy certain conditions. A primary condition is that the state implement a policy "that assures all handicapped children the right to a free appropriate public education.". . .

A "free appropriate public education" is explicitly defined as "special education and related services." "Related services" are defined as

> transportation, and such development corrective, and other *supportive services (including* speech pathology and audiology, psychological services, physical and occupational therapy, recreation and *medical* and counseling *services, except that such medical services shall be for diagnostic and evaluation purposes only) as may be required to assist a handicapped child to benefit from special education,* and includes the early identification and assessment of handicapping conditions in children.

The issue in this case is whether CIC is a "related service" that petitioner is obliged to provide to Amber. We must answer two questions: first, whether CIC is a "supportive servic[e] . . . required to assist a handicapped child to benefit from special education"; and second, whether CIC is excluded from this definition as a "medical servic[e]" serving purposes other than diagnosis or evaluation.

A

The Court of Appeals was clearly correct in holding that the CIC is a "supportive servic[e] . . . required to assist a handicapped child to benefit from special education." It is clear on this record that, without having CIC services available during the school day, Amber cannot attend school and thereby "benefit from special education." CIC services therefore fall squarely within the definition of "supportive services."

As we have stated before, "Congress sought primarily to make public education available to handicapped children" and "to make such access meaningful." A service that enables a handicapped child to remain at school during the day is an important means of providing the child with the meaningful access to education that Congress envisioned. The Act makes specific provision for services, like transportation, for example, that do no more than enable a child to be physically present in class, and the Act specifically authorizes grants for schools to alter buildings and equipment to make them accessible to the handicapped. Services like CIC that permit a child to remain at school during the day are no less related to the effort to educate than are services that enable the child to reach, enter, or exit the school.

We hold that CIC services in this case qualify as a "supportive servic[e] . . . required to assist a handicapped child to benefit from special education."

B

We also agree with the Court of Appeals that provision of CIC is not a "medical servic[e]," which a school is required to provide only for purposes of diagnosis or evaluation. We begin with the regulations of the Department of Education, which are entitled to deference. The regulations define "related services" for handicapped children to include "school health services," which are defined in turn as "services provided by a qualified school nurse or other qualified person." "Medical services" are defined as "services provided by a licensed physician." Thus, the Secretary has determined that the services of a school nurse otherwise qualifying as a "related service" are not subject to exclusion as a "medical service," but that the services of a physician are excludable as such.

This definition of "medical services" is a reasonable interpretation of congressional intent. Although Congress devoted little discussion to the "medical services" exclusion, the Secretary could reasonably have concluded that it was designed to spare schools from an obligation to provide a service that might well prove unduly expensive and beyond the range of the competence. From this understanding of congressional purpose, the Secretary could reasonably have concluded that Congress intended to impose the obligation to provide school nursing services.

Congress plainly required schools to hire various specially trained personnel to help handicapped children, such as "trained occupational therapists, speech therapists, psychologists, social workers and other appropriately trained personnel." School nurses have long been a part of the educational system, and the Secretary could therefore reasonably conclude that school nursing services are not the sort of burden that Congress intended to exclude as a "medical service." By limiting the "medical services" exclusion to services of a physician or hospital, both far more expensive, the Secretary has given a permissible construction to the provision.

Petitioner's contrary interpretation of the "medical services" exclusion is unconvincing. In petitioner's view, CIC is a "medical service," even though it may be provided by a nurse or trained layperson; that conclusion rests on its reading of Texas law that confines CIC to uses in accordance with a physician's prescription and under a physician's ultimate supervision. Aside from conflicting with the Secretary's reasonable interpretation of congressional intent, however, such a rule would be anomalous. Nurses in petitioner's school district are authorized to dispense oral medication and administer emergency injections in accordance with a physician's prescription. This kind of service for nonhandicapped children is difficult to distinguish from the provision of CIC to the handicapped. It would be strange indeed if Congress, in attempting to extend special services to handicapped children, were unwilling to guarantee them services of a kind that are routinely provided to the non-handicapped.

To keep in perspective the obligation to provide services that relate to both the health and educational needs of handicapped students, we note several limitations that should minimize the burden petitioner fears. First, to be entitled to related services, a child must be handicapped so as to require special education. In the absence of a handicap that requires special education, the need for what otherwise might qualify as a related service does not create an obligation under the Act.

Second, only those services necessary to aid a handicapped to benefit from special education must be provided, regardless how easily a school nurse or layperson could furnish them. For example, if a particular medication or treatment may appropriately be administered to a handicapped child other than during the school day, a school is not required to provide nursing services to administer it.

Third, the regulations state that school nursing services must be provided only if they can be performed by a nurse or other qualified person, not if they must be performed by a physician. It bears mentioning that here not even the services of a nurse are required; as is conceded a layperson with minimal training is qualified to provide CIC.

Finally, we note that respondents are not asking petitioner to provide *equipment* that Amber needs for CIC. They seek only the *services* of a qualified person at the school.

We conclude that the provision of CIC to Amber is not subject to exclusion as a "medical service," and we affirm the Court of Appeals' holding that CIC is a "related service" under the Education of the Handicapped Act.

Case law since the *Tatro* decision has indicated that while the EAHCA does not mandate constant nursing care as a related service, other types of health services, such as sectioning, would be required.[21] A decision by the Second Circuit sets out a standard for these decisions, which is likely to provide guidance in future cases.

DETSEL V. BOARD OF EDUCATION

820 F.2d 587 (2d Cir. 1987)
Per Curiam:

Plaintiff Melissa Detsel, a severely handicapped child, . . . appeals from a final judgment . . . dismissing her complaint seeking to compel defendants Board of Education of the Auburn Enlarged City School District, to provide her with nursing services pursuant to the Education of All Handicapped Children Act. . . . We conclude that the complaint was properly dismissed.

We are unpersuaded by plaintiffs' argument that the district court gave insufficient deference to the decision in Department of Education v. Katherine D., 727 F.2d 809 (9th Cir. 1983) . . . which ordered a school board to provide nursing services. Plaintiffs acknowledge that Melissa needs a fulltime person trained to monitor her respiratory status "constantly" and to assist her with her physical needs while she attends school, and that the service must be provided by "at least a licensed practical nurse" and "cannot be adequately provided by a regular school nurse who must care for other children." . . . In contrast, the opinions of the Ninth Circuit and the Hawaii district court make plain that Katherine D. needed care that was intermittent, not constant, and which did not require as much expertise ("It is indisputable that even a lay person could have been trained to provide the services Katherine required.").

OTHER RELATED SERVICES

A number of other potential questions arise under the issue of related services. One area of controversy involves interpreters for deaf children in the classroom. The *Rowley* case involved that issue. While the *Rowley* decision did not require an interpreter, it left the door open for a different result if the factual circumstances were different.[22] It should be noted that there is a substantial rift in philosophy between advocates of the *aural* method (those promoting teaching deaf children to speak and read lips) and advocates of *signing* as the primary mode of communication. This debate makes it even more difficult to resolve questions about the obligation to provide interpreters. It should also be noted that the related services provision does not require that the school purchase a hearing aid for the child; however, the school is to ensure that hearing aids are functioning properly.[23]

SUMMARY

Although the EAHCA specifically defines which related services are to be provided to handicapped children who qualify for special education, this issue remains the subject of debate and litigation. Concerns about transportation, psychological services, and health services are constantly raised. It is no coincidence that these are also generally the most expensive related services. For that reason, schools are more likely to object to providing these services, and parents are most likely to request the school to provide them.

Transportation as a related service raises questions about the actual extent of transportation service to be provided. That is, What is meant by door-to-door service? When must transportation be provided? How much time can be spent in transit? How much supervision and assistance are necessary? Can parents be reimbursed for the costs of providing transportation themselves? The issue of the extent of transportation is not well resolved by the courts. Neither is the question of when transportation must be provided. Issues of time in transit and supervision are usually addressed in state regulations. What is not clear from such requirements, however, is whether the parents may bring an action for damages if injuries occur as a result of noncompliance with state requirements. One issue that is somewhat consistently treated by the courts is reimbursement for parent-provided transportation. If the school had an obligation to provide the transportation and failed to do so, generally parents will be permitted to recover the costs they incur in carrying out the service themselves. An issue likely to be subject to future litigation is whether disciplinary measures can be taken to deny a handicapped student access to transportation. These cases are likely to follow the reasoning that courts begin to apply with regard to disciplinary measures for handicapped students generally.

As a general rule, courts will require the school to provide psychological services when these are necessary for the child to benefit from education. Whether these services will be viewed as medical services—and therefore not within the related services definition, when they are provided by a psychiatrist—is not clearly resolved. It would seem that the issue should not be answered based on who is providing the services but rather on the nature of the service itself. Because psychological counseling can be provided by either a psychologist or a psychiatrist, it is arguable that it should be a covered related service in either case when it is necessary for the child to benefit from education.

Like psychological counseling, health services, which are in the nature of medical services, need not be provided by the school. The only exception is medical service for diagnostic and evaluation purposes. The Supreme Court addressed this issue in 1984 in *Irving Independent School District v. Tatro.* In holding that catheterization is a required related service, the Court focused on the fact that catheterization is a school health service and not a medical service that had to be performed by a licensed physician. One factor mentioned in that case is likely to be relevant to future litigation involving health services. The Court noted that catheterization is not unduly expensive or disruptive so as to be unreasonably burdensome.

QUESTIONS AND PROBLEMS

1. Why should social service agencies acquiesce to the authority of the state educational agency to coordinate and require service delivery?

2. The Hatfield family lives at the end of a "hollow" in rural West Virginia. The lack of paved roads prevents regular school buses from getting closer than two miles from the Hatfield home. Jimmy Hatfield is orthopedically impaired and cannot walk to the bus pickup point. His IEP indicates that transportation is to be provided as a special service. Must the school purchase a special vehicle that can reach the Hatfield home?

3. What provision in the EAHCA or its regulations would relate to ensuring that bus drives do not shout at emotionally disturbed children who are on the bus?

4. Philip is an adolescent with a behavior disorder resulting from alcohol and drug problems. He rides the regular school bus each day and because he lives in a large metropolitan area, bus transportation is essential if he is to attend school. After several incidents

of misbehavior on the bus, he is told that he can no longer ride the school bus. Because his parents are unable to take Philip to school, he has effectively been excluded from school. Is there any remedy under the EAHCA?

5. In *Hurry v. Jones,* the court notes in a footnote that the school argued that the parents should be required to mitigate damages. Is that argument valid? Why or why not?

6. In *Hurry v. Jones,* the school did not address the regulation's validity because of its reliance on the issue of a good-faith standard, a standard that changed during the litigation. Tactically, what should the school's attorney have done?

7. Ricky has a normal IQ, and he has had no major problems until he reached high school and fell in with a bad crowd. His parents are both career-oriented and have had little time for Ricky in recent years. Ricky has turned to drugs and alcohol to the point where he is having serious problems in school, and clearly needs drug counseling. Must the school pay for this service? Suppose Ricky's parents have an annual income of $250,000?

8. In the *Max M.* case, would the school have fared better had it insisted that Max attend the therapy sessions with Frank Brull or that family therapy take place?

9. What if Texas law required that CIC be performed only by a physician? Would the result in *Tatro* have been different?

10. Karen is a six-year-old with a condition requiring that a tracheal tube be permanently placed in her throat. She has no mental handicaps requiring special education. Occasionally the tube becomes clogged, and a relatively simple emergency procedure is required to clear the tube. If it is not performed within a few minutes, Karen could die. The teacher in the regular classroom in which Karen is to be placed has been told of the situation and that training for the procedure will be provided to the teacher before Karen begins class. The teacher is concerned about liability should something go wrong. In addition, she feels that teachers should not be required to perform these procedures. Is the school required to admit Karen? May the teacher refuse to have Karen in the class? If so, what steps should the teacher take to protect herself from liability? What if the teacher's union agreement or contract states that teachers are not required to perform such services?

11. In light of the *Detsel* opinion, at what point is a health service *constant* as opposed to *intermittent*?

NOTES

1. 20 U.S.C. § 1402(17). *See also* L. Rothstein, Rights of Physically Handicapped Persons § 2.19 (1984) and cumulative supplements.
2. 34 C.F.R. § 300.600.
3. 20 U.S.C. § 1412(6).
4. 20 U.S.C. § 1413(a)(13).
5. *See,* for example, California Government Code on Interagency Responsibilities for Related Services, A.B. 3632, Chapter 1747, Statutes of 1984, As Amended by AB 882, Chapter 1274, Statutes 1985.
6. *See,* H.R. Turnbull III, Free Appropriate Public Education: The Law and Children with Disabilities 120–22. (1986).
7. 34 C.F.R. § 300.13(b)(13).

8. *Id.*

9. Cohn v. School Board, 450 So.2d 1238 (Fla. 1984).

10. Clomon v. Monroe City School Board, 490 So.2d 691 (La. Ct. App. 1986).

11. See Chapter 19.

12. In Kennedy v. Board of Education, 337 S.E. 2d 905 (W. Va. 1985), the school had to purchase a special vehicle to reach a child because the regular school bus could not use unpaved mountain roads.

13. TRANSPORTING HANDICAPPED STUDENTS: A RESOURCE MANUAL AND RECOMMENDED GUIDE-LINES FOR SCHOOL TRANSPORTATION AND SPECIAL EDUCATION PERSONNEL (1985), prepared by Dr. Linda F. Bluth, Coordinator Division of Instructional Support Services, Baltimore Public Schools. (Available from the National Association of State Directors of Special Education, 2021 K Street, N.W. #31, Washington, D.C. 20006.

14. Taylor v. Board of Education, 649 F. Supp. 1253 (N.D.N.Y. 1986).

15. 20 U.S.C. § 1401(17); 34 C.F.R. § 300.13(b)(6) & (8) & (11).

16. 34 C.F.R. § 300.13(b)(1)(v) & (b)(12)(v).

17. 34 C.F.R. § 300.13(b)(6).

18. 34 C.F.R. § 300.13(b)(8).

19. 34 C.F.R. § 300.13(b)(2) & (11).

20. *See* L. ROTHSTEIN, RIGHTS OF PHYSICALLY HANDICAPPED PERSONS § 2.19 fn.187 (1984) and cumulative supplement.

21. See RPHP § 2.19 cases cited in cumulative supplement.

22. 102 S.Ct. 3051 n. 28. *See also* Chapter 8.

23. 34 C.F.R. § 300.303.

CHAPTER 10

Residential Placements

Residential placements are contemplated by the EAHCA regulations:

> If placement in a public or private residential program is necessary to provide special education and related services to a handicapped child, the program, including non-medical care and room and board, must be at no cost to the parents of the child.
>
> Comment. This requirement applies to placements which are made by public agencies for educational purposes, and includes placements in State-operated schools for the handicapped, such as a State school for the deaf or blind.[1]

The need for residential placements arises in primarily two different situations. First is the severely or profoundly handicapped[2] individual who needs highly intensive programming, such as a child who is autistic. While some of these children can be educated in a regular day program, for others the educational programming is so integrated into the teaching of self-help skills, etc., and behavior modification programming, that a residential placement may be necessary. Another group of individuals whose parents have increasingly been seeking residential placements are children (especially adolescents) who have serious emotional problems, in some cases relating to drug and alcohol dependency.

These situations can be contrasted with the mildly or moderately mentally retarded student such as a child with Down syndrome, who in years past might well have been placed in an institution or "residential placement." These individuals are now either being deinstitutionalized or are no longer being institutionalized in the first place.

Residential placements are important issues for educational agencies to address because they can be extremely expensive, even as much as $75,000 per year.[3]

That can be a very large portion of a local school district's budget. Several questions must be addressed in looking at residential placements under the EAHCA. These questions include (1) is the program the least restrictive appropriate placement? (2) must all of the costs be borne by the school district? and (3) what if there is no appropriate accredited placement available?[4] Some additional policy questions also might be raised. These include whether the programming, such as toilet training and other self-help skills, is really "education" that must be provided to profoundly handicapped children and whether adolescents with drug-related or emotional problems resulting primarily from family situations should be provided expensive placements at public expense, particularly where the parents are financially well situated.

While some of these questions are addressed by existing law, many are not, and they raise complex social problems.

LEAST RESTRICTIVE
APPROPRIATE PLACEMENT

In the context of the mainstreaming principle, namely the general philosophy of providing education in the least restrictive setting, a placement in a residential program is usually viewed as very restrictive. In spite of its restrictive nature, the placement will be considered appropriate if it is necessary for the child to benefit from education. There is, however, a significant degree of difficulty in separating educational and noneducational needs in this area, and in some cases the placement may result from medical, social, or emotional problems separate from the learning process.

The following case is the earliest major decision on residential placements. It still is cited as a standard on this issue.

KRUELLE V. NEW CASTLE COUNTY SCHOOL DISTRICT

642 F.2d 687 (3d Cir. 1981)
[Paul Kruelle] is profoundly retarded and is also afflicted with cerebral palsy. At age thirteen he has the social skills of a six-month-old child and his I.Q. is well below thirty. [H]e cannot walk, dress himself, or eat unaided. He is not toilet trained. He does not speak, and his receptive communication level is extremely low. In addition to his physical problems, he has had a history of emotional problems which result in choking and self-induced vomiting when experiencing stress. . . .

[T]he district court concluded that Paul required a greater degree of consistency than many other profoundly retarded children. Specifically, it held that the present educational program [a day program] provided by the [school district] was not a free appropriate public education within the meaning of the Act. Then, in a supplemental order, the district court directed the State Education Board to provide Paul with a full-time residential program. . . .

Significantly, all parties concede that Paul needs full-time assistance from the state of Delaware beyond that available in any day school program. It is also uncontroverted that the Education Act specifically provides for residential placement in certain instances. The question, then, is whether the trial judge correctly construed the Education Act as requiring more continuous supervision for Paul than he was receiving under the [day program] in order to meet the standard of a free appropriate education.

Based on our careful review of the record, we cannot find that the district court erred in holding that the six-hour day provided by the [day] program was an inappropriate education given the terms of the Act. The trial judge's conclusion that Paul required more continuous care is supported generally by the logic of [prior case law].

The school district centers its challenge on the proposition that here the residential placement is required only for reasons of medical and domiciliary care, not for educational purposes. But . . . the concept of education is necessarily broad with respect to persons such as Paul. "Where basic self-help and social skills such as toilet training, dressing, feeding and communication are lacking, formal education begins at that point." And Congress was clearly aware of children with needs similar to those of Paul, and was quite conscious of the foundational nature of their education. The Education Act unqualifiedly provides for a free appropriate education for all handicapped children, "regardless of the severity of their handicap," . . .

Analysis must focus, then, on whether full-time placement may be considered necessary for educational purposes, or whether the residential placement is a response to medical, social or emotional problems that are segregable from the learning process. This Court is not the first to attempt to distinguish between residential placement that is a necessary predicate for learning and the provision of services that are unrelated to learning skills. One of the early cases to grapple with this issue, . . . actually collapsed the distinction by declaring the impossibility of separating emotional and educational needs in complex cases. [That] case is almost indistinguishable on the facts from the present case. It also involved the same issue: whether placement was required for emotional problems and was therefore the responsibility of the parents or social service agencies or whether full-time placement was a necessary ingredient for learning. [That] court enjoined the school board from denying a sixteen-year-old multiply-handicapped epileptic free placement in a residential academic program because it found the social, emotional, medical and educational problems to be so intertwined "that realistically it is not possible for the court to perform the Solomon-like task of separating them." However, as later cases demonstrate, the claimed inextricability of medical and educational grounds for certain services does not signal court abdication from decision-making in difficult matters. Rather, the unseverability of such needs is the very basis for holding that the services are an essential prerequisite for learning. . . .

[H]ere, consistency of programming and environment is critical to Paul's ability to learn, for the absence of a structured environment contributed to Paul's choking and vomiting which, in turn, interferes fundamentally with his ability to learn. [U]ltimately any life support system or medical aid can be construed as related to a child's ability to learn. But this would ignore the very limitations the legislation provides. The statutory language requires courts to assess the link between the supportive service or educational placement and the child's learning needs. Thus, . . . inasmuch as the statute comprehends only services "as may be required to assist a handicapped child to benefit from special education," "a life support service would not be a related service if it did not have to be provided during school hours, but instead could be performed at some other time." The relevant question in the present case is whether residential placement is part and parcel of a "specially designed instruction . . . to meet the unique needs of a handicapped child.". . . And we cannot conclude that the district judge misapplied the statutory standard in determining that "because of his combination of physical and mental handicaps, [Paul] requires a greater degree of consistency of programming than many other profoundly retarded children" and that "it would appear that full-time care is necessary in order to allow Paul to learn." Indeed, it would be difficult to conceive of a more apt case than Paul's for which the unique needs of a child required residential placement. . . .

Of course, before ordering residential placement, a court should weigh the mainstreaming policy embodied in the Education Act which encourages placement of the child in the least restrictive environment. The district judge here, however, carefully undertook such a calculation. He noted that in the past attempts to provide in-home care and after-school instruction had been singularly unsuccessful; all had occasioned regression for Paul. Once a court concludes that residential placement is the only realistic option for learning improvement, the question of "least restrictive" environment is also resolved. "Only when alternatives exist must the court reach the issue of which is the least restrictive." If day school cannot provide an appropriate education it is, by definition, not a possible alternative.

The standard for decision making in the *Kruelle* case is only one approach to making decisions about residential placements. While this probably represents the current trend of majority opinion, there are other judicial approaches that have been used. One commentator has categorized and analyzed four major approaches.[5]

First is the "uneducable approach." The premise is that for certain extremely low functioning populations educational residential placements are not required because these children are "uneducable." Although a minority view, it still has recent judicial adherents.

Second is the "separate and balance" approach.

This approach involves an attempt to separate a child's educational needs from other needs including those commonly referred to as medical, custodial, social, emotional, and behavioral. The next step is to determine which of the needs are most responsible for necessitating the residential placement. If it is adjudged that the child's educational needs are not primarily responsible for the placement, the school district is not obligated under the [EAHCA].[6]

One problem with this approach is that "[i]t is often . . . impossible to draw neat lines between the various needs. . . ."[7] Another problem is that the placement may address only the primary needs of the child because many residential programs have a primary emphasis.

The third approach is referred to as the "intertwined needs approach."[8] This approach initially attempts to separate the needs but recognizes that in certain cases, such as multiple and severely handicapped children, this will not be possible. This approach, however, does not really assign responsibility to the school district for the placement.

It is the fourth approach that was used in the *Kruelle* decision, namely an "intertwined needs" approach that added an "educational link" component.[9] The test first determines that the needs are not severable, and then asks if the placement is "necessary for the child to benefit from education." This test seems to be the one adopted in a significant number of rulings. The danger of applying this approach, however, is in a restricted view of what it means to benefit from education. Some courts tend to look only at academic progress.[10] At the other extreme is the question as to whether requiring a residential placement that mandates psychiatric services is a violation of the EAHCA provision exempting educational agencies from providing medical services.[11]

The commentator's suggested approach would be that

> [D]ecision makers should acknowledge that social, behavioral, and other such difficulties, in and of themselves, warrant remedial intervention as educational needs rather than as opposed to or impacting upon educational needs.[12]

A few courts and administrative decision-makers have adopted this approach.[13]

It is important to understand that the EAHCA does not require schools to provide the *best* program, but they must provide an appropriate program. Even though parents may not like the program the school is offering, as long as what the school is offering is appropriate, that is all the educational agency is required to provide. Parents may, of course, choose to place their child in an alternative program at their own cost, as long as those programs meet state requirements.

A residential placement can mean a variety of settings—from the traditional "institution" to a group home or foster care. It could be argued that placement in a more "normal" setting should be made whenever appropriate because of the importance of complying with the mainstreaming mandate. Like any special education placement, a residential placement should be reviewed at least annually. States may set higher standards for an appropriate placement, as the following decision demonstrates.

DAVID D. V. DARTMOUTH SCHOOL COMMITTEE

775 F.2d 411 (1st Cir. 1985)

The only factual matter truly at issue is whether David's special needs are severe enough to warrant a full-time, residential program or whether, instead, David is being educated to the degree legally imposed as a minimum standard by attendance at a special education day program with some supplementary services in the local school district.

David is a seventeen-year-old adolescent with Down's Syndrome, who learns and has skills at the kindergarten level. Although he has been gaining academic skills during the time he has been a student at the Dartmouth school, he has in recent years exhibited a range of seriously inappropriate behavior showing little or no self-control in unstructured or unfamiliar situations. David's parents are concerned that some of the behavior he has been exhibiting will result in his being unable to become a productive adult with a job in a sheltered workshop and denial of his access to and living within the mainstream community. Such has been predicted by special education professionals as the likely outcome, given the range, gravity and frequency of his inappropriate behavior. The parents maintain that the Dartmouth School Committee (Town) has not taught and will not be able to teach David self-control, rendering the IEP the Town proposed for him fatally deficient. The district court agreed with the parents and reversed the decision of the state educational agency. The court expressed the additional concern that David will come into conflict with the law if he persists in a lack of self-control.

The evidence presented at both the administrative hearing and at trial showed that David has repeatedly and unrelentingly engaged in sexual and aggressive behavior directed at persons and animals. He has repeatedly grabbed at students' genitals, lain on the floor of his classroom attempting to look up female students' dresses, tried to touch female staff and students' breasts, and tried to embrace complete strangers. He has repeatedly attempted to engage in sexual play with neighborhood dogs. He has entered neighbors' homes uninvited and has refused to leave. In every valuative setting, David was observed engaging in seriously inappropriate behavior of a sexual and aggressive nature.

The district court carefully reviewed the testimony of special educational professionals who had had experience with David. Except for his classroom teacher, each recounted and characterized David's behavior as extreme even when compared with that of students with similar cognitive functioning. . . .

All parties to the case agreed that social and personal skills including sex education are part of David's special education needs and that his educational program should effectively address these objectives. The conclusion of all four of the independent evaluators was the same: that David needed a comprehensive 24-hour, highly structured special education program that would address his social and behavioral needs in a consistent way by a trained staff throughout his waking hours. These experts, whom the district court credited, uniformly believed that given the frequency and intensity of his unacceptable actions, the Dartmouth IEP would not be sufficient to address David's need for continuous training. They were of the opinion that learning the self-control essential to living in the mainstream community would take from one to two years, and after that, David could and should be returned to the community. . . .

[The court then addressed the issue of whether the state could have more stringent standards than the EAHCA and have these enforced through EAHCA procedures.]

We do not think Congress envisioned having handicapped childrens' plans subject to double legal standards dependent solely upon the aggrieved party's choice of forum. Neither do we discern any intention that the federal Act preempt and reduce all state standards to the federal minimum. Rather, we think Congress contemplated, and due process requires, that a consistent body of law would be applied throughout all stages of the due process hearing system. Congress intertwined federal and state standards into one body of law, and did not leave EHA cases dependent upon whether an appeal is taken to a state or federal court.

The next question is whether a state's overall substantive standard for determining the sufficiency of a handicapped child's IEP is to be treated differently from other substantive requirements mandated by the state. The Congress explicitly defined a free appropriate public education as an education which "meets the standards of the State educational agency" and expressly authorized review of the question whether the education actually provided (or proposed) met those standards. Where a state has chosen to provide by law greater benefits to handicapped children than the federal Act requires, we believe Congress explicitly mandated that the courts—both federal and state—determine whether those state standards have been met. We need not decide at this time the extent of what constitutes "relevant" state substantive law; we hold only that a state's overall standard for evaluating the IEPs of handicapped children is incorporated by the federal Act. . . .

We now turn to the district court's decision, which we have no difficulty affirming in its entirety. The overwhelming evidence showed that a change in David's IEP was warranted. The district judge carefully reviewed the administrative findings, received additional evidence, and discussed David's needs as a unique individual, rather than as an abstract representative of the category of children with Down's syndrome. She found that while David was making progress in some of the academic areas within the Dartmouth School Committee's classroom, his inappropriate sexual behavior continued unabated and posed a serious threat to David's ability to live in the community. The importance of "maximizing [David's] potential for eventual placement in a community-based program or private employment" had already been identified by the state hearing officer as an appropriate objective of the IEP.

The district judge was especially concerned that, although David had performed relatively well in the rather cloistered and familiar environment of the school he had been attending for several years, in less familiar situations, or where relatively unsupervised, he frequently showed little or no self-control in his conduct towards other persons. The court pointed to a variety of situations where this had occurred, including David's being sent home from a camp for handicapped youths, and his rejection from other programs. The court was especially concerned because some of the special education experts who evaluated David regarded his lack of self-control and related behavior grave enough to warrant rejection of him from developmentally disabled service programs, and predicted that he would not be admitted to sheltered workshops for employment or community-based programs. As the court concluded, the evidence uniformly shows that the behavior problem in unstructured or unfamiliar situations has become less controlled over the past two years in the Dartmouth Schools rather than improved.

The district court also found that since Massachusetts law mandated a level of substantive benefits superior to that of the federal Act, the state standard would be utilized as determinative of what was an "appropriate" education for the child. The court noted that the Massachusetts Supreme Judicial Court "in a recent decision interpreted [state education law] as requiring the Department of Education to administer special education programs 'to assure the maximum possible development of a child with special needs.'" Since both the federal and state Acts require that education be provided in the least restrictive environment, the district court stated the issue as "whether Dartmouth's IEP addresses plaintiff's special educational needs so as to assure him maximum possible development in the least restrictive environment consistent with that goal." We think that the court both phrased and answered the question correctly.

COST ISSUES

If residential placement is necessary for the child to benefit from education, then the school is responsible for paying not only the educational expenses but also the cost of room and board and transportation costs to and from the residential placement (although the frequency of such trips is unclear). The school is not required to pay for medical expenses involved in a residential placement.[14]

Because residential placements are expensive, particularly if the placement is in an out-of-state and/or private facility, there is an incentive for educational agencies to develop programs and services that would alleviate the need to have residential placements.

Such programs and services would include extended day programming, support service in the home, respite care, family counseling, and training parents in behavior management and other skills. It is important to recognize that it is stressful to have a severely handicapped child with behavior and emotional problems in the home. For some parents there may be a conflict of interest between the need for relief of family stress and the best interests of the child. Providing support services in the home, in some cases, would help to achieve the mainstreaming goal of least restrictive environment (LRE). Exhausted parents, however, may prefer relief to accomplishing mainstreaming. While these feelings are understandable, the EAHCA does not address the preferences of parents but rather the interest of the child.

Because of the costly nature of these services, disputes often arise over which educational agency (local or state) is responsible for these costs. This is also an issue that is ripe for interagency disputes. These issues are addressed more fully in Chapter 13.

LACK OF AVAILABLE PLACEMENT

A problem that arises in some cases is when there is no appropriate placement available in the state. It is well settled that, if necessary, the student must be sent to an out-of-state placement, which schools are reluctant to do because of cost. The more difficult problem arises when the only appropriate placement is an unaccredited program and the state will not fund placements in unaccredited programs. One possible way around this might be for an accredited school simply to contract for a private program to provide the services under the supervision of the school. As yet, no consistent judicial viewpoint exists on these issues.[15] The following court ruling exemplifies some of the difficult issues.

ANTKOWIAK V. AMBACH

838 F.2d 635 (2d Cir. 1988)

Since the age of ten, Lara Antkowiak has suffered from emotional disturbances and anorexia nervosa. She became anxious and upset about her schoolwork, although she was a bright child with an I.Q. of 143. Lara's schooling was disrupted by three lengthy stays at Strong Memorial Hospital ("Strong" or "the hospital") in Rochester between October 1983 and May 1985, necessitated by her condition. During this period, her ability to function educationally declined to the point that even efforts by the hospital's special education teacher to tutor her individually failed. Lara regularly refused to attend class. Even when she did, Lara stared out the window, was unresponsive, and occasionally became hostile.

In late 1984, Lara's parents, at the hospital staff's suggestion, applied to the Buffalo City School District Committee on the Handicapped ("COH") to arrange for an appropriate special education placement for Lara upon her discharge from Strong. After initially rejecting the application, the COH, upon further investigation, on February 27, 1985 found that Lara could not function in a regular classroom. Accordingly, the COH developed an individualized education plan ("IEP") for Lara and recommended placement for her at a residential educational facility. Rosalie Wiggle, coordinator of the COH, made six applications to in-state residential facilities, but each refused to accept Lara. The COH then applied to the Hedges Treatment Center ("Hedges") of the Devereux Foundation in Malvern, Pennsylvania, which accepted Lara. Therefore, on March 21, Ms. Wiggle applied to the SED [State Education Department] for the Commissioner of Education's approval of a contract with Hedges.

Pursuant to an earlier telephone conversation, Edward McDonald, a regional associate of the SED in the Office for the Education of Children with Handicapping Conditions, notified Ms. Wiggle on April 17, 1985 that Lara's placement at Hedges would not be approved because the SED had imposed a moratorium on new admissions there. The regional associate recommended three approved in-state facilities, and Ms. Wiggle applied to them. Each declined to accept Lara.

While the COH was seeking a placement for Lara, Strong informed her parents that Lara no longer needed acute medical treatment and would be discharged by April 24. In response, on April 23 Dr. Antkowiak brought an action on behalf of his daughter in the Western District of New York, in which he sought an order forcing the SED to place Lara at Hedges and interim injunctive relief preventing Strong from discharging Lara until an alternative placement was found. Thereafter, Dr. Antkowiak visited two residential treatment facilities at the SED's suggestion, but each of them determined that they could not meet Lara's needs. Ms. Wiggle did not seek further recommendations from the regional associate after both the COH and the Antkowiaks had looked into those facilities suggested by the SED, because Dr. Antkowiak placed Lara in Hedges at his own expense on May 15, 1985. Lara received academic instruction in the Devereux Day School at Hedges. After Lara's placement, the complaint was amended, and Strong was dismissed as a defendant in the suit.

Plaintiff moved for a preliminary injunction to require the SED to approve Lara's placement. Chief Judge Curtin found that Lara had not exhausted state administrative remedies first as the EHA requires, since the SED had made no formal adjudication of Lara's case in rejecting the COH's recommendation. He ordered plaintiff to "immediately resume the [s]tate administrative process."

The Antkowiaks thus sought a hearing through the board of education as required by law. The school district and Lara's parents stipulated that Lara was emotionally disturbed and needed placement at Hedges. The hearing officer found Lara in need of a residential placement, agreed with the COH's recommendation and, on December 26, 1985, ordered Lara's placement at Hedges. On January 24, 1986, the SED advised the school district that the placement could not be approved. Although Hedges was by then once again on the SED's approved list, it was approved only for children at least 14 years old; Lara was only 12. Further, the Devereaux Day School at Hedges had never been approved by, or even sought approval from, the SED. [Procedural information omitted.]

Following a bench trial, Chief Judge Curtin found that no other placement was identified as appropriate for Lara despite the court's repeated requests for a recommendation from the SED. The court also found that Hedges "is a suitable placement for Lara and meets most, if not all, of her needs." The court dismissed the importance of Hedges' unapproved status. Chief Judge Curtin noted that Lara, who had turned 14 one week before the decision, was now within the SED's approved age range for Hedges, and that there was "no indication that Lara is not receiving all the benefits and rights at Hedges that she would receive at" an in-state school. The related services that Hedges provided to Lara were found "necessary to enable her to derive any benefit from" the instruction she was receiving. The court therefore ordered the state to effect immediately the Hedges placement at state expense, and, finding that Congress implicitly abrogated the states' eleventh amendment immunity in enacting the EHA, ordered the state to retroactively reimburse Lara's tuition at Hedges during the period of her private placement.

Lara left Hedges in June 1987. Her parents enrolled her in a private school in Buffalo that was not a part of her original, and only, IEP from the COH.

The district court found that the Commissioner "refused to provide Lara with the free, appropriate education to which she is entitled under the EHA" because the SED had declined to place Lara at Hedges, despite the determinations of COH and the hearing officer, but had not come forward with an appropriate alternative placement. The court further found that Hedges was "a suitable placement for Lara and satisfies the requirements of her IEP," noting that the Commissioner did not dispute this. Accordingly, Chief Judge Curtin ordered the Commissioner to effect Lara's placement. We conclude, however, that the district court had no authority to do so in this case.

The EHA requires that handicapped children in private placements have the same right as those handicapped students placed in facilities of the state. "In all such instances" where handicapped children are provided special education and related services at private facilities, the state determines whether the facility meets the same standards "that apply to [s]tate and local educational agencies." Thus, the EHA "expressly incorporates [s]tate educational standards" and "the [s]tate has an obligation to insure that the school meets application [s]tate educational standards" when a private placement is made under the EHA. The requirement that the Commissioner approve all contracts between local school boards and private schools for the placement of handicapped children is such a standard. Neither a local school board nor the SED can approve a placement at a private school consistent with the EHA unless the Commissioner specifically approves of a facility prior to placement, in accordance with section 4402(2)(b)(2).

The SED's Office for the Education of Children with Handicapping Conditions, through the Division of Program Monitoring, maintains an "approved list" of private and out-of-state schools eligible to contract for the education of handicapped students from New York. Out-of-state schools must seek approval by application to the SED, and the division monitors compliance by out-of-state schools with New York's standards and approves placements at such schools recommended at the local level.

At trial, Hanna Flegenheimer, director of the Program Monitoring Division, testified that the SED closed new admissions to the Hedges in 1985 because (1) Hedges was not licensed in its home state as the SED required for approval, (2) "seclusion rooms" were purportedly used there, and (3) the SED was concerned about a school policy that would allow students at least 14 years old to sign themselves out of treatment. Hedges thus was not available as a placement when the SED refused to approve the Buffalo COH's contract with the facility. Nor was Hedges available when the hearing officer ordered Lara's placement there in December 1985.

Neither the SED nor the Buffalo School Board could place and fund Lara in an unapproved private school "without violating the EHA's requirement that handicapped children be educated at public expense only in those private schools that meet [s]tate educational standards." The hearing officer had no jurisdiction to compel either the school or the state to violate federal law, and thus her decision was void to the extent that it ordered Lara's placement at Hedges without the Commissioner's approval. Likewise, the district court could not order Lara's placement at Hedges without forcing the SED to violate the EHA. Although the SED reopened Hedges for new admissions of students ages 14–21 in January 1986, Lara was then only 12. Even though Lara turned 14 a week before the court's final decision in this case, the court still could not properly order Lara's placement at Hedges without the Commissioner's approval of the contract. Moreover, the SED has never approved the Devereux Day School, which Lara attended for her academic program. In fact, Hedges' campus unit administrator testified at trial that the Day School had never sought SED approval "because it served primarily Pennsylvania day students and few out-of-state students."

We observe that this case has been complicated significantly by the unusual procedural posture in which it unfolded prior to appeal. The Antkowiaks' premature resort to the federal forum without exhausting their administrative remedies, the hearing officer's decision to order relief that was in part beyond her jurisdiction to afford, and the Commissioner's use of a compulsory review procedure where the hearing officer's decision had not been appealed by the parties, have contributed to the absence of a proper resolution of Lara's case. In enacting the EHA, Congress expressly sought to place on the parents and the local educational agency "the primary responsibility for developing," through their cooperative efforts, "a plan to accommodate the needs of each individual handicapped child." Accordingly, the Antkowiaks and the Buffalo City School District were obliged to continue seeking an appropriate placement for Lara in cooperation with the regional office of the SED. However, because the emphasis in this case has been upon litigation against the state, rather than upon the cooperation among the parents, school board and SED envisioned by the Act, Lara remained in an unapproved placement for which her parents cannot obtain the sanction of the EHA.

Another issue involving placement concerns state-imposed caps on the amount of reimbursement available for residential placements. In one state, this policy was struck down through legislation. If a particular program is the only appropriate one available and it is more expensive than the state reimbursement policy will allow, to prohibit payment amounts to noncompliance with the EAHCA mandate of providing appropriate education at no cost.[16]

One final problem that arises in residential placements is what happens if the parents are dissatisfied with the public school placement, challenge the school's placement through due process procedures, and place their child in a residential placement in the interim. The problem arises as to who is responsible for paying the costs of the placement pending the resolution of the question. Because due process procedures can take months and even years if the administrative decisions are challenged in court, this is a very important issue. The resolution of that problem is discussed in Chapter 17.

SUMMARY

A residential placement is inherently a restrictive placement. The student is separated from family and from nonhandicapped peers. In extreme situations, however, placement may be necessary for the needs of the student. Residential placements necessary for the child to benefit from education must be paid for by the educational agency. The public cost is to include room and board as well as the educational component of the placement. Only medical expenses need not be paid by the educational agency. Because of the high cost of such placements, schools are reluctant to approve them. As a result, this issue is frequently subject to resolution by the courts, which have taken a variety of approaches to determining when the residential placement is necessary. While a single judicial test has yet to be consistently applied, there is a general recognition of the fact that educational needs and other needs are often inextricably intertwined, and where such needs are not severable, the placement will be made if this is what is necessary for the child to benefit from education.

Because of the high cost of such placements, courts are likely to begin developing the application of cost as a factor in educational decision making in cases of this sort.

There is a developing body of law, which as yet has few clear guidelines, relating to the issue of what responsibilities fall on the educational agency when the only appropriate placement is a residential placement and there is no available appropriate placement that the state will approve. Future litigation can be expected to address these issues. It is unlikely, however, that a clear determination of the requirements to be applied in these cases will occur very quickly.

QUESTIONS AND PROBLEMS

1. Eddie is a seriously emotionally disturbed child, age 9, with some autistic-type behaviors. In order for Eddie to benefit from education he needs a great deal of behavior modification, and this must be provided on a 24-hour basis to avoid daily regression. Understandably, the parents, who both work in blue-collar jobs, have been unable to control Eddie's behavior, and they are concerned about the fact that their other son, Wally, age 5, is not given a sufficient amount of attention. They would like to have Eddie placed in a residential program, at a cost of $35,000 annually. Does the school have to pay for this? *Should* the school have to pay for this? What if the parents are not willing to carry out school-provided parent training? Is foster care appropriate?

2. Sandra is fifteen. Until recently she had no apparent serious problems. Last year, however, her parents got divorced, she broke up with her boyfriend, and her grades began to suffer. Sandra lives with her father, who is an engineer at a petroleum company and

makes $60,000 per year. She has had episodes of running away and suicide "attempts." Her father would like to have her placed in a private residential program whose cost is $50,000 annually. What kind of facts must be developed in order for the school to be required to pay for such a placement?

3. What if the counseling needed for a child to benefit from education is provided in the residential setting by a psychiatrist? Is this a "medical expense" to be paid by the parents?

4. Educational programming for nonhandicapped children could potentially be adversely affected if scarce resources have to be used for expensive residential placements. Could such a situation be the basis for a reverse discrimination lawsuit by parents of the nonhandicapped children? Could cost ever be a legitimate defense?

5. The court in *Antkowiak* was critical of the parents' failure to exhaust administrative remedies. Given the fact that the factual issues were not in dispute, and that the educational agency had proposed no appropriate placement, what purpose would be served by seeking review at the state level?

6. What relief is available to parents, such as the Antkowiaks, who are not offered any appropriate placement? Was the Hedges school an "inappropriate" placement? If not, then why was it not an approved school?

NOTES

1. 34 C.F.R. § 300.302. *See also* 20 U.S.C. § 1412(2)(B); 1413(a)(4)(B).
2. L. Rothstein, *Educational Rights of Severely and Profoundly Handicapped Children,* 61 Neb. L. Rev. 586 (1982).
3. In Clevenger v. Oak Ridge School Board, 744 F.2d 514 (6th Cir. 1984), the court held that cost considerations could not be a factor in placing a seriously emotionally disturbed child in an $88,000/year residential placement.
4. *See* L. Rothstein, Rights of Physically Handicapped Persons §§ 2.19 & 2.20 (1984) and cumulative supplements.
5. Cichon, *Educability and Education: Filling the Cracks in Service Provision Responsibility Under the Education for All Handicapped Children Act of 1975,* 48 Ohio St. L.J. 1089, 1114–28 (1987).
6. *Id.* at 1116.
7. *Id.* at 1117.
8. *Id.* at 1119–21.
9. *Id.* at 1121.
10. *Id.* at 1123.
11. *Id.* at 1123, citing Clevenger v. Oak Ridge School Board, 744 F. 2d 514 (6th Cir. 1984).
12. Cichon, *supra* note 5, at 1126.
13. *Id.* at 1127, citing David D. v. Dartmouth School Committee, 615 F. Supp. 639 (D. Mass. 1984), *aff'd,* 775 F.2d 411 (4th Cir. 1985).
14. 34 C.F.R. § 300.302.
15. *See* RPHP § 2.20, cases cited at note 196.
16. *See* RPHP § 2.20, note 217, cumulative supplement.

CHAPTER 11

Placements in Private Day Schools

Chapter 10 addressed issues that occur when a residential placement is made because of a student's emotional or health needs. As was noted, some of those placements will be in private schools because there is not an appropriate public school placement available. The chapter noted the problems that arise in separating educational from noneducational needs, in placing a child in a nonaccredited private school, and in financing the cost of expensive placements when there is a per-pupil cap on residential placements.

This chapter addresses situations where parents have chosen to place their child in a private day school. The major issue is how the educational agency can provide special education and related services to handicapped students not within the public school system and not placed by the public school system. The chapter focuses on providing these services when the parents have chosen to make a private school placement for personal reasons, but where the children need special education and related services.[1] Particular attention is paid to problems that arise when a child is being educated in a parochial school.

Whether the parents place the child in a private school or the educational agency does so, the EAHCA requires that the public educational agency make special education and related services available to the child.[2] A number of services could fall into the category of special education and related services. For most services, the issue is not whether to provide the services but the location for providing them.

NONPAROCHIAL SCHOOLS

Special education and related services can be provided in nonparochial private day schools by a number of means. In a school with a small population of handicapped students, the service might be provided by an itinerant teacher. In other situations, a public school teacher or therapist may remain at the same private school site at all times. Services may also be provided by paying a private school employee for the costs of providing the services.

Some state constitutions prohibit public funds from being used to support private purposes. Several judicial decisions have found certain types of support to private schools to fall within the ban on supporting private purposes[3] It may be necessary in some states, therefore, to require that the services of a public school employee, be provided outside of regular working hours. In states with stringent requirements in this regard, it may be impermissible for the state to provide equipment or physical plant renovations at the private school.

While one solution is to allow services at the public school site, this can create significant logistical and administrative problems in moving children back and forth from public site to private site. This has the additional adverse result of requiring children to spend time in transit rather than in learning.

PAROCHIAL SCHOOLS

Even greater problems arise in trying to provide special education and related services to students in parochial schools.[4] This is because of constitutional concerns over separation of church and state.

The First Amendment and Educational Services

The first amendment to the United States Constitution provides that "Congress shall make no law respecting the establishment of religion, or prohibiting the free exercise thereof. . . ." This means that federal grant statutes, such as the EAHCA, must not support the establishment of religion. In the area of educational services in general, the Supreme Court has held that not all public educational services provided to parochial schools will be considered to establish religion. The test to determine what support is permissible is found in the case of *Lemon v. Kurtzman*.[5] The Supreme Court permits government services that (1) have a secular purpose, (2) have a primary effect of neither advancing nor inhibiting religion, and (3) do not involve the state in excessive entanglement with religion. In the *Lemon* case, the Supreme Court held that salary supplements for teachers of nonreligious subjects in parochial schools would not be permitted.

The specifics of which types of services are considered to be permissible and how these services may or may not be provided have been the subject of a number of judicial decisions. Many issues are not well resolved. There does seem to be a general rule that assistance that is indirect, rather than direct, is more likely to be permitted.[6] It is not always easy, however, to determine which aid is direct and which is indirect.

Direct Government Aid

It is apparently permissible for the federal government to provide direct government assistance through grants of federal property (such as land) to parochial institutions. The validity of state property grants to a religious institution depends on state law. State *grants* of property are distinguished from *sale* of state property, which is apparently usually permissible.[7]

Direct financial support, such as reimbursement for instructional services, is clearly impermissible under the *Lemon* case, which dealt directly with that issue. The concern in that case was the problem of entanglement that the Court thought would occur in monitoring school employees in sectarian schools.[8]

In 1985, the Supreme Court, in *Aguilar v. Felton*[9] provided guidance as to the application of these standards to special education services. In a decision in which only five Justices joined, the Court found that it was unconstitutional to provide Chapter 1 programs (federal programs for educationally deprived children from low income families) in New York parochial schools. These programs involved remedial instruction and guidance services similar to many special educational services. The Court was concerned about the fact that because the service was "provided in the form of teachers, ongoing inspection [would be] required to ensure the absence of a religious message. . . . [T]he scope and duration of [the] program would require a permanent and pervasive State presence in the sectarian schools receiving aid."[10] The Court further noted that the administrative cooperation required to maintain the program would result in excessive entanglement.

> Administrative personnel of the public and parochial school systems must work together in resolving matters related to schedules, classroom assignments, problems that arise in the implementation of the program, requests for additional services, and the dissemination of information regarding the program. Furthermore, the program necessitates "frequent contacts between the regular and the remedial teachers (or other professionals) in which each side reports on individual students needs, problems encountered, and results achieved."[11]

The Court did, however, permit provision of these services at "a neutral site off the premises of the religious school."[12] It seems that the standard in this type of direct aid depends not so much on *what* is provided, but *where* it is provided.[13]

One type of direct benefit that is likely to occur with respect to handicapped students is that of diagnostic, counseling, and therapy services. The Supreme Court has had difficulty in deciding how to treat these services, but it appears that there is a distinction between therapy, guidance, and counseling, which are viewed as direct services and which must not be provided at the parochial school site, and diagnostic services, which may be provided at the school or reimbursed if provided at the religious school.[14]

Indirect Government Aid

In addition to diagnostic services, which are viewed as indirect, several other types of services are apparently permissible for public schools to provide at the parochial school site or to reimburse. These services include state-mandated testing (such as sweep-screening under the EAHCA),[15] textbooks, instructional materials, supplies and equipment,[16] and transportation.[17]

Even though it is probably permissible under the federal Constitution to provide these services, many states view such assistance as impermissible. And, even though the federal Constitution permits certain services, and a particular state may permit the provision of certain services, that does not mean that the service *must* be provided in all cases.

Practical Problems in Implementation

As was noted previously, the *Lemon* case makes the provision of instruction and other direct services impermissible at the parochial school site. As a result, many special education services will have to be provided in the regular public school classroom. The child must in these situations spend time traveling back and forth between the parochial school and the public school. The following case excerpt demonstrates the problems that can occur by requiring that the education be provided at a site other than the parochial school.

BOARD OF EDUCATION V. WIEDER

531 N.Y. Supp. 2d 889 (Ct. App. 1988)
This appeal centers on a struggle between the Board of Education of the Monroe-Woodbury Central School District, and parents and handicapped children of Kiryas Joel, an incorporated village of Satmarer Hasidim located within the school district. No one disputes that State and Federal law require the Board of Education to make special services available to these handicapped children. The conflict arises over where the services are to be offered—whether in the public schools, or in the religiously affiliated private schools of Kiryas Joel, or elsewhere. . . .

As the pleadings are framed, plaintiff Board of Education demands judgment declaring that the law compels it to furnish special education and related services of an instructional, remedial and therapeutic nature only in regular public school classes and programs, and declaring that it is without authority to provide such services separately. At the other extreme, defendants' counterclaim demands a declaration that the Board must furnish these services in classes conducted on the premises of the school the children attend for their normal educational instruction.

Approximately 150 Satmarer children are the true subjects of this controversy, with handicaps such as mental retardation, deafness, speech and language impairments, emotional disorders, learning disabilities, Down's syndrome, spina bifida and cerebral palsy.

Kiryas Joel is a community of Hasidic Jews. Apart from separation from the outside community, separation of the sexes is observed within the village. Yiddish is the principal language of Kiryas Joel; television, radio and English language publications are not in general use. The dress and appearance of the Hasidim are distinctive—the boys, for example, wear long side curls, head coverings and special garments, and both males and females follow a prescribed dress code. Education is also different: Satmarer children generally do not attend public schools, but attend their own religiously affiliated schools within Kiryas Joel. Boys are enrolled in the United Talmudic Academy (UTA) and girls in Bais Rochel, a UTA affiliate. With an apparent over-all goal that children should continue to live by the religious standards of their parents, "Satmarer want their school to serve primarily as a bastion against undesirable acculturation, as a training ground for Torah knowledge in the case of boys, and, in the case of girls, as a place to gather knowledge they will need as adult women.". . .

Plaintiff's reading of Education law § 3602-c [state law] is overbroad and must be rejected. That section does not mandate that a board can provide special services to private school handicapped children only in regular classes and programs of the public schools, and not elsewhere.

Upon request of a parent, guardian or custodian of a handicapped student, boards of education of all school districts must offer services to pupils who are residents of the State and who attend nonpublic schools in their district. "Services" include "education for students with handicapping conditions, and counseling, psychological and social work services related to such instruction provided during the regular school year for pupils enrolled in a nonpublic school located in a school district, provided that such instruction is given to pupils enrolled in the public schools of such district." Subdivision (9) provides: "Pupils enrolled in nonpublic schools for whom services are provided pursuant to the provisions of this section shall receive such services in regular classes of the public school and shall not be provided such services separately from pupils regularly attending public schools.". . .

While insisting in its complaint that section 3602-c(9) must be read literally as the exclusive vehicle for providing special services to handicapped private school students, plaintiff now embraces the Appellate Division's modification of that proposition, urging that, to the maximum extent possible—and consistent with other laws mandating services at specific places, and with individual exceptions for hardship—section 3602-c compels, and authorizes, school districts to offer programs and services to private school handicapped students only in regular public school classes and programs, and not elsewhere. We disagree.

We conclude that section 3602-c authorizes services to private school handicapped children and affords them an option of dual enrollment in public schools, so that they may enjoy equal access to the full array of specialized public school programs; if they become part-time public school students, for the purpose of receiving the special services, the statute directs that they be integrated with other public school students, not isolated from them. The statute does not limit the right and responsibility of educational authorities in the first instance to make placements appropriate to the educational needs of each child, whether the child attends public or private school. Such placements may well be in regular public school classes and programs, in the interests of mainstreaming or otherwise, but that is not a matter of statutory compulsion under section 3602-c. . . .

The view that the statute affords an added double-enrollment option—rather than dictating the sole or presumptive means for affording services—is in harmony with the scheme of State and Federal regulation pertaining to services for handicapped school children.

The [EAHCA] regulations of the United States Department of Education specify, in particular, that while the public agency is not required to pay for a child's private school education, it is to make services available to the nonpublic school children; each local education agency is to "provide special education and related services designed to meet the needs of private school handicapped children residing in the jurisdiction of the agency." (34 CFR 300.452.)

To implement the goals declared by Federal law, New York has adopted an extensive statutory and regulatory scheme. Several pertinent points may be distilled from these laws. First, the paramount principle that guides State law is concern for a handicapped child's educational needs, whether in public or private school. All handicapped children residing within a school district are to be afforded suitable educational opportunities according to their individual needs, in a manner that enables them to participate in regular education services when appropriate. Second, the statutes and regulations vest in State educational authorities broad responsibility for tailoring programs to a child's individual needs in the least restrictive environment, considering the appropriateness of the resources of the regular education program. Third, to this end, the authorities have a wide choice of programs and services, including home instruction, itinerant teachers and counseling and psychological services. The Education Law permits contracts with private facilities, even out-of-State facilities, where such services are deemed necessary for a child's appropriate education. From the scope of services and programs, it is plain that not all services can even be furnished in "regular classes of the public school."

While the Appellate Division's reading of the Education Law § 3602-c would recognize limited exceptions from the general mandate for public school services to avoid inconsistency and individual hardship, we believe the better reading is that this provision in the first instance imposes no such mandate but leaves educational authorities to fashion an appropriate program for each child within statutory guidelines and constitutional constraints.

We therefore conclude that plaintiff's contention should be rejected: it is neither compelled to make services available to private school handicapped children only in regular public school classes and programs, nor without authority to provide otherwise.

That plaintiff may be free of the claimed restraint of Education Law § 3602-c(9) does not, however, establish defendants' contention that the services must be provided within their own schools, or even at a neutral site.

Defendants' contention that State and Federal statutes mandate provision of services to nonpublic school children on the premises of the schools they normally attend requires little discussion. Without reaching any constitutional implications of the contention, there is no such statutory requirement. Indeed, as the foregoing discussion indicates, such a general compulsion would be inconsistent with the regulatory scheme, which contemplates that the placement of children in programs will be guided generally by their individual educational needs in the least restrictive environment. This statutory claim advanced by defendants is therefore without merit.

Similarly, on this record defendants have been denied no constitutional right by the children's public school placements.

Considerable doubt has been voiced . . . , that the alternate setting contemplated by defendants could even be a genuinely neutral, public site, free of identification with defendants' beliefs. The point is made that the fear and trauma of leaving the language, life-style and environment of Kiryas Joel and mixing with others—defendants' stated grounds for refusing to attend the public schools—of necessity mean that any acceptable alternate site designated to address those concerns could never be truly neutral. We see an even more fundamental flaw in defendants' position: on this record, defendants' statutory entitlement to special services does not carry with it a constitutional right to dictate where they must be offered.

Defendants' constitutional "right" to services in their own schools or at a neutral site, as asserted in this court, rests on their contention that the Board's public school placements interfere with the free exercise of their sincere religious beliefs guaranteed by the State and Federal Constitutions (N.Y. Const., art. I, § 3; U.S. Const. 1st Amend.), that compelling the children to attend regular public school classes and programs forces them to choose between following the precepts of their religion and foregoing benefits on the one hand, and accepting benefits while violating their religious beliefs on the other.

But that is not the claim defendants asserted and supported below. Defendants in their submissions to the trial court insisted that, as a class, they should be exempted from public school placements only for nonreligious reasons—most particularly because of the emotional impact on the children of traveling out of Kiryas Joel. They made no showing that any sincere religious beliefs were threatened by requiring limited public school attendance, only for special services. Thus, there is no basis here for the constitutional right now asserted by defendants and found by the trial court. Whether a school board might, as a matter of choice, offer certain services to defendant children at a neutral site (as plaintiff allegedly is doing for services to other children) without running afoul of the Establishment Clause is a question not presented by this case, because no such proposal is before us.

We therefore conclude that the Appellate Division correctly denied defendants' motion for summary judgment and dismissed their counterclaim: they have demonstrated no right to the relief they request.

While the facts in this case are somewhat unusual, they demonstrate the tension between protecting religious freedom and providing education.

PROCEDURAL SAFEGUARDS FOR PRIVATE SCHOOL PLACEMENTS

The EAHCA regulations provide that whether the child is placed by the public agency or by the parents, to the extent that special education is being provided (or should be provided) by the public agency, the due process procedures of the EAHCA are available to ensure that the program is appropriate and to decide financial questions.[18]

The individualized educational program is to be developed with participation of personnel from the private school.[19] It is the responsibility of the public agency to initiate and conduct the meetings to provide special education to children placed in nonpublic school settings.[20] It is also the responsibility of the public agency to identify handicapped children in the private schools.[21]

SUMMARY

The fact that a child's parents have chosen to place the child in a private school—either nonparochial or parochial—does not necessarily relieve the public educational agency from an obligation to provide special education or related services. As a general rule, if the parents request such services from the public educational agency, the agency must make these services available on the same basis and with the same procedural protections as for children who attend the public school regularly.

Making special education available to children who are not physically in attendance at the public school building can present administrative and logistical problems. Such problems are not a defense, however, to the general obligation to provide such services.

A child placed in a parochial school presents additional difficulties. Because of the first amendment requirements relating to separation of church and state, the Supreme Court prohibits any direct aid to parochial schools. This seems to prevent the provision of special education services at the parochial school site. Where the public school might be able to provide speech therapy at a nonparochial school by sending an itinerant teacher to the private school site, this is impermissible if the school is church related. The result is that services for such children must be provided by transporting the children to the public school site or at least to some neutral setting, such as a mobile unit. What remains unresolved is what is required in extreme cases where the religion itself includes principles of nonintegration with those outside the religion. It is unclear whether the school must make these services available at a neutral site.

QUESTIONS AND PROBLEMS

1. If the EAHCA requires that services must be made available to a child placed in a private school, and a state has a constitutional provision interpreted to prevent any aid to private enterprises, which provision takes precedence?

2. In the *Aguilar* case, the Court noted with concern that monitoring the Chapter 1 programs at the school site would be impermissible because of the entanglement through frequent contracts between regular and remedial professionals. This was the basis of requiring that the education program for the disadvantaged be provided at a neutral site rather than the parochial school site. In fact, in many instances it is essential that the special educator or provider of related services keep an ongoing dialogue with the regular classroom teacher to identify problems. Will the fact that special education must be provided at a neutral site eliminate the possibility of frequent contact?

3. The *Aguilar* decision requires that special education and related services be made available at a neutral site. This will necessitate additional transportation to the neutral site. Who is to pay for this: the public school program or the private parochial school? Does the EAHCA address this?

4. If special education programming is to be given at a neutral site or public school for pa-

rochial school students, additional time in transit will frequently become a necessity. How can this be balanced if it is determined that for a child's program to be "appropriate" the child should not spend an undue amount of time in transit?

5. Do parents who place their children in parochial schools simply forego some of their children's right to an "appropriate" education?

6. Certain special education services need to be made available in the regular classroom. How can this be accomplished when a child is attending a parochial school? Can mainstreaming be accomplished in a case where a parochial student must be provided programming at a site different from the one that the child regularly attends?

NOTES

1. *See* L. ROTHSTEIN, RIGHT OF PHYSICALLY HANDICAPPED PERSONS § 2.20 (1984) and cumulative supplements.
2. 34 C.F.R. §§ 300.403(a) & 300.450–.452.
3. *See* W. VALENTE, EDUCATION LAW: PUBLIC and PRIVATE § 21.123 (1985).
4. *Id.* at §§ 21.127–.139.
5. 403 U.S. 602 (1971), *rehearing denied,* 404 U.S. 876 (1971).
6. VALENTE, *supra* note 3, at § 21.124.
7. *Id.* at § 21.125–.126.
8. *Id.* at § 21.127.
9. 473 U.S. 402 (1985).
10. *Id.* at 412–13.
11. *Id.* at 413.
12. *Id.* at 421 (O'Connor, dissent). *See also* VALENTE, § 21.12.
13. VALENTE. § 21.128.
14. Wolman v. Walter, 433 U.S. 229 (1977). *See also* VALENTE, *supra* note 3, at § 21.136.
15. Wolman v. Walter, 433 U.S. 229 (1977). *See* VALENTE § 21.129.
16. *Id.* Wolman, VALENTE § 21.135.
17. Wolman, VALENTE § 21.134.
18. 34 C.F.R. § 300.400–.452.
19. *Id.* at § 300.347.
20. *Id.* at § 300.348.
21. *Id.* at § 300.128.

CHAPTER 12

Special Problems
of Secondary Students

Most of the case law on special education has focused on elementary-age children. This is usually the age at which the initial placement decision and educational planning occurs. There are, however, several issues that have unique impact on students at the secondary-school level.

The uniqueness occurs as a result of two major factors. First, students at the secondary-school level have unique behavior and social problems that can affect their physical and emotional development. Students who may have had no handicapping condition prior to adolescence may develop emotional or behavior and/or substance abuse problems as a result of social pressures, lack of self-esteem, or family problems. The severity of these problems may require the student to have counseling or even residential placement in order to benefit from education. These problems may even result in incarceration as a result of criminal conduct.

The second unique factor is that the secondary-school level is the end of the line for receiving services under the EAHCA. Once the student graduates from high school, the EAHCA no longer requires that the individual receive special education and related services. The student may be eligible for vocational rehabilitation services or may be protected from discrimination by Section 504 of the Rehabilitation Act or state laws. The entitlement to a special education program and due process protections under the EAHCA, however, usually ends at graduation. Thus, the impending termination of services raises two major issues. One is what event—graduation, reaching a certain age, etc.—terminates the obligation. Another is how to ensure that public school programs provide appropriate vocational education and other programs to facilitate the transition to the world of adulthood, employment, and independence.

The following sections focus on these issues. The issue of services for students with emotional or behavioral problems requiring counseling or residential placement has been discussed in previous chapters.[1]

GRADUATION REQUIREMENTS

The issue of graduation requirements involves two different questions of obligation by educational agencies. The first is whether diploma requirements may be imposed on handicapped students. The second is whether there is any obligation to a handicapped student once the diploma has been awarded.

Diploma Requirements

In Chapter 6 it was noted in discussing testing and evaluation of handicapped students that it is legally valid to require minimum competency tests of all students, including handicapped students.[2] The lead case on this issue is *Debra P. v. Turlington,*[3] in which the court recognized the validity of such exams, but held that in that case there was inadequate notice of the requirements. That case did not involve handicapped students. The following opinion follows the *Debra P.* analysis, but directly involves handicapped students.

BROOKHART V. ILLINOIS STATE BOARD OF EDUCATION

697 F.2d 179 (7th Cir. 1983)

Plaintiffs are fourteen handicapped elementary and secondary students who are challenging a Peoria School District (School District) requirement that they pass a "Minimal Competency Test" (M.C.T.) in order to receive a high school diploma.

Plaintiffs manifested a broad spectrum of handicapping conditions. One student was physically handicapped, one was multiply handicapped, and four were educably mentally handicapped. The other eight were learning disabled.

In the spring of 1978, the School District decided to require all students eligible for graduation of 1980 to pass an M.C.T. as a prerequisite to receipt of a diploma. The test is given each semester. It contains three parts—reading, language arts, and mathematics—and a student must score 70% on each part in order to receive a diploma. If a student fails any particular part, he is eligible to retake that part until he passes or becomes 21 years of age. . . .

Students who do not pass, but otherwise qualify for graduation, receive a Certificate of Program Completion at graduation time, and may continue to take the M.C.T. until age 21.

After the M.C.T. policy was adopted in 1978, the School District undertook to notify students of the additional requirement through distribution of circulars in the schools, individual mailings to some parents, and repeated announcements in the mass media. . . .

Plaintiffs claim that the M.C.T. as applied to handicapped students violates federal and state statutes, as well as the due process and equal protection clauses of the Fourteenth Amendment. We note at the outset that in analyzing these claims deference is due the School District's educational and curricular decisions. The School District's desire to ensure the value of its diploma by requiring graduating students to attain minimal skills is admirable, and the courts will interfere with educational policy decisions only when necessary to protect individual statutory or constitutional rights. . . .

[T]he EHA does not require "specific results," but rather only mandates access to specialized and individualized educational services for handicapped children. Denial of diplomas to handicapped children who have been receiving the special education and related services required by the Act, but are unable to achieve the educational level necessary to pass the M.C.T., is not a denial of a "free appropriate public education."

Plaintiffs further contend that the imposition of the M.C.T. violates the EHA and corresponding regulation mandating that "no single procedure shall be the sole criterion for determining an appropriate educational program for a child."

Yet plaintiffs admit that graduation requirements in Peoria are threefold: earning seventeen credits, completing State requirements such as a constitution test and a consumer education course, and passing the M.C.T. In the face of this admission, passing the M.C.T. is clearly not the sole criterion for graduation.

1. Rehabilitation Act of 1973

Plaintiffs also argue that application of the M.C.T. requirement constitutes unlawful discrimination under Section 504 of the Rehabilitation Act of 1973 (RHA), providing:

> No otherwise qualified handicapped individual in the United States . . .
> shall, solely by reason of his handicap, be excluded from the participation
> in, be denied the benefits of, or be subjected to discrimination under any
> program or activity receiving Federal financial assistance. . . .

Supreme Court [has] held that an "otherwise qualified" individual entitled to the protection of Section 504 is "one who is able to meet all of a program's requirements in spite of his handicap.". . .

The statute does not require "an educational institution to lower or to effect substantial modification of standards to accommodate a handicapped person."

Plaintiffs in this case have no grounds on which to argue that the contents of the M.C.T. are discriminatory solely because handicapped students who are incapable of attaining a level of minimal competency will fail the test. Altering the content of the M.C.T. to accommodate an individual's inability to learn the tested material because of his handicap would be a "substantial modification," as well as a "perversion" of the diploma requirement. A student who is unable to learn because of his handicap is surely not an individual who is qualified in spite of his handicap. Thus denial of a diploma because of inability to pass the M.C.T. is not discrimination under the RHA.

However, an otherwise qualified student who is unable to disclose the degree of learning he actually possesses because of the test format or environment would be the object of discrimination solely on the basis of his handicap. It is apparent, as the district court said, that "to discover a blind person's knowledge, a test must be given orally or in braille . . . ." [F]ederal law requires administrative modification to minimize the effects of plaintiffs' handicaps on any future examinations. . . .

Plaintiffs' final argument is that the School District provided them inadequate notice of the M.C.T. requirement, thus depriving them of a protected liberty or property interest without due process of law. Although the issues in this case do not fit easily into a traditional procedural due process analysis, we conclude, after close consideration, that the School District failed to satisfy constitutional requirements.

The first question to be decided is whether the plaintiffs have a protected liberty or property interest at stake. Denial of a diploma clearly affects a student's reputation. It attaches a "stigma" that will have potentially disastrous effects for future employment or educational opportunities. Though the Supreme Court held that injury to reputation alone does not implicate a liberty interest, it went on to say in the same opinion that liberty interests are implicated when injury to reputation is combined with "governmental action [that] deprived the individual of a right previously held under state law." It was the removal of the right or interest "from the recognition and protection previously afforded by the State, which we found sufficient to invoke the procedural guarantees contained in the Due Process Clause of the Fourteenth Amendment."

Plaintiffs in this case have more than merely an interest in protecting their reputations and avoiding the stigma attached to failure to receive a high school diploma. They, too, had a right conferred by state law to receive a diploma if they meet the requirements imposed prior to 1978: completion of seventeen course credits and fulfillment of the State's graduation requirements. In changing the diploma requirement, the governmental action by the School District deprived the individual of a right or interest previously held under state law. Plaintiffs thus have a liberty interest sufficient to invoke the procedural protections of the due process clause.

The consequence of identifying a protected liberty interest is that governmental action cannot be used to deprive an individual of that interest without due process of law. Traditionally, a procedural due process right means "an opportunity to be heard on the factual basis underlying the loss of a liberty or property interest. . . . "

This case does not fit into the traditional procedural due process mold. Plaintiffs here do not contest the factual basis underlying the loss of a liberty interest; in fact, they admit that they did not pass the M.C.T. Rather, they demand procedures which would provide sufficient notice of the M.C.T. to enable them to prepare adequately to satisfy the new requirement.

We think that procedural due process protections are flexible enough to encompass notice of this kind. The issue arose . . . in *Debra P. v. Turlington,* where the Fifth Circuit stated its view that inadequate notice to students that they would be required to pass an exit examination before qualifying for diploma violated procedural due process. . . .

[W]e hold that plaintiffs were entitled to notice permitting reasonable preparation for the M.C.T. . . .

We must now consider whether the notice provided to plaintiffs was sufficient to satisfy constitutional requisites. The older eleven plaintiffs were informed that they were subject to the M.C.T. requirement during their junior year in high school. The State Superintendent found they therefore had approximately one and a half years to master the skills necessary to pass the M.C.T., the district court found that all plaintiffs had notice of the M.C.T. requirement one year prior to graduation. Despite the fact that plaintiffs had between a year and a year and a half to be exposed to the material on the M.C.T., the record shows that individual petitioners lacked exposure to as much as 90% of the material tested.

Plaintiffs' educational programs were developed in accordance with 20 U.S.C. §1414(a)(5) requiring that each handicapped student receive an individualized educational program (IEP).

[T]he record reflects that the plaintiffs' programs of instruction were not developed to meet the goal of passing the M.C.T., but were instead geared to address individual educational needs. Since plaintiffs and their parents knew of the M.C.T. requirements only one to one and a half years prior to the students' anticipated graduation, the M.C.T. objectives could not have been specifically incorporated into the IEP's over a period of years. If they were incorporated at all, it could only have been during the most recent year and a half. . . .

[P]arents had only a year to a year and a half to evaluate properly their children's abilities and redirect their educational goals. We agree with the parents and the State Board that this was insufficient time to make an informed decision about inclusion or exclusion of training on M.C.T. objectives. . . .

The private interest at stake here is an interest in protecting reputation and in qualifying for future employment opportunities. The governmental interest in upgrading the value of a diploma is also significant. However, the risk of an erroneous deprivation of plaintiffs' interest in this case is overwhelming because of the near-total lack of exposure to the material tested. Requiring earlier notice and the attendant opportunity to learn the material will greatly decrease the risk of erroneous deprivation. . . .

Though we are unable on this record to define "adequate notice" in terms of a specific number of years, the School District can be assured that the requirement would be satisfied if one of the following two conditions for adequate notice is met. The School District can, first, ensure that handicapped students are sufficiently exposed to most of the material that appears on the M.C.T., or second, they can produce evidence of a reasoned and well-informed decision by the parents and teachers involved that a particular high school student will be better off concentrating on educational objectives other than preparation for the M.C.T.

We turn finally to the question of remedy. Plaintiffs argue that the only proper remedy is issuance of diplomas, . . . The School District suggests that plaintiffs should be denied diplomas, but allowed more time to participate in remedial classes and further opportunities to take the M.C.T.

Plaintiffs argue that it is impossible to put them back in the position that they would have been in had they received adequate notice while still in school. Several are employed and would be forced to leave their jobs in order to participate in the remedial program and prepare for the M.C.T. Eleven plaintiffs have been away from school for over two years, since June of 1980, and it would be difficult, both psychologically and academically, for them to make up for lost time. They ask, essentially, why they should endure these hardships when the School District was at fault for providing inadequate notice.

We agree with the School District that, in theory, the proper remedy for a violation of this kind is to require it to provide free, remedial, special education classes to ensure exposure to the material tested on the M.C.T., and a reasonable opportunity for plaintiffs to learn that material. In this particular case, however, it is unrealistic to assume that eleven of these plaintiffs would be able to return to school without undue hardship. Consequently, the School District may not require those plaintiffs to pass the M.C.T. as a prerequisite for a diploma.

The judgement of the district court is reversed with directions to order the School District to issue high school diplomas to the eleven plaintiffs who satisfy the remaining graduation requirements.

Although competency requirements are likely to be upheld as valid, many educational agencies have implemented a practice of awarding a certificate of achievement to special education students. Such a certificate, while a good means of recognizing effort, should not be viewed as the equivalent of a diploma so as to relieve the agency of further responsibility to provide services to that student.

Compensatory Relief

The *Brookhart* case involved the situation where the educational agency did not want to award the diploma because the student had not completed the minimum competency requirements. The reverse of this is not an uncommon occurrence. An educational agency interested in eliminating the continuing obligation to educate certain difficult students — such as adolescents with severe behavioral problems — may simply award the diploma and claim that once the diploma has been awarded there is no further obligation to provide education. Problems can also arise where a student actually does meet the minimum competency requirements for graduation, but who has not been appropriately educated up to that point.

Chapter 17 will discuss this issue further, but it is important to address part of that issue here. At what point does the obligation to provide education end? Is it at the point the diploma has been awarded? What if the diploma is awarded in spite of the fact that minimum competency has not been met, or if the diploma has been earned but the student was not appropriately educated?

Answers to these questions are not clear. Case law is inconsistent from state to state. Some states have taken the position that providing remedial education is something that the educational agency *may* do, but is not required to do after a student graduates. Still others have taken the position that their state statutes actually preclude them from providing education once the diploma has been awarded. An argument can be made that awarding a diploma in a clearly inappropriate case (such as to a behavior-disordered student who clearly has not met the requirements), or providing grossly inappropriate educational programming, constitutes educational malpractice. (This theory has not been widely accepted, however, and is explored further in Chapter 16.) Such an award may also be a violation of procedural due process.

In sum, it should be noted that the law in this area is not clear. In many instances reliance on state statutes and regulations will be necessary to determine the requirements. The EAHCA provides little guidance.[4] The only point on which there seems to be some guidance is that awarding a diploma constitutes a change in placement, and the school is obligated to advise the parents of the due process protections of the EAHCA.[5]

School Attendance Requirements

In many states, students are not required to attend school beyond a certain age, usually around 14 to 16. This raises an interesting question as to whether a student who is receiving special education may elect to stop attending school. For example, a student who has reached 16 in a state where 16 is the cutoff for mandatory attendance may wish to stop attending school. If that student is receiving some programming for a learning disability, for example, what is the obligation of the school to try to keep that student in school? Is there any greater obligation for that student than there is for a student who is not receiving special education? What happens if the parents do not care? Is there any greater obligation to try to persuade the parents to "force" the child to attend because the student is receiving special education? Once the student becomes 18, the parents no longer have the legal power to force the student to attend anyway.

These issues have not really been addressed at all by the courts, but they raise an interesting dilemma. If the student simply stops attending, and the school makes no effort to try to keep the student in school, can the student later claim negligence by the school? Is there a heightened duty to special education students by virtue of the fact that educational programming may be more essential for them than for other students?

While current law does not seem to resolve these questions, school administrators would do well to develop policies to address these questions.

INCARCERATED JUVENILES

Special education and adolescents who are incarcerated in detention facilities raise two issues. Neither issue is well resolved, although there is increasing interest in studying these issues.

The first issue is whether an individual who has been receiving special education must be provided the special education in the detention facility. While there is little case law on this issue, what there is seems to indicate that it must be provided. For example, in *Green v. Johnson,*[6] the court held that incarcerated individuals under the age of 22 (the upper age limit requirement in Massachusetts) must be provided special education. In that case, the individuals involved had been receiving special education before their incarceration. A more difficult question is the obligation of the educational agency to identify incarcerated individuals as needing special education. The second major issue involving incarcerated juveniles is whether the handicapping condition may be a factor in the behavior of the individual that resulted in being incarcerated. There has been a significant amount of interest in studying the relationship of handicapping conditions (particularly learning disabilities) to antisocial behavior that results in criminal conduct. One theory is that perhaps if appropriate educational programming were provided to some of these individuals, the misconduct would not have occurred and the student would not be incarcerated. The debate on this issue is not well resolved, and it will probably continue for some time.

VOCATIONAL EDUCATION

For many handicapped students, preparation for the outside world of independence and employment will require some type of vocational training rather than an emphasis on academics. Many students will not be qualified to attend institutions of higher education. Thus, it is important for this group to have the advantage of public education to prepare for the transition to a world where comprehensive programming will not be available as it is under the EAHCA.

In spite of the importance of vocational training, vocational education teachers are woefully unprepared for the presence of handicapped students in the classroom. There has been a lack of development of special vocational programs just for handicapped students and a lack of adaptation of general vocational programs to incorporate and include special education students. For example, a secondary school that has an automobile repair training program may exclude the handicapped student by having certain qualifications for the program that cannot be met by the handicapped student. Is that permissible under the EAHCA or Section 504 of the Rehabilitation Act?

Federal law requires that 10% of federal vocational funding provided to public schools must be allocated to serving handicapped students.[7] There is little guidance as to how this funding should be used, however. The states have an obligation to match federal funding. There is also a federal incentive program to provide funding for demonstration programs for job training, but this does not really provide any comprehensive mandate.[8]

One area where there is some relevant law relates to personnel training. Vocational education teachers, like all other teachers, are supposed to be adequately prepared for the presence of special education students. This will mean that the teacher in a woodshop class or a home economics class, for example, will need to be aware of the limitations of students with handicapping conditions and to be aware of the need to provide appropriate instructions or adequate supervision. In *Collins v. School Board,*[9] the issue of liability was raised where a substitute teacher in the shop class was negligent when an emotionally handicapped student was sexually assaulted by another student. It will be important to set up mechanisms for communicating special needs to vocational education teachers so that liability does not result. A student with a learning disability may have difficulty understanding instructions on certain machinery in a shop class. A student with cerebral palsy may be a risk in operating an electric mixer in a home economics class. While immunity and other defenses may in some cases protect the school from liability[10] it is better to rely on prevention and to be sure personnel are adequately prepared.

SUMMARY

Students in their teenage years present two major issues relating to special education. The emotional upheaval that normally goes with adolescence can trigger even greater problems for a student with handicaps. Moreover, nonhandicapped individuals may become so emotionally distraught as a result of the changes in their lives during this period that they can actually become emotionally disturbed and be categorized as handicapped. Thus, it is particularly critical that students in this age range be given appropriate special education and, to the extent possible, that this education prepare these students for the transition into the world of work.

One issue relating to special education for teenagers is whether the educational agency can impose competency requirements for graduation. Such requirements might adversely affect students with certain handicapping conditions. As a general rule, courts have upheld the legality of minimum competency testing for the award of a diploma as long as adequate notice has been given. A related issue, less well resolved, is whether a state is no longer obligated to provide any special education once the diploma is awarded. Courts have reached a wide disparity of results in addressing this question. Similarly, they have not reached any conclusion on whether there is a remedy against an educational agency that awards a diploma to a student who has not met the minimum competency requirements generally imposed.

Students in this age group occasionally end up in juvenile detention settings. Those students who have previously been identified as handicapped are required by the EAHCA to be provided special education and related services even while in detention. Theoretically, there should be some mechanism within the judicial system that would ensure that students not yet identified as handicapped could be evaluated. A growing body of social science research indicates a relationship between learning disabilities and juvenile delinquency, making this a group that is important to reach. As a practical matter, however, the logistics of providing educational services to this transitory population are difficult. Perhaps the fact that this is not a group that is very likely to have strong parental advocates accounts for the fact that there is little case law addressing issues relating to special education and incarcerated juveniles.

Students in this age group who are handicapped are also less likely to attend institutions of higher education than are their nonhandicapped peers. This makes vocational education a very important program for high school students with handicaps. Unfortunately, although the need is extremely high, the training that vocational education teachers receive does not currently provide any significant preparation for teaching students with special needs. And the little existing case law relating to these issues seems primarily to be cases in which vocational education personnel are being sued for inappropriate supervision. This fact alone demonstrates the importance of placing a high priority on training vocational education teachers to teach handicapped students.

QUESTIONS AND PROBLEMS

1. Is there harm done to the public by awarding a student a diploma when the student had not completed competency requirements? Is this different from a situation involving higher education? That is, is it less harmful to award a high school diploma because of inadequate notice than it would be to award a nursing certificate to a student who had not met minimal competency requirements?

2. If a school district treats a certificate of achievement for a special education student as equivalent to a diploma, are those students who receive such a certificate still entitled to a free appropriate public education (FAPE)? If so, for how long?

3. In *Brookhart,* the court found the notice inadequate as to these handicapped students. If the notice is adequate for nonhandicapped students, might they claim reverse discrimination because they must pass the M.C.T., but the handicapped students are not required to?

4. What would be the practical problems of providing special education to a juvenile incarcerated in a detention center? How can mainstreaming (i.e., LRE) in a detention center be accomplished?

5. Would it be permissible to allocate all vocational training funds for handicapped students to separate programs? Should *all* vocational training programs integrate handicapped and nonhandicapped students?

NOTES

1. See Chapters 9 and 10.
2. At least half of the states have such requirements.
3. 730 F.2d 1405 (11th Cir. 1984).
4. *See* L. ROTHSTEIN, RIGHTS OF PHYSICALLY HANDICAPPED PERSONS (RPHP) §§ 2.13 & 2.40 (1984) and cumulative supplements.
5. *See generally* Max M. v. Illinois State Board of Education, 629 F. Supp. 1504, 1509 (N.D. Ill. 1986).
6. 513 F. Supp. 965 (D. Mass. 1981). *See also* RPHP § 2.13.
7. 20 U.S.C. § 2301. *See also* THE EDUCATION OF THE HANDICAPPED ADOLESCENT: THE TRANSITION FROM SCHOOL TO WORKING LIFE (1983) and THE EDUCATION OF THE HANDICAPPED ADOLESCENT: INTEGRATION IN THE SCHOOL (1981).
8. 49 Fed. Reg. 18390 (Apr. 30, 1984).
9. 471 So. 2d 560 (Fla. Dist. Ct. App. 1985).
10. See Chapters 15 and 19.

CHAPTER 13

Cost Issues

FREE APPROPRIATE PUBLIC EDUCATION

Under the EAHCA, free appropriate public education means, among other things, education "provided at public expense, under public supervision and direction, and without charge."[1] States providing this service to handicapped children in compliance with the EAHCA mandates are eligible to receive supportive funding from the federal government under the funding formula mentioned in Chapter 3. Because special education on average costs about twice as much per pupil as regular education, cost issues are a major concern for state and local educational agencies. For certain types of placements, such as residential placements, the concern is even greater. While the EAHCA funding provides a subsidization for special education, the federal funding does not cover all of the additional costs of providing special education and related services.

Cost issues have been mentioned previously in several chapters, and there will be additional issues raised in subsequent chapters. This chapter reviews those issues raised elsewhere. It also addresses in greater detail some of those same issues and some new ones not raised elsewhere in this book.

What Expenses Are Covered under the EAHCA?

The first issue to address is which costs are covered under the EAHCA; that is, which costs must be paid for at public expense?

Educational Programming. The educational programming and related services themselves are, of course, covered, but it is not always easy to identify when a particular service is part of the educational program and which related services are covered under the EAHCA. The discussion on residential placements in Chapter 10 indicated that where the placement is necessary for educational purposes, both the cost of room and board and the educational services must be paid by the educational agency. The medical expenses of such a placement, however, need not be paid by the educational agency.

Another issue that occasionally arises is whether certain programs such as teaching self-help skills are really "education" that must be paid under the EAHCA.[2] A similar question could arise in a context where a comatose child is being provided regular muscle therapy or being provided background music to try to bring the child out of the coma. Is that education? These issues are not really addressed to a great extent by the courts, so there is little clear resolution of these questions, but they may be more clearly defined in the future.

Related Services. In addition to educational programming, the educational agency must pay for related services, including identification and assessment services, needed to enable the child to benefit from special education.[3]

Chapter 9 discussed these issues and illustrated how expensive some related services, such as transportation, can be.[4] The *Tatro*[5] case involving catheterization as a related service pointed out that while some services may be defined to be medical services, which are not related services under the EAHCA, whenever the service is a related service within the EAHCA, it must be provided at no cost.

Assessment services fall within the category of related services. As the *Seals v. Loftis*[6] decision illustrated, it can become quite costly to complete all of the necessary assessments to determine the child's handicapping condition. If these assessments are necessary to determine the special education program, they must be paid for by the school, even if the parents have insurance benefits to cover these expenses in certain instances.

Procedural Protections. One area that has not been previously discussed very deeply is the right to procedural safeguards to ensure that the EAHCA has been complied with. These procedural safeguards include a right to have a hearing when there is disagreement over a child's handicap, placement, program, etc.; a right to be represented at the hearing; a right to a record of the hearing; a right to appeal to the state administrative agency; and a right to seek review in court. It should be pointed out that having certain procedural rights does not always mean that these rights must be provided at no cost. The EAHCA offers clarification on most of these issues. Although the school is not required to pay for the cost of representation unless the parents are prevailing parties,[7] the educational agency is obligated for the other costs of the due process hearing itself. These costs include payment to the hearing officer, the cost of tape-recording or transcribing the proceedings, and the cost of sending copies of the findings of fact to the parents.[8] These are not minor costs, and as a practical matter, educational agencies often weigh the cost of the administrative proceedings in deciding whether to grant the parents' request for a service or program. Cost of conducting an administrative review at the state level are also borne by the educational agency.[9]

Questions relating to attorneys' fees and costs such as expert witnesses, production of documentary evidence, and other costs of representation are treated separately. Basically, however, it can be noted at this point that these costs are initially paid by the parents, but they may be reimbursed if they are prevailing parties.

School Records. In preparation for a placement decision or a hearing, parents may wish to obtain copies of their child's school records. Their rights of access are discussed more fully in Chapter 15. It should be noted here, however, that while parents have a right to examine and obtain copies of school records, the school may charge a reasonable fee for providing copies unless doing so would preclude parents from access to due process.[10] A fee for search and retrieval may not be charged to the parents.[11]

Budgetary Constraints on Educational Agencies

Technically, if it is determined that a particular program or service is necessary for a handicapped child to receive an appropriate education under the EAHCA, it must be provided regardless of cost.[12]

There is nothing in the statute or regulations that permits budgetary constraints to be a defense when a school fails to provide mandated special education and related services, but it is arguable that the *Mills* case, which was a foundation for passage of the EAHCA, provides that

> If sufficient funds are not available to finance all of the services and programs that are needed and desirable in the system, then the available funds must be expended equitably in such a manner that no child is entirely excluded from a publicly supported education consistent with his needs and ability to benefit therefrom.[13]

Assuming the *Mills* view is a correct interpretation of the EAHCA, one can imagine the difficulty of determining how to cut back all programming. Perhaps the complexity of doing so explains the fact that this defense is rarely raised by the educational agencies. While there is not clear guidance from current judicial interpretation of the EAHCA, two major decisions indicate that cost may be a legitimate factor in determining whether certain services must be provided.

In *Irving Independent School District v. Tatro,*[14] the Supreme Court, in discussing whether catheterization must be provided as a related service, the Court stated that it would be reasonable for the Secretary of Education to conclude that the medical services exclusion was "designed to spare schools from an obligation to provide a service that might well prove unduly expensive. . . . " Another major case in which cost was raised as an issue is *Roncker v. Walter,*[15] in which the major issue was whether it was appropriate to place severely retarded children in separate schools. The court held that "Cost is a proper factor to consider since excessive spending on one handicapped child deprives other handicapped children."

But the court cautioned against a conservative view of when a particular service would benefit only one handicapped child, in its statement that

> Cost is no defense . . . if the school district has failed to use its funds to provide a proper continuum of alternative placements. . . . The provision of such alternative placements benefits all handicapped children.

Case law also supports the school's selection of the less expensive placement where there is a choice between appropriate placements.[16]

It would seem, therefore, that while the circumstances under which cost can be used as a defense have yet to be clearly delineated, educational agencies will have that avenue available in certain instances. These instances are likely to be extreme cases, however. The following case is an example of one such extreme case.

BEVIN H. V. WRIGHT

666 F. Supp. 71 (W.D. Pa. 1987)

Bevin H. is a 7-year-old girl who suffers severe mental and physical handicaps. At issue here is whether the School District, under the Education for all Handicapped Children Act (EAHCA), must bear the cost of nursing services necessary to enable Bevin to attend school. . . .

At this writing, Bevin is 7 years old and resides with her parents. She suffers from multiple handicaps, principally Robinow syndrome (fetal face syndrome), severe broncho-pulmonary dysplasia, profound mental retardation, spastic quadriplegia, seizure disorder and hydrocephalus. She is also legally blind. She breathes through a tracheostomy tube and is fed and medicated through a gastrostomy tube.

As Bevin neared school age, her parents sought an educational program to improve on her severely delayed development. In 1984 the Pittsburgh School District agreed to admit Bevin to its Pioneer School in a special curriculum for handicapped children, with the stipulation that Bevin's parents would bear the cost of the nursing services and related equipment which Bevin required. The parents agreed to this arrangement. It is undisputed that without these nursing services, Bevin would be unable to attend school.

In October 1984, Bevin was placed in a classroom with 6 other handicapped children. The Individualized Educational Program (IEP) developed for Bevin in consultation with her parents provides the auditory, visual and tactile stimulation and fine and gross motor development. The goal is to improve Bevin's awareness of and interaction with the world around her. All parties agree that, with the exception of the nursing services issue, this program is the most appropriate and least restrictive educational plan for Bevin.

For the 1984–85 year, Bevin's parents agreed to provide the full-time nurse and related equipment which Bevin requires at all times. The cost of this nursing service, from the time Bevin leaves home in the morning until she returns home from school in the afternoon, is about $1,850 per month and was paid for by the parents' health insurance. The fact that the District did not have to pay for these services was apparently a salient factor in the District's decision to admit Bevin to a classroom.

Unfortunately, Bevin's insurance coverage has a ceiling of $500,000 and by the time this suit was filed her medical needs had already consumed $120,000. In addition to the $1,850 per month for the attending nurse for school, Bevin's other routine medical expenses are between $500 and $1,000 per month. The prospect of exhausting Bevin's medical coverage prompted her parents to request that the School District assume the expense of the nurse who must care for Bevin in school. The District refused, prompting the institution of administrative proceedings and ultimately this action.

The services Bevin requires at school are extensive. The attending nurse must accompany Bevin to and from school. She is responsible for the care and cleaning of the tracheostomy and gastrostomy tube. She administers a constant oxygen supply to Bevin. She supervises positioning for physical and occupational therapy. She administers chest physical therapy each day to break up mucous, and must suction the mucous from the lungs. Above all though, the nurse must remain with Bevin at all times because of the constant possibility of a mucous plug in the tracheostomy tube. Such a plug is a common event, occurring several times each day, and must be cleared by the nurse within 30 seconds to prevent injury to Bevin.

In the 1984–85 school year, Bevin attended class from 8:30 A.M. to 12:30 P.M., Monday through Thursday, with a full school day on Friday. On a typical school day, the nurse accompanies Bevin to school in a cab, suctioning the tracheostomy tube as needed. On arrival at school, Bevin is fed through the gastrotomy tube. She then has a classroom session with her teacher and classmates. This is followed by a period of chest physical therapy in which mucous is suctioned from the lungs. Bevin returns to class for further activities and is then escorted home by the nurse. Because of the nature of Bevin's condition, and specifically because of the possibility of a mucous plug interfering with breathing, the nurse is with Bevin every moment of the school day.

In contrast to Bevin, her 6 classmates, all with multiple handicaps, do not require the extensive nursing attention which Bevin requires. Although each of these children has a tracheostomy, each is able to care for and clear the tube without assistance. The class is conducted by a teacher and 2 aides, but no nurse is assigned to the class.

There is some dispute about the amount of progress that Bevin has made in her educational program. Bevin's mother and nurse report that Bevin's interaction with people has increased, that she is more aware of familiar voices and sounds, and she appears to express feelings of joy. Standing activities have improved weight-bearing capacity and permitted growth. On the other hand, Bevin's teacher indicates that while some progress has been noted, it is inconsistent and minimal. However, as noted above, there is no dispute that this program is the most appropriate and least restrictive for Bevin. Alternative programs such as at-home instruction or residential placement have not been presented to the court. . . .

Plaintiffs contend that "related services" as defined by the [EAHCA] regulations include the daily nursing care which makes it possible for Bevin to attend school. Defendants argue that this nursing care is actually "medical services" not provided for diagnosis or evaluation and is therefore specifically excluded from "related services". . . .

We have set forth above in some detail the facts in the present case. The services required are varied and intensive. They must be provided by a nurse, not a layperson. They are time-consuming and expensive. Above all, the life threatening prospect of a mucous plug demands the constant attention of the nurse. Because of this need for constant vigilance, a school nurse or any other qualified person with responsibility for other children within the school could not safely care for Bevin.

It is the "private duty" aspect of Bevin's nursing services which distinguished this case from the other, [which] all involved intermittent care which could be provided by the school district at relatively little expense in both time and money. The services Bevin requires are far beyond those, and to place that burden on the school district in the guise of "related services" does not appear to be consistent with the spirit of the act and the regulation.

We are also fortified in our conclusion by the decision in *Board of Education v. Rowley,* 458 U.S. 176 (1982). Although the Act presumes that all handicapped children are entitled to some form of education tailored to their individual needs and abilities, it does not require school districts to provide the best possible education without regard to expense. While no alternative educational programs for Bevin have been presented to us, we recognize that the Act is not restricted in application to classroom settings but envisions the need for specialized programs. Such an alternative may be appropriate for Bevin but the issue is not before us.

We do not intend to intimate that "related services" are only those services which can be provided at low cost to the district or which can be performed by existing school personnel. To the contrary, the states reap the benefit of federal monies and the Act presumes that compliance with its tenets may require special services or the hiring of additional personnel at considerable expense. We simply hold that on the facts of the present case, the nursing services required are so varied, intensive and costly, and more in the nature of "medical services" that they are not properly includable as "related services."

It should be noted that while the educational agency's fiscal status for the most part is irrelevant to deciding its obligation to provide services, the parents' right to services for the child is not dependent on family income. Parents with an annual income of a million dollars have as much right to free special education for their child as do parents on welfare.

As a policy matter, this may seem troublesome. As a practical matter, however, the transaction costs of determining a sliding scale of parental obligation based on their resources would be extremely burdensome. Since access to a free regular education is not based on income, it is really questionable whether special education should be so conditioned. The difference, of course, is that regular education costs about the same for each child. Special education can be vastly more expensive for certain programs.

WHICH PUBLIC AGENCY IS RESPONSIBLE?

Assume that the program or placement has been determined to be one that is appropriate to the child in question. In other words, a determination has been made that a particular program should be paid for at public expense. The issue of which public agency is responsible may still be undecided.

First, there are issues as to whether the placement is one that the state educational agency should be responsible for instead of the local agency. And if it determined that a particular program is to be a local responsibility, the question may become one of residency; that is, which local school district has responsibility for a particular child?

And there are further questions in some cases as to whether the educational agencies (local or state) are responsible at all. It may be that in some cases, social service agencies such as departments of welfare, corrections, or health have total or partial financial or programmatic responsibility. Where careful interagency agreements have not been worked out, these issues are more likely to arise.

State Versus Local Agency Responsibility

While the state educational agency has the primary and ultimate responsibility for providing special education under the EAHCA, states have a great deal of latitude in deciding whether to provide direct services themselves or to permit local agencies to provide direct services. In actuality, in most states it is the local agencies that have been given the primary responsibility of providing direct services for most types of placements. In some states, certain expensive placements such as residential programs and placements in schools for the deaf are arranged for and paid for by the state rather than the local educational agency.

The question that can arise is what happens if the local educational agency does not provide the services it is supposed to provide according to the state established system of resource allocation. Is it the state's obligation to take care of placements when the local educational agency has failed to do so? This issue was recently addressed in the decision of *Doe v. Maher,* by the Ninth Circuit. The case, which addressed the issue of whether a child could be removed from the classroom for a disciplinary reason, was ultimately decided by the Supreme Court. The Supreme Court addressed the discipline and removal issues, but did not really rule directly on the issue of state responsibility, although the State Superintendent of Public Instruction sought review of that issue. The Court was evenly divided on the issue, and thus the Ninth Circuit decision holding the state responsible was affirmed.

The following excerpt is only a small portion of the Ninth Circuit's opinion. Although the issue has not been resolved by the Supreme Court, other circuit courts have reached results similar to the Ninth Circuit's disposition of the state agency responsibility issue.

DOE V. MAHER

793 F.2d 1470, 1491 (9th Cir. 1986)
The state contends that the district court erred in enjoining it to provide services directly whenever, in any individual case, it determines that a local educational agency is unable or unwilling to maintain programs of free appropriate public education for handicapped students. According to the state, section 1414(d) of the EAHCA requires it to provide services directly, not in individual instances of local inaction, but only when localities maintain no programs of special education whatsoever.

We think the state conceives its role under section 1414(d) too narrowly. When read in its entirety, the provision imposes on the state a broader duty. Although the state stresses the language in 20 U.S.C. section 1414(d)(1) (1982) that speaks of the state's responsibility for direct action when the locality fails to maintain "programs" of free appropriate education, section 1414(d)(3) specifically requires direct action when a local education agency "has one or more handicapped children who can best be served by a regional or State center designed to meet the needs of such children." *Id.* It would seem incontrovertible that, whenever the local agency refuses or wrongfully neglects to provide a handicapped child with a free appropriate education, that child "can best be served" on the regional or state level. . . .

Although the state has broad responsibilities under the EAHCA, those responsibilities are not absolute. The state is not obligated to intervene directly in an individual case whenever the local agency falls short of its responsibilities in some small regard. The breach must be significant (as in this case), the child's parents or guardian must give the responsible state officials adequate notice of the local agency's noncompliance, and the state must be afforded a reasonable opportunity to compel local compliance.

Residency Issues

In addition to disputes regarding responsibility between state and local educational agencies, disputes can arise regarding which local educational agency or which state is responsible for the education of a particular child. These issues usually reach the formal dispute resolution level when expensive placements such as residential placements or other expensive programming is involved.

The EAHCA is not very helpful in clarifying these types of residency issues. Resolution is usually found by examining state education and state residency statutes. Problems arise in cases where a residential placement has been made and the parents have later moved, when the child is placed in a foster home or with a guardian or someone other than the parents, and if the child is a ward of the state. It is difficult to find any national trend in how these cases are being resolved because so much depends on individual state law.[17] The following judicial opinion is an example of the type of analysis that courts are likely to consider in these cases.

CATLIN V. AMBACH

655 F. Supp. 161 (N.D.N.Y. 1986)
Plaintiff, Dunbar Elliot ("Dell") Catlin, is a 13-year-old child who was born in New York City on April 22, 1973. Shortly after Dell was born, his parents Daniel and Dundeen Catlin learned that Dell had been born with Down's Syndrome. After several consultations, the Catlins decided to place Dell in a family home with Samuel and Elizabeth Conde ("the Condes") in Edmeston, New York. Dell went to Edmeston directly from the hospital and has lived there continuously since that time. He has never resided with his natural parents and has never even visited their home.

The Catlins pay for the cost of Dell's care in Edmeston and no part of those costs is paid by any social service agency. It is not controverted that the Catlins have always intended that Dell reside with the Condes. The center of Dell's civic, social, religious and family life is in Edmeston, New York. The Condes' is the only home Dell has ever known and the people with whom he resides are his "family." Dell refers to the Condes as "Mama" and "Dad" and has longstanding, extended family relationships with two of the Condes' natural children who reside in the area.

Dell shares a room with another child, one year younger than he, who, like Dell, has lived in Edmeston since shortly after his birth. The relationship between Dell and his roommate is brotherly; they attend school together and have become virtually inseparable over the years. Both the Catlins and the Condes believe that it would be extremely harmful for Dell to leave Edmeston and the setting the Condes have provided him.

The Condes are completely responsible for day-to-day decisions regarding Dell's care and supervision.

Selection of schools was not a factor in choosing to place Dell in Edmeston with the Condes. Since 1978, when he came of school age, Dell has attended the BOCES-Mt. Vision School in Edmeston, based upon the recommendation of the Edmeston School District Committee of the Handicapped. The placement has been reviewed each year and has been reaffirmed on each of those occasions. The Catlins never attended any of the meetings related to Dell's placement; the school district has dealt solely with the Condes on all matters related to Dell and his education.

Up to mid-1985, the Catlins resided in New York State, within the Bedford Central School District. From the time the child started attending school through 1985, the Bedford Central School District assumed financial responsibility for his tuition and paid that tuition to the Edmeston Central School District.

In the summer of 1985 the Catlins moved from their home in Bedford to the State of Massachusetts. The Bedford Central School District advised the Nantucket Public School System that "now that the family has moved to Nantucket, we are no longer responsible for tuition and the burden of Dunbar's education falls on your school district." The Bedford Central School District also informed the Edmeston Central School District that Bedford would no longer pay Dell's tuition. . . .

[The issue in this case is whether the Edmeston School District or another locality bears responsibility for Dell's education.]

. . . All parties agree that the only remaining issue is the State's determination of Dell's residence. Plaintiffs' first claim hinges on an equal protection challenge to the New York residence rule as applied in the present case.

[In the present case,] an intermediate scrutiny standard applies in cases where the classifications, "while not facially invidious, nonetheless give rise to recurring constitutional difficulties; in these limited circumstances we have sought the assurance that the classification reflects a reasoned judgment consistent with the ideal of equal protection by inquiring whether it may fairly be viewed as furthering a substantial state interest." Given that the Commissioner's application of the statute affects a subclass of children by limiting their access to a state-created right, and given the importance of education for this society, the application of the New York residence statute is subject to the *intermediate standard* of furthering a substantial goal of the state.

New York Education Law places the obligation to provide schooling without payment of tuition on the school district in which the child resides. N.Y. Educ.L. section 3202(1) (McKinney 1981). The Commissioner's finding that Dell was not a resident of Edmeston School District for educational purposes was based on section 3202(4)(b) of the New York Education Law, which states:

> b. Children cared for in free family homes and children cared for in family homes at board, when such family homes shall be the actual and only resi-

> dence of such children and when such children are not supported or maintained at the expense of a social services district or a state department or agency, shall be deemed residents of the school district in which such family home is located.

Although the statutory language would seem to point directly to deeming the child a resident "of the school district in which such family home [at board] is located," the Commissioner concluded that, since the Catlins had financial control over Dell, Dell's residence is that of his natural parents.

The Commissioner's conclusions are specifically as follows: (1) It is undisputed that Dell is cared for in a family home at board which is licensed by the Department of Social Services, and that he is not supported by a social services district or a state department or agency. (2) The Board's decision is that the family home at board in which Dell resides is not his actual and only residence, because the child's parents continue to have parental authority and control over the child and are financially responsible for him. (3) A child's residence is presumed to be that of his parents, even if the child is not physically present in the parent's home; the presumption can be overcome by demonstrating that the parent neither exercises control over the child nor is financially responsible for the child. (4) The Catlins continue to be financially responsible for their son's support and maintenance; the responsibility delegated to the Condes can be terminated at any time. Thus, the Commissioner concluded that there was no basis upon which to conclude that the residence of the child should not be deemed to be that of his natural parents.

The State contends that the Commissioner's findings are only an application of constitutionally acceptable bona fide residence requirements. Furthermore, the State contends that "the same public interests and State interests in applying a bona fide residence test under traditional standards are present in this case."

A bona fide residence requirement, appropriately defined and uniformly applied, furthers the substantial state interest in assuring that services provided for its residents are enjoyed only by residents. A bona fide residence requirement simply requires that the person does establish residence before demanding the services that are restricted to residents.

The question before this court is, therefore, whether the New York residence requirement, as applied, does further the substantial state interests.

The interests on the child's side are fairly easy to identify. It is not controverted that Dell's reason for the claim to residence in Edmeston School District is not solely to benefit from the free school system. Dell's social, civic and actual family life centers around the home the Condes have provided. It is also uncontroverted that unless the Edmeston School District assumes the cost of Dell's education, Dell will have to move, probably to Massachusetts, for the Catlins could not bear the cost of the child's tuition in New York. Moving Dell would disrupt his world as he has always known it, with results which presumably would be very harmful to him. Or the child would have to be removed from school, remaining in Edmeston, also with serious detriment resulting for him.

The State's interests are [first] "local control over the operation of schools; local autonomy has long been thought essential both to the maintenance of community concern and support for the public schools and to the quality of the educational process.". . . This case presents no problem whatsoever with local autonomy. All decisions regarding Dell's education have been made pursuant to consultation with the Condes, and primarily, if not absolutely, according to their judgment. Another related interest, proper planning and operation of the schools, would not be affected at all by allowing Dell to remain in Edmeston at the school district expense.

Other concerns related to the planning problems that would result from substantial school population fluctuations, simply are not present in this case.

Other possible arguments, regarding the school district's interest in assuming that services provided for residents are enjoyed only by residents, could be read as an interest in limiting education to children of those who support the school system as taxpayers. This argument, and the closely related one of preservation of resources, have been clearly rejected as legitimate state interests absent a clear showing of the state's purpose.

Another argument reflects the interest school districts have in having somebody with whom "a school official may deal . . . effectively and authoritatively in matters of punishment, educational progress and medical needs." The Edmeston School District's recognition of the Condes as the persons responsible for decisions regarding Dell's education makes this a moot issue. De facto, the Condes are the persons in charge of Dell's education and the school district has never challenged their authority.

The court concludes therefore, that the State has failed to show that the New York residency statute, as applied in this case, furthers any substantial state interest. As applied in this case, the New York residence requirement offends the Equal Protection Clause of the Fourteenth Amendment. Other grounds for plaintiffs' claims need not be addressed.

Given that the Edmeston School District has continued to provide Dell with school services during this dispute, this judgment is limited to invalidating the Commissioner's determination as to residence.

Obligations of Other Social Service Agencies

Under the EAHCA, the state educational agency has the primary responsibility of ensuring the provision of special education to all handicapped children within the state. That does not preclude state lawmakers and administrators from implementing programs whereby social service agencies other than the educational agency bear at least some of the financial and/or programmatic responsibility for the placement of a handicapped child. One problem that can arise is the issue of what happens if the educational agency has never had the opportunity to participate in a placement decision made by another social service agency. The following case illustrates the importance of ensuring that the educational agency is involved in the process.

IN RE TODD P.

509 A.2d 140 (N.H. 1986)
In 1980, the Henniker school system found that Todd P. was educationally handicapped, and it established an individual education plan (IEP) for him. In September 1983, Todd began attending the Hillsboro-Deering Middle School, which found that he was emotionally disturbed. In January 1984, the Hillsboro-Deering School District established an IEP for Todd, finding that Todd's educational needs could be ad-

dressed within the school district. The IEP provided for psychological counselling, parent consultation, and academic monitoring.

In March 1984, Todd was adjudicated a delinquent child, ... The court ordered that Todd be placed outside the home, and placed Todd on probation. The court subsequently found that Todd was guilty of violating its order, and ordered that he be detained at the Youth Development Center (YDC), subject to a suspension of the order upon a petition showing "either [an] alternative placement or other good cause." On March 23, 1984, the court suspended Todd's placement at the YDC on the condition that Todd be placed at the Chamberlain School. He resided at the Chamberlain School until August 1985. He is now out of the placement system. . . .

The sole issue before the court was whether the Town of Henniker or, rather, the school district was liable for the educational portion of the expenses of Todd's Chamberlain School placement. . . .

The school district appealed to this court, asserting that the district court is without authority to review the substance of an IEP developed by the school district. It argues that the district court has no jurisdiction to issue liability orders against a school district for an educational program that was not part of an IEP established by it. We agree.

The issues before us arise out of the tangled interrelationship of New Hampshire's juvenile justice system and special education laws. This interrelationship is the result of the fact that many children are both delinquent and educationally handicapped. Todd's needs, which stem from both his delinquency and his educational handicap, must be addressed through both the juvenile justice statutes and the special education laws. . . .

The district court has the authority to issue liability orders against the town declared the legally liable unit. This provision also grants the district court the authority to issue a liability order against a school district for educational expenses incurred. Todd's expenses at the Chamberlain School, however, were not voluntarily chosen by the school district as part of the IEP developed, and therefore were not chargeable to the school district. . . .

The school district's lack of participation in Todd's placement by the juvenile court permitted it in this case to evade its financial responsibility for Todd's special education needs. The juvenile court's disruption of special education services may be remedied by ensuring its awareness of the child's educational needs. The school district's participation in the juvenile justice process will permit the juvenile court to place a child on the basis of both the child's delinquency and his or her special education needs, and to assign liability accordingly. On its own initiative, the school district should review a child's IEP after a delinquency adjudication, or the district court may order review. If the school district refuses to review the IEP, or its decision after review is still unsatisfactory to the parents or legal guardian of the educationally handicapped child, they may take an appeal.

Hillsborough county asserts that because the special education administrative appeals process does not provide for the participation of the legally liable unit in a delinquency proceeding, exhaustion of administrative remedies is a futile requirement. Although the legally liable unit under the juvenile justice laws may not participate in the administrative appeals process, parents of a child involved in a delinquency adjudication have an incentive to appeal a school district's decision because the legally liable unit has a right of reimbursement against the parents for the expenses of the placement charged to it. The administrative process is not futile here because the State

Board of Education, or the superior court or federal district court, has the power to determine that the IEP is inadequate. Without the use of this administrative process, however, no administrative record exists to guide the court in evaluating the substance of an IEP.

Once a child is placed by the juvenile court, and the school district is ordered to review the child's IEP, the school district is financially responsible for the educational portion of the placement while administrative remedies are pursued. The assumption is that the special education portion of a placement under the juvenile justice laws is the responsibility of the school district.

In this case, however, the Peterborough District Court determined liability after Todd's placement had taken place, and the school district had not been ordered to review the IEP. No administrative appeal was pending. The district court had the authority to order a review of Todd's IEP, but had no authority to issue a liability order against the school district for the educational expenses of a placement that the school district had not established as part of Todd's IEP. Todd's placement at the Chamberlain School was the result of a delinquency adjudication, and the legally liable unit is responsible for the expenses of that placement.

PRIVATE OBLIGATIONS

As was mentioned earlier in this chapter, the income of the parent is irrelevant in a determination that the education should be provided at no cost by the school. An issue that is likely to arise increasingly is the question of whether certain expenses should be borne by private insurance companies of the public educational agency. The *Seals v. Loftis* opinion excerpted in Chapter 6 should be reviewed at this point. The result in that case is probably the appropriate outcome in any case involving special education—namely if the payment by the private insurance company will reduce the lifetime benefits or in any other way have an adverse financial impact on the family insurance benefits available to it, the parents should not be required to use their insurance benefits to cover educational expenses. These expenses include the cost of special education and related services.

The less clear issue is whether the private insurance company can raise the educational agency's obligation to provide special education and related services as a defense against its own obligation to pay certain expenses in instances where the parents are willing to have their insurance benefits cover certain expenses, or where the obligation of the insurance company to pay would not affect the parents' benefits. This issue is too complex to address here. The resolution will depend both on the terms of the insurance contract between the parents and the insurance company and on the judicial interpretation of the validity and meaning of these contract terms.

SUMMARY

The EAHCA requires that special education and related services be provided to eligible students at public expense. There are those who might suggest that at least certain expensive services should be paid for by parents on an ability-to-pay basis.

At present, however, the EAHCA does not apply this standard, and parents are not required to pay for these services regardless of their income.

The special education and related services that are to be publicly funded include not only the educational services but also the cost of procedural protections of the administrative hearing. What is not covered within the public expense mandate is the parents' cost of legal representation (attorneys' fees and costs) unless the parent is successful in the matter.

Regardless of their success at the initial administrative level, parents have a right to have a record of the hearing and a copy of the findings provided at public expense. The EAHCA does not require that the school disseminate the student's records free of charge unless this would, in effect, prevent access to due process.

While courts seem to scrutinize cost defenses fairly rigorously, it would seem that cost can be used as a legitimate reason for limiting the type and level of special education programming needed by a student. Cost cannot be a defense, however, if the result would be a total denial of any education to a particular student. As the number of cases in which expensive quasi-medical and other extraordinary services increases, it is likely the courts will begin to define more clearly the circumstances under which educational agency budgetary constraints will be a defense. Although a significant number of judicial opinions have addressed cost as an issue, there is not yet a clear standard by which to evaluate such cases.

Another issue lacking clear definition is the question of public interagency responsibility. The EAHCA contemplates that other public funding sources (such as human services, health services, etc.) as well as private sources (insurance) should be used to pay for some special education and related services programming. Unfortunately, the EAHCA lacks any mechanism whereby state educational agencies can exert pressure on other public agencies to play a supporting role. As a result, cooperative efforts exist only by virtue of state statutory mandate or interagency agreements developed voluntarily. While it is clear that such coordination is more efficient at accomplishing the goal of ensuring that children with handicaps receive appropriate services, there is not yet any consistent policy in this regard from one state to the next.

As to the responsibility of the educational agency, it is clear that the state agency bears the primary responsibility for providing the services, and in fact probably has the ultimate responsibility for directly providing the services if a local educational agency fails to do so. As to which state has responsibility, this depends generally on the residency of the child. In most cases this is easily determined. But in cases where the child does not actually reside with the natural parents, difficulties can arise in determining the responsible state. The EAHCA does not provide any specific guidance on this issue. The resolution instead will depend on how individual states define residency in the relevant statutes and policies and how state laws principles resolve disputes when more than one state is involved. Because of the EAHCA principle that special education is to be provided at no cost to the parents, private insurance can be required as a funding source only where it is clear that this will have no adverse economic impact (such as reduced lifetime benefit or increased premiums) on the parents.

QUESTIONS AND PROBLEMS

1. Suppose a child had been in a residential placement for several years and the child's file contained 250 documents in it. Would it be reasonable to allow the parent an opportunity to review the file and request only specified documents?

2. What would be considered a reasonable fee for photocopying?

3. Suppose a $20,000 vehicle was needed to provide transportation to an orthopedically impaired student who lived at the end of an unpaved mountain road. What if the local agency's entire budget was very low because of poor local economic tax base? What if there were no chalk in the classrooms? What if the entire state in that district had a low economic base? Who would set these priorities?

4. To what extent was the result in *Bevin* related to the "nature of the services" and to what extent was it a cost issue?

5. Could the *Roncker* argument, that spending benefiting only one student is a factor in using cost as a defense, be used by a school district to deny residential placement to a student because it will only benefit one individual?

6. In the *Catlin* case, could the Massachusetts school district in which the Catlins now reside be found to be obligated to pay for Dell's education? This issue was not decided in the case. If so, as a practical matter, how could they evaluate Dell and place him?

7. Keeping in mind the *Todd P.* case, as a practical matter how will schools be aware of a delinquency proceeding and know when to participate? How can juvenile court judges be apprised of the EAHCA and its requirements?

NOTES

1. 201 U.S.C. 1402(a)(18); 34 C.F.R. sec. 300.4. *See also* L. ROTHSTEIN RIGHTS OF PHYSICALLY HANDICAPPED PERSONS § 2.18 (1984) and cumulative supplements.
2. Rothstein, *Educational Rights of Severely and Profoundly Handicapped Children,* 61 NEB. L. REV. 586 (1982).
3. 20 U.S.C. § 1402(a)(17).
4. In the *Espino* case in Chapter 8, the expense involved was the cost of air-conditioning a classroom.
5. *See* Chapter 9.
6. *See* Chapter 6.
7. *See* Chapter 18.
8. 34 C.F.R. § 300.506 & 300.508.
9. *See* Chapter 14.
10. 34 C.F.R. §§ 300.562(b)(2) & 300.566.
11. 34 C.F.R. § 300.566(b).
12. In Clevenger v. Oak Ridge School Board, 744 F.2d 514 (6th Cir. 1984), the court held that cost concerns would not be relevant where the only appropriate placement was an $88,000 residential program.
13. Mills v. Board of Education, 348 F. Supp. 866, 876 (D.D.C. 1972).
14. 468 U.S. 883, 892 (1984). See Chapter 9 for an excerpt from the case.
15. 700 F.2d 1058, 1063 (6th Cir. 1983). See Chapter 8 for a portion of the case decision. *See also* Department of Education v. Katherine D., 727 F.2d 809 (9th Cir. 1984).

16. Mark & Ruth A. v. Grant Wood Area Educ. Agency, 795 F.2d 52 (8th Cir. 1986) and Springdale School District 50 v. Grace, 693 F.2d 41 (8th Cir. 1982).
17. For citations to a number of cases addressing these issues, see RPHP § 2.18 & cumulative supplements.

CHAPTER 14

Due Process Procedures under the EAHCA

The substantive right to a free appropriate public education might well be an empty promise without the procedural safeguards mandated by the EAHCA.[1] One of the major features of the procedural protections is the opportunity for parental participation in all decision making affecting the education of a child who is eligible for special education. The EAHCA and the implementing regulations spell out in great detail the procedural safeguards and the points at which parental involvement is guaranteed.

NOTICE AND CONSENT

A key element to procedural due process is *notice*. Without notice of plans and proposed decisions, parental involvement would often be nonexistent.

The EAHCA requires *written* notice *before* the agency

   (i) proposes to initiate or change, or
   (ii) refuses to initiate or change, the identification, evaluation, or educational placement of the child or the provision of an appropriate public education. . . . [2]

Requirement of notice is based on constitutional due process principles recognized in *Mills*. The EAHCA expands on the general constitutional guarantee by specifying not only when notice is required but also the form of the notice and its content.

Notice must be in writing and must be in a form understandable to the general public.[3] It must be in the native language of the parents or other mode of communication if that is not feasible. In the *Rowley*[4] case, for example, the school had set up a telecommunications device for the deaf (TDD) telephone hookup not only to notify Amy Rowley's deaf parents of their procedural rights but also to allow frequent discussion of Amy's educational progress.

The regulations provide no guidance as to when it might be infeasible to provide notice in a particular language or mode of communication. It could be speculated that proposing a program for a child whose parents' native language is Hindi, but who also communicate in English, might be permitted to provide the notice in English. It is suggested that variations will probably only be permitted under the infeasibility standard where the alternative notice is reasonably designed to provide actual notice to the parents.

If parents do not communicate in written form, the educational agency must take steps to ensure that there is appropriate translation that is understood by the parents. The agency must have written evidence of what was provided.[5]

The content of the notice must include not only a description of the action proposed or refused, an explanation of why, and a description of options that were considered and why they were rejected, but it must also include a full explanation of all of the procedural safeguards available under the EAHCA. This information must be in *every* notice provided relating to identification, evaluation, or placement. Notice must also include a description of the procedures, tests, or other factors used in making the proposal or refusal.[6]

It is not sufficient for the educational agency simply to provide notice to the parents. The parents must *consent* to the action before it can occur. Consent is required whenever the "educational agency wants to conduct a preplacement evaluation" or make an initial placement in a special education program.[7] Consent is not required, however, for changes in the child's program after the initial placement.[8] Although consent is not required, the notice requirements are still in place. If the parent objects to the change, and seeks administrative or other judicial review of the proposed change, the change may not occur until the resolution of the complaint, unless both sides agree otherwise.[9] This issue is discussed more fully later in this chapter.

What this means is that if, for example, the educational agency initially identifies a child through sweep-screening as being potentially eligible for special education, the agency must provide notice and obtain consent before doing further evaluations of the child as an individual. If the parent fails to consent to an evaluation, it is arguable that it is incumbent upon the school district to request a hearing. Failure to do so opens up the potential for liability later under an "educational malpractice" theory as discussed in Chapter 16.

The agency must also provide notice and obtain consent before making an initial placement into a program of special education and related services. Once a child is placed, however, the agency may make changes in the child's program without parental consent as long as prior notice has been given. And if the parents, upon receiving prior notice of the proposed change, object to it by filing for a hearing, the change may not take place until the dispute is resolved. There are some notable exceptions in emergency situations that will be discussed later in this chapter.

In Chapter 6, the *Quackenbush* case illustrated the possible consequences that can occur when the educational agency fails to comply with the notice requirements. What that case and other cases seem to indicate is that failure to comply with the notice requirement is a per se violation of the EAHCA. It is not entirely clear what the consequences of such a violation might be, but it is possible that if the violation is made in bad faith and has serious consequences, such as those in *Quackenbush,* there is the potential for financial liability on the part of the educational agency or perhaps some of the individuals involved in the process.[10]

THE INDIVIDUALIZED EDUCATIONAL PROGRAM

Once a child has been identified as being in need of special education and related services, the child is usually tested and evaluated to determine specific needs and problems. Chapter 6 discussed in detail the problems and issues surrounding the evaluation process. Once the various evaluations have been completed (subject to the notice and consent requirements, of course), the next step is usually the development of the individualized educational program (IEP). This is in some ways the most important step in the process, for it has the potential to make or break the child's educational future. The IEP is developed at a meeting[11] that includes a representative or representatives from the educational agency, the teacher, the parent(s), and the child—in appropriate circumstances. Other individuals, such as the child's physician or a specialist in a particular area, may be present in appropriate situations. Where the child has been evaluated for the first time, a member of the evaluation team or someone familiar with the evaluation procedures and the results in the particular case must be present. Whenever a placement in a private school or a parochial school is contemplated, a representative of that school should also be present, if possible.[12]

Development of the IEP is an extremely important opportunity for parental participation.[13] The EAHCA regulations recognize the importance of requiring parental attendance at this meeting by requiring that notice of the meeting must be provided in a timely fashion to ensure attendance and by requiring that meetings be scheduled at mutually agreeable times and locations. The notice given of the meeting is to include a specification of the time, place, participants, and the purpose of the meeting.

Even with the best of efforts by an educational agency, the unfortunate fact is that there will be instances when the parents cannot or will not attend an IEP meeting. The agency must, however, attempt to use other methods of participation, such as telephone communication. The agency must also document in detail its attempts to ensure parental participation. Such documentation would include records of telephone calls made or attempted, copies of correspondence, and records of attempts at actual contact with the parents.

When it is completed, the IEP itself must include the following: a statement of the child's present level of educational performance, a statement of annual goals (including short-term objectives), a statement of the specific services and program to be provided and the extent of participation in the regular program, the projected dates and duration of the services, and the criteria and procedures for determining whether the short-term objectives have been met. An assessment of whether the goals are being met must be made on at least an annual basis. If the parents request a copy of the IEP it must be given to them.

At the meeting itself a representative of the school will usually explain the proposed IEP. There should usually be discussion and clarification, and there may well be changes based on these discussions. Parents must be given an opportunity to suggest additions, deletions, or other changes to what the school proposes. Once the document is finalized, the educational agency must obtain parental consent before actually implementing the program at least for an initial placement.[14] The EAHCA does not require that the consent be in writing. As a practical matter, this is the simplest way for the agency to prove consent, and it is probable that most, if not all, local agencies designate a place for a signature on the IEP to indicate parental consent.

Refusal to consent does not automatically trigger an impartial hearing under the EAHCA. State law may indicate the process for proceeding with an educational program where there is no consent. Absent state law on this issue, the hearing procedures of the EAHCA will apply.[15]

Before addressing the hearing process, one final point should be noted regarding the IEP. That point relates to accountability. The IEP is not a contract to assure a particular level of performance at the end of a specified period of time. Rather, it is a statement of goals and services to meet those goals and standards to measure progress. In recognition of the purpose of the IEP, the EAHCA "does not require accountability on the part of an educational agency, teacher, or other individual."[16] While the school and its representatives may not be accountable for not achieving certain goals and objectives, this does not mean that there may not be accountability for failing to follow a course of conduct reasonably designed to achieve those goals and objectives or for failing to provide the agreed-upon services.

IMPARTIAL DUE PROCESS HEARING

When there is disagreement about a proposed identification, evaluation, or placement or refusal to do so, either party (the parents or the educational agency) may request a due process hearing.[17] Notice of the right to a hearing must be included in the notice of the proposed placement, etc. State law determines whether the state educational agency or a local or regional agency is responsible for conducting the hearing. Some states have developed intermediate mediation steps.

If a hearing is requested, the hearing must be held and final decision by the hearing office must be reached and a copy of the decision mailed to the parties within 45 days of the request for a hearing.[18] The 45 days includes any time required for mediation. States may not require the parents to submit to mediation before making the hearing request and the beginning of the 45-day period. Extensions for good reasons may be granted by the hearing officer at the request of either party.[19] Compliance with time requirements can be particularly important for certain placements, such as a preschool program, which is likely to continue only for the duration of the school year.

Sometimes the request for a hearing is sufficient to convince the educational agency that the parent is serious about pursuing a particular course of conduct, and the educational agency may reconvene the IEP committee and change its IEP as a result. The agency, however, may believe that its proposed IEP is appropriate, and that what the parents want is either too expensive and/or inappropriate for the child, and they may proceed through the hearing process rather than changing the proposal. Educational agencies are increasingly in a precarious position, however, because of amendments to the EAHCA regarding attorneys' fees.[20] If the parents eventually prevail, the educational agency may become obligated to pay attorneys' fees and costs. As a result, sometimes educational agencies agree to parental desires in spite of the fact that the agency believes its program to be appropriate.

Once the hearing is requested, the parents must be informed of available free or low-cost legal and other services.[21] The parents have a right to have counsel and special education advocates present at the hearing.[22] All of the costs of the hearing, except costs of representation, are paid by the educational agency.

The formality of the hearings is subject to state discretion to a large degree. Some states require that formal rules of evidence be complied with. This can have the de facto result that parents must be represented by counsel to be appropriately represented. Others are less formal both in regard to who may represent the parents and what types of evidence may be presented.

Although states have discretion in certain respects, the EAHCA requires that parties have the right to present evidence and confront, cross-examine, and compel attendance of witnesses. In addition, the parties have a right to a verbatim record of the hearing and a copy of written findings of fact and decisions. Any evidence that is to be presented at the hearing must be disclosed to the other party at least five days before the hearing or it may be prohibited at the hearing. Parents may have the child present and request that the hearing be open at their discretion.[23] Parents may choose to have a closed hearing if they are concerned about the stigma and harm to the child. On the other hand, parents may wish to expose the school to public scrutiny if they believe that bad faith or other misconduct is an issue.

The hearing itself is conducted by a hearing officer appointed by the local or state educational agency. One of the essential features of the EAHCA due process procedures is that the hearing officer must be *impartial.*[24] This means that the individual may not be an employee of the agency involved in educating or caring for the child or anyone having a personal or professional conflict of interest or who could not be objective. In the early years after passage of the EAHCA, there was confusion about whether certain individuals were impartial. In 1984, the U. S. Department of Education declared that state education employees could be hearing officers if they could establish impartiality. Some states allow education officials who are employed in localities other than the child's residence to act as hearing officers. Other states require that hearing officers be attorneys. Regardless of which types of individuals act as hearing officers, most states spell out specific qualifications, such as knowledge about handicapping conditions or knowledge about special education generally. There is a wide variation among states on these qualifications. Some states even have panels of hearing officers, although this adds to the expense incurred by the educational agency in conducting the hearing.

There has not been extensive litigation on the issue of hearing officers, but there have been some interesting cases. In one decision, an appellate court held that university personnel who had participated in formulating state special education policies were not impartial.[25]

At the hearing itself the process depends on the established procedures noted previously. The parents have a right to introduce independent evaluations as evidence at the hearing. Who bears the cost of these evaluations depends on whether the educational agency's evaluation was appropriate. If the agency's evaluation is appropriate, the parents still have the right to have the independent evaluation considered, but the parents must pay for it.[26] If the hearing officer requests an independent evaluation, the public agency must pay for the cost of the evaluation, regardless of whether the school's initial evaluation was appropriate or not.[27]

After conducting the hearing, the hearing officer must make a written finding of fact and decisions. There has been much disagreement about the authority of the hearing officer. It is clear that the hearing officer may make findings regarding whether the child has been appropriately identified, or whether the educational agency has been remiss in reevaluating on a regular basis, or other findings of this type. The hearing officer may also determine that a particular program or placement site is inappropriate under the EAHCA. What is not clear is whether the hearing officer has the authority to order the educational agency to make a particular placement or to order reimbursement. The authority to order attorneys' fees is similarly unresolved, although this issue has received a great deal of attention as an issue. It is probable that this is something that will eventually be resolved either by Department of Education clarification or by judicial consensus.

ADMINISTRATIVE AND JUDICIAL REVIEW

Once the hearing decision has been reached and transmitted to the parties, either party may seek review by appealing to the state educational agency. The review is based on the entire hearing record and any additional evidence necessary. Reviewing officials have the discretion to allow oral or written argument. Based on the review of this information, the reviewing official must make an independent decision and provide written findings and a decision to the parties. This must be done within 30 days after review was sought.[28] Extensions may be granted by the hearing or reviewing officer. Some states conduct the initial hearing at the state level. In those states there is no state agency review. Any party seeking review from a state level hearing must seek relief in court.[29]

When a matter is not resolved after a review by the state administrative agency or after a state-level hearing, either party may bring an action in state or federal court.[30] There have been instances where parents have sought relief by going to court initially, without first seeking resolution through the administrative avenues. In those cases, the courts have fairly consistently required that administrative remedies be exhausted before seeking judicial action, at least where it would not be futile to exhaust administrative remedies.[31] While the EAHCA does not specifically state a deadline either in the statute or in the regulations, judicial decisions have indicated that state statutes of limitations for similar types of actions will be applied in deciding how much time a party has to seek judicial review of the administrative decision.[32] In the judicial action, new evidence may be presented, and the decision of the state agency is usually accorded a substantial degree of deference.

All of this can be time-consuming and costly. In the early years of the EAHCA, the fact that the child was to remain in the current placement and the fact that parents were not entitled to attorneys' fees often resulted in a significant amount of foot-dragging by the school. A 1985 Supreme Court decision requiring reimbursement in some cases and the Handicapped Children's Protection Act of 1986 providing for attorneys' fees to be paid to prevailing parents have probably eliminated a great deal of delay that occurred in the past.

BURDEN OF PROOF

The EAHCA is silent as to which party bears the burden of proof in prevailing at the administrative or the judicial level. There are those who suggest that the party wishing to place a child in the more restrictive setting bears the burden of justifying why that is permissible under the least restrictive setting requirement. There are others who suggest that whenever there is a change in placement, the party seeking the change bears the burden. There is simply very little that has been clearly established on this issue.

At the administrative-review level, there is also little guidance from the regulations. The state agency is to consider the hearing record and additional evidence if necessary, but nothing is stated as to who bears the burden.

At the judicial review level, there is somewhat greater clarity. If the findings of the state education agency are supported by the record, the findings are conclusive.[33] For good cause, the complaint may be remanded for further consideration. As the Supreme Court in *Rowley* pointed out, courts will generally defer to the discretion of the educational agencies.[34]

WHEN ARE DUE PROCESS PROCEDURES TRIGGERED?

It is essential for the EAHCA to be effective that the due process requirements of the EAHCA be implemented at critical points in the process. Notice is required whenever the educational agency proposes to initiate or change the identification, evaluation, or placement or the provision of education, or refuses to do so. Consent is required for preplacement evaluations and initial placement. The opportunity for a hearing and review is available to all of these points.

The critical question that can arise is whether a particular action constitutes a change in placement, so as to require notice and the triggering of the procedural safeguards. The following section addresses temporary removals from a classroom and whether these constitute a change in placement. There are other situations that raise this question also. Several judicial opinions have addressed a variety of issues. As a general rule, minor changes, such as moving the class to a different room, or changing a feeding program for a profoundly handicapped child, or slightly increasing transportation time, are not considered to require notice.

It could prove unreasonably cumbersome to require that the agency notify the parents of minor variations. In the instance of a child for whom even minor variations would be important, the IEP could reflect the fact that not even minor variations would be made without notice.

STATUS OF CHILD PENDING FINAL DECISION AND DISCIPLINARY REMOVAL

The EAHCA provides that during the pendency of administrative and judicial proceedings, the child is to remain in the present educational placement.[35] This is known as the "stay-put" provision. If the child has not been previously placed in public school, the child must be placed in the public school program pending resolution. This requirement is subject to parental consent. The educational agency and the parents can agree to alternate placements pending resolution of the dispute.

The stay-put provision has given rise to a significant amount of litigation, primarily relating to disciplinary removals. The first issue to be resolved is whether there has been a change in placement at all by virtue of disciplinary removal from a classroom. A second issue results when a temporary removal is required for emergency reasons. What circumstances justify such a removal and for how long may the removal be permitted? Related to that issue is the question of what must be provided in terms of educational services during the removal. The following

Supreme Court decision addressed the issue of disciplinary removals and provided a significant degree of guidance as to these issues.

HONIG V. DOE

108 S. Ct. 592 (1988)
Justice BRENNAN delivered the opinion of the Court.

As a condition of federal financial assistance, the Education of the Handicapped Act requires States to ensure a "free appropriate public education" for all disabled children within their jurisdictions. In aid of this goal, the Act establishes a comprehensive system of procedural safeguards designed to ensure parental participation in decisions concerning the education of their disabled children and to provide administrative and judicial review of any decisions with which those parents disagree. Among these safeguards is the so-called "stay-put" provision, which directs that a disabled child "shall remain in [his or her] then current educational placement" pending completion of any review proceedings, unless the parents and state or local educational agencies otherwise agree. 20 U.S.C sec. 1415(e)(3). Today we must decide whether, in the face of this statutory proscription, state or local school authorities may nevertheless unilaterally exclude disabled children from the classroom for dangerous or disruptive conduct growing out of their disabilities. In addition, we are called upon to decide whether a district court may, in the exercise of its equitable powers, order a State to provide educational services directly to a disabled child when the local agency fails to do so. . . .

The EHA confers upon disabled students an enforceable substantive right to public education in participating States, and conditions federal financial assistance upon a State's compliance with the substantive and procedural goals of the Act. . . .

The primary vehicle for implementing these congressional goals is the "individualized educational program" (IEP), which the EHA mandates for each disabled child. . . .

The Act establishes various procedural safeguards that guarantee parents both an opportunity for meaningful input into all decisions affecting their child's education and the right to seek review of any decisions they think inappropriate. . . .

The "stay-put" provision at issue in this case governs the placement of a child while these often lengthy review procedures run their course in directs that:

> During the pendency of any proceedings conducted pursuant to [sec. 1415], unless the State or local educational agency and the parents or guardian otherwise agree, the child shall remain in the then current educational placement of such child. . . . Sec. 1415(e)(3).

The present dispute grows out of the efforts of certain officials of the San Francisco Unified School District (SFUSD) to expel two emotionally disturbed children from school indefinitely for violent and disruptive conduct related to their disabilities. In November 1980, respondent John Doe assaulted another student at the Louise Lombard School, a developmental center for disabled children. Doe's April 1980 IEP identified him as a socially and physically awkward 17-year-old who experienced considerable difficulty controlling his impulses and anger. Among the goals set out in his IEP was "[i]mprovement in [his] ability to relate to [his] peers [and to] cope with frustrating situations without resorting to aggressive acts." Frustrating situations, however, were an unfortunately prominent feature of Doe's school career: physical abnormalities, speech difficulties, and poor grooming habits had made him the target of teasing and ridicule as early as the first grade; his 1980 IEP reflected his continuing difficulties with peers, noting that his social skills had deteriorated and that he could tolerate only minor frustration before exploding.

On November 6, 1980, Doe responded to the taunts of a fellow student in precisely the explosive manner anticipated by his IEP: he choked the student with sufficient force to leave abrasions on the child's neck, and kicked out a school window while being escorted to the principal's office afterwards. Doe admitted his misconduct and the school subsequently suspended him for five days. [The maximum permitted in California at that time.] Thereafter, his principal referred the matter to the Student Placement Committee (SPC or Committee) with the recommendation that Doe be expelled. On the day the suspension was to end, the SPC notified Doe's mother that it was proposing to exclude her child permanently from SFUSD and was therefore extending his suspension until such time as the expulsion proceedings were completed. The Committee further advised her that she was entitled to attend the November 25 hearing at which it planned to discuss the proposed expulsion.

After unsuccessfully protesting these actions by letter, Doe brought this suit against a host of local school officials and the state superintendent of public education. Alleging that the suspension and proposed expulsion violated the EHA, he sought a temporary restraining order cancelling the SPC hearing and requiring school officials to convene an IEP meeting. . . .

Respondent Jack Smith was identified as an emotionally disturbed child by the time he entered the second grade in 1976. School records prepared that year indicated that he was unable "to control verbal or physical outburst[s]" and exhibited a "[s]evere disturbance in relationships with peers and adults." Further evaluations subsequently revealed that he had been physically and emotionally abused as an infant and young child and that, despite above average intelligence, he experienced academic and social difficulties as a result of extreme hyperactivity and low self-esteem. Of particular concern was Smith's propensity for verbal hostility; one evaluator noted that the child reacted to stress by "attempt[ing] to cover his feelings of low self-worth through aggressive behavior[,] . . . primarily verbal provocations."

Based on these evaluations, SFUSD placed Smith in a learning center for emotionally disturbed children. His grandparents, however, believed that his needs would be better served in the public school setting and, in September 1979, the school district acceded to their requests and enrolled him at A.P. Giannini Middle School. His February 1980 IEP recommended placement in a Learning Disability Group, stressing the need for close supervision and highly structured environment. Like earlier evaluations, the February 1980 IEP noted that Smith was easily distracted, impulsive, and anxious; it therefore proposed a half-day schedule and suggested that the placement be undertaken on a trial basis.

At the beginning of the next school year, Smith was assigned to a full-day program; almost immediately thereafter he began misbehaving. School officials met twice with his grandparents on October 1980 to discuss returning him to a half-day program; although the grandparents agreed to the reduction, they apparently were never apprised of their right to challenge the decision through EHA procedures. The school officials also warned them that if the child continued his disruptive behavior—which included stealing, extorting money from fellow students, and making sexual comments to female classmates—they would seek to expel him. On November 14, they made good on this threat, suspending Smith for five days after he had made further lewd comments. His principal referred the matter to the SPC, which recommended exclusion from SFUSD. As it did in John Doe's case, the Committee scheduled a hearing and extended the suspension indefinitely pending a final disposition in the matter. On November 28, Smith's counsel protested these actions on grounds essentially identical to those raised by Doe, and the SPC agreed to cancel the hearing and to return Smith to a half-day program at A.P. Giannini or to provide home tutoring. Smith's grandparents chose the latter option and the school began home instruction on December 10; on January 6, 1981, an IEP team convened to discuss alternative placements.

After learning of Doe's action, Smith sought and obtained leave to intervene in the suit. . . .

Respondent John Doe is now 24 years old and, accordingly, is no longer entitled to the protections and benefits of the EHA, which limits eligibility to disabled children between the ages of three and 21. See 20 U.S.C. sec. 1412(2)(B). It is clear, therefore, that whatever rights to state educational services he may yet have as a ward of the State, the Act would not govern the State's provision of those services, and thus the case is moot as to him. Respondent Jack Smith, however, is currently 20 and has not yet completed high school. Although at present he is not faced with any proposed expulsion or suspension proceedings, and indeed no longer even resides within the SFUSD, he remains a resident of California and is entitled to a "free appropriate public education" within that State. His claims under the EHA, therefore, are not moot if the conduct he originally complained of is "capable of repetition, yet evading review." Given Smith's continued eligibility for education services under the EHA, the nature of his disability, and petitioner's insistence that all local school districts retain residual authority to exclude disabled children for dangerous conduct, we have little difficulty concluding that there is a "reasonable expectation," *ibid.,* that Smith would once again be subjected to a unilateral "change in placement" for conduct growing out of his disabilities were it not for the state-wide injunctive relief issued below.

III

The language of sec. 1415(e)(3) is unequivocal. It states plainly that during the pendency of any proceedings initiated under the Act, unless the state or local educational agency and the parents or guardians of a disabled child otherwise agree, "the child *shall* remain in the then current educational placement." Faced with this clear directive, petitioner asks us to read a "dangerousness" exception into the stay-put provision on the basis of either of two essentially inconsistent assumptions: first, that Congress thought the residual authority of school officials to exclude dangerous students from the classroom too obvious for comment; or second, that Congress inadvertently failed to provide such authority and this Court must therefore remedy the oversight. Because we cannot accept either premise, we decline petitioner's invitation to re-write the statute.

Petitioner's arguments proceed, he suggests, from a simple, common-sense proposition: Congress could not have intended the stay-put provision to be read literally, for such a construction leads to the clearly unintended, and untenable, result that school districts must return violent or dangerous students to school while the often lengthy EHA proceedings run their course. We think it clear, however, that Congress very much meant to strip schools of the *unilateral* authority they had traditionally employed to exclude disabled students, from school. In so doing, Congress did not leave school administrators powerless to deal with dangerous students; it did, however, deny school officials their former right to "self-help," and directed that in the future the removal of disabled students could be accomplished only with the permission of the parents or, as a last resort, the courts.

As noted above, Congress passed the EHA after finding that school systems across the country had excluded one out of every eight disabled students from classes. In drafting the law, Congress was largely guided by the recent decisions in *Mills* . . . and *PARC* . . . , both of which involved the exclusion of hard-to-handle disabled students. . . .

Congress attacked such exclusionary practices in a variety of ways. It required participating States to educate all disabled children, regardless of the severity of their disabilities, 20 U.S.C. sec. 1412(2)(C), and included within the definition of "handicapped" those children with serious emotional disturbances. Sec. 1401(1). It further provided for meaningful parental participation in all aspects of a child's educational placement, and barred schools, through the stay-put provision, from changing that placement over the parent's objection until all review proceedings were completed. Recognizing that those proceedings might prove long and tedious, the Act's drafters did not intend sec. 1415(e)(3) to operate inflexibly, and therefore allowed for interim placements where parents and school officials are able to agree on one. Conspicuously, absent from sec. 1415(e)(3), however, is any emergency exception for dangerous students. We are therefore not at liberty to engraft onto the statute an exception Congress chose not to create.

Our conclusion that sec. 1415(e)(3) means what it says does not leave educators hamstrung. The Department of Education has observed that, "[w]hile the [child's] placement may not be changed [during any complaint proceeding], this does not preclude the agency from using its normal procedures for dealing with children who are endangering themselves or others." Comment following 34 CFR sec. 300.513(1987). Such procedures may include the use of study carrels, timeouts, detention, or the restriction of privileges. More drastically, where a student poses an immediate threat to the safety of others, officials may temporarily suspend him or her for up to 10 school days. This authority, which respondent in no way disputes, not only ensures that school administrators can protect the safety of others by promptly removing the most dangerous of students, it also provides a "cooling down" period during which officials can initiate IEP review and seek to persuade the child's parents to agree to an interim placement. And in those cases in which the parents of a truly dangerous child adamantly refuse to permit any change in placement, the 10-day respite gives school officials an opportunity to invoke the aid of the courts under sec. 1415(e)(2), which empowers courts to grant any appropriate relief.

Petitioner contends, however, that the availability of judicial relief is more illusory than real, because a party seeking review under sec. 1415(e)(2) must exhaust time-consuming administrative remedies, and because under the Court of Appeals' construction of sec. 1415(e)(3), courts are as bound by the stay-put provision's "automatic injunction," as are schools. It is true that judicial review is normally not available under sec. 1415(e)(2) until all administrative proceedings are completed, but as we have previously noted, parents may by-pass the administrative process where exhaustion would be futile or inadequate. . . . While many of the EHA's procedural safeguards protect the rights of parents and children, schools can and do seek redress through the administrative review process, and we have no reason to believe that Congress meant to require schools alone to exhaust in all cases, no matter how exigent the circumstances. The burden in such cases, of course, rests with the school to demonstrate the futility or inadequacy of administrative review, but nothing in sec. 1415(e)(2) suggests that schools are completely barred from attempting to make such a showing. Nor do we think that sec. 1415(e)(3) operates to limit the equitable powers of district courts such that they cannot, in appropriate cases, temporarily enjoin a dangerous disabled child from attending school. . . .

In short then, we believe that school officials are entitled to seek injunctive relief under sec. 1415(e)(3) in appropriate cases. In any such action, sec. 1415(e)(3) effectively creates a presumption in favor of the child's current education placement which school officials can overcome only by showing that maintaining the child in his or her current placement is substantially likely to result in injury either to himself or herself, or to others. In the present case, we are satisfied that the District Court, in enjoining the state and local defendants from indefinitely suspending respondent or otherwise unilaterally altering his then current placement, properly balanced respondent's interest in receiving a free appropriate public education in accordance with the procedures and requirements of EHA against the interest of the state and local school officials in maintaining a safe learning environment for all their students.

IV

We believe the courts below properly construed and applied sec. 1415(e)(3), except insofar as the Court of Appeals held that a suspension in excess of 10 school days does not constitute a "change of placement." We therefore affirm the Court of Appeals judgment on this issue as modified herein. Because we are equally divided on the question whether a court may order a State to provide services directly to a disabled child where the local agency has failed to do so, we affirm the Court of Appeals; judgment on this issue as well [requiring the state to provide services when the local agency refuses to do so].

The Supreme Court resolved some issues as to disciplinary removal in the *Honig* case. Did the justices decide the issue left open in the following case?

S-1 V. TURLINGTON

635 F.2d 342 (5th Cir. 1981)
cert. denied *454 U.S. 1030 (1981)*

Plaintiffs S-1, S-2, S-3, S-4, S-5, S-6, and S-8, were expelled from Clewiston High School, Hendry County, Florida, in the early part of the 1977–78 school year and for the entire 1978–79 school year for alleged misconduct.* Each was expelled for the remainder of the 1977–78 school year and for the entire 1978–79 school year, the maximum time permitted by state law. All of the plaintiffs were classified as either educable mentally retarded (EMR), mildly mentally retarded, or EMR/dull normal. It is undisputed that the expelled plaintiffs were accorded the procedural protections required by *Goss v. Lopez,* 419 U.S. 565 (1975). Except for S-1, they were not given, nor did they request hearings to determine whether their misconduct was a manifestation

---

* The misconduct upon which the expulsions were based ranged from masturbation or sexual acts against fellow students to willful defiance of authority, insubordination, vandalism, and the use of profane language.

of their handicap. Regarding S-1, the superintendent of Hendry County Schools determined that because S-1 was not classified as seriously emotionally disturbed, his misconduct, as a matter of law, could not be a manifestation of his handicap.

At all material times, plaintiffs S-7 and S-9 were not under expulsion orders. S-7 was not enrolled in high school by his own choice. In October, 1978, he requested a due process hearing to determine if he had been evaluated or if he had an individualized educational program. S-9 made a similar request; S-9's guardian had consented to the individualized educational program being offered her during that school year. The superintendent denied both students' requests, but offered to hold conferences in order to discuss the appropriateness of their individualized educational programs.

Plaintiffs initiated this case alleging violations of their rights under the Education for all Handicapped Children Act (EHA) and section 504 of the Rehabilitation Act of 1973. . . .

Florida, and the Hendry County School Board, are recipients of federal funds under both section 504 and the EHA. The children in this suit are clearly handicapped within the meaning of both section 504 and the EHA. The parties agree that a handicapped student may not be expelled for misconduct which results from the handicap itself. It follows that an expulsion must be accompanied by a determination as to whether the handicapped student's misconduct bears a relationship to his handicap. From a practical standpoint, this is the only logical approach. How else would a school board know whether it is violating section 504?

Defendant local officials argue that they complied with section 504. As support for their position, they state that they determined, in the expulsion proceedings, that the plaintiffs were capable of understanding rules and regulations or right from wrong. They also assert that they found, based upon a psychological evaluation, that plaintiffs' handicaps were not behavioral handicaps (as it would be if plaintiffs were classified as seriously emotionally disturbed), thereby precluding any relationship between the misconduct and the applicable handicap. We cannot agree that consideration of the above factors satisfies the requirement of section 504. A determination that a handicapped student knew the difference between right and wrong is not tantamount to a determination that his misconduct was or was not a manifestation of his handicap. The second prong of the school officials' argument is unacceptable. Essentially, what the school officials assert is that a handicapped student's misconduct can never be a symptom of his handicap, unless he is classified as seriously emotionally disturbed. With regard to this argument, the trial court stated:

> The defendants concede that a handicapped student cannot be expelled for misconduct which is a manifestation of the handicap itself. However, they would limit application of this principle to those students classified as "seriously emotionally disturbed." In the Court's view such a generalization is contrary to the emphasis which Congress has placed on individualized evaluation and consideration of the problems and needs of handicapped students.

We agree. In addition, the uncontradicted testimony elicited at the preliminary injunction hearing suggests otherwise. At the hearing, a psychologist testified that a connection between the misconduct upon which the expulsions were based and the plaintiffs' handicaps may have existed. She reasoned that "a child with low intellectual functions and perhaps the lessening of control would respond to stress or respond to a threat in the only way that they feel adequate, which may be verbal aggressive behavior." She further testified that an orthopedically handicapped child, whom she had consulted,

> [w]ould behave in an extremely aggressive way towards other children and provoke fights despite the fact that he was likely to come out very much on the short end of the stick. That this was his way of dealing with stress and dealing with a feeling of physical vulnerability. He would be both aggressive and hope that he would turn off people and as a result provoke an attack on him.

The record clearly belies the school officials' contention.

FIRST ISSUE
With regard to plaintiff S-1, the trial court found that the school officials entrusted with the expulsion decision determined at the disciplinary proceedings that S-1's misconduct was unrelated to his handicap. The trial court, however, held that this determination was made by school board officials who lacked the necessary expertise to make such a determination. The trial court arrived at this conclusion by holding that an expulsion is a change in educational placement. Under 45 CFR §121a.533(a)(3) and 45 CFR §84.35(c)(3), evaluations and placement decisions must be made by a specialized and knowledgeable group of persons. [The court went on to hold that expulsion is a change in placement].

SECOND ISSUE
The school officials point out that a group of persons entrusted with the educational placement decision could never decide that expulsion is the correct placement for a handicapped student, thus insulating a handicapped student from expulsion as a disciplinary tool. They further state that Florida law does not contemplate this result because expulsion is specifically provided for under Florida law as a disciplinary tool for all students. While the trial court declined to decide the issue whether a handicapped student can ever be expelled, we cannot ignore the gray areas that may result if we do not decide this question. We therefore find that expulsion is still a proper disciplinary tool under the EHA and section 504 when proper procedures are utilized and under proper circumstances. We cannot, however, authorize the complete cessation of educational services during an expulsion period.

THIRD ISSUE
State defendants focus their attention on the fact that, with the exception of S-1, none of the expelled plaintiffs raised the argument, until eleven months after expulsion, that they could not be expelled unless the proper persons determined that their handicap did not bear a causal connection to their misconduct. By this assertion, we assume that state defendants contend that the handicapped students waived their right to this determination. The issue is therefore squarely presented whether the burden of raising the question whether a student's misconduct is a manifestation of the student's handicap is on the state and local officials or on the student. The EHA, section 504, and their implementing regulations do not prescribe who must raise this issue. In light of the remedial purposes of these statutes, we find that the burden is on the local and state defendants to make this determination. Our conclusion is buttressed by the fact

that in most cases, the handicapped students and their parents lack the wherewithal either to know or to assert their rights under the EHA and section 504.

FOURTH ISSUE
The next issue is whether the EHA and its implementing regulations required the local defendants to grant S-7 and S-9 due process hearings. The school officials suggest that because S-7 had voluntarily withdrawn from school, he was not entitled to a due process hearing. With regard to S-9, the school officials assert that because she had previously agreed to the educational program being offered her during the school year, she was not entitled to a due process hearing. They also suggest that the conference offered by the superintendent was an adequate substitute for the due process hearings. They cite 45 CFR 121a506 as support for their argument. Under this regulation, the Department of Health, Education and Welfare (HEW) (now Health and Human Services), states in a comment that mediation can be used to resolve differences between parents and agencies without the development of an adversarial relationship.

The Justice Department, as amicus curiae, and the trial court, point out that under 20 U.S.C. §1415(b)(1), parents and guardians of handicapped children must have "an opportunity to present complaints with respect *to any matter* relating to the identification, evaluation, or educational placement of the child, or the provision of a free appropriate public education to such child." (Emphasis added.) The statute also states, in section 1415(b), that "whenever a complaint has been received under paragraph (1) of this subsection, the parents or guardians shall have an opportunity for an impartial due process hearing. . . . " No exception is made for handicapped students who voluntarily withdraw from school or previously agree to an educational placement. With regard to defendants' argument under 45 CFR §121a.506, HEW states in the same comment that mediation may not be used to deny or delay a parent's rights under this subpart. In the circumstances, the trial judge correctly found that plaintiffs S-7 and S-9 were entitled to due process hearings. . . .

CONCLUSION
Accordingly, we hold that under the EHA, section 504, and their implementing regulations: (1) before a handicapped student can be expelled, a trained and knowledgeable group of persons must determine whether the student's misconduct bears a relationship to his handicapping condition; (2) an expulsion is a change in educational placement thereby invoking the procedural protections of the EHA and section 504; (3) expulsion is a proper disciplinary tool under the EHA and section 504, but a complete cessation of educational services is not; (4) S-7 and S-9 were entitled to due process hearings; and, (5) the trial judge properly entered the preliminary injunction against the state defendants. In the circumstances, the trial judge did not abuse his discretion in entering the injunction.
AFFIRMED.

SUMMARY

A key feature of the effectiveness of the EAHCA in ensuring that special education will be available to those entitled to it is the procedural safeguards available under the Act. The Act and the regulations are fairly specific about the procedural requirements. These include notice to the parents at any point when a change in the identification, evaluation, or placement of the child is proposed or refused. Both the form and the content of the notice are specified, including written notice in a manner understandable to the parents to whom it is provided. Parental participation continues in the actual development of the individualized educational program (IEP). Parents not only have a right to notice but they must also give their consent before most special education actions can occur.

When there is disagreement over any of these decisions, either the school or the parents may request an impartial due process hearing. This administrative hearing incorporates numerous basic procedural protections—a right to have representation, a right to present evidence and examine witnesses, and a right to a record and the results of the hearing. States may add additional requirements for the hearings as long as these do not conflict with the EAHCA framework. A party aggrieved by the decision at this level may seek review at the state administrative agency level, and ultimately in state or federal court. There are specified EAHCA time frames within which all of these decisions must occur with the exception of a deadline for appealing to court. Judicial appeal deadlines have generally been found to be those that apply to similar actions in each state.

Most of the procedural requirements are fairly straightforward, and there has not been a substantial amount of litigation addressing these issues. One area that has received some attention by the courts is the question of who may serve as an impartial hearing officer. As yet there is not a substantial body of case law from which to draw many clear guidelines.

Another issue that has been raised, but has not yet been well settled, is what remedies are available to parents where procedural requirements are not complied with. Some courts have left open the possibility of damages, but this is far from settled. Another unresolved question is who bears the burden of proof in administrative and judicial actions. The EAHCA is silent, and courts have not addressed this issue extensively, although it does seem clear that educational agencies will generally be given a great deal of deference in their educational decision making.

The procedural issue receiving the greatest amount of judicial attention involves disciplinary removals. The issue is whether a temporary removal of a student with a handicap for disciplinary reasons can occur without triggering the procedural requirements of the EAHCA. A related issue is whether a child with a handicap can ever be completely removed from the education program because of disciplinary problems. The Supreme Court has provided some guidance on these questions. In the *Honig v. Doe* decision in 1988, the Court held that a removal for more than 10 days constitutes a change in placement and such a removal triggers the due process procedures. Shorter removals can be made in extreme circumstances where there is danger to self or others without resort to the EAHCA due process procedures. No clear resolution, however, has been reached as to whether repeated short-term removals are permissible or whether a child can ever be totally denied special education because of disciplinary problems.

QUESTIONS AND PROBLEMS

1. What kind of notice would be required in a case where parents are illiterate?
2. Suppose a child had a record of severe anxiety on standardized tests. Would the school be required to state in the notice to parents that the test would be in a standardized form? Should it make a difference whether the school is aware of the child's aversion to such tests? See *Healy v. Ambach,* 103 A.D.2d 565, 481 N.Y.S.2d 809 (1984).
3. What remedy is there if the educational agency does not comply with the deadlines for rendering decisions?
4. The regulations permit extensions to be granted, but with no statement as to the basis for granting extensions. Should this issue be clarified?
5. After *Honig v. Doe,* is there any way that a handicapped child can be expelled from school?
6. *Honig* allows short-term suspensions for disciplinary reasons. Removals longer than 10 days constitute a change in placement. Is there anything to prevent a school from engaging in a series of short-term removals?
7. What evidence should the school submit to justify judicial approval for long-term removal?
8. Does this decision resolve disciplinary removals from transportation?

NOTES

1. 20 U.S.C. § 1415–1416; 34 C.F.R. § 300.500–.589. *See also* L. Rothstein, Rights of Physically Handicapped Persons § 2.23–2.36 (1984) and cumulative supplements.
2. 20 U.S.C. § 1415(b)(1)(C).
3. 34 C.F.R. § 300.505(b).
4. *See* Chapter 7.
5. 34 C.F.R. § 300.505(c).
6. *Id.* at § 300.505(a).
7. *Id.* § 300.504(b).
8. *Id.* § 300.504 (Comment 1).
9. *Id.* § 300.513.
10. *See* Chapter 16.
11. 34 C.F.R. § 300.344.
12. 34 C.F.R. § 300.347–300.348.
13. 34. C.F.R. § 300.345.
14. *Id.* § 300.504(b).
15. *Id.* § 300.504(c).
16. *Id.* § 300.349.
17. *Id.* § 300.506.
18. *Id.* § 300.512(a).
19. *Id.* 300.512(c).
20. *See* Chapter 18.
21. 34 C.F.R. § 300.506(c).
22. *Id.* § 300.508(a)(1).
23. *Id.* § 300.508.
24. *Id.* § 300.507.
25. Mayson v. Teague, 749 F.2d 652 (11th Cir. 1984).

26. 34 C.F.R. § 300.503(b)(c).
27. *Id.* at § 300.503(d).
28. *Id.* §§ 300.510 & 300.512(b)
29. *Id.* §§ 300.506(b) & 300.510(a).
30. *Id.* § 300.511.
31. *See* RPHP § 2.34.
32. 20 U.S.C. § 1415.
33. *See* RPHP, cases cited in § 2.28 and cumulative supplement.
34. *See* Chapter 7.
35. C.F.R. § 300.513.

CHAPTER 15

Other Procedural Issues

PROCEDURES FOR VIOLATIONS
OF SECTION 504 AND SECTION 1983

As was noted in Chapter 3, Section 504 of the Rehabilitation Act prohibits recipients of federal financial assistance, such as educational agencies, from discriminating against otherwise qualified individuals with handicaps. In theory, this would seem to provide a statutory basis for parents to challenge educational agency practices that discriminate against students with handicaps.

Similarly, the equal protection and due process clauses of the fourteenth amendment to the U.S. Constitution would seem to provide a basis for challenging unequal treatment of students with handicaps and denial of procedural protections to that group.[1] Section 1983 of the Civil Rights Act[2] is the statutory basis through which constitutional and federal statutory violations can be redressed. It provides that individuals deprived of rights, privileges, or immunities of the Constitution or federal laws may bring action in court. It would therefore seem that Section 1983 could be used to claim not only violations of the Constitution (such as was claimed in *PARC* and *Mills*), but also for violations of Section 504 of the Rehabilitation Act and the EAHCA.

For several years it was unsettled whether Section 504 and/or Section 1983 could be the basis for claiming redress in special education cases. This was an important issue because the EAHCA was unclear whether damages and attorney's fees were available. It was not until a 1984 Supreme Court decision that this issue was resolved to some degree.

As was noted in the *Smith v. Robinson*[3] decision, it will be an unusual situation for Section 504 or the Constitution to provide a basis for a legal action where special education is at issue. The *Smith v. Robinson* decision clarified that the

EAHCA provides the exclusive avenue for relief for the vindication of constitutional claims and statutory rights under Section 504 in most instances.

Where there has been a denial of access to the procedural safeguards of the EAHCA or where a child does not fit within the definition of handicapped student under the EAHCA, it is possible that the EAHCA will not provide relief. In those instances, reliance on Section 504 of the Rehabilitation Act and Section 1983 of the Civil Rights Act will be necessary. A student with AIDS, but who is not in need of special education, would need to resort to Section 504 or the Constitution rather than the EAHCA for relief. Where a practice or procedure is widespread or is stated or de facto policy, it will also be important to consider redress through Section 504 or Section 1983. Although reliance on constitutional and Section 504 theories will be the exception, it is still important to know the procedures for bringing such actions.

Complaints under Section 504 can be filed with the Department of Education within 180 days of the violation. The complaint should be sent to the Office for Civil Rights of the Department of Education in the region where the school district is located. The complaint need not be on any particular form in order for investigation to proceed, but it must contain the following:

1. The name, address, and telephone number of the complaining party.
2. The basis for the complaint, such as handicap discrimination.
3. Who has been affected by the discrimination—individuals or groups of individuals.
4. The name and address of the discriminating agency if known.
5. The approximate date of the discriminatory conduct.
6. A brief description of what happened.
7. The signature of the complaining party.[4]

An administrative investigation follows. Because of the fact that administrative action in such cases is generally futile to resolution of the individual situation, the majority of courts permit individuals to bring actions directly in court. While Section 504 complaints are not a viable avenue for remedying many types of practices that may affect only one individual—because the EAHCA often preempts Section 504 and because Section 504 is often too cumbersome for special education type cases—it is important to recognize Section 504 as a tool for remedying systemic practices and policies. For example, a practice of always conducting special education classes in separate, segregated facilities could be attacked through a complaint to the Office for Civil Rights. An investigation could lead to an order for the school to stop the practice, and this would then affect all special education students in the school. An individual complaint using EAHCA due process procedures will often only resolve the situation for one student. For that reason, it is important that both advocacy groups and parents concerned about overall policy and practice recognize the value of the administrative complaint procedure under Section 504. Not only may such groups bring direct actions but they are not required to exhaust administrative remedies (including filing a complaint with the

Department of Education) when it would be futile.[5] The advantage of a Section 504 action over an EAHCA action is that a 1986 statutory amendment to the Rehabilitation Act clarified that states are not immune from actions under Section 504.[6] Neither judicial resolution nor congressional amendment has completely resolved the question as to whether states are immune from certain types of actions, such as damage suits, under the EAHCA. The issue of immunity is discussed in more detail in Chapter 19.

Like Section 504 cases, constitutional claims will be the exception after *Smith v. Robinson.* In a post-*Smith v. Robinson* decision, the Fourth Circuit[7] recognized the continuing validity of a Section 1983 action for procedural violations of the EAHCA. In that case, the parents had initially obtained a favorable disposition of their claim through EAHCA procedures, but the school had never implemented the program. Other procedural violations would include a failure to comply with EAHCA time requirements, a failure to review or reevaluate on schedule, or a refusal to hold an IEP meeting.[8] Disciplinary policies that run afoul of due process requirements have also been the basis for Section 1983 suits.[9] Constitutional violations are filed directly in court, without resort to any administrative agency. There is no immunity from a constitutional claim. The difficulty, however, is in proving that the violation is one not remediable under the EAHCA.

The disadvantage of either Section 504 or Section 1983 actions is that they do not have the built-in deadlines that the EAHCA due process hearing and administrative review do. Therefore, once a claim is filed, the speed with which the claim is resolved may well depend on how crowded the docket in the jurisdiction is or whether the judge can be convinced to grant preliminary relief.

The importance of these two mechanisms for redress, however, is the fact that Section 504 provides an avenue for relief for students falling outside the protection of the EAHCA, and Section 1983 provides a mechanism for ensuring that the procedural safeguards are followed.

EDUCATIONAL RECORDS

The issue of educational records has been mentioned previously,[10] but a few points should be emphasized. There are four major issues that relate to school records: (1) accuracy, (2) access, (3) cost, and (4) destruction.

As to all of these issues, the Family Education Rights and Privacy Act (FERPA)[11] must be read in addition to the EAHCA. Basically, under these statues, parents have a right to ensure that educational records are correct, and disputes over these matters can be resolved in EAHCA due process procedures.[12] Because of the stigma that may attach to inaccurate information, or the fact that benefits may be denied if educational records do not reflect a student's disability status accurately, this becomes an important issue. Also, because of concern about entitlement to benefits in the future, parents may want to ensure that the agency policy on handling old records does not result in important information being destroyed.[13]

Again, because of the stigma that may attach, it can be important to know who has access to records. FERPA, the EAHCA, and state confidentiality laws are fairly restrictive about allowing access only to those who have a privileged reason.[14] Adherence to proper policies has become even more important to protect children with AIDS. A teacher, who has no real need to know, but who has access to a record indicating that a child has AIDS, can destroy the privacy of the family if the teacher is indiscreet about telling others. The fact that there is a legal remedy for the parents is of little comfort in such cases. It is far better to implement the protective procedures in the first place.

In addition to the question of what educational personnel or other third parties may obtain access to records, it can often become critical for parents to have access to records—in order to evaluate whether the student's school records are accurate, and in some instances to use as evidence at a due process hearing. There is no question that parents may inspect and review all educational records under the EAHCA.[15] The issue of medical records becomes a bit more complex. Medical records that have been used as part of the basis for making an educational placement must be included as part of the records to which parents have access. The right of access to medical records other than those used in placement decisions is covered under state law.

The next question that arises is whether the parents must pay for copies of educational records. As a general rule, the answer is that reasonable charges may be assessed.[16] Given that it may well be deemed reasonable to charge 50 cents to $1.00 for one page, the parent of a severely handicapped child who has hundreds of pages of school records can end up paying hundreds of dollars just to get the records. The EAHCA does provide that if the cost would in effect prevent the parents from obtaining access to records, the charge must be waived. In addition, the Handicapped Children's Protection Act of 1986[17] may allow for reimbursement for the cost of copying records, if these are seen as related costs in an action where the parents prevail.

MOOTNESS

The Constitution prevents the judicial resolution of any case or controversy that has already been settled.[18] As such, mootness is a defense to any action under the EAHCA, Section 504, or the Constitution. An exception to the mootness doctrine is allowed when the issue before the court is one that is capable of repetition, but which evades review. It is not difficult to imagine any number of special education controversies that might fall under this type of exception. For example, if a placement involved whether a state was required to provide a full day of kindergarten to a particular handicapped child, then the amount of time it could take to go through the IEP, the due process hearing, and the administrative review could mean that by the time the case had reached the level of judicial decision making, the child is no longer eligible for a kindergarten program. In such a case, it would be appropriate for the court to resolve the issue by making a declaratory judgment as to the general policy at issue, even though it would not necessarily affect the particular child involved in the case.

Disciplinary cases also can raise issues of mootness. Often the disciplinary action—whether it concerns class discipline or removal—is over at the time of the legal action. Particularly where there has been no serious harm, the claim would seem moot. If the disciplinary action is part of an ongoing practice or policy, the case would seem to meet the standard of being repeated, yet escaping review.

Educational agencies frequently claim that graduation renders placement a moot issue. The portion of the *Honig v. Doe* opinion on that issue should be reviewed at this point.[19] That opinion states that graduation does not necessarily moot a claim. It should also be pointed out that in cases where damages, reimbursement, or compensatory education are being sought as remedies, the fact that an individual was no longer age eligible for special education would also be irrelevant.

SUMMARY

The EAHCA is the procedural framework through which most disagreements about the education of a child with a handicap will to resolved. There are cases, however, in which it may be necessary to resort to Rehabilitation Act or constitutional protections. The 1984 Supreme Court decision in *Smith v. Robinson* settled that these avenues of redress are only available in cases where the EAHCA does not provide any substantive protection for the student's situation. This holding does not preclude a parent from filing a complaint with the Department of Education for violation of Section 504 of the Rehabilitation Act. Such complaints are to be filed within 180 days of the conduct and are to include information specific enough for the Department of Education to conduct an investigation into the situation. These administrative investigations are of benefit primarily in cases where a general practice or policy of an educational agency is affecting a large group of students with handicaps.

Where the educational agency has denied the parents access to the procedural protections of the EAHCA, courts have generally been consistent in recognizing the right to bring an action under Section 1983 of the Civil Rights Act. This is the jurisdictional statute for redressing federal statutory and constitutional violations.

In enforcing any procedural right, issues of student records often come into play. The EAHCA, the Family Education Rights and Privacy Act, and state law must all be referenced to determine issues of accuracy, access, cost, and destruction of school records. This is not an issue receiving a great deal of discussion in the courts in the context of special education cases.

Unless there is currently an unresolved dispute at issue, courts are prevented by the Constitution from making declarations about policies and practices. Because of the time it often takes to resolve controversies, there are often occasions in the educational setting where a case may become moot before it can be heard in court. Cases that are capable of repetition but that evade review are exceptions to the mootness doctrine, and courts are permitted to address the general practice or policy in these cases, although its application to the named individual may already have been resolved.

QUESTIONS AND PROBLEMS

1. In what types of cases might an individual be able to seek redress under Section 504 of the Rehabilitation Act or Section 1983, where the EAHCA does not provide appropriate substantive protection?
2. If it were to be decided by the Supreme Court that an individual could not recover damages under the EAHCA, and thus it could be said that the EAHCA does not provide an adequate remedy in a particular situation involving special education, could that be a basis for claiming that Section 504 should be allowed as a basis for recovery so that damages could be recovered? (This assumes that Section 504 does permit damages as a remedy).
3. It has generally been held that there is no private relief for a violation of FERPA. If that is so, what is the parents' recourse if a school negligently allows information on a student's record indicating that the student has AIDS to be disclosed to the media?

NOTES

1. *See* Chapter 5.
2. 42 U.S.C. § 1983.
3. *See* Chapter 3.
4. See 45 C.F.R. § 807. The U.S. Department of Education is located at 400 Maryland Avenue, S.W., Washington, D.C. 20202. Regional offices are located in Boston, New York City, Philadelphia, Atlanta, Chicago, Dallas, Denver, San Francisco, and Seattle.
5. L. ROTHSTEIN, RIGHTS OF PHYSICALLY HANDICAPPED PERSONS §§ 2.32, 2.35 & 2.36 (1984).
6. Pub. L. No. 99–506, 100 Stat. 1807 (1986), 29 A.S.C. § 701. *See also* RPHP § 2.42.
7. Robinson v. Pinderhughes, 810 F.2d 1270 (4th Cir. 1987).
8. *See, e.g.* Mrs. W. v. Tirrozzi, 832 F.2d 748 (2d Cir. 1987); Manecke v. School Board, 762 F.2d 912 (11th Cir. 1985).
9. Hayes v. Unified School District, 669 F. Supp. 1519 (D. Kan. 1987); Doe v. Rockingham County School Board, 658 F. Supp. 403 (W.D. Va. 1987).
10. *See* Chapter 3.
11. 20 U.S.C. § 1232(g). This is often known as the Buckley Amendment.
12. 34 C.F.R. § 300.567(c). *See also* RPHP § 2.21.
13. 34 C.F.R. § 300.573. The Education General Administrative Regulations also provide that educational records should usually be retained for five years and destroyed after that point. 34 C.F.R. § 75.734.
14. *See generally* RPHP § 2.21.
15. 20 U.S.C. § 1415(b)(a)(A); 34 C.F.R. § 300.502. *See also* RPHP § 2.29.
16. 34 C.F.R. § 300.566(a).

17. *See* Chapter 18.
18. U.S. Const., art. III. *See also* RPHP § 2.31.
19. *See* Chapter 14.

CHAPTER 16

Special Education Malpractice

Ever since the advent of a national program of special education for handicapped students in 1975, there has been an influx of students with a variety of handicapping conditions into the mainstream of public schools. The presence of handicapped children raises the potential for misconduct to occur when educational personnel are not adequately trained or prepared for children with special needs.

As a policy matter, schools and school personnel should be held accountable for at least gross misconduct; but, historically, courts have rejected "educational malpractice" as a theory of liability. More recently, however, courts have begun to look more favorably on these cases.[1] The best means to avoid liability is for educational policymakers and administrators to ensure that educators and other school personnel are adequately prepared for the demands of mainstreaming handicapped students.

In this chapter special education malpractice is used as an umbrella term covering misconduct that could potentially be remedied through common law tort actions, EAHCA claims for remedies with financial obligations, and "constitutional torts" under Section 1983 of the Civil Rights Act. The application of these theories is discussed later in this chapter.

It should be noted here, however, that this use of terminology is somewhat broader than what is intended by many commentators when using this term. The term *education malpractice* is most often used in a context of common law tort. In the late 1970s and early 1980s, there was a flurry of litigation in the regular education context using this theory.[2] These claims often stemmed from parental dissatisfaction with the fact that while the child was being passed from grade to grade, the child was failing to learn basic skills such as reading and math. The parents would then bring a malpractice action claiming that the failure was a result of the school's breach of its duty to educate. These claims were overwhelmingly rejected by the courts, primarily because of the judicial attitude that there was neither a clear duty nor proof of causation.

Unfortunately, the blanket rejection of these claims was carried over to a large extent to claims involving special education. Courts often adopted the general reasoning of the regular education "why Johnny can't read" cases, without examining significant differences in the duty and other elements between regular and special education malpractice claims.

INJURIES AND REMEDIES

To ensure appropriate education is provided according to the EAHCA mandates, extensive practices and procedures are built into the law. Despite the fact that more than a dozen years have passed since the EAHCA became law, some educational personnel have not been adequately trained for this mandate, and some administrators do not comply with the clear administrative requirements. The mandate that handicapped children attend public schools and participate in the regular classroom to the maximum extent appropriate creates the potential for numerous injuries of the type previously described.

Actual physical injury could result from inadequate supervision of the physically or mentally impaired child in the regular classroom, in the playground setting, or in situations such as woodworking class. Physical injury could also result where the in-class discipline is inappropriate or where the bus driver or other educational employee who was negligently hired assaults a child.

Psychological or emotional damage could result where either the teacher ridicules or permits other children to ridicule a handicapped child, or even where a teacher simply fails to give any attention to the child. Emotional damage can also result if a child spends too much time on the bus because of the injury to concentration and stress on the child, or where inappropriate disciplinary measures damage the child's self-esteem.

Finally, damage to the child's educational development and even to the child's potential to earn a living can result from a variety of failures in the educational system—failure to provide a timely evaluation, program development, or implementation (as mandated by EAHCA requirements); improper suspension or expulsion of a handicapped child; failure to appropriately identify, evaluate, or place a handicapped child; or the total failure to implement an appropriate program as agreed upon.

The question is: What remedies are appropriate to compensate for these injuries? In some cases injunctive relief will be sufficient—that is, simply requiring the school to stop doing what it is doing or to start doing something else. In others, where the parents have unilaterally placed their child in an appropriate program while they dispute the school's recommended placement, a reimbursement of their expenses will adequately redress or remedy the situation.

But what if the injury results in hospital bills for physical injuries, or bills to psychiatrists or psychologists for counseling to remedy emotional damage? What if the parents cannot afford to make a unilateral placement in an expensive residential program pending a five-year litigation process, and the child remains in a grossly inappropriate program in the meantime? The damage in such cases can only be remedied by providing compensatory education or money damages for remedial education or money damages for lost potential earnings.

OBSTACLES TO DAMAGE AWARDS

There are four main reasons (other than finding no fault) why courts have not traditionally awarded money damages.

Public Policy

The first reason is public policy. As a matter of policy, some courts deem it inappropriate to require educational agencies (which are supported by the taxpayer) to provide compensation for misconduct—even in some cases where the misconduct resulted in serious damage.[3] Some courts have applied this public policy reasoning but have recognized that at least in cases where there has been bad faith or serious harm to the child, compensation could be required of the school.

   The other policy reason that courts have been reluctant to permit recovery for injuries caused as a result of misconduct toward handicapped children in the educational process is a general public policy reason. Courts are generally deferential to educational institutions in their decision making, and they do not want to get into the business of second-guessing educational practices.[4] While that makes sense for many educational decisions—such as whether a particular teacher should be given tenure or whether a particular textbook or curriculum is appropriate—it does not always make sense with respect to special education decisions.

No Duty Exists

The elements of common law tort actions are (1) a duty to adhere to a particular standard of conduct or to exercise reasonable care, (2) a breach of the duty or a violation of a standard, (3) a causal connection between the breach and the injury, and (4) resulting injury.[5]

   Another reason why courts have not traditionally awarded money damages is that courts have often found that the duty element of negligence is not present. The early cases denying recovery on negligence theories, because of findings that no clear standards of practice or clear duty existed, should not be relied on as the basis for not applying a malpractice theory. Most early special education malpractice decisions involved factual settings where the conduct in question arose before there were clearly established standards of practice relating to handicapped students as a result of the EAHCA. Because standards of practice have been clarified as a result of the EAHCA, in many instances it should no longer be valid to claim that the "duty" element of a malpractice case has not been met.

Private Actions under the Education for All Handicapped Children Act

There is no question that if the parents dispute the school's decision to evaluate, dispute also the school's assessment of a child's status, or the proposed placement, or a proposed change in placement, the parents have a right under the EAHCA to seek redress through an impartial hearing, review by the state agency, and ultimately review in the courts.

What is less clear is whether the parents may go directly to court if the issue is not a dispute about the appropriateness of an evaluation or placement. What if the issue is a claim that the due process rights of the EAHCA have not been complied with or that the program has never been implemented as agreed upon, or that the school has failed to reevaluate in the time frame required under the EAHCA? Can the parents bring an action in court without going through administrative procedures? More important, what are the remedies available to them in these situations?

While the Supreme Court has not specifically ruled on the issue, there is a growing body of case law establishing that parents need not exhaust administrative remedies before claiming relief for EAHCA violations, where it would be futile to do so.[6] Cases involving noncompliance with procedural safeguards and denial of access to administrative procedures would be examples of situations where resort to administrative remedies would be futile.

The issue where the courts have been less consistent is the issue of remedies. While declaratory and injunctive relief are clearly available under the EAHCA, the availability of other remedies is more problematic. Availability of reimbursement as a remedy was only clearly established in 1985 when the Supreme Court decided the case of *Burlington School Committee v. Department of Education.*[7]

Burlington answers the question about the availability of reimbursement as a remedy under the EAHCA, and this would resolve situations where the parents have the financial resources to pay for residential placements or other expenses pending resolution of a dispute. The decision does not resolve, however, what remedy is available to the parents who cannot afford to make the unilateral placement, but who ultimately prevail in a dispute where the school's placement turns out to be inappropriate. In those cases can the parents recover damages to cover costs of remedial tutoring or lost potential earnings? Can the school be required to provide compensatory education to make up for the time lost during the dispute? On these issues there is a difference of opinion.

Some courts hold that damages are *never* available as a remedy.[8] Others hold that damages may be available, but do not specify under what circumstances.[9] In other jurisdictions, damages are available only in situations where there is a danger to the child's physical health or where the school has acted in bad faith.[10]

As for compensatory relief, the availability of such relief may depend on whether it is viewed as equivalent to damages. The reasoning in the *Burlington* decision holding that reimbursement is not the same as damages, because "reimbursement merely requires [payment of] expenses that . . . should have [been] paid all along,"[11] would lend itself to a similar result when looking at compensatory education. If the school wrongfully denied an educational program, providing compensatory education is simply paying for services it was required to provide all along. At least one circuit court, however, has ruled that compensatory education is equivalent to damages.[12]

Immunity

Under the eleventh amendment to the U.S. Constitution, states and state agencies are immune from suits not based on violations of the Constitution. The exceptions are where Congress has specifically abrogated immunity (as it now has for violations of Section 504 of the Rehabilitation Act), or where the state has waived immunity.[13] After *Smith v. Robinson*,[14] Section 504 or the Constitution will ordinarily not be available as a vehicle for remedying a problem that can be redressed through the EAHCA. The question then becomes whether states are immune from damage claims under the EAHCA.

At this point the circuit courts are inconsistent on this issue. Rulings in the Seventh[15] and Ninth[16] Circuit courts indicate that states are immune. The First[17] and Third[18] Circuit courts seem to find that states are *not* immune. Adding to the complexity surrounding the immunity issue is the question of whether the immunity doctrine protects local school districts or state officials or educational employees such as bus drivers and teachers. This issue is more fully addressed in Chapter 19.

TRENDS IN AWARDING DAMAGES AND COMPENSATORY EDUCATION IN MISCONDUCT CASES

Supervision and Related Conduct

Because in many situations a handicapped child is in greater need of supervision than is a nonhandicapped child of the same age, it is important for administrators to recognize that heightened duty and to ensure that all personnel are appropriately trained to meet their obligations.

There have been several cases in the past several years in which supervision of handicapped children has been at issue. These cases have mixed results.

Several cases involving handicapped children have resulted in findings of liability or have left open the possibility of liability. In *Collins v. School Board*,[19] a directed verdict in favor of the school was reversed and the case was remanded for findings in a suit claiming that the substitute teacher in a shop class had been negligent in supervising the class, when an emotionally handicapped student was sexually assaulted by another student.

In *Hopkins v. Spring Independent School District,*[20] the court found that the state would not be immune from liability for leaving a child with cerebral palsy unsupervised, and who subsequently suffered head injuries as a result of being pushed into a stack of chairs. Liability by the school board was found in *Clomon v. Monroe City School Board,*[21] when a four-year-old deaf child was struck and killed after alighting from the bus because the bus driver did not make sure she reached safety. Ironically, the claim in that case was brought by the driver who killed the child, claiming severe emotional trauma. The court held in *DeFalco v. Deer Lake School District,*[22] that the teacher, school nurse, and principal might all be liable under Section 1983 of the Civil Rights Act for failing to provide medication to a student with hypoglycemia in a timely manner. In *Barbin v. State,*[23] an award of $185,000 was upheld when a deaf seventh grader was improperly supervised in woodworking class and the injury that resulted permanently impaired the child's finger-spelling skills. Perhaps the most dramatic instance of liability is the $400,000 damage award in *Rodriguez v. Board of Education,*[24] where a trainable mentally retarded child suffered severe head injuries after being negligently supervised during play period.

There have been a number of cases, however, in which no liability has been found. The reasons have included findings that there was no negligence. The primary reason, however, is the application of the immunity defense. The court in *Braun v. Board of Education*[25] found that there had not been negligence when an epileptic student manager suffered a seizure while standing on a ladder to make scoreboard alterations. Immunity was a defense in *Hicks v. Walker County School District,*[26] where a handicapped child was assaulted on the bus by two other handicapped children but the bus driver was not wilful, malicious, or acting in bad faith. In another bus driver case, a mixed result was reached. *Doe A. v. Special School District,*[27] involved a bus driver who had beaten and sexually abused handicapped students on the bus. The claim was brought under Section 1983 of the Civil Rights Act, and the court found the action permissible as against the bus driver but not against the school district or school administrators.

In at least some of the cases, the injury may have resulted not only from a failure to supervise but also from a failure on the part of the school to adequately prepare personnel for the heightened awareness necessary to supervise handicapped students. Because of the tendency of some courts to apply the immunity defense when raised against school districts and administrators, it would seem that in many cases only the individual supervisor will be held liable. In cases involving particular egregious misconduct, this policy seems to be wrong. In *Lopez v. Houston Independent School District,*[28] the court found that although a school bus driver may have been liable for negligence in not stopping lengthy fights on the bus, the bus driver's supervisors had not been callously indifferent and therefore were immune. It would seem that if this standard were to be applied in a case where a child had been seriously injured and sustained extensive medical expenses, an injustice might be done because the bus driver may well not have the resources to compensate the parents for those expenses.

One possible avenue for seeking redress might be through a direct action under the EAHCA. If a handicapped child's IEP states that the child is to have an assistant on the bus, or that the bus should be provided with a supervisor in addition to the driver, a violation of this requirement might give rise to direct action in court. Because the right to bring such actions is not clearly settled, and the availability of damages under the EAHCA is even less well settled, there seems to be a gap in coverage at least for some instances of negligence in supervision in states with strong immunity policies.

Infliction of Emotional Distress

Like negligent supervision, a claim of infliction of emotional distress is probably going to be brought under a tort theory, or in extreme cases, under Section 1983 of the Civil Rights Act. It will not be the type of injury where a claim under the EAHCA will ordinarily be appropriate. There is not a great deal of case law on this issue, but it would seem that cases alleging infliction of emotional distress will face the same obstacle of immunity in many jurisdictions. Unless the infliction of emotional distress reaches the level of a constitutional claim under Section 1983, there may well be problems of immunity.

The *Clomon* case, mentioned previously[29] involved a claim of emotional trauma for negligently supervising a child getting off the bus. While in that case liability was found, immunity is probably going to be a defense in some jurisdictions. *Doe A. v. Special School District* is such a case.[30] In that case immunity prevented claims against the school district and school administrators although there was evidence of negligent supervision of a bus driver who beat and sexually abused handicapped children over a long period of time.

Violations of EAHCA Requirements

Ever since *Smith v. Robinson* there have been a number of rulings that indicate that if there is a denial of access to due process procedures and other substantive rights available under the EAHCA, rather than a dispute over the appropriateness of the educational program, a claim can be made directly either under the EAHCA or under Section 1983 of the Civil Rights Act. What is essential in those cases is a claim that there was a total denial or at least a substantial denial of access to the EAHCA rights and procedures. It is unclear, however, whether damages are available in such cases. If damage claims are limited to instances where there is bad faith or a serious physical injury, many injuries will go unredressed. For example, the child whose parents cannot afford unilateral placement, but who ultimately prevail in proving that the school's placement was inappropriate, may have spent several years in an inappropriate placement. Such a wrongful placement could result in a serious detriment to the child's educational development, although it would not necessarily result in serious physical harm or even have been caused by bad faith. It is questionable whether "policy reasons" should prevent recovery of damages in such cases.

Inappropriate Disciplinary Action

Inappropriate discipline can be of two kinds. First, using corporal punishment or another disciplinary measure that is inappropriate in a particular circumstance can result in emotional damage to a sensitive child, particularly one who is already emotionally disturbed or one who has a behavior problem. Second, improper classroom discipline can also result in physical injury to the child. The theories for remediation of these injuries in most instances follow the theories for improper supervision or infliction of emotional distress. In other words, courts may either be inclined to find that there was no duty in a particular case, or that immunity is a defense even if there was improper conduct.

In *Cole v. Greenfield-Central Community Schools,*[31] the court found that it was permissible to paddle and tape shut the mouth of a hyperactive and emotionally disturbed child where this was used as a last resort with an extremely disruptive child. While the result may be correct in this case, there is a question whether a court would find liability should it turn out that the disciplinary measures in this case were extreme and inappropriate and caused serious emotional damage to the child. In *Jefferson v. Ysleta Independent School District,*[32] the court ruled that tying an eight-year-old to a chair and denying her access to the bathroom was improper discipline. While the youngster was not handicapped in that case, it seems likely that other courts would find that "a competent teacher knew or should have known [that such punishment] was constitutionally impermissible," particularly in cases involving handicapped children.

The second type of inappropriate discipline involves disciplinary removal of a student. This could include suspension (temporary removal) or expulsion (permanent removal). As Chapter 14 demonstrated, there is now some degree of clarity about the circumstances under which either type of disciplinary measure may be imposed legally within the requirements of the EAHCA.[33]

The wrongful removal of a student can have serious detrimental effects on a student, particularly when it is a long-term removal. These effects can include damage to the academic progress of the student as well as negative psychological effects due to embarrassment and other factors.

Misconduct in Identification, Evaluation, Placement, and Programming

This is the type of issue that is most frequently considered to fall within the area of educational malpractice. And it is in this area that the courts have traditionally been particularly reluctant to intervene. The case most frequently cited for the proposition that there is no viable cause of action for special education malpractice involves an issue of inappropriate identification and placement. In *Hoffman v. Board of Education,*[34] the New York Court of Appeals found although Daniel Hoffman had been misidentified as mentally retarded and had wrongfully been placed in a class of mentally retarded children when he was not retarded, because of judicial deference to educational decision-makers, the lower court award of $750,000 in damages was dismissed. In that same vein, a later decision in New York rejected a special education malpractice case for misidentification in *Torres v. Little Flower Children's Services*,[35] although a court in that state had only one year earlier upheld a $1.5 million damage award involving a physician who had improperly relied on an IQ test in recommending a child's placement in an institution.[36]

In the early years after the EAHCA was passed, it seemed that courts would continue to reject special education malpractice cases of this type. But in recent years, there seems to be an increase in the willingness to bring such cases, and at least some courts are beginning to find liability for misconduct in identification, placement, and programming types of issues. Not surprisingly, a New York ruling in *DeRosa v. City of New York*[37] held that there is no cause of action based on an educational malpractice theory for alleged negligent placement of a deaf child in a class for mentally retarded students. And in Pennsylvania a similar result was reached in a case involving the improper placement of a learning-disabled student in a class of mentally retarded students.[38]

Interestingly, a court in New York has recognized educational malpractice as a basis for recovery, when a school district with knowledge that a student had psychological problems that could worsen if left untreated did not notify the student's mother.[39] Another court in New York, this time a federal court using the EAHCA as the theoretical basis for the case, found that the City of New York was not in compliance with the EAHCA for failing to evaluate and place children in a timely manner.[40]

While not proof of judicial attitude, a case in Connecticut was recently settled for $2,000 in damages plus $2,500 in attorneys' fees when the school failed to implement (through administrative errors) a program that had been agreed upon for a handicapped student.[41] This payment of damages is particularly significant because the parents had incurred no out-of-pocket expenses and the child had not suffered egregiously, and the situation was remedied. The payment was deemed to be one that would prompt more diligence by the school.

Probably the most well-known case involving a claim of misconduct in identification and placement is the case of Karen Morse.[42] Although she had been diagnosed as being learning disabled, she was not provided with appropriate educational programming for two or three years. Although the school agreed to provide compensatory education for one year, she had to seek judicial intervention to obtain further relief. In early 1987, the New Hampshire Department of Education ordered the school to pay $17,000 to compensate her for her costs incurred in seeking additional remedial education after she had graduated from high school. It is likely that litigation will increase regarding appropriate methodology for certain situations, such as for learning-disabled and deaf children. In cases where the appropriate methodology is far from settled, it is likely that courts will defer to reasonable judgment of the educational agency, as they did in *Rowley.*

TRENDS IN LIABILITY

There are still too few cases to draw any sweeping conclusions about the future of special education malpractice. There does seem to be, however, at least a crack in the dam of judicial refusal to consider special education malpractice. And there is certainly an increased tendency for parents to litigate in cases where they believe the school has acted inappropriately.

Some of the courts have remediated school misconduct under EAHCA or Section 1983 theories, and these cases have not been brought using malpractice theories. Other cases, however, have resulted in a finding of liability and damage awards where the case theory is in terms of common law malpractice or at least tort language rather than statutory language.

A judicial willingness to recognize a duty toward handicapped children in public schools, and to move away from the total deference to educational decision-makers and away from a general reluctance to order damages against public schools as a policy matter, seems to be at least a minor trend. It may be that where an injury has resulted from serious misconduct, the courts will order the injury to be remedied. Perhaps courts will not order compensation for pain and suffering, lost potential earnings, or punitive damages, but they will at least remediate out-of-pocket expenses already incurred or provide for the cost of compensatory education.

Schools should take seriously the EAHCA requirement that educational agencies implement a comprehensive system of personnel development. The specter of accountability is an important incentive to schools to ensure that their personnel are adequately trained and their procedures and practices are appropriate for the challenges and obligations imposed on the public school system by the mainstreaming mandate of the EAHCA. State certification requirements, local hiring practices, and colleges of education should take account of this issue in ensuring that the regular classroom teacher, not just the special educator, is trained in handicapping conditions, behavior management, and legal requirements.

SUMMARY

The presence of students with handicaps in the public education system creates the potential for a number of types of misconduct, particularly where educational personnel have not been adequately prepared or trained to meet the needs of this population of students. Whether educational personnel or educational agencies should be held accountable for injuries that occur as a result of such misconduct is a difficult and complex issue.

As a general rule, courts have been disinclined to hold educators liable for misconduct, with the major exception being failure to supervise, thus resulting in physical injuries as a direct result. This judicial deference has usually prevented parents from recovering damages of any type against educational personnel and agencies for claims involving infliction of emotional distress, violations of EAHCA requirements, improper disciplinary action, or misconduct in identification, evaluation, placement, and programming. This is generally true even when parents can demonstrate actual physical injury, psychological or emotional damage, or damage to the child's educational development.

In addition to the general tendency of courts not to hold educators liable, there are a number of other obstacles to such actions, particularly where damage awards are sought as a remedy. These obstacles include: failure to find that the elements of negligence are present, rulings that there is no private action for damages under the EAHCA, and the application of immunity doctrines in these cases.

In general, it is not likely that parents will be able to recover damages for misconduct toward their handicapped children. There is a slowly growing body of judicial law that has recognized that educators should be held accountable for their misconduct, particularly when the conduct has been in bad faith or is particularly egregious.

QUESTIONS AND PROBLEMS

1. In which of the following instances would the EAHCA address the problem, and in which would a tort action of some type be more appropriate? In examining these situations, which individual within the school system should be held accountable and why?

   a. Connie is six and has a learning disability that prevents her from processing verbal instructions. She is a first grader, placed in the regular classroom for most of the day. She and her classmates have been told not to play near the swings. Connie walks in front of a swing during recess on the first day, is knocked down, and breaks her arm.

   b. Zack is autistic, and his parents want to have Zack placed in a full-day, rather than a half-day, kindergarten program. When the IEP meeting fails to result in agreement, his parents request a due process hearing, the request being made on June 30. The school does not hold the hearing until September, and does not render a decision until November.

   c. Mark (age 10) has a behavior disorder requiring psychological counseling. He is in the regular classroom for most of the day, but frequently runs out of the classroom. The teacher deals with this by tying Mark into his seat. His parents find out about this after it has gone on for six months.

   d. Diane is a third grader with Down syndrome. She is educably mentally retarded and has been placed in the regular classroom for most of the day during kindergarten, first grade, and second grade. She has made excellent progress in learning academic skills such as counting and reading. Diane's IEP indicates that she is to continue learning these skills in the regular classroom. Mrs. Green, the third-grade teacher, is 57 and attends the IEP conference. Although Mrs. Green says nothing at the conference, she is philosophically opposed to mainstreaming mentally retarded children. She thinks the experience and demands are too frustrating and that the best thing for them is to "just love them" so they'll be happy. Once Diane arrives in the classroom, Mrs. Green places her at a table and gives her coloring and simple puzzles to do for most of the time each day. At the end of the year Diane's progress review indicates that she has lost most of the skills she had gained before beginning third grade. What if the principal becomes aware of Mrs. Green's conduct?

2. How can educational institutions best avoid liability by ensuring that their personnel are adequately trained?

3. What can regular education teachers who are concerned that they have not been adequately prepared for handicapped children in the classroom do to protect themselves from liability?

4. As a policy matter, is it wise to allow parents to collect tort damages against school systems, whose resources are already stretched, when the result will be that all other children will be "penalized" by educational dollars going to pay damage awards?

NOTES

1. For an in-depth analysis of this issue, see Rothstein, *Accountability for Professional Misconduct in Providing Education to Handicapped Children,* 14 J.L. & EDUC. 349 (1985). *See also,* Rothstein, *Special Education Malpractice, 43,* EDUC. L. REP. 1249 (1988) and L. ROTHSTEIN, RIGHTS OF PHYSICALLY HANDICAPPED PERSONS § 2.22 (1984).

2. *See generally* Elson, *A Common Law Remedy for the Educational Harms Caused by Incompetent or Careless Teaching,* 73 NW. U.L. REV. 641 (1978).

3. *See, e.g.,* Torres v. Little Flower Children's Services, 61 N.Y. 2d 119, 474 N.E. 2d 223, 485 N.Y.S. 2d 15 (1984), *cert. denied,* 106 S. Ct. 181 (1985) (misclassification of child).

4. *Hoffman v. Board of Education,* 49 N.Y.2d 121, 400 N.E. 2d 317, 424 N.Y.S. 2d 376 (1979).

5. *See* W. PROSSER & W. KEETON, LAW OF TORTS § 30 (5th ed. 1984).

6. *See* Chapter 14.

7. 471 U.S. 359 (1985). *See* Chapter 17.

8. Miener v. Missouri, 673 F.2d 969 (8th Cir.), *cert. denied,* 459 U.S. 909 (1982).

9. Manecke v. School Board, 762 F.2d 912 (11th Cir. 1985). *See also* RPHP § 2.39 (cumulative supplement) for breakdown of circuit court opinions on this issue.

10. Anderson v. Thompson, 658 F.2d 1205 (7th Cir. 1981). The Supreme Court in Smith v. Robinson, 468 U.S. 992 (1984) noted the various lower court opinions on damages, but did not indicate whether any of those standards were correct.

11. 471 U.S. at 370–71.

12. Alexopulos v. San Francisco Unified School District, 817 F.2d 551 (9th Cir. 1987). *See also* RPHP § 2.40.

13. *See* Chapter 19.

14. *See* RPHP § 2.42 cumulative supplement. *See also* Chapter 3.

15. Gary A. v. New Trier High School District No. 203, 796 F.2d 940 (7th Cir. 1986).

16. Doe v. Maher, 793 F.2d 1470 (9th Cir. 1986). There are several rulings from the Ninth Circuit that relate to other aspects of this issue, such as liability for local school districts. *See* RPHP § 2.42 cumulative supplement.

17. David D. v. Dartmouth School Committee, 775 F.2d 411 (1st Cir. 1985).

18. Geis v. Board of Education, 774 F.2d 575 (3d Cir. 1985).

19. 471 So. 2d 560 (Fla. App. 4th 1985).

20. 706 S.W.2d 325 (1986), *aff'd.* 722 S.W. 2d 741 (Tex. 1987).

21. 490 So. 2d 691 (La. App. 1986).

22. 663 F. Supp. 1108 (W.D. Pa. 1987). *See* Chapter 15.

23. 506 So. 2d 888 (La. App. 1987).
24. 104 A.D.2d 978, 480 N.Y.S.2d 901 (N.Y. 1984).
25. 151 Ill. App. 3d 787, 502 N.E.2d 1076 (1986).
26. 172 Ga. App. 428, 323 S.E.2d 231 (1984).
27. 637 F. Supp. 1138 (E.D. Mo. 1986).
28. 817 F.2d 351 (5th Cir. 1987).
29. *See* note 21 *supra.*
30. *See* note 27 *supra.*
31. 657 F. Supp. 56 (S.D. Ind. 1986).
32. 817 F.2d 303 (5th Cir. 1987). *See also* Juneau v. Louisiana Board of Elementary & Secondary Education, 506 So. 2d 756 (La. 1987) where the court held a school nurse could be dismissed for unauthorized use of aversive stimuli on handicapped students.
33. *See* Honig v. Doe, 108 S. Ct. 592 (1988).
34. 49 N.Y.2d 121, 400 N.E.2d 317, 424 N.Y.S.2d 376 (1979).
35. 64 N.Y.2d 119, 47 N.E.2d 223, 485 N.Y.S.2d 15 (1984), *cert. denied,* 474 U.S. 864 (1985).
36. Snow v. State, 98 A.D.2d 442, 469 N.Y.S.2d 959 (1983) (physician improperly relied on IQ test).
37. 517 N.Y.S.2d 754 (App. Div. 1987).
38. Agostine v. School District of Philadelphia, 527 A.2d 193 (Pa. Commwlth. 1987).
39. Savino v. Board of Education, 123 A.D.2d 315, 506 N.Y.S.2d 210 (1986).
40. P. v. Ambach, C.A. No. 79 C 270 (E.D.N.Y. 1986).
41. P. v. New Haven Board of Education, C.A. No. N84-64 (D. Conn., filed Feb. 6, 1984).
42. Reported by the news media.

CHAPTER 17

Reimbursement and Compensatory Education

As the material on due process procedures demonstrates, very detailed procedures protect the interests of children entitled to services under the EAHCA. While there are a number of deadlines set for complying with the procedures, the process can be a long one, particularly if the final administrative decision is appealed to court. The dilemma for parents in such cases is where to place the child pending the decision. Unlike employment cases, where at least some retroactive compensation (in the form of back wages, reinstatement, and the like) can be provided for a wrongful employment decision, the development of a child cannot be put on hold and compensated for adequately later. This is particularly true for younger children.

REIMBURSEMENT

The regulations under the EAHCA require the child to remain in the current placement pending a final decision. This can be problematic where the parents are concerned that the current placement is inappropriate or may even create a serious risk for the child. Many parents have placed their children in expensive residential or other programs and paid for them pending resolution of the placement dispute. Until *Burlington School Committee v. Department of Education* was decided by the Supreme Court, it was not clear whether parents could be reimbursed for these "self-help" placements. The *Burlington* case answers the major question about reimbursement, but leaves a number of questions unanswered.

BURLINGTON SCHOOL COMMITTEE V. DEPARTMENT OF EDUCATION

471 U.S. 359 (1985)
Justice REHNQUIST delivered the opinion of the Court.

The Education of the Handicapped Act requires participating state and local educational agencies "to assure that handicapped children and their parents or guardians are guaranteed procedural safeguards with respect to the provision of free appropriate public education" to such handicapped children. These procedures include the right of the parents to participate in the development of an "individualized education program" (IEP) for the child and to challenge in administrative and court proceedings a proposed IEP with which they disagree. Where as in the present case review of a contested IEP takes years to run its course—years critical to the child's development—important practical questions arise concerning interim placement of the child and financial responsibility for that placement. This case requires us to address some of those questions.

Michael Panico, the son of respondent Robert Panico, was a first grader in the public school system of petitioner Town of Burlington, Massachusetts, when he began experiencing serious difficulties in school. It later became evident that he had "specific learning disabilities" and thus was "handicapped" within the meaning of the Act. This entitled him to receive at public expense specially designed instruction to meet his unique needs, as well as related transportation. The negotiations and other proceedings between the Town and the Panicos, thus far spanning more than 8 years, are too involved to relate in full detail; the following are the parts relevant to the issues on which we granted certiorari.

In the spring of 1979, Michael attended the third grade of the Memorial School, a public school in Burlington, Mass., under an IEP calling for individual tutoring by a reading specialist for one hour a day and individual and group counseling. Michael's continued poor performance and the fact that Memorial School encompassed only grades K through 3 led to much discussion between his parents and Town school officials about his difficulties and his future schooling. Apparently the course of these discussions did not run smoothly; the upshot was that the Panicos and the Town agreed that Michael was generally of above average to superior intelligence, but had special educational needs calling for a placement in a school other than Memorial. They disagreed over the source and exact nature of Michael's learning difficulties, the Town believing the source to be emotional and the parents believing it to be neurological.

In late June, the Town presented the Panicos with a proposed IEP for Michael for the 1979–1980 academic year. It called for placing Michael in a highly structured class of six children with special academic and social needs, located at another Town public school, the Pine Glen School. On July 3, Michael's father rejected the proposed IEP and sought review by respondent Massachusetts Department of Education's Bureau of Special Education Appeals [BSEA]. A hearing was initially scheduled for August 8, but was apparently postponed in favor of a mediation session on August 17. The mediation efforts proved unsuccessful.

Meanwhile the Panicos received the results of the latest expert evaluation of Michael by specialists at Massachusetts General Hospital, who opined that Michael's "emotional difficulties are secondary to a rather severe learning disorder characterized by perceptual difficulties" and recommended "a highly specialized setting for children with learning handicaps . . . such as the Carroll School," a state approved private school for special education located in Lincoln. Believing that the Town's proposed placement of Michael at the Pine Glen School was inappropriate in light of Michael's needs, Mr. Panico enrolled Michael in the Carroll School in mid-August at his own expense, and Michael started there in September.

The BSEA held several hearings during the fall of 1979, and in January 1980 the hearing officer decided that the Town's proposed placement at the Pine Glen School was inappropriate and that the Carroll School was "the least restrictive adequate program within the record" for Michael's educational needs. The hearing officer ordered the Town to pay for Michael's tuition and transportation to the Carroll School for the 1979–1980 school year, including reimbursing the Panicos for their expenditures on these items for the school year to date.

The Town sought judicial review of the State's administrative decision in the United States District Court for the District of Massachusetts naming Mr. Panico and the State Department of Education as defendants. In November 1980, the District Court granted summary judgment against the Town. The Court of Appeals vacated the judgment.

In the meantime, the Town had refused to comply with the BSEA order, the District Court had denied a stay of that order, and the Panicos and the State had moved for preliminary injunctive relief. The State also had threatened outside of the judicial proceedings to freeze all of the Town's special education assistance unless it complied with the BSEA order. Apparently in response to this threat, the Town agreed in February 1981 to pay for Michael's Carroll School placement and related transportation for the 1980–1981 term, none of which had yet been paid, and to continue paying for these expenses until the case was decided. But the Town persisted in refusing to reimburse Mr. Panico for the expenses of the 1979–1980 school year. When the Court of Appeals disposed of the state claim, it also held that under this status quo none of the parties could show irreparable injury and thus none was entitled to a preliminary injunction. The court reasoned that the Town had not shown that Mr. Panico would not be able to repay the tuition and related costs borne by the Town if he ultimately lost on the merits, and Mr. Panico had not shown that he would be irreparably harmed if not reimbursed immediately for past payments which might ultimately be determined to be the Town's responsibility.

On remand, the District Court entered an extensive pretrial order on the Town's federal claim. In denying the Town summary judgment, it ruled that 20 U.S.C. sec. 1415(e)(3) did not bar reimbursement despite the Town's insistence that the Panicos violated that provision by changing Michael's placement to the Carroll School during the pendency of the administrative proceedings. The court reasoned that sec. 1414(e)(3) concerned the physical placement of the child and not the right to tuition reimbursement or to procedural review of a contested IEP. The court also dealt with the problem that no IEP had been developed for the 1980–1981 or 1981–1982 school years. It held that its power under sec. 1414(e)(2) to grant "appropriate" relief upon reviewing the contested IEP for the 1979–1980 school year included the power to grant relief for subsequent school years despite the lack of IEPs for those years. In this connection, however, the court interpreted the statute to place the burden of proof on the Town to upset the BSEA decision that the IEP was inappropriate for 1979–1980 and on the Panicos and the State to show that the relief for subsequent terms was appropriate.

After a 4-day trial, the District Court in August 1982 overturned the BSEA decision, holding that the appropriate 1979–1980 placement for Michael was the one proposed by the Town in the IEP and that the parents had failed to show that this placement would not also have been appropriate for subsequent years. Accordingly, the court concluded that the Town was "not responsible for the cost of Michael's education at the Carroll School for the academic years 1979–80 through 1981–82."

In contesting the Town's proposed form of judgment embodying the court's conclusion, Mr. Panico argued that, despite finally losing on the merits of the IEP in August 1982, he would be reimbursed for his expenditures in 1979–1980, that the Town should finish paying for the recently completed 1981–1982 term, and that he should not be required to reimburse the Town for its payments to date, apparently because the school terms in question fell within the pendency of the administrative and judicial review contemplated by sec. 1415(e)(2). The case was transferred to another District Judge and consolidated with two other cases to resolve similar issues concerning the reimbursement for expenditures during the pendency of review proceedings. [Lower court proceedings omitted.] We granted certiorari, only to consider the following two issues: whether the potential relief available under sec. 1415(e)(2) includes reimbursement to parents for private school tuition and related expenses, and whether sec. 1415(e)(3) bars such reimbursement to parents who reject a proposed IEP and place a child in a private school without the consent of local school authorities.

The *modus operandi* of the [EAHCA] is the "individualized educational program." The IEP is in brief a comprehensive statement of the educational needs of a handicapped child and the specially designed instruction and related services to be employed to meet those needs. The IEP is to be developed jointly by a school official qualified in special education, the child's teacher, the parents or guardian, and, where appropriate, the child. In several places, the Act emphasizes the participation of the parents in developing the child's educational program and assessing its effectiveness.

Apparently recognizing that this cooperative approach would not always produce a consensus between the school officials and the parents, and that in any disputes the school officials would have a natural advantage, Congress incorporated an elaborate set of what it labeled "procedural safeguards" to insure the full participation of the parents and proper resolution of substantive disagreements. . . .

The Act also provides for judicial review in state or federal court to "[a]ny party aggrieved by the findings and decision" made after the due process hearing. The Act confers on the reviewing court the following authority:

> [T]he court shall receive the records of the administrative proceedings, shall hear additional evidence at the request of a party, and, basing its decision on the preponderance of the evidence, shall grant such relief as the court determine is appropriate. Sec. 1415(e)(2).

The first question on which we granted certiorari requires us to decide whether this grant of authority includes the power to order school authorities to reimburse parents for their expenditures on private special education for a child if the court ultimately determines that such placement, rather than a proposed IEP, is proper under the Act.

We conclude that the Act authorizes such reimbursement. The statute directs the court to "grant such relief as [it] determines is appropriate." The ordinary meaning of these words confers broad discretion on the court. The type of relief is not further specified, except that it must be "appropriate." Absent other reference, the only possible interpretation is that the relief is to be "appropriate" in the light of the purpose of the Act. As already noted, this is principally to provide handicapped children with "a free appropriate public education which emphasizes special education and related services designed to meet their unique needs." The Act contemplates that such education will be provided where possible in regular public schools, with the child participating as much as possible in the same activities as nonhandicapped children, but the Act also provides for placement in private schools at public expense where this is not possible. In a case where a court determines that a private placement desired by the parents was proper under the Act and that an IEP calling for placement in a public school was inappropriate, it seems clear beyond cavil that "appropriate" relief would include a prospective injunction directing the school officials to develop and implement at public expense an IEP placing the child in a private school.

If the administrative and judicial review under the Act could be completed in a matter of weeks, rather than years, it would be difficult to imagine a case in which such prospective injunctive relief would be sufficient. As this case so vividly demonstrates, however, the review process is ponderous. A final judicial decision on the merits of an IEP will in most instances come a year or more after the school term covered by that IEP has passed. In the meantime, the parents who disagree with the proposed IEP are faced with 3 choices: go along with the IEP to the detriment of their child if it turns out to be inappropriate or pay for what they consider to be the appropriate placement. If they choose the latter course, which conscientious parents who have adequate means and who are reasonably confident of their assessment normally would, it would be an empty victory to have a court tell them several years later that they were right but that these expenditures could not in a proper case be reimbursed by the school officials. If that were the case the child's right to a *free* appropriate public education, the parents' right to participate fully in developing a proper *IEP*, and all of the procedural safeguards would be less than complete. Because Congress undoubtedly did not intend this result, we are confident that by empowering the court to grant "appropriate" relief Congress meant to include retroactive reimbursement to parents as an available remedy in a proper case.

In this Court, the Town repeatedly characterizes reimbursement as "damages," but that simply is not the case. Reimbursement merely requires the Town to belatedly pay expenses that it should have paid all along and would have borne in the first instance had it developed a proper IEP. Such a post-hoc determination of financial responsibility was contemplated in the legislative history. . . .

Regardless of the availability of reimbursement as a form of relief in a proper case, the Town maintains that the Panicos have waived any right they otherwise might have to reimbursement because they violated sec. 1415(e)(3), which provides:

> During the pendency of any proceedings conducted pursuant to [sec. 1415], unless the State or local educational agency and the parents or guardian otherwise agree, the child shall remain in the then current educational placement of such child. . . .

We need not resolve the academic question of what Michael's "then current placement" was in the summer of 1979, when both the Town and the parents had agreed that a new school was in order. For the purposes of our decision, we assume that the Pine Glen School, proposed in the IEP, was Michael's current placement and, therefore, that the Panicos did "change" his placement after they had rejected the IEP and had set the administrative review in motion. In so doing, the Panicos contravened the conditional command of sec. 1415(e)(3) that "the child shall remain in the then current educational placement."

As an initial matter, we note that the section calls for agreement by *either* the *State or the local educational agency.* The BSEA's decision in favor of the Panicos and the Carroll School placement would seem to constitute agreement by the State to the change of placement. The decision was issued in January 1980, so from then on the Panicos were no longer in violation of sec. 1415(e)(3). This conclusion, however, does not entirely resolve the instant dispute because the Panicos are also seeking reimbursement for Michael's expenses during the fall of 1979, prior to the State's concurrence in the Carroll School placement.

We do not agree with the Town that a parental violation of sec. 1414(e)(3) constitutes a waiver of reimbursement. The provision says nothing about financial responsibility, waiver, or parental right to reimbursement at the conclusion of judicial proceedings. Moreover, if the provision is interpreted to cut off parental rights to reimbursement, the principal purpose of the Act will in many cases be defeated in the same way as if reimbursement were never available. As in this case, parents will often notice a child's learning difficulties while the child is in a regular public school program. If the school officials disagree with the need for special education or the adequacy of the public school's program to meet the child's needs, it is unlikely they will agree to an interim private school placement, while the review process runs its course. Thus, under the Town's reading of sec. 1415(e)(3), the parents are forced to leave the child in what may turn out to be an inappropriate educational placement or to obtain the appropriate placement only by sacrificing any claim for reimbursement. The Act was intended to give handicapped children both an appropriate education and a free one; it should not be interpreted to defeat one or the other of those objectives.

The legislative history supports this interpretation, favoring a proper interim placement pending the resolution of disagreements over the IEP: . . . .

We think at least one purpose of sec. 1415(e)(3) was to prevent school officials from removing a child from the regular public school classroom over the parents' objection pending completion of the review proceedings. As we observed in *Rowley,* the impetus for the Act came from two federal court decisions, which arose from the efforts of parents of handicapped children to prevent the exclusion or expulsion of their children to private institutions or warehousing them in special classes. We also note that sec. 1415(e)(3) is located in a section detailing procedural safeguards which are largely for the benefit of the parents and the child.

This is not to say that sec. 1415(e)(3) has no effect on parents. While we doubt that this provision would authorize a court to order parents to leave their child in a particular placement, we think it operates in such a way that parents who unilaterally change their child's placement during the pendency of review proceedings, without the consent of state or local school officials, do so at their own financial risk. If the courts ultimately determine that the IEP proposed by the school officials was appropriate, the parents would be barred from obtaining reimbursement for any interim period in which their child's placement violated sec. 1415(e)(3). This conclusion is supported by the agency's interpretation of the Act's application to private placements by the parents:

(a) If a handicapped child has available a free appropriate public education and the parents choose to place the child in a private school or facility,

the public agency is not required by this part to pay for the child's education at the private school or facility. . . .
(b) Disagreements between a parent and a public agency regarding the availability of a program appropriate for the child, and the question of financial responsibility, are subject to the due process procedures under [sec. 1415].

In cases decided subsequent to the *Burlington* decision, courts have reached a number of conclusions in a variety of factual settings in which the parents sought reimbursement.[1] In one case the court held that the school need not reimburse transportation expenses when the parents had chosen to place the student in a private school setting.[2] A different decision resulted in a reimbursement for transportation and babysitting when the school refused to provide the services.[3]

In one interesting decision it was held that because the parents did not take advantage of ample opportunities to participate in the IEP, they could not be reimbursed for a unilateral placement.[4] And several courts have found that reimbursement for out-of-state placements are not required when the school has not been able to adequately assess the child.[5]

The conclusion that can be drawn from these cases is that while unilateral placement carries some risk, the pre-*Burlington* position taken by some courts—that a unilateral placement by a parent violates the "stay-put" requirement and is not subjected to reimbursement—is no longer the case. The *Burlington* decision reaches a reasonably good balance between the interests of the child and the concerns of the educational agency. Where the school has not provided an appropriate placement, parents may be reimbursed. As the problems illustrate, however, there are still some unanswered questions and some policy inequities.

COMPENSATORY EDUCATION

Where a student has been improperly educated in the past, one of the means of redressing the problem can be by providing compensatory education.[6] This remedy under the EAHCA has been a topic of debate in a number of judicial decisions, with inconsistent results. The following is an example of a situation in which compensatory education would be ordered.

JEFFERSON COUNTY BOARD OF EDUCATION V. BREEN

853 F.2d 853 (11th Cir. 1988)

In November 1974, at age seven, Alice Breen sustained a closed head injury in an automobile accident near Mobile, Alabama. She emerged from the resulting coma with a multitude of physical and emotional problems such as impaired memory, attention, perception, and judgment. Since the accident she has engaged in impulsive behavior, self-mutilation, and suicide attempts.

Alice was placed in various public and private schools with marginal success. By the fall of 1979 she began experiencing severe psychiatric problems and had become violent. In September and December 1982 Alice was admitted to the Psychiatric Unit of

University Hospital in Birmingham; the December admission was prompted by suicide attempts. From January until August 1983, Alice was under the care of Dr. Otto Eisenhardt at Hillcrest Hospital.

Alice was next treated at the Engel Day Treatment Center in Birmingham, Alabama. Apparently dissatisfied with the program at Engle, Mrs. Breen (Alice's mother) withdrew Alice in November 1983. In December 1983 and January 1984 Mrs. Breen contacted the Jefferson County Board of Education regarding an appropriate placement for Alice. The Board recommended that Alice be enrolled at Berry High School in Jefferson County and be provided a self-contained classroom with regular classes part-time.

Alice's stay at Berry was short-lived, however. She spent from April 9 to April 20, 1983 at Hillcrest Hospital recovering from a suicide attempt. She returned to Berry on April 27 but six days later overdosed on an over-the-counter drug and was admitted to Children's Hospital in Birmingham under the care of Dr. Thomas Vaughan. Alice was discharged on July 9, but readmitted two weeks later. Dr. Vaughan recommended that Alice be placed at the Ranch [Treatment Center in Austin, Texas] and on September 17, 1984 she was admitted there.

Over the next fifteen months Alice received therapeutic, educational, and related services seven days per week, twenty-four hours per day. Mrs. Breen's insurance paid for all but $9,715.26 of the costs.

Shortly after Alice enrolled in the Ranch Mrs. Breen met with the Jefferson County School Board to discuss an appropriate placement for Alice. Mrs. Breen rejected the Board's proposal that Alice be enrolled at Gilmore-Bell High School because it did not provide services twenty-four hours per day, seven days per week.

At Mrs. Breen's request a hearing was held to determine whether the Jefferson County Board of Education was obligated to pay for Alice's care at the Ranch or whether by providing instate care the Board could satisfy its duty under the Act to provide an "appropriate education." The hearing officer upheld Mrs. Breen's decision to place Alice at the Ranch, concluding that a residential program was required. The hearing officer's decision was affirmed by a state administrative review officer. The review officer found that "[p]rior efforts to educate Alice in day programs were not successful." Further, "the entire group of services provided at The Ranch Treatment Center is of the type needed for Alice to be educated. The unseverability of Alice's needs met by such services is the reason for concluding that such services are an essential prerequisite for Alice's learning."

In late 1985, while the administrative proceedings were pending, Alice checked out of the Ranch and returned home. Her condition rapidly deteriorated and hospitalization was once again necessary. Alice spent most of the summer of 1986 in Brookwood Hospital and upon discharge became violent toward her mother. Over the next year Alice was frequently in and out of the psychiatric unit of University Hospital in Birmingham.

On September 8, 1986 the Board filed this lawsuit in the United States District Court for the Northern District of Alabama. The Board acknowledged that Alice required residential services, but argued that she should be placed at Bryce Hospital, a state mental hospital in Tuscaloosa, Alabama.

The district court disagreed and ordered the Board to pay Alice's $9,715.26 outstanding balance at the Ranch, to immediately place her at the Ranch, and to provide her with two years of compensatory education beyond her twenty-first birthday.

The district court placed great weight on the opinion of the Director of

Neuropsychology at Bryce Hospital, Dr. Goff, who believed that Bryce did not have the facilities to adequately address Alice's problems. Dr. Goff reasoned that Alice's problems require a comprehensive treatment program combining behavioral intervention and cognitive remediation with an educational program.

The district court also considered the opinions of Dr. Julia Hannay, Professor and Director of Clinical Neuropsychology Training at the University of Houston and one of the founders of the Alabama Head Injury Foundation, and Dr. Tom Boll, Professor of psychology and the Director of the Comprehensive Head Injury Center at the University of Alabama in Birmingham. The common thread running through both opinions is that Bryce does not have the residential facilities needed to treat head injured patients such as Alice. Dr. Hannay believed that Bryce could provide a safe environment for Alice, but it could not treat her problems. Dr. Boll states that there were no facilities in the entire State of Alabama capable of providing Alice with the care she needs.

We have little difficulty deciding that the district court correctly ordered the Board to reimburse the Breens for their out-of-pocket expenses. Because the Ranch was ultimately determined to be the appropriate placement for Alice, "[r]eimbursement merely required the [Board] to belatedly pay expenses that it should have paid all along. . . ." [Citing *Burlington*]. Further, we agree with the district court that the equities weigh heavily in favor of full reimbursement.

The second issue is closely related to the first in that the district court ordered the two additional years in response to the Board's failure to provide an appropriate education prior to the court's order. Compensatory education, like retroactive reimbursement, is necessary to preserve a handicapped child's right to a free education. Without it, the child's right would depend upon his or her parent's ability to fund the education during the years of administrative proceedings and federal court litigation. Also, providing a compensatory education should serve as a deterrent against states unnecessarily prolonging litigation in order to decrease their potential liability. We believe that the district court correctly ordered the Board to provide Alice with two years' compensatory education.

One of the issues that is debated is whether compensatory education is in essence "damages" from which a state agency might be held to be immune in a particular jurisdiction. While this reasoning was adopted by the Ninth Circuit,[7] it can be criticized in light of the *Burlington* case, in which the Court found that reimbursement should not be characterized as "damages" because these are expenses that should have been paid all along had a proper IEP been developed. This reasoning is applied in the *Breen* case. Certainly compensatory education should be seen in the same light—these are expenses that are being borne to compensate for expenses that should have been paid in the first place. Whether this reasoning will ultimately be adopted by the Supreme Court remains to be seen. In those jurisdictions that do allow damages as a remedy, it can be important whether bad faith was involved.

One additional factor that can add to the complexity of this problem is when the student has either graduated or has gone beyond the age for which special education is mandated. In some states, compensatory education is actually prohibited; in others it is discretionary.

SUMMARY

The EAHCA itself does not state whether there are any circumstances in which parents may be reimbursed for the costs they incur in making a placement themselves, or whether there might be circumstances under which the school might be required to provide compensatory education if the school had failed to provide an appropriate education.

The Supreme Court, however, has provided a significant degree of resolution at least on the issue of reimbursement. The Court in *Burlington School Committee v. Department of Education* in 1985 held that reimbursement could be ordered as a remedy in appropriate cases. These cases are where the parents have made an appropriate placement on their own and the school has failed to provide an appropriate placement. While this opinion provides important guidance by permitting reimbursement in these cases, it leaves open some unresolved issues, including whether the parents can be fully reimbursed when their placement is in an expensive program and less expensive alternatives are reasonably available. Also unresolved is whether the school can be reimbursed when it agrees to fund the parentally selected placement pending dispute resolution, and the school's proposed placement is ultimately found to be appropriate. What remedy is available to the parents who cannot afford to fund a placement pending dispute resolution is also unsettled. If the parents ultimately prevail in demonstrating that the school's placement is inappropriate, can the school be required to provide compensatory education to make up for the lost time that occurred during the inappropriate placement? While as yet unresolved, it would seem that courts are likely to rely on the same reasoning of the *Burlington* decision—that such a remedy is essential to carrying out the goals of the EAHCA.

QUESTIONS AND PROBLEMS

Rhoda Markum is 16. A private psychiatrist has diagnosed her as emotionally disturbed. Upon entering high school, the school recommends Rhoda for an in-school placement that the parents believe to be inappropriate. They think Rhoda needs a highly intensive program that integrates educational programming and counseling. Because of their concern about Rhoda's education and the time it will take to resolve the dispute over the placement, they put Rhoda into a private residential program (School A) where she receives programming year round. The program costs $40,000 per year, which the parents pay. Two years after the parents' unilateral placement, the final judicial decision found that the school's recommended placement is not appropriate, and that the program in which Rhoda has been placed by her parents is appropriate. During the judicial proceedings, the school presented evidence that although it was not the program recommended by the school, there was another appropriate residential program (School B) available at the time of Rhoda's initial placement in School A. The cost of the program at School B is $15,000 per year.

1. If the court were to find that School B is an appropriate placement, and that there was space in the program for Rhoda, how much, if anything, should the school be required to reimburse the parents?

2. Suppose both School A and School B were appropriate placements and that School B had been offered at the time the parents placed Rhoda in School A. Should the school have to reimburse the parents at least $15,000 for each year, since it would have to pay that anyway?

3. Suppose that instead of refusing to pay the $40,000, the school agrees to pay the yearly costs pending resolution of the case, but contests its obligation to do so. Are the parents required to reimburse the school if it is later determined that the school's program was appropriate?

4. If it is determined that a student has been provided an inappropriate program for two years, should any compensatory education order be limited to two years? What if the inappropriate programming occurred in primary grades or in preschool, where "lost" time is difficult to compensate because of the importance of that developmental stage?

NOTES

1. *See* L. ROTHSTEIN, RIGHTS OF PHYSICALLY HANDICAPPED PERSONS (1984), § 2.39A cumulative supplement. Appellate court decisions addressing this issue include Evans v. District No. 17, 841 F.2d 824 (8th Cir. 1988); Board of Education v. Dienelt, 843 F.2d 813 (4th Cir. 1988); Hudson v. Wilson, 828 F.2d 1059 (4th Cir. 1987); Gregory K. v. Longview School District, 811 F.2d 1307 (9th Cir. 1987); Jenkins v. Florida, 815 F.2d 629 (11th Cir. 1987); Wexler v. Westfield Board of Education, 784 F.2d 176 (3d Cir. 1986); Gary A. v. New Trier High School District, 796 F.2d 940 97th Cir. 1986); McKenzie v. Smith, 771 F.2d 1527 (D.C. Cir. 1985); Cain v. Yukon Public Schools, 775 F.2d 15 (10th Cir. 1985).
2. Work v. McKenzie, 661 F. Supp. 225 (D.D.C. 1987).
3. Taylor v. Board of Education, 649 F. Supp. 1253 (N.D.N.Y. 1986).
4. Scituate School Committee v. Robert B., 620 F. Supp. 1224 (D.R.I. 1985).
5. Evans v. District No. 17, 841 F.2d 824 (8th Cir. 1988); Lenoff v. Farmington Public Schools, 680 F. Supp. 921 (E.D. Mich. 1988). In one particularly extreme case, the court held that the placement of an autistic child 8,000 miles from the school (in Tokyo, Japan) would limit reimbursement.
6. *See* RPHP § 2.39, 2.40. Drew P. v. Clarke County School District, 676 F. Supp. 1559 (M.D. Ga. 1987).
7. Alexopulos v. San Francisco Unified School District, 817 F.2d 555 (9th Cir. 1987).

CHAPTER 18

Attorneys' Fees

ARE THEY ALLOWED?

The 1975 EAHCA was silent as to whether attorney's fees and costs incurred in the administrative due process and judicial proceedings of special education cases could be recovered by parents. Early cases did not really address whether there is an implied right to attorneys' fees and costs, because most cases were brought using a combination of Section 504 and Section 1983 claims. These statutes clearly provide that attorneys' fees may be recovered.[1]

Until *Smith v. Robinson,*[2] however, it was unclear whether one could use Section 504, Section 1983, and the EAHCA in combination to obtain relief in special education cases. Ever since that 1984 decision, it is clear that unless the EAHCA does not provide appropriate relief, Section 504 and Section 1983 are unavailable as avenues of redress. It thus became important to determine whether the EAHCA provides for attorneys' fees.

The Handicapped Children's Protection Act (HCPA) of 1986[3] was passed by Congress as an amendment to the EAHCA. It provides for the award of reasonable attorneys' fees and costs to parents who are prevailing parties. What follows are the specific provisions of that amendment.

Handicapped Children's Protection Act of 1986

Award of Attorney's Fees
SEC. 2. Section 615(e)(4) of the Education of the Handicapped Act is amended by inserting "(A)" after the paragraph designation and by adding at the end thereof the following new subparagraphs:
    (B) In any action or proceeding brought under this subsection, the court, in its

discretion, may award reasonable attorneys' fees as part of the costs to the parents or guardian of a handicapped child or youth who is the prevailing party.

(C) For the purpose of this subsection, fees awarded under this subsection shall be based on rates prevailing in the community in which the action or proceeding arose for the kind and quality of services furnished. No bonus or multiplier may be used in calculating the fees awarded under this subsection.

(D) No award of attorneys' fees and related costs may be made in any action or proceeding under this subsection for services performed subsequent to the time of written offer of settlement to a parent or guardian, if—

(i) the offer is made within the time prescribed by Rule 68 of the Federal Rules of Civil Procedure or, in the case of an administrative proceeding, at any time more than ten days before the proceeding begins;

(ii) the court or administrative officer finds that the relief finally obtained by the parents or guardian is not more favorable to the parents or guardian than the offer of settlement.

(E) Notwithstanding the provisions of subparagraph (D), an award of attorneys' fees and related costs may be made to a parent or guardian who is the prevailing party and who was substantially justified in rejecting the settlement offer.

(F) Whenever the court finds that—

(i) the parent or guardian, during the course of the action or proceeding, unreasonably protracted the final resolution of the controversy;

(ii) the amount of the attorneys' fees otherwise authorized to be awarded unreasonably exceeds the hourly rate prevailing in the community for similar services by attorneys of reasonably comparable skill, experience, and reputation; or

(iii) the time spent and legal services furnished were excessive considering the nature of the action or proceeding, the court shall reduce, accordingly, the amount of the attorneys' fees awarded under this subsection.

(G) The provisions of subparagraph (F) shall not apply in any action or proceeding if the court finds that the State or local educational agency unreasonably protracted the final resolution of the action or proceeding or there was a violation of section 615 of this Act.

Effect of Education of the Handicapped Act on Other Laws

SEC. 3. Section 615 of the Education of the Handicapped Act is amended by adding at the end thereof the following new subsection:

"(f) Nothing in this title shall be construed to restrict or limit the rights, procedures, and remedies available under the Constitution, title V of the Rehabilitation Act of 1973, or other Federal statutes protecting the rights of handicapped children and youth, except that before the filing of a civil action under such laws seeking relief that is also available under this part, the procedures under subsections (b)(2) and (c) shall be exhausted to the same extent as would be required had the action been brought under this part.". . .

SEC. 5. The amendment made by section 2 shall apply with respect to actions or proceedings brought under section 615(e) of the Education of the Handicapped Act after July 3, 1984, and actions or proceedings brought prior to July 4, 1984, under such section which were pending on July 4, 1984.

Section 2(D) of the amendment was designed to encourage settlement of disputes. Litigation during the next few years will determine whether that goal has been accomplished.

The attorneys' fees amendment has been criticized by some as stirring up litigation by encouraging the involvement of attorneys. Others, however, believe that the availability of attorneys' fees will make it more likely that due process will be a reality because attorneys will be willing to represent parents.

WHAT IS A PREVAILING PARTY?[4]

While the HCPA amendment clarifies that attorneys' fees are available, there still remain unanswered questions. Many of these issues are in the early litigation stages and will probably be resolved as this litigation reaches the appellate level in more jurisdictions.

When a party obtains all the relief sought, it is simple to demonstrate that the party prevailed. In the *Rollison v. Biggs* decision, excerpted later in this chapter, the court applied a standard that prevailing parties are only those that succeed on a significant issue that achieved some of the benefit sought.[5] Another trial-level court found that the parents had prevailed in some, but not all, of their claims, and were thus entitled to fees and costs.[6] There are also decisions permitting recovery where the case was resolved through settlement.[7] Although a substantial amount of litigation addresses these issues, it is too early to draw any sweeping conclusions about the standards that will be applied in these cases.

RECOVERY IN ADMINISTRATIVE ACTIONS

One of the issues about which there has been much debate in the courtroom is whether attorneys' fees are available for administrative proceedings. On one hand the amendment provides that fees are to be awarded by a court, implying that they are available only for judicial proceedings. On the other hand, the amendment states that they are available for "any action or *proceeding,*" arguably including administrative proceedings in the coverage.

Whereas the strong weight of judicial opinion seems to be in favor of awarding fees in administrative proceedings, one exception is the following case.

ROLLISON V. BIGGS

660 F. Supp. 875 (D. Del. 1987)
The [Congressional] committee reports cite *New York Gaslight Club v. Carey,* 447 U.S. 54 (1980), for the proposition that prevailing parties in administrative proceedings

are entitled to a court-ordered fee award. After the HCPA was enacted, however, the Supreme Court characterized the relevant passage in *Carey* as erroneous dicta, and held that under 42 U.S.C. § 1988 plaintiffs may not recover fees for prevailing in administrative proceedings. Because Congress intended that the HCPA be construed consistent with other fee-shifting statutes, the rules of *Crest Street* applies in special education cases brought under the EAHCA just as the rule applies in other civil rights cases.

There are cases that hold that in EAHCA cases counsel fees may be recovered in federal court for work done at the administrative level where the underlying merits never reach the court. These cases, however, ignore the overriding congressional intent to have the HCPA attorneys' fees provision interpreted consistent with all other civil rights fee-shifting statutes.

Another basic reason plaintiffs cannot recover attorneys' fees for work performed at the administrative level exists in this case. Plaintiffs may be considered prevailing parties in the administrative proceedings only if they succeeded on any significant issue in the proceedings that achieved some of the benefit plaintiffs sought from administrative review of the decision to deny their financial aid request.

Both the local hearing officer and the state level review officer, however, denied plaintiffs' request for tuition reimbursement. Moreover, nothing in the record of the administrative proceedings suggests that plaintiffs sought—or benefited from—the prospective change in procedures ordered by the local hearing officer or that any attorney time was spent on this issue. Plaintiffs cannot be said to have prevailed at the administrative level in any genuine way.

WHAT EXPENSES ARE RECOVERABLE?

Types of Expenses

The amendment provides for the award of "*reasonable* attorneys' fees" and related costs. The obvious question concerns what expenses are deemed reasonable. The statute itself provides some further guidance by noting that fees are to be based on rates prevailing in the community where the action arose for the type of services offered. Furthermore, the court making the award has the discretion to reduce the amount of fees if the request is excessive, in either the hourly rate or the time spent. There is not yet a well-developed body of case law interpreting these requirements. One additional point made clear by the statute, however, is that no multiplier or bonus can be used in making these awards. This means that a court does not have the discretion to award double attorneys' fees or another type of bonus as a punitive measure.

One issue that has been addressed by at least one federal circuit court is whether lay advocates may be awarded attorney's fees. A 1988 Third Circuit decision held that lay advocates could be denied attorneys' fees.[8] This does not mean that lay advocates could not be advisors in EAHCA matters, but that payment to such individuals does not fall within the attorneys' fees amendment. It is unclear how likely this issue is to be raised in the courts. One problem that could occur should courts find lay advocates entitled to attorneys' fees is the difficulty in determining what would be a reasonable rate for such individuals.

Expenses after Settlement Offer

Congress recognized the potential for protracted litigation should there not be a disincentive to unnecessary attorneys' fees and costs. That recognition is manifested in the settlement portion of the amendment that provides that once a reasonable settlement offer is made, attorneys' fees for services performed after the offer will not be available. Where a settlement places the parents in the position of a prevailing party, the fact that a settlement occurs does not mean that the presettlement fees are not recoverable. To provide otherwise would potentially discourage settlement agreements.

The post-settlement ban on fees only applies where the offer is a timely offer and the relief obtained by the parents is less favorable than the settlement offer. There is even a loophole to this limitation, however. If the rejection of the settlement was substantially justified, the parents may at the court's discretion recover post-settlement costs and fees. Factors indicating substantial justification for rejecting the offer might be claims involving novel or unusual circumstances not well resolved by the courts, unreasonable settlement offers, and offers made in situations where the parents had reason to suspect bad faith in implementation.

The amendment attempts to strike a balance between the need to provide these costs to ensure access to due process, and the need to avoid unnecessarily protracted controversies and litigation costs.

The following case provides an illustration of how an early decision applying the attorneys' fees amendment has viewed the various requirements.

BARBARA R. V. TIROZZI

665 F. Supp. 141 (D. Conn. 1987)
Plaintiffs are children and parents who were unable to obtain decisions from state educational agencies concerning their claims that the defendant Department of Children and Youth Services failed to provide them with appropriate special education while the children were residents at Long Lane juvenile correctional center. Plaintiffs alleged that the Connecticut State Board of Education was violating the fourteenth amendment due process rights of mentally handicapped children. Defendants allegedly failed to adhere to the "procedural safeguards" provisions of the Education for all Handicapped Children Act. . . . Specifically, plaintiffs alleged that defendants (1) regularly failed to hold hearings and render decisions within forty-five days of receiving a request for same; (2) repeatedly violated the requirement that hearing officers be independent; and (3) illegally limited the issues which could be raised at these hearings. From data supplied by defendants for 343 hearings over a six-year period, the average time from the date a hearing was requested to the day when a decision was issued was one hundred sixty-seven days; in only 6 of 343 hearings was a decision rendered within forty-five days.

Defendants denied wrongdoing and the existence of a requirement that hearings be held and decisions rendered within forty-five days of receipt of a request.

After attempts at settlement proved fruitless, the parties engaged in substantial discovery. Thereafter the parties agreed to a Consent Decree clearly delineating the due process rights of handicapped children in this state. Plaintiffs claim that the Consent Decree incorporates the procedural guarantees they sought to vindicate, thereby entitling them to attorney fees as a "prevailing party" under 42 U.S.C. § 1988. Alternatively, plaintiffs argue their entitlement to attorney fees under the Handicapped Children's Protection Act of 1986, 20 U.S.C. § 1415(e), which not only provided for attorney fees in EHA cases but made them retroactive.

Discussion

I.
A "prevailing party" in a 42 U.S.C. § 1983 action to vindicate constitutional rights is entitled to reasonable attorney fees. 42 U.S.C. § 1988. . . .

A.
Defendants rely on *Bonar v. Ambach,* 771 F.2d 14 (2d Cir. 1985), and *McKenzie v. Smith,* 771 F.2d 1527 (D.C. Cir. 1985), for the proposition that *Smith v. Robinson* makes the EHA, not § 1983, plaintiffs' exclusive remedy. Although attorney fees were there held not available for plaintiffs who pursue their rights under the EHA, the courts left open the possibility—as did *Smith*—of attorney fee awards under § 1988 where plaintiffs are forced to go outside the EHA to obtain relief. As stated in *Smith:*

> [W]hile Congress apparently had determined that local and state agencies should not be burdened with attorney's fees to litigants who succeed, through resort to the procedures outlined in the EHA, in requiring those agencies to provide free schooling, there is no indication that agencies should be exempt from a fee award where plaintiffs have had to resort to judicial relief to force the agencies to provide them the process they were constitutionally due.

468 U.S. at 1014-15, n. 17, 104 S.Ct. at 3470, n.17.
. . . Plaintiffs here sought from defendants the timely hearings mandated by state and federal law—precisely the situation exempted by *Smith* from its holding that EHA provides the exclusive remedy in cases involving the rights of mentally handicapped school children. Accordingly, plaintiffs are not ineligible for attorney fees pursuant to § 1988.

B.
Yet, even if the EHA were plaintiffs' exclusive remedy, the 1986 amendment to the EHA authorized attorney fee awards in EHA cases retroactive to July 3, 1984—the day before *Smith* was decided. The clear intent of Congress was to negate *Smith.* Accordingly, plaintiffs are eligible for attorney fees under the EHA.

C.
Whether under EHA or § 1988, plaintiffs must establish that they prevailed to be eligible for attorney fees. A plaintiff is a "prevailing party" if he or she has succeeded "on any significant issue in litigation which achieves some of the benefit the parties sought

in bringing suit." The fact that the litigation ended by a settlement does not preclude plaintiffs from claiming attorney fees as a "prevailing party."

The Consent Decree herein provides in detail for scheduling EHA hearings and decisions to ensure compliance with what it is specifically acknowledged to be "the 45 day time limit provided by state law . . . and the time limit provided in [federal regulations]." When viewed in light of defendants' significant and repeated departures from the forty-five day time limit before this action was brought, and the lack of any procedure established to assure adherence to the time limits fixed by law, the Consent Decree establishes the most important of plaintiffs' objectives: to force the state to recognize its responsibility to hold hearings and render decisions within forty-five days of receiving a request for an EHA hearing as the law required.

It is true that plaintiffs dropped their second claim regarding the issues which could be raised at EHA hearings and their third claim regarding the independence of hearing officers. The second claim was abandoned, however, only after the Connecticut legislature enacted a measure, drafted by counsel for plaintiffs, which accorded handicapped children equivalent relief. These facts do not detract from the fact that plaintiffs prevailed on a principal issue in the law suit—the lack of timely hearings and decisions. Where two or more claims challenge a single procedure or practice, it is inappropriate to refuse to award a reasonable attorney fee where one claim was successful. . . . Here, at most, a small amount of attorney time was spent on the issues not resolved in the Consent Decree, and all three issues in the complaint concern state compliance with EHA hearing regulations. Accordingly, plaintiffs have prevailed on an issue central to their suit and attorney fees related thereto will be awarded. . . .

II.

Plaintiffs have submitted affidavits in support of their motion. Counsel's professional background and experience is fully described and the time spent on this case is documented through computer printouts.

Attorney Crockett, who has been with Legal Services since December 1968 and who has concentrated his practice in the area of special education for the past five years, claims 254.85 hours at a requested hourly rate of $125, for a total of $31,856.25. After reviewing the hours and noting some excesses, for example, that 24 hours were expended drafting the complaint, the 254.85 will be reduced by 20%, for a total of 203.88 hours found to have been reasonably expended in this case. The hourly rate found to be reasonable is $110, for a total fee award of $22,426.80.

There is a claim for 19.11 hours at $50 per hour, for a total of $955.50 for the services of a computer programmer. The hours and rate are deemed to be reasonable and the $955.50 is, therefore, approved.

There is a claim for costs of $466.34 and $431.01 for transcripts from two depositions, which is approved, for a total of $897.35.

Attorney Crockett has submitted a supplemental motion for an award for his time spent responding to defendants' objections to his earlier filed motion for attorney fees. Thirty (30) hours is found reasonably to have been required and, at $110 per hour, $3,300 is allowed.

Attorney Mary Conklin, who helped out in support of plaintiff's motion for attorney fees, is allowed 24 hours at $80 per hour, for a total of $1,920. Her travel time will be allowed, 2.5 hours, at $50 per hour, or $125. The total allowed for her is thus $2,045.

Accordingly, a total award of attorney fees in the amount of $29,624.65 shall enter on behalf of the plaintiffs.

So Ordered.

SUMMARY

Before 1984 it was unclear whether parents could recover attorneys' fees and other legal costs incurred in attaining appropriate special education and related services for their children. The EAHCA was silent on the question, and while attorneys' fees and costs are permitted in Section 504 and constitutional actions, it was unsettled whether either of these types of actions could be the basis for resolving special education disputes.

The 1984 *Smith v. Robinson* Supreme Court decision declared that, except in cases where the EAHCA does not provide substantive protection, Section 504 and constitutional actions could not be used to redress special education disputes. The Court also held that the EAHCA does not permit the recovery of attorneys' fees and costs. Because of the importance of true parental participation in carrying out the goals of the EAHCA and the recognition that reasonable access to legal recourse requires that attorneys' fees and costs be available to successful parents, Congress amended to EAHCA to allow attorneys' fees and costs to be recovered in appropriate situations.

The attorneys' fees amendment offers an incentive for both parties to seek prompt resolution and a disincentive to needlessly protracting a dispute. New issues require resolution as a result of this amendment to the EAHCA. The statute does not specify whether fees are recoverable in administrative actions or only in judicial actions. The weight of judicial authority has thus far held that they are available in administrative actions. There also appears to be a majority of opinion finding that where a dispute is resolved through settlement, the fees may be recovered if the parents succeed on a significant issue. The other major issue receiving judicial attention is the question of whether the retroactivity of the amendment is constitutional. So far, the general result has been to find the retroactive application to be constitutional.

While not receiving enormous amounts of attention in the courts, there are some developments relating to what types of expenses are recovered and whether such fees are available to lay advocates. These decisions have yet to provide any demonstrable patterns.

QUESTIONS AND PROBLEMS

1. Is there any requirement that a parent select the least expensive attorney available?
2. What if an attorney is selected from another city, but attorneys in the home city are available. Can travel expenses be justified in such a case?

3. Is there any basis for permitting a higher than usual hourly rate for an attorney who is an expert in special education law?

NOTES

1. 29 U.S.C. § 794(d); 42 U.S.C. § 1988. *See also* L. ROTHSTEIN, RIGHTS OF PHYSICALLY HANDI-CAPPED PERSONS § 2.41 (1984).
2. 468 U.S. 992 (1984). See Chapter 3 for the case opinion.
3. 20 U.S.C. § 1415(e)(4).
4. R. WEINER, P.L. 94–142: IMPACT ON THE SCHOOLS 78–80 (1985).
5. 669 F. Supp. 875, 877–78 (D. Del. 1987).
6. Garland Independent School District v. Wilks, 657 F. Supp. 1163 (N.D. Tex. 1987).
7. *See* RPHP § 2.41.
8. Arons v. New Jersey State Board of Education, 842 F.2d 58 (3d Cir. 1988).

CHAPTER 19

Immunity

TYPES OF IMMUNITY

Basically, two different types of immunity protect educational agencies from suits and certain remedial orders. First is common-law governmental immunity protecting states and state agencies from suits in state court. Second is eleventh amendment immunity protecting states and state agencies from suits in federal court. These doctrines are based on historical principles that the government can do no wrong. But these immunity protections are not absolute.

State law usually provides for some exemption from the common-law immunity doctrine. For example, state law may specify that the state will be liable for certain injuries resulting from school-related activities on school property or while at school-sponsored events. This would thus provide monetary recovery for injuries sustained by a child on the playground if there was inadequate supervision. These tort exceptions are usually enacted as a matter of public policy.

If a claim is based on a violation of a constitutionally protected right, the state will not be protected by either of the immunity doctrines. A constitutionally based claim can be brought against a state, state agency, or other government agency, and if monetary relief is awarded, the defendant will be obligated for the award.

Actions based on statutory grounds, however, are a different matter. The eleventh amendment of the U.S. Constitution provides immunity from federal statutory claims for states and state agencies. Even statutorily based claims can be brought against states and state agencies in two situations. The first is where the state has expressly waived immunity. The second is where Congress has specifically provided that states and state agencies are not immune from claims brought under specific statutes. In both situations the waiver or abrogation of immunity must be clear and unequivocal.

Immunity in Special Education Cases

While a 1986 amendment to the Rehabilitation Act of 1973[1] specifies that immunity shall not protect the states from Rehabilitation Act claims, the EAHCA is not so clear. Because the *Smith v. Robinson*[2] decision provides that the EAHCA is the exclusive avenue of redress for most special education claims, it becomes important whether immunity from certain types of EAHCA claims exists. There is no question that the federal government could withdraw federal funding for EAHCA violations, and that the courts can order injunctive relief. What is not clear, however, is whether remedies involving monetary relief can be ordered against states or state agencies. These remedies would include reimbursement, compensatory education, and damages. Although *Burlington School Committee v. Department of Education*[3] clarified that reimbursement is an appropriate remedy, it may be that this remedy is only recoverable from a local educational agency. It is not even entirely clear whether local educational agencies are subject to the eleventh amendment immunity doctrine that protects states.

A further issue involves the extent to which individuals in various positions and at different governmental levels are protected under the immunity doctrine. Are superintendents protected? Are school board members? What about teachers and bus drivers?

These issues are not resolved.[4] The following case excerpts provide a spectrum of views on these issues. The first two cases, *Doe v. Maher* and *Muth v. Central Bucks School District,* demonstrate two divergent circuit court opinions on the application of the immunity doctrine to states. The *Muth* decision is more recent and probably represents the weight of judicial opinion on state immunity and the EAHCA. The third decision, *Doe A. v. Special School District,* involves particularly outrageous conduct, and it focuses on immunity issues as they apply to individuals. It is difficult to draw any clear line of judicial unanimity or agreement on this issue. It is probable that future litigation will develop this issue more fully. Individual state statutes will also be relevant in ascertaining whether immunity exists, to the extent that the EAHCA is not viewed as overriding any state immunity doctrines.

DOE V. MAHER

793 F.2d 1470 (9th Cir. 1986)
[*Author's Note:* The Supreme Court decided some of the issues in this case under its ruling on this case titled *Honig v. Doe,* 108 S.Ct. (1987). The Court did not address the immunity issues decided in the Ninth Circuit decision.]

[The factual setting for this case involved the disciplinary expulsion of an emotionally disturbed student. The claims were brought against the local school district and the State Superintendent of Public Instruction. The relief sought included both injunctive relief and damages. The issue of damages against the local school district was not decided because of a settlement with that agency.]

The plaintiffs argue that the district court dismissed their EAHCA damage claims against the state based on an erroneous standard by which to measure a valid claim under the statute. We do not reach this issue because, whatever the proper standard, we hold that the state is shielded by the Eleventh Amendment from damage liability under the EAHCA. Doe and Smith cite two Ninth Circuit cases for the proposition that the State of California has waived its sovereign immunity with regard to the EAHCA. Although these cases formerly were controlling, they can carry no force in light of the Supreme Court's recent decision in *Atascadero State Hospital v. Scanlon,* 105 S.Ct. 3412. In *Scanlon,* the Court held that the State of California is immune from suits for monetary relief under sec. 504 of the Rehabilitation Act. We believe the Court's reasoning compels a similar result with respect to the EAHCA.

The Court began in *Scanlon* by determining that California had not waived its general immunity to suit in federal court. Although Art. III, sec. 5 of the California Constitution provides that "[s]uits may be brought against the State in such manner and in such courts as shall be directed by law," the Court held that this language did not satisfy the stringent test necessary for waiver under the Eleventh Amendment. "[F]or a State statute or constitutional provision to constitute a waiver of Eleventh Amendment immunity," the Court explained, "it must specify the State's intention to subject itself to suit in *federal court.*" The California Constitution did not so specify.

The Court next determined that Congress had not abrogated the states'·immunity in enacting the Rehabilitation Act. Acknowledging Congress's power to abrogate sovereign immunity pursuant to section 5 of the Fourteenth Amendment, the Court cautioned that congressional exercise of that power should be inferred only when such an intention is expressed "in unmistakable language in the statute itself." In the Court's estimation, the language in the Rehabilitation Act providing remedies for violations of section 504 did not meet this test.[*] Finally, the Court held that California had not tacitly consented to suit in federal court merely because "various provisions of the Rehabilitation Act are addressed to the States" and because California "participat[ed] in programs funded under the statute." The Act's language, the Court concluded, "falls far short of manifesting a clear intent to condition participation in the programs funded under the Act on a State's consent to waive its constitutional immunity."

Scanlon thus enunciated a three-step test for resolving sovereign immunity questions that we must apply: (1) Has the state expressly waived its general immunity to suit in federal court? (2) Has Congress expressed in unmistakable language its intent to abrogate states' sovereign immunity pursuant to section 5 of the Fourteenth Amendment? and (3) Does the act manifest a clear intent to condition a state's receipt of federal benefits on the state's waiver of its constitutional immunity? Applying each step of this test to EAHCA, we conclude that California retains its sovereign immunity from damage suits.

First, California has not waived its general immunity to suit in federal court. Second, Congress did not unequivocally express in the Act its intent to abrogate California's sovereign immunity. The EAHCA provision authorizing suits in federal courts provides in relevant part:

---

[*] [*Author's Note:* This case was apparently decided before the 1986 amendment to the Rehabilitation Act changed the Section 504 immunity rule of *Atascadero.*]

> Any party aggrieved by the findings and decision made under subsection (b) [providing for administrative review] . . . shall have the right to bring a civil action . . . in any State court of competent jurisdiction or in a district court of the United States without regard to the amount in controversy.

20 U.S.C. sec. 1415(e)(2). This language simply does not pass muster under the stringent *Scanlon* test. Third, although the EAHCA—like the Rehabilitation Act—imposes various duties on the states, it nowhere explicitly conditions their right to receive funds on the willingness to waive their sovereign immunity.

Thus, we affirm the district court's dismissal of the plaintiffs' damage claims under the EAHCA.

MUTH V. CENTRAL BUCKS SCHOOL DISTRICT

839 F.2d 113 (3d Cir. 1988)
[This case involved Alexander Muth, a learning-disabled student in elementary school who had related emotional problems. His father challenged the appropriateness of the placement developed by the school, and sought reimbursement for private school tuition incurred during the dispute. The claim was brought against the local school district and the Pennsylvania State Secretary of Education. In addition to addressing the appropriateness of the placement, and the violation of timetable limitations in the review process (a delay of a year from the request for a due process hearing until the final review decision was rendered), the court focused on eleventh amendment immunity.]

We next address the question, raised on appeal by the Secretary, of whether the 11th amendment to the Constitution bars reimbursement by the state of plaintiff's expenses. This is also an issue of statutory construction requiring plenary review.

The 11th amendment provides that:

> The Judicial power of the United States shall not be construed to extend to any suit in law or equity, commenced or prosecuted against one of the United States by Citizens of another State, or by Citizens or Subjects of any Foreign State.

U.S. Const. amend. XI. As the Secretary correctly points out, the 11th amendment has been consistently interpreted by the Supreme Court to preclude federal court suits against a state by the state's own citizens, and to preclude suits for equitable relief as well as damages. For 11th amendment purposes, a suit against a state official in his or her official capacity, as here, is the equivalent of a suit against the state, since the state is the real party in interest. Accordingly, we are confronted with the issue of whether the 11th amendment bars suits against a state in a federal court under the EHA.

Section 5 of the 14th amendment authorizes Congress to enforce the provisions of that amendment by "appropriate legislation." Utilizing this authority, Congress may abrogate the immunity from federal court suits bestowed on the states by the 11th amendment. However, if Congress chooses to override 11th amendment rights, it must make its intentions clear. So that immunity will prevail in the absence of a conscious congressional decision that it must be sacrificed to preserve 14th amendment values, the Supreme Court has declared that "Congress must express its intention to abrogate the eleventh amendment in unmistakable language in the statute itself." While the text of the federal legislation must bear evidence of such an intention, the legislative history may still be used as a resource in determining whether Congress's intention to lift the bar has been made sufficiently manifest.

The text of EHA and its legislative history leave no doubt that Congress intended to abrogate the 11th amendment immunity of the states. In the preamble of the Act, Congress declared it necessary to exercise its right under sec. 5 of the 14th amendment in order to assure equal protection of the law for handicapped children. Thus, in sec. 1400(b)(9), Congress expressly "finds that . . . it is in the national interest that the Federal government assist State and local efforts to provide programs to meet the educational needs of handicapped children in order to assure equal protection of the law."

The EHA then goes on to establish a national minimum standard for the education of handicapped children and to set up a detailed process for identifying handicapped children and ascertaining what the federal standard requires in each individual case. The state educational agency is responsible under the EHA to see that this process is successfully implemented. Moreover, if for any reason a local educational agency is unwilling or unable to provide a handicapped child with a "free appropriate public education," the state agency is required to step in and provide that education by contract or otherwise. Most importantly, the EHA not only confers substantive and procedural rights upon handicapped children and their parents vis-á-vis the state educational agency, it bestows upon them the right to seek judicial enforcement of those rights in a federal or state court.

Although a number of other courts of appeal have held that the EHA does not abrogate 11th amendment immunity, none have articulated a rationale as persuasive as that of the First Circuit and none have reached this result after the 1986 amendment to the EHA.

We now join the Court of Appeals for the First Circuit in holding that the EHA authorizes suits against states in a federal court. Since the "jurisdictional bar [of the 11th amendment] applies regardless of the nature of the relief sought," and there is thus no distinction to be made between actions for injunctive relief and for damages in the context of an EHA suit against a state agency, we hold that Congress, in authorizing such suits, must have contemplated that tuition reimbursement judgments . . . would be a part of sec. 1415(e) litigation.

DOE A. V. SPECIAL SCHOOL DISTRICT

637 F. Supp. 1138 (E.D. Mo. 1986)

Plaintiffs, nine handicapped children enrolled in the defendant Special School District [SSD] and their parents, allege that the defendants deprived them of their constitutional rights either by beating and sexually abusing the children or by failing to investigate and to act upon complaints of abuse.

Plaintiffs' first amended complaint contains nine counts. The first count alleges a sec. 1983 claim against the Board of Education and individual administrators of SSD for failing to provide handicapped students a safe and humane environment, including protection from sexual assaults. In Count II, plaintiffs allege that SSD maintained a *de facto* policy of failing to investigate complaints of abuse, actively inhibiting investigation of complaints and failing to train and monitor employees. In Count III, the minor plaintiffs allege that the acts of Cerny resulted from a *de facto* policy of defendant SSD in violation of the Fifth and Fourteenth Amendments and sec. 1983. Similarly, in Count IV the minor plaintiffs allege that the acts of Cerny resulted from a *de facto* policy of defendant SSD and violated plaintiffs' rights under the Fifth, Ninth, and Fourteenth Amendments and sec. 1983. Count V alleges that SSD allowed defendant Cerny to restrain the minor plaintiffs without probable cause in violation of the Fourth, Fifth and Fourteenth Amendments and sec. 1983. Count VI purports to state common law claims for assault, battery, and false imprisonment against defendants Cerny and SSD. In Count VII, the minor plaintiffs sue SSD, its Board, and its administrators for their negligent failure to supervise employees and to investigate complaints of abuse. In Count VIII, the plaintiff parents allege that the District, Board, and administrators deprived them of their rights to custody, care, and companionship in violation of the Fifth and Fourteenth Amendments and sec. 1983. In Count IX, the parents allege tortious interference with their custody rights. . . .

The complaint alleges the following facts: Defendant David Cerny was employed by SSD as a school bus driver. Between September, 1983 and February, 1985, defendant Cerny repeatedly molested the minor plaintiffs while they were passengers on his bus. These incidents occurred while the bus was stopped at a transfer point, a location at which the children would make connections between buses on their way to and from school. These incidents included . . . the confinement of the students in the school bus for one or more hours after the conclusion of the school day and completion of the bus route. In addition, Cerny frequently started and stopped the school bus so quickly that the students were thrown about the bus.

Due to their handicaps, the minor plaintiffs were incapable of resisting or protecting themselves from the assaultive and abusive behavior of Cerny. Despite complaints from parents, teachers and other employees of SSD, defendants SSD, its Board and its administrators failed to investigate the actions of Cerny. Indeed, defendant SSD concealed the actions of Cerny by discouraging any investigation of complaints. In addition, the defendants failed to develop a policy to provide training for the investigation of complaints and to screen employees for their propensity to abuse children. Also, the defendants failed to report Cerny's conduct to law enforcement and child protective agencies despite their statutory obligation to do so. As a result of these acts, the plaintiff children suffered serious physical, psychological, and emotional damage, requiring them to undergo medical and psychological treatment. The plaintiff parents have suffered mental anguish and lost the companionship of their children. The minor plaintiffs seek $24,000,000.00 in actual damages and $24,000,000.00 in punitive damages on each count; the parents seek $20,000,000.00 in actual damages and $40,000,000.00 in punitive damages on each count. . . .

I. Under Color of State Law

As defendant Cerny and the individual SSD defendants assert, Cerny's actions were taken as a private citizen and not under color of any state law authorizing him to operate a school bus. . . .

Here the district was obligated by statute to provide free transportation to handicapped students enrolled in this district. That statute also vests the Board of Education of the district with the authority to promulgate rules and regulations necessary to provide transportation. Under this mandate, SSD employed defendant Cerny to drive a school bus. This arrangement provided Cerny with custody of the children and opportunities to engage in the alleged conduct. Thus, defendant Cerny acted under color of state law.

II. Student Plaintiffs' Federal Cause of Action

Plaintiffs assert sec. 1983 claims based upon violations of their Fourth, Fifth, Ninth, and Fourteenth Amendment rights. As defendants argue, the alleged actions sound in tort and do not rise to the ignomy of constitutional violations. In response, plaintiffs assert that the alleged conduct "shocks the conscience" and, therefore, violates the minor plaintiffs' rights to substantive due process. This Court concludes that plaintiffs' allegations state a claim upon which relief may be granted. . . .

A public official is liable under sec. 1983 only if the official deprives an individual of a constitutional right. Section 1983 does not provide a remedy for violations of duties of care arising out of tort law. Remedies for these injuries must be sought in state court under traditional tort law principles. Thus, the crucial issue is whether plaintiffs allege any deprivation of *constitutional* rights. As plaintiffs allege, defendants' actions deprive them of liberty without due process of law as guaranteed by the Fourteenth Amendment. As such, plaintiffs purport to allege violations of their right to substantive due process.

The due process clause affords individuals far-reaching protection against intrusions by state officials. The Due Process Clause not only requires the Government to follow appropriate procedures when its agents decide to deprive any person of life, liberty or property, but also bars certain arbitrary Government actions regardless of the fairness of the procedures used to implement them. . . .

An important manifestation of "liberty" as guaranteed by substantive due process is the right to be free of state intrusions into personal privacy and bodily security. . . .

Though many cases involve adults physically injured by guards or police officers, the principles set forth apply with equal force to abuses by state officials in other contexts. . . .

This Court does not doubt that the constitutional rights of children to be free from harm is commensurate with the rights of adults in state custody. . . .

The alleged acts of defendant Cerny and the alleged tolerance of these acts by SSD and the individual defendants pass beyond the pale of common law torts. They shock the conscience of this Court. Thus, this Court finds the minor plaintiffs' allegations sufficient to state a claim against defendants under sec. 1983.

[The portion dismissing the parents' sec. 1983 claim based on loss of companionship is omitted.]

IV. State Law Causes of Action

In Counts VII and IX, minor plaintiffs and their parents allege that SSD, its Board, and its administrators failed to supervise defendant Cerny and to investigate complaints or abuse. The students allege physical and emotional damage. The parents allege emotional damage and loss of companionship. In defense of these claims, the individual SSD defendants assert official immunity. Plaintiffs' allegations present common law claims based upon state law. The gravamen of these complaints is that defendants failed to exercise reasonable care. Therefore, this Court must look to Missouri law to determine defendants' duty and to determine the scope of official immunity.

State officials acting within the scope of their authority are not liable for discretionary acts or omissions but may be liable for torts committed when acting in a ministerial capacity.

The characterization of an act as discretionary turns upon the degree of reason and judgment required for its execution. A discretionary act requires the exercise of judgment in determining how and whether an act should be done or course pursued. In contrast, ministerial acts are "of a clerical nature which a public officer is required to perform upon a given state of facts, in a prescribed manner, in obedience to the mandate of legal authority, without regard to his own judgment or opinion concerning the propriety of the act to be performed." These definitions do not create bright lines separating discretionary from ministerial acts. Rather, the question is one of degree, necessarily incapable of reduction to verbal formulas. . . .

Here, defendants are not engaged in the ministerial act of physically transporting students or maintaining buses for transportation. Rather, defendants formulate policies which are carried out by subordinates. As school district administrators, defendants are responsible for planning for transportation and ensuring the execution of their plans. Defendants' responsibilities require primarily the exercise of judgment rather than the performance of routine tasks. Thus, defendants are immune from liability for negligent selection, training, and supervision of defendant Cerny.

Plaintiffs also predicate their claims upon the negligent failure of SSD officials to report the alleged child abuse to the Missouri Division of Family Services. According to plaintiffs' allegations, the defendant officials received complaints concerning Cerny from parents and teachers. . . .

In Missouri, before an act is said to be negligent, there must exist a duty to the individual complaining. . . . The Missouri child abuse reporting statute creates a duty owed to the general public, not to specific individuals, and consequently the statute does not support a private cause of action in favor of individuals. Therefore, to the extent plaintiffs rely upon the Missouri statute they fail to state a cause of action. . . .

This Court does not agree with plaintiffs' characterization of defendants' actions as ministerial. The statute does not require school teachers and administrators to report every suspicion of abuse. Rather, the statute specifically requires reporting only when there is a *reasonable* cause to suspect abuse. This requirement calls for the exercise of a teacher's or administrator's professional judgment.

V. Sovereign Immunity

In Counts II, VI, VII, and IX, plaintiffs assert various common law tort claims against defendant SSD. In defense, SSD asserts the doctrine of sovereign immunity. The Missouri legislature [has] reestablished the doctrine of sovereign immunity abrogated by the Missouri Supreme Court. Section 437.600 provides two exceptions to sovereign immunity: 1) injuries resulting directly from the operation of motor vehicles, and 2) injuries caused by dangerous conditions on a public entity's property. These exceptions operate in opposition to the general legislative intent to revive sovereign immunity and therefore must be strictly construed. . . . Regarding the motor vehicle exception, the alleged actions must relate directly to the operation of the vehicle. In *Johnson,* plaintiff alleged that he was physically held by a school bus driver to permit another student to beat him. As the Missouri Court of Appeals held, the acts of the driver were not within the exception because the acts did not concern the operation of the bus. The court noted that "the only connection to the bus was the actors' presence therein." Plaintiff presents no principled distinction between *Johnson* and the facts of the instant case. Thus, the motor vehicle exception does not apply. The dangerous condition exception applies only to physical defects upon property. . . . Therefore, that exception to sovereign immunity does not apply, and defendants' motions to dismiss on this ground are granted.

In sum, defendants' motions to dismiss are denied as to the sec. 1983 claims of the minor plaintiffs based upon substantive due process. Defendants' motions are granted as to all state law claims, the sec. 1983 claims of the minor plaintiffs' parents based upon constitutional provisions other than the due process clause of the Fourteenth Amendment.

SUMMARY

The issue of immunity is a complex and difficult one. It is the subject of an extensive amount of litigation in numerous contexts in addition to special education and has been the subject of a substantial amount of scholarly discussion.

Basically, immunity is imposed as a policy matter to protect states and state agencies from liability for conduct that occurs even when such conduct has been injurious and wrongful. One major source of immunity is common-law governmental immunity protecting a state from actions by its citizens. The eleventh amendment of the U.S. Constitution is the second major source of immunity. It prohibits parties from bringing claims against states or their agencies based on federal statute. Neither of these sources can protect a state from misconduct that rises to the level of a constitutional violation. And waiver of immunity can occur either through a specific state statute waiving immunity or in the case of federal law where the federal statute clearly abrogates immunity.

The application of immunity principles to the special education context has provided differing levels of clarity. It is clear from a 1986 amendment to the Rehabilitation Act that states and state agencies are not immune from Section 504 claims. Although there are strong arguments that an abrogation of immunity is an obvious necessity to carry out EAHCA policy, this position has not been uniformly accepted by all courts addressing the issue. Even more complex is the application of immunity principles to individual educators—administrators, teachers, and other school personnel. While it is clear that local educational agencies are not protected under immunity principles, it is less clear whether immunity will apply to protect a school board member or bus driver, for example, in a particular factual setting. Given the difficulty of this issue, it is unlikely that complete clarity on these questions will occur for some time.

QUESTIONS AND PROBLEMS

1. Could the claims set forth in this chapter have been brought alleging violations of the EAHCA? If so, would that have precluded the Section 1983 claims?
2. As a practical matter, what should the parents in the *Doe* case have done when they realized the misconduct of the bus driver?
3. As a legal matter, what could the parents have done to stop the conduct as soon as they learned about it?
4. Assuming the bus driver would be found to be individually liable, would that provide a remedy to the parents and the children? Why or why not?
5. As a policy matter, does there need to be an adjustment to the immunity doctrine? If so, how would such a change best be accomplished?

NOTES

1. 29 U.S.C. § 701.
2. 468 U.S. 992 (1984). See Chapter 3.
3. 471 U.S. 359 (1985). See Chapter 17.
4. *See* L. ROTHSTEIN, RIGHTS OF PHYSICALLY HANDICAPPED PERSONS § 2.42 (1984) and cumulative supplement.

CHAPTER 20

The Status and Future
of Special Education Law

Numerous commentators have found the EAHCA to be positive and constructive legislation. They believe that it has already achieved the goals of the EAHCA to a substantial degree—that most handicapped children in this country are now receiving an appropriate education, without unreasonable disruption or consequences to the rest of regular education. Many believe that the teaching methodologies and the accountability resulting from the EAHCA have benefited *all* of education and that nonhandicapped children benefit in humanistic ways from the presence of handicapped children in the mainstream of public education.

Others counter that the EAHCA has brought unnecessary bureaucracy, paperwork, and costs to public education. Some find that while the EAHCA is a positive step for children with certain handicaps—such as mental retardation— that it is unduly burdensome when severely medically and psychologically involved children are seeking services. These critics suggest that the appropriate avenues for such services are health, social service, and welfare agencies rather than educational agencies.

What is perhaps a more appropriate reaction is not that the educational agency is the wrong agency, but that there is an enormous financial burden when educating children with severe medical and psychological needs, and that the funding for such programs needs to be rechanneled through the educational agencies. In addition, educational agencies need to be empowered at the state level to obtain support services from other agencies.

Litigation in the first 10 years after passage of the EAHCA focused on major policy questions: What is appropriate? What constitute medical services and what do not? What type of remedies are available under the EAHCA? How does the EAHCA interrelate with Section 504 and Section 1983? Are policies limiting the amount of service available permissible? How can testing be used to identify, evaluate, and place children?

During the early 1980s, attempts to deregulate the EAHCA proved an embarrassment to the U.S. Department of Education, and the major legislation that passed during that period only added to the substance of the EAHCA—by providing for additional programming for preschool children and infants—and by providing for attorneys' fees for parents who prevailed against the educational agencies.

The future of special education law will probably involve a fine-tuning of the EAHCA requirements. Cost issues are likely to recur. When can limited resources be used as a defense? Will damages or compensatory education be recoverable under the EAHCA? Will administrators or state or local agencies become accountable for financial awards? Will improvements in secondary and vocational education occur? How will schools be required to handle custodial and medical-type placements? How will interagency agreements and funding allocations be worked out? What types of extended services will be required? How will the preschool and infant programs work? What refinements will occur in disciplinary removals of handicapped children? How will children with AIDS be educated? And perhaps most important, to what extent will the mainstreaming requirement be implemented? What will become of the regular education initiative—the plan to make regular education more directly responsible for special education? Will the burden fall on the educational agency any time a placement outside the regular school is involved? Will the availability of attorneys' fees be a positive step—will it improve the quality of representation? Will it stir up unnecessary controversies? Or will it encourage schools to provide appropriate programming in the first place? Will mediation become more common?

Whether the EAHCA is a good program or not, it seems that for a variety of reasons it is here to stay. Special education probably requires more attention to legal issues than any other education program in schools today. For that reason, teachers, education administrators, and policymakers would do well to be informed on the basic requirements of the law and to take advantage of opportunities to update their information on a regular basis. Although the EAHCA may be a frustrating and demanding law for some on both sides because of its ambiguities and numerous requirements, it is certainly an interesting law.[1]

QUESTIONS AND PROBLEMS

1. Which of the issues noted above would best be resolved through litigation? Which through legislation? Which through regulation? Which through education?

NOTES

1. For discussions of the overall policy of the EAHCA, *see* H.R. Turnbull III, Free Appropriate Public Education: The Law and Children with Disabilities, ch. 11 & 12 (1986); and R. Weiner, P.L. 94–142: Impact on the Schools, ch. 11 (1985).

APPENDIX A*

Education and the American Legal System

In this appendix we look first at the role of state governments in education. Then we present the organization of U.S. court systems and indicate the way they relate to educational controversies.*

EDUCATION AND STATE GOVERNMENTS

Unlike most countries, the United States has no national system of education. In fact, the national Constitution is silent on the matter; however, under its tenth amendment, education is considered to be among the powers reserved to the states. Courts have accepted this interpretation of the Constitution, and the Supreme Court has repeatedly stated that federal courts may interfere with the actions of state and local school officials only when such actions somehow threaten a personal liberty or property right protected by the Constitution or violate federal law.

All 50 states provide in their constitutions for public education. With America's historic commitment to decentralized government and local control, states have delegated much power and responsibility over schooling to local governments. Such delegation is a choice made by the people of a state, who could, like the state of Hawaii, choose to have one statewide school district. In spite of the existence of local school districts, legally schools remain a responsibility of the state government; school officials, teachers, and staff are agents of the state when per-

*Appendix adapted from Louis Fischer, David Schimmel, and Cynthia Kelly, *Teachers and the Law* (New York: Longman, 1981). Reprinted by permission of Longman, Inc. From *School Law for Counselors, Psychologists, and Social Workers,* by Louis Fischer and Gail Paulus Sorenson (1985).

forming their official duties. This is a significant principle, because the Constitution only protects individuals against actions taken by the government.

The first 10 amendments to the Constitution (more commonly, the Bill of Rights) prohibit certain actions on the part of the federal government. The fourteenth amendment applies to actions by the states. Because all actions of school officials and school boards are "state actions," the fourteenth amendment prohibits certain arbitrary and discriminatory practices. What makes this all the more important is the historic development whereby all the guarantees of the first amendment, and many other provisions of the Bill of Rights, have been incorporated into the "liberty clause" of the fourteenth and thus made applicable to all the states. Although there is a complex and controversial legal history to this incorporation, for our purposes it will suffice to understand that all protections of the first amendment, and most protections of the other Bill of Rights provisions, apply to the actions of public school officials just as do those of the fourteenth amendment.

Thus, although states have the primary power and responsibility for public schools, their power must at all times be exercised consistently with the rights guaranteed in the national Constitution.

THE FEDERAL COURT SYSTEM

The U.S. Supreme Court is the only court specifically created by the Constitution (art. III, sec. 2); all other federal courts were established by Congress. Below the Supreme Court are 13 federal courts of appeal (see Figure A.1), and within each "circuit" or geographical area (except for one centralized federal court of appeals dealing with copyright and other specialized matters) are trial courts, called district courts. There are nearly 100 district courts, at least one in each state, though their exact number may change from time to time. School-related cases involving federal issues may be brought to trial in a district court; from this court an appeal may be taken to a court of appeals and eventually to the Supreme Court (see Figure A.2).

The Constitution specifies what cases the Supreme Court will consider (art. III, sec. 2, cl. 1). For all other federal courts, Congress determines which cases will be tried where, the route appeals will take, and the relationship of courts to the many administrative agencies of government. In general, federal courts take only two kinds of cases: (1) those that present substantial questions under federal laws and the Constitution, and (2) those involving different states or citizens of different states. Many cases present questions involving both federal and state laws and may initially be tried in either federal or state courts. If such a case is brought to trial in a federal court, however, the court must decide questions of state law according to the laws of the affected state. Conversely, if the case was initially filed in a state court, that court must follow the federal law governing that area.

Although decisions of the Supreme Court are applicable to the entire nation, the decisions of circuit courts are binding only within their territories; thus different rules may apply in different regions of the country until the Supreme Court decides the issue.

The Thirteen Federal Judicial Circuits

See 28 U.S.C.A. § 41

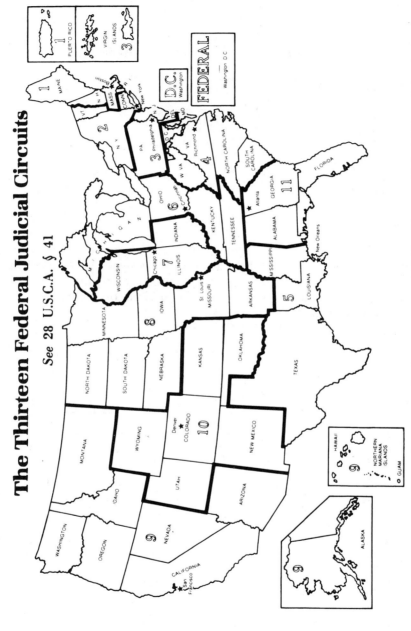

Figure A.1. The thirteen federal judicial circuits. (Courtesy of West Publishing Company, St. Paul, Minnesota.)

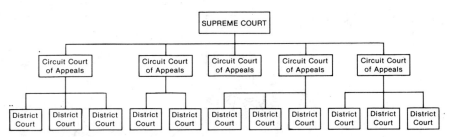

Figure A.2. The federal court system.

THE STATE COURT SYSTEM

Most school-related cases are litigated in state courts. Because these courts are created by state constitutions and legislatures, however, they vary considerably in titles, procedures, and jurisdiction. A general pattern among the states is a three-tiered system, excluding lower courts of special jurisdiction such as traffic courts and small claims courts (See Figure A.3).

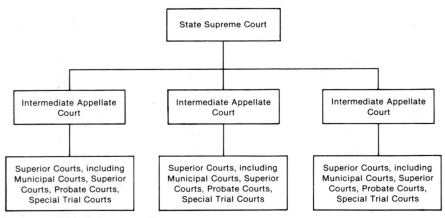

Figure A.3. A typical state court system.

At the foundation of the state court system, we find the trial courts, often organized along county lines. From these, appeals go to intermediate appeals courts and finally to the highest court of the state, variously named in different states. For example, the highest state court is named the Supreme Judicial Court in Massachusetts, the Court of Appeals in Kentucky, the Supreme Court of Errors in Connecticut, and the Supreme Court in California.

THE FUNCTIONS OF TRIAL AND APPEALS COURTS

A school-related controversy that cannot be resolved without a lawsuit first goes to a trial court. Here the facts are established and the relevant legal principles applied to the facts. If the case is appealed, the appellate court will not retry the case; it will usually accept the facts as established by the trial court unless it is very clear that evidence to support such facts was inadequate. The main concern of appeals courts is whether correct legal principles were applied to the facts determined by the court below it.

For example, a school may have expelled Student X for persistent acts of violence and classroom disruption. Student X could seek review of such action in a state trial court of general jurisdiction. If it were alleged that the student had been deprived of a constitutional right to due process, the case could be brought to a federal district court instead. (The student could still proceed in state court, however, because state courts have the power to decide issues of federal constitutional law.) Whichever trial court the student chose would hear evidence from both sides in order to determine what actually happened. Once the facts were established, the judge would apply the law to the facts and arrive at a decision. Even if the judge were a state judge, all laws applicable to the case, both federal and state, would be considered, because article VI of the U.S. Constitution provides that the "Constitution, and the Laws of the United States . . . shall be the supreme Law of the Land; and the Judges in every State shall be bound thereby." If the case were appealed, the appeals court would consider whether or not the principles of law were properly applied by the trial court.

The highest state court will be the final authority on legal questions related to the law of that state unless there is federal law on the same matter. The U.S. Supreme Court is the final authority on matters arising out of the Constitution, treaties, federal laws, or conflicts among state laws. In matters that involve only state laws, the state courts have the authoritative voice.

ADMINISTRATIVE BODIES

It is generally recognized today that the courts are overburdened and their calendars overcrowded. It is all too true that "justice delayed is justice denied," yet in many cities it takes over a year for a criminal case to come to trial and several years for a civil suit to be tried. This situation would be worse if we did not have administrative agencies acting in quasi-judicial capacities. Without a doubt, the largest and most detailed body of law, administrative rules and regulations, is created by agencies that regulate public affairs. Administrative law functions at both federal and state levels, and the lives of educators are heavily influenced by it.

HOW TO FIND REPORTS OF COURT CASES

Every county has a courthouse that contains a law library. Every law school has such a library, and most universities and colleges have legal collections. In each of these places a librarian can help one to find cases of interest. The following constitutes a brief introduction to legal research.

Appellate courts almost always publish their decisions. The decisions of the highest appellate court, the U.S. Supreme Court, can be found in the *United States Reports.* For example, the citation *Brown v. Board of Education of Topeka, Kansas,* 349 U.S. 294(1955), indicates that the case, decided in 1955, is reported in volume 349 of the *United States Reports* at page 294. Since Supreme Court cases are reported in several publications, the same case may be followed by the notations 75 S.Ct. 753, 99 L. Ed. 1083. This means that the same case also appears in volume 75 of the *Supreme Court Reporter* at page 753 and in volume 99 of the *Lawyers Edition* at page 1083. The most recent cases decided by the Supreme Court appear in a looseleaf volume called *United States Law Week,* cited, for example, as *Irving Independent School District v. Tatro,* 52 U.S.L.W. 5151 (July 5, 1984).

Recent cases decided by the U.S. Courts of Appeals are reported in West's *Federal Reporter, Second Series* (F.2d). For example, *Clark v. Whiting,* 607 F.2d 634 (4th Cir. 1979) would be found in volume 607 of the *Federal Reporter, Second Series* at page 634. The case was decided by the Fourth Circuit Court of Appeals in 1979. When a series becomes too long and thus the volume numbers too large, a second series is begun and cited, for example, "F.2d" rather than "F."

Decisions of the U.S. District Courts are reported in the *Federal Supplement* (F. Supp.), also published by West Publishing Company, and are cited in a manner similar to other federal court cases. For example, *Valencia v. Blue Hen Conference,* 476 F. Supp. 809 (D. Del. 1979), indicates that this case was decided by a district court in Delaware in 1979 and is reported in volume 476 of the *Federal Supplement* at page 809. The *Federal Supplement* does not yet have a second series.

The National Reporter System of the West Publishing Company, in addition to reporting the federal cases noted above, also reports cases from state courts. Most reported state appellate court decisions appear in the following volumes: *Atlantic Reporter* (A.), *North Eastern Reporter* (N.E.), *North Western Reporter* (N.W.), *Pacific Reporter* (P.), *South Eastern Reporter* (S.E.), *South Western Reporter* (S.W.), and *Southern Reporter* (So.). Cases from New York, including some trial court decisions, are available in West's *New York Supplement* (N.Y.S.); cases from California are contained in the *California Reporter* (Cal. Rptr.). Many of these same cases also appear in the respective regional reporters—the *North Eastern Reporter* and the *Pacific Reporter.*

In addition to reading cases, counselors and educators interested in a particular topic might go to one of the standard legal encyclopedias to gain an overview of the topic. The best-known of these encyclopedias are *Corpus Juris Secundum* (C.J.S.) and *American Jurisprudence 2d* (Am. Jur. 2d). School counselors, psychologists, social workers, and other professionals who want to know more about legal research may consult with a law librarian and/or read one of the standard guides on the subject. A good guide is Jacobstein and Merskey, *Fundamentals of Legal Research* (1981).

APPENDIX B

Sequential Listing of Major Special Education Law Developments

Brown v. Board of Education, 347 U.S. 483 (1954)
Established that separate but equal was not equal in education.
PARC v. Pennsylvania, 334 F. Supp. 1257 (E.D. Pa. 1971) and *Mills v. Board of Education,*
348 F. Supp. 866 (D.D.C. 1972)
Established the constitutional basis for providing education to handicapped children by finding that denial of education to handicapped children and denial of due process in so doing violates the fourteenth amendment to the constitution.
Rehabilitation Act of 1973 (Section 504) 29 U.S.C. Section 794
Recipients of federal financial assistance may not discriminate on the basis of handicap.
Education for All Handicapped Children Act—1975, 20 U.S.C. Sections 1400–1461
A grant statute to provide for the support of special education to states that implement a plan to provide a free appropriate public education to all handicapped children so that special education and related services will be available on an individualized basis; due process protection must be in place to ensure compliance.
Final Regulations for EAHCA passed—August 15, 1977
Now found at 34 C.F.R., Part 300.
Battle v. Commonwealth, 629 F.2d 269 (3d Cir. 1980)
Established that educational policies (such as one limiting the school year to 180 days) would violate the EAHCA if such policies denied handicapped students a free appropriate public education.
Board of Education v. Rowley, 458 U.S. 176 (1982)
An "appropriate" education under the EAHCA is found when a program of special education and related services is provided such that the child benefits from education and where the due process procedures have been followed in developing the program.
Irving Independent School District v. Tatro, 468 U.S. 883 (1984)
Catheterization and similar health-type services are "related services" because they need not be provided by a physician and are relatively simple procedures to provide. If these

services had been determined to be medical services, they would not be required under the EAHCA.

Smith v. Robinson, 468 U.S. 992 (1984)

Where the EAHCA provides the basis for protection in special education, it is the exclusive avenue of relief, and Section 504 and Section 1983 are not available.

Perkins Act—1984, 20 U.S.C. § 2301, 2332–34

Ten percent of all federal funding for vocational education must go toward the education of handicapped students. Vocational education is to be provided in the least restrictive environment. An important step toward recognizing the importance of special education in the secondary schools and as part of the transition to adulthood.

City of Cleburne v. Cleburne Living Center, 473 U.S. 432 (1985)

Mentally retarded individuals are not a suspect or even a quasi-suspect class for determining the appropriate level of constitutional scrutiny. The *Plyler v. Doe,* 202 U.S. (1982) decision, which provides that while education is not a fundamental right it deserves heightened scrutiny, will mean that although handicapped individuals will not be given any special deference by the courts, education will. This may be an important decision for addressing children with AIDS.

Burlington School Committee v. Department of Education, 471 U.S. 359 (1985)

Where the parents unilaterally place a child in an appropriate placement and the school did not provide an appropriate placement, the parents may receive reimbursement for the expenses incurred.

Handicapped Children's Protection Act of 1986, 20 U.S.C. Section 1415(e)(4)

An amendment to the EAHCA providing for attorney's fees and costs to be awarded to parents who are prevailing parties.

Education of the Handicapped Act Amendments of 1986, 20 U.S.C. §§ 1471 *et seq.* and 1419 *et seq.*

Provides for a phase-in of early intervention services for three- to five-year-olds, to be mandatory by 1990; also contains an incentive program for younger children.

School Board of Nassau County v. Arline, 107 S.Ct. 1123 (1987)

Contagious diseases are a handicap under Section 504 of the Rehabilitation Act, and individuals with these diseases are protected from discrimination in federal financially assisted programs, although the individuals must also be otherwise qualified. Risk to the health and safety of others, if actual, may deem the individual unqualified.

Preschool amendment regulations—1987, 34 C.F.R. Parts 301 and 303.

Civil Rights Restoration Act of 1987, 29 U.S.C. § 706(7)(8)(c)

Amended Section 504 of the Rehabilitation Act to clarify that *all* portions of an educational agency are considered to be part of the program; adopted the *Airline* characterization of contagious diseases as handicaps within the Rehabilitation Act.

Honig v. Doe, 108 S.Ct. 592 (1988)

Expulsion of a child for more than 10 days constitutes a change in placement for which all EAHCA due process protections must take place. Temporary removals are permissible for emergency situations.

APPENDIX C

Frequently Used Acronyms and Terms

BD	behavior disordered: often refers to a student whose behavior makes functioning in society difficult
case law	law developed by the courts through issuing judicial opinions
certiorari	a discretionary writ giving a superior court the jurisdiction to review the decision of a lower court
common law	law developed primarily by the courts; developed over time by usage and custom
consent	permission of the parents allowing the school to evaluate, assess, place or make another individualized decision about a child who is or who is thought to be handicapped
EAHCA or EHA	Education for All Handicapped Children Act
ED	emotionally disturbed: often refers to a student with a behavior disorder that results in the inability to control emotions
education malpractice	a broad term including a variety of types of misconduct by educators or employees of educational agencies, including improper supervision, infliction of emotional distress, improper discipline, or improper evaluation or placement of a handicapped child
EMR	educably mentally retarded (highest level of retardation, IQ approximately 50–70)
FAPE	free appropriate public education
HCPA	Handicapped Children's Protection Act of 1986: an amend-

	ment to the EAHCA providing for attorneys' fees and costs to parents in successful cases
IEP	Individualized Educational Program
FERPA	Family Educational Rights and Privacy Act (also commonly known as the Buckley Amendment): a federal statute relating to confidentiality and access involving student educational records
injunction	an order issued by a court requiring a party to do or refrain from doing something
IQ	intelligence quotient: an artificial number that is used to indicate mental development level
LD	learning disabled: an individual who has a disorder in the psychological processes in language that affects the ability to listen, think, speak, read, write, spell, or do math
LRE	least restrictive environment: often known as mainstreaming, the concept of placing a child in an environment that exposes the handicapped child to nonhandicapped children to the maximum extent appropriate
mainstreaming	one of the major principles of the EAHCA requiring that education of handicapped children be provided in the least restrictive environment appropriate to that child's needs
MR	mentally retarded
notice	information provided to parents regarding proposed action to be taken toward their child and information about their legal rights under the EAHCA.
P.L. 94–142	Education for All Handicapped Children Act
Section 504	referring to that portion of the Rehabilitation Act of 1973 that provides that recipients of federal financial assistance may not discriminate on the basis of handicap
stare decisis	legal precedent, binding holdings in similar previous cases
sweep screening	group assessments of children for a specific problem, such as vision or hearing
TMR	trainably mentally retarded (often refers to individuals with an IQ between 25 and 50)
tort law	the law of private or civil wrongs arising from a violation of a duty other than a contract duty

APPENDIX D

P.L. 94–142 Regulations

SUBPART A—GENERAL

Purpose, Applicability, and General Provisions Regulations

SUBPART B—STATE ANNUAL PROGRAM PLANS AND LOCAL APPLICATIONS

SUBPART C—SERVICES

Free Appropriate Public Education

Priorities in the Use of Part B Funds

Protection in Evaluation Procedures

Additional Procedures for Evaluating Specific Learning Disabilities

Least Restrictive Environment

Confidentiality of Information

Department Procedures

SUBPART A—GENERAL

Purpose, Applicability, and General Provisions Regulations

§ 300.1 Purpose.

The purpose of this part is:

(a) To insure that all handicapped children have available to them a free appropriate public education which includes special education and related services to meet their unique needs.

(b) To insure that the rights of handicapped children and their parents are protected,

(c) To assist States and localities to provide for the education of all handicapped children, and

(d) To assess and insure the effectiveness of efforts to educate those children. (20 U.S.C. 1401 Note)

§ 300.2 Applicability to State, local, and private agencies.

(a) *States.* This part applies to each state which receives payments under Part B of the Education of the Handicapped Act.

(b) *Public agencies within the State.* The annual program plan is submitted by the State educational agency on behalf of the State as a whole. Therefore, the provisions of this part apply to all political subdivisions of the State that are involved in the education of handicapped children. These would include:

(1) The State educational agency, (2) local educational agencies and intermediate educational units, (3) other State agencies and schools (such as Departments of Mental Health and Welfare and State schools for the deaf or blind), and (4) State correctional facilities.

(c) *Private schools and facilities.* Each public agency in the State is responsible for insuring that the rights and protections under this part are given to children referred to or placed in private schools and facilities by that public agency. (See §§ 300.400–300.403) (20 U.S.C. 1412(1), (6); 1413(a); 1413(a)(4)(B))

Comment. The requirements of this part are binding on each public agency that has direct or delegated authority to provide special education and related services in a State that receives funds under Part B of the Act, regardless of whether that agency is receiving funds under Part B.

§ 300.3 Regulations that apply to assistance to States for education of handicapped children.

(a) *Regulations.* The following regulations apply to this program of Assistance to States for Education of Handicapped Children.

(1) The Education Department General Administrative Regulations (EDGAR) in 34 CFR Part 76 (State-Administered Programs) and Part 77 (Definitions).

(2) The regulations in this Part 300.

(b) *How to use regulations; how to apply for funds.* The "Introduction to Regulations of the Department" at the beginning of EDGAR includes general information to assist in—

(1) Using regulations that apply to Department programs; and

(2) Applying for assistance under a Department program. (20 U.S.C. 1221e-3(a)(1))

Definitions

Comment. Definitions of terms that are used throughout these regulations are included in this subpart. Other terms are defined in the specific subparts in which they are used. Below is a list of those terms and the specific sections and subparts in which they are defined.

Consent (Section 300.500 of Subpart E)

Destruction (Section 300.560 of Subpart E)

Direct services (Section 300.370(b)(1) of Subpart C)

Evaluation (Section 300.500 of Subpart E)

First priority children (Section 300.320(a) of Subpart C)

Independent educational evaluation (Section 300.503 of Subpart E)

Individualized education program (Section 300.340 of Subpart C)

Participating agency (Section 300.560 of Subpart E)

Personally identifiable (Section 300.500 of Subpart E)

Private school handicapped children (Section 300.450 of Subpart D)

Public expense (Section 300.503 of Subpart E)

Second priority children (Section 300.320(b) of Subpart C)

Special definition of "State" (Section 300.700 of Subpart G)

Support services (Section 300.370(b)(2) of Subpart C)

[42 FR 42476, Aug. 23, 1977, as amended at 45 FR 22531, Apr. 3, 1980. Redesignated at 45 FR 77368, Nov. 21, 1980]

§ 300.4 Free appropriate public education.

As used in this part, the term "free appropriate public education" means special education and related services which:

(a) Are provided at public expense, under public supervision and direction, and without charge.

(b) Meet the standards of the State educational agency, including the requirements of this part,

(c) Include preschool, elementary school, or secondary school education in the State involved, and

(d) Are provided in conformity with an individualized education program which meets the requirements under §§ 300.340–300.349 of Subpart C.
(20 U.S.C. 1401(18))

§ 300.5 Handicapped children.

(a) As used in this part, the term "handicapped children" means those children evaluated in accordance with §§ 300.530–300.534 as being mentally retarded, hard of hearing, deaf, speech impaired, visually handicapped, seriously emotionally disturbed, orthopedically impaired, other health impaired, deaf-blind, multi-handicapped, or as having specific learning disabilities, who because of those impairments need special education and related services.

(b) The terms used in this definition are defined as follows:

(1) "Deaf" means a hearing impairment which is so severe that the child is impaired in processing linguistic information through hearing, with or without amplification, which adversely affects educational performance.

(2) "Deaf-blind" means concomitant hearing and visual impairments, the combination of which causes such severe communication and other developmental and educational problems that they cannot be accommodated in special education programs solely for deaf or blind children.

(3) "Hard of Hearing" means a hearing impairment, whether permanent or fluctuating, which adversely affects a child's educational performance but which is not included under the definition of "deaf" in this section.

(4) "Mentally retarded" means significantly subaverage general intellectual functioning existing concurrently with deficits in adaptive behavior and manifested during the developmental period, which adversely affects a child's educational performance.

(5) "Multihandicapped" means concomitant impairments (such as mentally retarded—blind, mentally retarded-orthopedically impaired, etc.), the combination of which causes such severe educational problems that they cannot be accommodated in special education programs solely for one of the impairments. The term does not include deaf-blind children.

(6) "Orthopedically impaired" means a severe orthopedic impairment which adversely affects a child's educational performance. The term includes impairments caused by congenital anomaly (e.g., clubfoot, absence of some member, etc.), impairments caused by disease (e.g., poliomyelitis, bone tuberculosis, etc.), and impairments from other causes (e.g., cerebral palsy, amputations, and fractures or burns which cause contractures).

(7) "Other health impaired" means (i) having an autistic condition which is manifested by severe communication and other developmental and educational problems; or (ii) having limited strength, vitality or alertness, due to chronic or acute health problems such as a heart condition, tubercu-

losis, rhematic fever, nephritis, asthma, sickle cell anemia, hemophilia, epilepsy, lead poisoning, leukemia, or diabetes, which adversely affects a child's educational performance.

(8) "Seriously emotionally disturbed" is defined as follows:

(i) The term means a condition exhibiting one or more of the following characteristics over a long period of time and to a marked degree, which adversely affects educational performance:

(A) An inability to learn which cannot be explained by intellectual, sensory, or health factors;

(B) An inability to build or maintain satisfactory interpersonal relationships with peers and teachers;

(C) Inappropriate types of behavior or feelings under normal circumstances;

(D) A general pervasive mood of unhappiness or depression; or

(E) A tendency to develop physical symptoms or fears associated with personal or school problems.

(ii) The term includes children who are schizophrenic. The term does not include children who are socially maladjusted, unless it is determined that they are seriously emotionally disturbed.

(9) "Specific learning disability" means a disorder in one or more of the basic psychological processes involved in understanding or in using language, spoken or written, which may manifest itself in an imperfect ability to listen, think, speak, read, write, spell, or to do mathematical calculations. The term includes such conditions as perceptual handicaps, brain injury, minimal brain disfunction, dyslexia, and developmental aphasia. The term does not include children who have learning problems which are primarily the result of visual, hearing, or motor handicaps, of mental retardation of emotional disturbance or of environmental, cultural, or economic disadvantage.

(10) "Speech impaired" means a communication disorder such as stuttering, impaired articulation, a language impairment,

or a voice impairment, which adversely affects a child's educational performance.

(11) "Visually handicapped" means a visual impairment which, even with correction, adversely affects a child's educational performance. The term includes both partially seeing and blind children.
(Authority: 20 U.S.C. 1401(1), (15))
[42 FR 42476, Aug. 23, 1977, as amended at 42 FR 65083, Dec. 29, 1977. Redesignated at 45 FR 77368, Nov. 21, 1980, and further amended at 46 FR 3866, Jan. 16, 1981]

§ 300.6 Include.

As used in this part, the term "include" means that the items named are not all of the possible items that are covered, whether like or unlike the ones named.
(Authority: 20 U.S.C. 1417(b))

§ 300.7 Intermediate educational unit.

As used in this part, the term "intermediate educational unit" means any public authority, other than a local educational agency, which:

(a) Is under the general supervision of a State educational agency;

(b) Is established by State law for the purpose of providing free public education on a regional basis; and

(c) Provides special education and related services to handicapped children within that State.
(Authority: 20 U.S.C. 1401 (22))

§ 300.8 Local educational agency.

(a) [Reserved]

(b) For the purposes of this part, the term "local educational agency" also includes intermediate educational units.
(Authority: 20 U.S.C. 1401 (8))
[42 FR 42476, Aug. 23, 1977, as amended at 45 FR 22531, Apr. 3, 1980. Redesignated at 45 FR 77368, Nov. 21, 1980]

§ 300.9 Native language.

As used in this part, the term "native language" has the meaning given that term by section 703(a)(2) of the Bilingual Education

Act, which provides as follows:

The term "native language", when used with reference to a person of limited English-speaking ability, means the language normally used by that person, or in the case of a child, the language normally used by the parents of the child.
(Authority: 20 U.S.C. 880b-1(a)(2); 1401(21))

Comment. Section 602(21) of the Education of the Handicapped Act states that the term "native language" has the same meaning as the definition from the Bilingual Education Act. (The term is used in the prior notice and evaluation sections under § 300.505(b)(2) and § 300.532(a)(1) of Subpart E.) In using the term, the Act does not prevent the following means of communication:

(1) In all direct contact with a child (including evaluation of the child), communication would be in the language normally used by the child and not that of the parents, if there is a difference between the two.

(2) If a person is deaf or blind, or has no written language, the mode of communication would be that normally used by the person (such as sign language, braille, or oral communication).

§ 300.10 Parent.

As used in this part, the term "parent" means a parent, a guardian, a person acting as a parent of a child, or a surrogate parent who has been appointed in accordance with § 300.514. The term does not include the State if the child is a ward of the State.
(Authority: 20 U.S.C. 1415)

Comment. The term "parent" is defined to include persons acting in the place of a parent, such as a grandmother or stepparent with whom a child lives, as well as persons who are legally responsible for a child's welfare.

§ 300.11 Public agency.

As used in this part, the term "public agency" includes the State educational agency, local educational agencies, intermediate educational units, and any other political subdivision of the State which are responsible for providing education to handicapped children.
(Authority: 20 U.S.C. 1412(2)(B); 1412(6); 1413(a))

§ 300.12 Qualified.

As used in this part, the term "qualified" means that a person has met State educational agency approved or recognized certification, licensing, registration, or other comparable requirements which apply to the area in which he or she is providing special education or related services.
(Authority: 20 U.S.C. 1417(b))

§ 300.13 Related services.

(a) As used in this part, the term "related services" means transportation and such developmental, corrective, and other supportive services as are required to assist a handicapped child to benefit from special education, and includes speech pathology and audiology, psychological services, physical and occupational therapy, recreation, early identification and assessment of disabilities in children, counseling services, and medical services for diagnostic or evaluation purposes. The term also includes school health services, social work services in schools, and parent counseling and training.

(b) The terms used in this definition are defined as follows:

(1) "Audiology" includes:

(i) Identification of children with hearing loss;

(ii) Determination of the range, nature, and degree of hearing loss, including referral for medical or other professional attention for the habilitation of hearing;

(iii) Provision of habilitative activities, such as language habilitation, auditory training, speech reading (lip-reading), hearing evaluation, and speech conservation;

(iv) Creation and administration of programs for prevention of hearing loss;

(v) Counseling and guidance of pupils, parents, and teachers regarding hearing loss; and

(vi) Determination of the child's need for group and individual amplification, selecting and fitting an appropriate aid, and evaluating the effectiveness of amplification.

(2) "Counseling services" means services provided by qualified social workers, psychologists, guidance counselors, or other qualified personnel.

(3) "Early identification" means the implementation of a formal plan for identifying a disability as early as possible in a child's life.

(4) "Medical services" means services provided by a licensed physician to determine a child's medically related handicapping condition which results in the child's need for special education and related services.

(5) "Occupational therapy" includes:

(i) Improving, developing or restoring functions impaired or lost through illness, injury, or deprivation;

(ii) Improving ability to perform tasks for independent functioning when functions are impaired or lost . . .

(iii) Preventing, through early intervention, initial or further impairment or loss of function.

(6) "Parent counseling and training" means assisting parents in understanding the special needs of their child and providing parents with information about child development.

(7) "Physical therapy" means services provided by a qualified physical therapist.

(8) "Psychological services" include:

(i) Administering psychological and educational tests, and other assessment procedures;

(ii) Interpreting assessment results;

(iii) Obtaining, integrating, and interpreting information about child behavior and conditions relating to learning.

(iv) Consulting with other staff members in planning school programs to meet the special needs of children as indicated by psychological tests, interviews, and behavioral evaluations, and

(v) Planning and managing a program of psychological services, including psychological counseling for children and parents.

(9) "Recreation" includes:

(i) Assessment of leisure function;

(ii) Therapeutic recreation services;

(iii) Recreation programs in schools and community agencies; and

(iv) Leisure education.

(10) "School health services" means services provided by a qualified school nurse or other qualified person.

(11) "Social work services in schools" include:

(i) Preparing a social or developmental history on a handicapped child;

(ii) Group and individual counseling with the child and family;

(iii) Working with those problems in a child's living situation (home, school, and community) that affect the child's adjustment in school; and

(iv) Mobilizing school and community resources to enable the child to receive maximum benefit from his or her educational program.

(12) "Speech pathology" includes:

(i) Identification of children with speech or language disorders;

(ii) Diagnosis and appraisal of specific speech or language disorders;

(iii) Referral for medical or other professional attention necessary for the habilitation of speech or language disorders;

(iv) Provisions of speech and language services for the habilitation or prevention of communicative disorders; and

(v) Counseling and guidance of parents, children, and teachers regarding speech and language disorders.

(13) "Transportation" includes:

(i) Travel to and from school and between schools,

(ii) Travel in and around school buildings, and

(iii) Specialized equipment (such as special or adapted buses, lifts, and ramps), if required to provide special transportation for a handicapped child.
(20 U.S.C. 1401 (17))

Comment. With respect to related services, the Senate Report states:

The Committee bill provides a definition of "related services," making clear that all such related services may not be required for each individual child and that such term includes early identification and assessment of handicapping conditions and the provision of services to minimize the effects of such conditions.
(Senate Report No. 94–168, p. 12 (1975))

The list of related services is not exhaustive and may include other developmental, corrective, or supportive services (such as artistic and cultural programs, and art, music, and dance therapy), if they are required to assist a handicapped child to benefit from special education.

There are certain kinds of services which might be provided by persons from varying professional backgrounds and with a variety of operational titles, depending upon requirements in individual States. For example, counseling services might be provided by social workers, psychologists, or guidance counselors; and psychological testing might be done by qualified psychological examiners, psychometrists, or psychologists, depending upon State standards.

Each related service defined under this part may include appropriate administrative and supervisory activities that are necessary for program planning, management, and evaluation.

§ 300.14 Special education.

(a) (1) As used in this part, the term "special education" means specially designed instruction, at no cost to the parent, to meet the unique needs of a handicapped child, including classroom instruction, instruction in physical education, home instruction, and instruction in hospitals and institutions.

(2) The term includes speech pathology, or any other related service, if the service consists of specially designed instruction, at no cost to the parents, to meet the unique needs of a handicapped child, and is considered "special education" rather than a "related service" under State standards.

(3) The term also includes vocational education if it consists of specially designed instruction, at no cost to the parents, to meet the unique needs of a handicapped child.

(b) The terms in this definition are defined as follows:

(1) "At no cost" means that all specially designed instruction is provided without charge, but does not preclude incidental fees which are normally charged to non-handicapped students or their parents as a part of the regular education program.

(2) "Physical education" is defined as follows:

(i) The term means the development of:

(A) Physical and motor fitness;

(B) Fundamental motor skills and patterns; and

(C) Skills in aquatics, dance, and individual and group games and sports (including intramural and lifetime sports).

(ii) The term includes special physical education, adapted physical education, movement education, and motor development.
(20 U.S.C. 1401 (16))

(3) "Vocational education" means organized educational programs which are directly related to the preparation of individuals for paid or unpaid employment, or for additional preparation for a career requiring other than a baccalaureate or advanced degree.
(20 U.S.C. 1401 (16))

Comment. (1) The definition of "special education" is a particularly important one under these regulations, since a child is not handicapped unless he or she needs special education. (See the definition of "handicapped children" in § 300.5) The definition of "related services" (section 300.13) also depends on this definition, since a related service must be necessary for a child to benefit from special education. Therefore, if a child does not need special education, there can be no "related services," and the child (because not "handicapped") is not covered under the Act.

(2) The above definition of vocational education is taken from the Vocational Education Act of 1963, as amended by Pub. L. 94–482. Under that Act, "vocational education" includes industrial arts and consumer and homemaking education programs.

SUBPART B—STATE ANNUAL PROGRAM PLANS AND LOCAL APPLICATIONS

SUBPART C—SERVICES

Free Appropriate Public Education

§ 300.300 Timeliness for free appropriate public education.

(a) *General.* Each State shall insure that free appropriate public education is available to all handicapped children aged three through eighteen within the State not later than September 1, 1978, and to all handicapped children aged three through twenty-one within the State not later than September 1, 1980.

(b) *Age ranges 3–5 and 18–21.* This paragraph provides rules for applying the requirement in paragraph (a) of this section to handicapped children aged three, four, five, eighteen, nineteen, twenty, and twenty-one:

(1) If State law or a court order requires the State to provide education for handicapped children in any disability category in any of these age groups, the State must make a free appropriate public education available to all handicapped children of the same age who have that disability.

(2) If a public agency provides education to non-handicapped children in any of these age groups, it must make a free appropriate public education available to at least a proportionate number of handicapped children of the same age.

(3) If a public agency provides education to 50 percent or more of its handicapped children in any disability category in any of these age groups, it must make a free appropriate public education available to all of its handicapped children of the same age who have that disability.

(4) If a public agency provides education to a handicapped child in any of these age groups, it must make a free appropriate public education available to that child and provide that child and his or her parents all of the rights under Part B of the Act and this part.

(5) A State is not required to make a free appropriate public education available to a handicapped child in one of these age groups if:

(i) State law expressly prohibits, or does not authorize, the expenditure of public funds to provide education to nonhandicapped children in that age group; or

(ii) The requirement is inconsistent with a court order which governs the provision of free public education to handicapped children in that State.

(20 U.S.C. 1412(2)(B); Sen. Rept. No. 94–168 p. 19 (1975))

Comment. 1. The requirement to make free appropriate public education available applies to all handicapped children within the State who are in the age ranges required under § 300.300 and who need special education and related services. This includes handicapped children already in school and children with less severe handicaps, who are not covered under the priorities under § 300.321.

2. In order to be in compliance with § 300.300, each State must insure that the requirement to identify, locate, and evaluate all handicapped children is fully implemented by public agencies throughout the State. This means that before September 1, 1978, every child who has been referred or is on a waiting list for evaluation (including children in school as well as those not receiving an education) must be evaluated in accordance with §§ 300.530–300.533 of Subpart E. If, as a result of the evaluation, it is determined that a child needs special education and related services, an individualized education program must be developed for the child by September 1, 1978, and all other applicable requirements of this part must be met.

3. The requirement to identify, locate, and evaluate handicapped children (commonly referred to as the "child find system") was enacted on August 21, 1974, under Pub. L. 93–380. While each State needed time to establish and implement its child find system, the four year period between August 21, 1974, and September 1, 1978, is considered to be sufficient to insure that the system is fully operational and effective on a State-wide basis.

Under the statute, the age range for the child find requirement (0–21) is greater than the mandated age range for providing free appropriate public education (FAPE). One reason for the broader age requirement under "child find" is to enable States to be aware of and plan for younger children who will require special education and related services. It also ties in with the full educational opportunity goal requirement, which has the same age range as child find. Moreover, while a State is not required to provide "FAPE" to handicapped children below the age ranges mandated under § 300.300, the State may, at its discretion, extend services to those children, subject to the requirements on priorities under §§ 300.320–300.324.

§ 300.301 Free appropriate public education—methods and payments.

(a) Each State may use whatever State, local, Federal, and private sources of support are available in the State to meet the requirements of this part. For example, when it is necessary to place a handicapped child in a residential facility, a State could use joint agreements between the agencies involved for sharing the cost of that placement.

(b) Nothing in this part relieves an insurer or similar third party from an otherwise valid obligation to provide or to pay for services provided to a handicapped child.
(20 U.S.C. 1401 (18); 1412(2)(B))

§ 300.302 Residential placement.

If placement in a public or private residential program is necessary to provide special education and related services to a handicapped child, the program, including non-medical care and room and board, must be at no cost to the parents of the child.
(20 U.S.C. 1412(2)(B); 1413(a)(4)(B))

Comment. This requirement applies to placements which are made by public agencies for educational purposes, and includes placements in State-operated schools for the handicapped, such as a State school for the deaf or blind.

§ 300.303 Proper functioning of hearing aids.

Each public agency shall insure that the hearing aids worn by deaf and hard of hearing children in school are functioning properly.
(20 U.S.C. 1412(2)(B))

Comment. The report of the House of Representatives on the 1978 appropriation bill includes the following statement regarding hearing aids:

In its report on the 1976 appropriation bill the Committee expressed concern about the condition of hearing aids worn by children in public schools. A study done at the Committee's direction by the Bureau of Education for the Handicapped reveals that up

to one-third of the hearing aids are malfunctioning. Obviously, the Committee expects the Office of Education will ensure that hearing impaired school children are receiving adequate professional assessment, follow-up and services.
(House Report No. 95–381, p. 67 (1977))

§ 300.304 Full educational opportunity goal.

(a) Each State educational agency shall insure that each public agency establishes and implements a goal of providing full educational opportunity to all handicapped children in the area served by the public agency.

(b) Subject to the priority requirements under §§ 300.320–300.324, a State or local educational agency may use Part B funds to provide facilities, personnel, and services necessary to meet the full educational opportunity goal.
(20 U.S.C. 1412(2)(A); 1414(a)(1)(C))

Comment. In meeting the full educational opportunity goal, the Congress also encouraged local educational agencies to include artistic and cultural activities in programs supported under this part, subject to the priority requirements under §§ 300.320–300.324. This point is addressed in the following statements from the Senate Report on Pub. L. 94–142:

The use of the arts as a teaching tool for the handicapped has long been recognized as a viable, effective way not only of teaching special skills, but also of reaching youngsters who had otherwise been unteachable. The Committee envisions that programs under this bill could well include an arts component and, indeed, urges that local educational agencies include the arts in programs for the handicapped funded under this Act. Such a program could cover both appreciation of the arts by the handicapped youngsters, and the utilization of the arts as a teaching tool per se.

Museum settings have often been another effective tool in the teaching of handicapped children. For example, the Brooklyn Museum has been a leader in developing exhibits utilizing the heightened tactile sensory skill of the blind. Therefore, in light of the national policy concerning the use of museums in federally supported education programs enunciated in the Education Amendments of 1974, the Committee also urges local educational agencies to include museums in programs for the handicapped funded under this Act.
(Authority: Senate Report No. 94–168, p. 13 (1975))

§ 300.305 Program options.

Each public agency shall take steps to insure that its handicapped children have available to them the variety of educational programs and services available to non-handicapped children in the area served by the agency, including art, music, industrial arts, consumer and homemaking education, and vocational education.
(Authority: 20 U.S.C. 1412(2)(A); 1414(a)(1)(C))

Comment. The above list of program options is not exhaustive, and could include any program or activity in which nonhandicapped students participate. Moreover, vocational education programs must be specially designed if necessary to enable a handicapped student to benefit fully from those programs; and the set-aside funds under the Vocational Education Act of 1963, as amended by Pub. L. 94–482, may be used for this purpose. Part B funds may also be used, subject to the priority requirements under §§ 300.320–300.324.

§ 300.306 Nonacademic services.

(a) Each public agency shall take steps to provide nonacademic and extracurricular services and activities in such manner as is necessary to afford handicapped children an equal opportunity for participation in those services and activities.

(b) Nonacademic and extracurricular services and activities may include counseling services, athletics, transportation, health services, recreational activities, special interest groups or clubs sponsored by the public agency, referrals to agencies which provide assistance to handicapped persons, and employment of students, including both employment by the public agency and assistance in making outside employment available.

(Authority: 20 U.S.C. 1412(2)(A); 1414(a)(1)(C))

§ 300.307 Physical education.

(a) *General.* Physical education services, specially designed if necessary, must be made available to every handicapped child receiving a free appropriate public education.

(b) *Regular physical education.* Each handicapped child must be afforded the opportunity to participate in the regular physical education program available to non-handicapped children unless:

(1) The child is enrolled full time in a separate facility; or

(2) The child needs specially designed physical education, as prescribed in the child's individualized education program.

(c) *Special physical education.* If specially designed physical education is prescribed in a child's individualized education program, the public agency responsible for the education of that child shall provide the services directly, or make arrangements for it to be provided through other public or private programs.

(d) *Education in separate facilities.* The public agency responsible for the education of a handicapped child who is enrolled in a separate facility shall insure that the child receives appropriate physical education services in compliance with paragraphs (a) and (c) of this section.

(Authority: 20 U.S.C. 1401(16); 1412(5)(B); 1414(a)(6))

Comment. The Report of the House of Representatives on Pub. L. 94–142 includes the following statement regarding physical education:

Special education as set forth in the Committee bill includes instruction in physical education, which is provided as a matter of course to all non-handicapped children enrolled in public elementary and secondary schools. The Committee is concerned that although these services are available to and required of all children in our school systems, they are often viewed as a luxury for handicapped children. . . .

The Committee expects the Commissioner of Education to take whatever action is necessary to assure that physical education services are available to all handicapped children, and has specifically included physical education within the definition of special education to make clear that the Committee expects such services, specially designed where necessary, to be provided as an integral part of the educational program of every handicapped child.

(Authority: House Report No. 94–332, p. 9 (1975))

Priorities in the Use of Part B Funds

§ 300.320 Definitions of "first priority children" and "second priority children."

For the purposes of §§ 300.321–300.324, the term:

(a) "First priority children" means handicapped children who:

(1) Are in an age group for which the State must make available free appropriate public education under § 300.300; and

(2) Are not receiving any education.

(b) "Second priority children" means handicapped children, within each disability, with the most severe handicaps who are receiving an inadequate education.

(Authority: 20 U.S.C. 1412(3))

Comment. After September 1, 1978, there should be no second priority children, since States must insure, as a condition of receiving Part B funds for fiscal year 1979, that all handicapped children will have available a free appropriate public education by that date.

NOTE: The term "free appropriate public education," as defined in § 300.4 of Subpart A, means "special education and related services which . . . are provided in conformity with an individualized education program. . . . "

New "First priority children" will continue to be found by the State after September 1, 1978 through on-going efforts to identify, locate, and evaluate all handicapped children.

§ 300.321 Priorities.

(a) Each State and local educational agency shall use funds provided under Part B or the Act in the following order of priorities:

(1) To provide free appropriate public education to first priority children, including the identification, location, and evaluation of first priority children.

(2) To provide free appropriate public education to second priority children, including the identification, location, and evaluation of second priority children.

(3) To meet the other requirements in this part.

(b) The requirements of paragraph (a) of this section do not apply to funds which the State uses for administration under § 300.620.

(Authority: 20 U.S.C. 1411 (b)(1)(B),(b)(2)(B), (c)(1)(B),(c)(2)(A)(ii))

(c) State and local educational agencies may not use funds under Part B of the Act for preservice training.

(Authority: 20 U.S.C. 1413(a)(3); Senate Report No. 94–168, p. 34 (1975))

Comment. Note that a State educational agency as well as local educational agencies must use Part B funds (except the portion used for State administration) for the priorities. A State may have to set aside a portion of its Part B allotment to be able to serve newly identified first priority children.

After September 1, 1978, Part B funds may be used:

(1) To continue supporting child identification, location, and evaluation activities;

(2) To provide free appropriate public education to newly identified first priority children;

(3) To meet the full educational opportunities goal required under § 300.304, including employing additional personnel and providing inservice training, in order to increase the level, intensity and quality of services provided to individual handicapped children; and

(4) To meet the other requirements of Part B.

§ 300.322 First priority children—school year 1977–1978.

(a) In school year 1977–1978, if a major component of a first priority child's proposed educational program is not available (for example, there is no qualified teacher), the public agency responsible for the child's education shall:

(1) Provide an interim program of services for the child; and

(2) Develop an individualized education program for full implementation no later than September 1, 1978.

(b) A local educational agency may use Part B funds for training or other support services in school year 1977–1978 only if all of its first priority children have available to them at least an interim program of services.

(c) A State educational agency may use Part B funds for training or other support services in school year 1977–1978 only if all first priority children in the State have available to them at least an interim program of services.

(20 U.S.C. 1411 (b), (c))

Comment. This provision is intended to make it clear that a State or local educational agency may not delay placing a previously unserved (first priority) child until it has, for example, implemented an inservice training program. The child must be placed. After the child is in at least an interim program, the State or local educational agency may use Part B funds for training or other support services needed to provide that child with a free appropriate public education.

§ 300.323 Services to other children.

If a State or a local educational agency is providing free appropriate public education to all of its first priority children, that State or agency may use funds provided under Part B of the Act:

(a) To provide free appropriate public education to handicapped children who are not receiving any education and who are in the age groups not covered under § 300.300 in that State; or

(b) To provide free appropriate public education to second priority children; or

(c) Both.

(20 U.S.C. 1411 (b)(1)(B), (b)(2)(B), (c)(2)(A)(ii))

§ 300.324 Application of local educational agency to use funds for the second priority.

A local educational agency may use funds provided under Part B of the Act for second priority children, if it provides assurance satisfactory to the State educational agency in its application (or an amendment to its application);

(a) That all first priority children have a free appropriate public education available to them;

(b) That the local educational agency has a system for the identification, location, and evaluation of handicapped children, as described in its application; and

(c) That whenever a first priority child is identified, located, and evaluated, the local educational agency makes available a free appropriate public education to the child.

(20 U.S.C. 1411 (b)(1)(B), (c)(1)(B); 1414(a)(1)(C)(ii))

Individualized Education Programs

§ 300.340 Definition.

As used in this part, the term "individual-

ized education program" means a written statement for a handicapped child that is developed and implemented in accordance with §§ 300.341–300.349.

(20 U.S.C. 1401(19))

§ 300.341 State educational agency responsibility.

(a) *Public agencies.* The State educational agency shall insure that each public agency develops and implements an individualized education program for each of its handicapped children.

(b) *Private schools and facilities.* The State educational agency shall insure that an individualized education program is developed and implemented for each handicapped child who:

(1) Is placed in or referred to a private school or facility by a public agency; or

(2) Is enrolled in a parochial or other private school and receives special education or related services from a public agency.

(20 U.S.C. 1412 (4), (6); 1413(a)(4))

Comment. This section applies to all public agencies, including other State agencies (e.g., departments of mental health and welfare), which provide special education to a handicapped child either directly, by contract or through other arrangements. Thus, if a State welfare agency contracts with a private school or facility to provide special education to a handicapped child, that agency would be responsible for insuring that an individualized education program is developed for the child.

§ 300.342 When individualized education programs must be in effect.

(a) On October 1, 1977, and at the beginning of each school year thereafter, each public agency shall have in effect an individualized education program for every handicapped child who is receiving special education from that agency.

(b) An individualized education program must:

(1) Be in effect before special education and related services are provided to a child; and

(2) Be implemented as soon as possible following the meetings under § 300.343.

(20 U.S.C. 1412 (2)(B), (4), (6); 1414(a)(5); Pub. L. 94–142, Sec. 8(c) (1975))

Comment. Under paragraph (b)(2), it is expected that a handicapped child's individualized education program (IEP) will be implemented immediately following the meetings under § 300.343. An exception to this would be (1) when the meetings occur during the summer or a vacation period, or (2) where there are circumstances which require a short delay (e.g., working out transportation arrangements). However, there can be no undue delay in providing special education and related services to the child.

§ 300. 343 Meetings.

(a) *General.* Each public agency is responsible for initiating and conducting meetings for the purpose of developing, reviewing, and revising a handicapped child's individualized education program.

(b) *Handicapped children currently served.* If the public agency has determined that a handicapped child will receive special education during school year 1977–1978, a meeting must be held early enough to insure that an individualized education program is developed by October 1, 1977.

(c) *Other handicapped children.* For a handicapped child who is not included under paragraph (b) of this action, a meeting must be held within thirty calendar days of a determination that the child needs special education and related services.

(d) *Review.* Each public agency shall initiate and conduct meetings to periodically review each child's individualized education program and if appropriate revise its provisions. A meeting must be held for this purpose at least once a year.

(20 U.S.C. 1412(2)(B), (4), (6); 1414(a)(5))

Comment. The dates on which agencies must have individualized education programs (IEPs) in effect are specified in § 300.112 (October 1, 1977, and the beginning of each school year thereafter). However, except for new handicapped children (i.e., those evaluated and determined to need special education after October 1, 1977, the timing of meetings to develop, review, and revise IEPs is left to the discretion of each agency.

In order to have IEPs in effect by the dates in § 300.342, agencies could hold meetings at the end of the school year or during the summer preceding those dates. In meeting the October 1, 1977 timeline, meetings could be conducted up through the October 1 date. Thereafter, meetings may be held any time throughout the year, as long as IEPs are in effect at the beginning of each school year.

The statute requires agencies to hold a meeting at least once each year in order to review, and if appropriate revise, each child's IEP. The timing of those meetings could be on the anniversary date of the last IEP meeting on the child, but this is left to the discretion of the agency.

§ 300.344 Participants in meetings.

(a) *General.* The public agency shall insure that each meeting includes the following participants:

(1) A representative of the public agency, other than the child's teacher, who is qualified to provide, or supervise the provision of, special education.

(2) The child's teacher.

(3) One or both of the child's parents, subject to § 300.345.

(4) The child, where appropriate.

(5) Other individuals at the discretion of the parent or agency.

(b) *Evaluation personnel.* For a handicapped child who has been evaluated for the first time, the public agency shall insure:

(1) That a member of the evaluation team participates in the meeting; or

(2) That the representative of the public agency, the child's teacher, or some other

person is present at the meeting, who is knowledgeable about the evaluation procedures used with the child and is familiar with the results of the evaluation.
(20 U.S.C. 1401(19); 1412 (2)(B), (4), (6); 1414(a)(5))

Comment. 1. In deciding which teacher will participate in meetings on a child's individualized education program, the agency may wish to consider the following possibilities:

(a) For a handicapped child who is receiving special education, the "teacher" could be the child's special education teacher. If the child's handicap is a speech impairment, the "teacher" could be the speech-language pathologist.

(b) For a handicapped child who is being considered for placement in special education, the "teacher" could be the child's regular teacher, or a teacher qualified to provide education in the type of program in which the child may be placed, or both.

(c) If the child is not in school or has more than one teacher, the agency may designate which teacher will participate in the meeting.

2. Either the teacher or the agency representative should be qualified in the area of the child's suspected disability.

3. For a child whose primary handicap is a speech impairment, the evaluation personnel participating under paragraph (b)(1) of this section would normally be the speech-language pathologist.

§ 300.345 Parent participation.

(a) Each public agency shall take steps to insure that one or both of the parents of the handicapped child are present at each meeting or are afforded the opportunity to participate, including:

(1) Notifying parents of the meeting early enough to insure that they will have an opportunity to attend; and

(2) Scheduling the meeting at a mutually agreed on time and place.

(b) The notice under paragraph (a)(1) of this section must indicate the purpose, time, and location of the meeting, and who will be in attendance.

(c) If neither parent can attend, the public agency shall use other methods to insure parent participation, including individual or conference telephone calls.

(d) A meeting may be conducted without a parent in attendance if the public agency is unable to convince the parents that they should attend. In this case the public agency must have a record of its attempts to arrange a mutually agreed on time and place such as:

(1) Detailed records of telephone calls made or attempted and the results of those calls.

(2) Copies of correspondence sent to the parents and any responses received, and

(3) Detailed records of visits made to the parent's home or place of employment and the results of those visits.

(e) The public agency shall take whatever action is necessary to insure that the parent understands the proceedings at a meeting, including arranging for an interpreter for parents who are deaf or whose native language is other than English.

(f) The public agency shall give the parent, on request, a copy of the individualized education program.
(20 U.S.C. 1401(19); 1412 (2)(B), (4), (6); 1414(a)(5))

Comment. The notice in paragraph (a) could also inform parents that they may bring other people to the meeting. As indicated in paragraph (c), the procedure used to notify parents (whether oral or written or both) is left to the discretion of the agency, but the agency must keep a record of its efforts to contact parents.

§ 300.346 Content of individualized education program.

The individualized education program for each child must include:

(a) A statement of the child's present levels of educational performance;

(b) A statement of annual goals, including

short term instructional objectives;

(c) A statement of the specific special education and related services to be provided to the child, and the extent to which the child will be able to participate in regular educational programs;

(d) The projected dates for initiation of services and the anticipated duration of the services; and

(e) Appropriate objective criteria and evaluation procedures and schedules for determining, on at least an annual basis, whether the short term instructional objectives are being achieved.

(20 U.S.C. 1401(19); 1412 (2)(B), (4), (6); 1414(a)(5); Senate Report No. 94–168, p. 11 (1975))

§ 300.347 Private school placements.

(a) *Developing individualized education programs.* (1) Before a public agency places a handicapped child in, or refers a child to, a private school or facility, the agency shall initiate and conduct a meeting to develop an individualized education program for the child in accordance with § 300.343.

(2) The agency shall insure that a representative of the private school facility attends the meeting. If the representative cannot attend, the agency shall use other methods to insure participation by the private school or facility, including individual or conference telephone calls.

(3) The public agency shall also develop an individualized educational program for each handicapped child who was placed in a private school or facility by the agency before the effective date of these regulations.

(b) *Reviewing and revising individualized education programs.* (1) After a handicapped child enters a private school or facility, any meetings to review and revise the child's individualized education program may be initiated and conducted by the private school or facility at the discretion of the public agency.

(2) If the private school or facility initiates and conducts these meetings, the public agency shall insure that the parents and an agency representative:

(i) Are involved in any decision about the child's individualized education program; and

(ii) Agree to any proposed changes in the program before those changes are implemented.

(c) *Responsibility.* Even if a private school or facility implements a child's individualized education program, responsibility for compliance with this part remains with the public agency and the State educational agency.

(20 U.S.C. 1413(a)(4)(B))

§ 300.348 Handicapped children in parochial or other private schools.

If a handicapped child is enrolled in a parochial or other private school and receives special education or related services from a public agency, the public agency shall:

(a) Initiate and conduct meetings to develop, review, and revise an individualized education program for the child, in accordance with § 300.343; and

(b) Insure that a representative of the parochial or other private school attends each meeting. If the representative cannot attend, the agency shall use other methods to insure participation by the private school, including individual or conference telephone calls.

(20 U.S.C. 1413(a)(4)(A))

§ 300.349 Individualized education program—accountability

Each public agency must provide special education and related services to a handicapped child in accordance with an individualized education program. However, Part B of the Act does not require that any agency, teacher, or other person be held accountable if a child does not achieve the growth projected in the annual goals and objectives.

(20 U.S.C. 1412(2)(B); 1414(a) (5), (6); Cong. Rec. at H7152 (daily ed., July 21, 1975))

Comment. This section is intended to relieve concerns that the individualized education program constitutes a guarantee by the public agency and the teacher that a child will progress at a specified rate. However, this section does not relieve agencies and teachers from making good faith efforts to assist the child in achieving the objectives and goals listed in the individualized education program. Further, the section does not limit a parent's right to complain and ask for revisions of the child's program, or to invoke due process procedures, if the parent feels that these efforts are not being made.

Direct Service by the State Educational Agency

§ 300.360 Use of local educational agency allocation for direct services.

(a) A State educational agency may not distribute funds to a local educational agency, and shall use those funds to insure the provision of a free appropriate public education to handicapped children residing in the area served by the local educational agency, if the local educational agency, in any fiscal year:

(1) Is entitled to less than $7,500 for that fiscal year (beginning with fiscal year 1979);

(2) Does not submit an application that meets the requirements of §§ 300.220–300.240;

(3) Is unable or unwilling to establish and maintain programs of free appropriate public education;

(4) Is unable or unwilling to be consolidated with other local educational agencies in order to establish and maintain those programs; or

(5) Has one or more handicapped children who can best be served by a regional or State center designed to meet the needs of those children.

(b) In meeting the requirements of paragraph (a) of this section, the State educational agency may provide special education and related services directly, by contract, or through other arrangements.

(c) The excess cost requirements under §§ 300.182–300.186 do not apply to the State educational agency.
(20 U.S.C. 1411(c)(4); 1413(b); 1414(d))

Comment. Section 300.360 is a combination of three provisions in the statute (Sections 611(c)(4), 613(b), and 614(d)). This section focuses mainly on the State's administration and use of local entitlements under Part B.

The State educational agency, as a recipient of Part B funds is responsible for insuring that all public agencies in the State comply with the provisions of the Act, regardless of whether they receive Part B funds. If a local educational agency elects not to apply for its Part B entitlement, the State would be required to use those funds to insure that a free appropriate public education (FAPE) is made available to children residing in the area served by that local agency. However, if the local entitlement is not sufficient for this purpose, additional State or local funds would have to be expended in order to insure that "FAPE" and the other requirements of the Act are met.

Moreover, if the local educational agency is the recipient of any other Federal funds, it would have to be in compliance with Subpart D of the regulations for section 504 of the Rehabilitation Act of 1973 (34 CFR Part 104). It should be noted that the term "FAPE" has different meanings under Part B and section 504. For Example, under Part B, "FAPE" is a statutory term which requires special education and related services to be provided in accordance with an individualized education program (IEP). However, under section 504, each recipient must provide an education which includes services that are "designed to meet individual educational needs of handicapped persons as adequately as the needs of nonhandicapped persons are met. . . . " Those regulations state that implementation of an IEP, in accordance with Part B, is one means of meeting the "FAPE" requirement.

§ 300.361 Nature and location of services.

The State educational agency may provide special education and related services under § 300.360(a) in the manner and at the location it considers appropriate. However, the manner in which the education and services are provided must be consistent with the requirements of this part (including the least restrictive environment provisions in §§ 300.550–300.556 of Subpart E).
(20 U.S.C. 1414(d))

§ 300.370 Use of State educational agency allocation for direct and support services.

(a) The State shall use the portion of its allocation it does not use for administration to provide support services and direct services in accordance with the priority requirements under §§ 300.320–300.324.

(b) For the purposes of paragraph (a) of this section:

(1) "Direct services" means services provided to a handicapped child by the State directly, by contract, or through other arrangements.

(2) "Support services" includes implementing the comprehensive system of personnel development under §§ 300.380–300.388, recruitment and training of hearing officers and surrogate parents, and public information and parent training activities relating to a free appropriate public education for handicapped children.
(20 U.S.C. 1411(b)(2), (c)(2))

§ 300.371 State matching.

Beginning with the period July 1, 1978–June 30, 1979, and for each following year, the funds that a State uses for direct and support services under § 300.370 must be matched on a program basis by the State from funds other than Federal funds. This requirement does not apply to funds that the State uses under § 300.360.
(20 U.S.C. 1411(c)(2)(B), (c)(4)(B))

Comment. The requirement in § 300.371 would be satisfied if the State can document that the amount of State funds expended for each major program area (e.g., the comprehensive system of personnel development) is at least equal to the expenditure of Federal funds in that program area.

§ 300.372 Applicability of nonsupplanting requirement.

Beginning with funds appropriated for Fiscal Year 1979 and for each following Fiscal Year, the requirement in section 613(a)(9) of the Act, which prohibits supplanting with Federal funds, does not apply to funds that the State uses from its allocation under § 300.706(a) of Subpart G for administration, direct services, or support services.
(20 U.S.C. 1411(c)(3))

Comprehensive System of Personnel Development

§300.380 Scope of system.

Each annual program plan must include a description of programs and procedures for the development and implementation of a comprehensive system of personnel development which includes:

(a) The inservice training of general and special educational instructional, related services, and support personnel;

(b) Procedures to insure that all personnel necessary to carry out the purposes of the Act are qualified (as defined in § 300.12 of Subpart A) and that activities sufficient to carry out this personnel development plan are scheduled; and

(c) Effective procedures for acquiring and disseminating to teachers and administrators of programs for handicapped children significant information derived from educational research, demonstration, and similar projects, and for adopting, where appropriate, promising educational practices and materials developed through those projects.
(20 U.S.C. 1413(a)(3))

§ 300.381 Participation of other agencies and institutions.

(a) The State educational agency must insure that all public and private institutions of higher education, and other agencies and organizations (including representatives of handicapped, parent, and other advocacy organizations) in the state which have an interest in the preparation of personnel for the education of handicapped children, have an opportunity to participate fully in the development, review, and annual updating of the comprehensive system of personnel development.

(b) The annual program plan must describe the nature and extent of participation under paragraph (a) of this section and must describe responsibilities of the State educational agency, local educational agencies, public and private institutions of higher education, and other agencies:

(1) With respect to the comprehensive system as a whole, and

(2) With respect to the personnel development plan under § 300.383.
(20 U.S.C. 1412(7)(A): 1413(a)(3))

§ 300.382 Inservice training.

(a) As used in this section, "inservice training" means any training other than that received by an individual in a full-time program which leads to a degree.

(b) Each annual program plan must provide that the State educational agency:

(1) Conducts an annual needs assessment to determine if a sufficient number of qualified personnel are available in the State; and

(2) Initiates inservice personnel development programs based on the assessed needs of State-wide significance related to the implementation of the Act.

(c) Each annual program plan must include the results of the needs assessment under paragraph (b)(1) of this section, broken out by need for new personnel and need for retrained personnel.

(d) The State educational agency may enter into contracts with institutions of higher education, local educational agencies or other agencies, institutions, or organizations (which may include parent, handicapped, or other advocacy organizations), to carry out:

(1) Experimental or innovative personnel development programs;

(2) Development or modification of instructional materials; and

(3) Dissemination of significant information derived from educational research and demonstration projects.

(e) Each annual program plan must provide that the State educational agency insures that ongoing inservice training programs are available to all personnel who are engaged in the education of handicapped children, and that these programs include:

(1) The use of incentives which insure participation by teachers (such as released time, payment for participation, options for academic credit, salary step credit, certification renewal, or updating professional skills);

(2) The involvement of local staff; and

(3) The use of innovative practices which have been found to be effective.

(f) Each annual program plan must:

(1) Describe the process used in determining the inservice training needs of personnel engaged in the education of handicapped children;

(2) Identify the areas in which training is needed (such as individualized education programs, non-discriminatory testing, least restrictive environment, procedural safeguards, and surrogate parents);

(3) Specify the groups requiring training (such as special teachers, regular teachers, administrators, psychologists, speech-language pathologists, audiologists, physical education teachers, therapeutic recreation specialists, physical therapists, occupational therapists, medical personnel, parents, volunteers, hearing officers, and surrogate parents);

(4) Describe the content and nature of training for each area under paragraph (f)(2) of this section;

(5) Describe how the training will be pro-

vided in terms of (i) geographical scope (such as Statewide, regional, or local), and (ii) staff training source (such as college and university staffs, State and local educational agency personnel, and non-agency personnel);

(6) *Specify:* (i) The funding sources to be used, and

(ii) The time frame for providing it; and

(7) Specify procedures for effective evaluation of the extent to which program objectives are met.

(20 U.S.C. 1413(a)(3))

§ 300.383 Personnel development plan.

Each annual program plan must: (a) Include a personnel development plan which provides a structure for personnel planning and focuses on preservice and inservice education needs;

(b) Describe the results of the needs assessment under § 300.382(b)(1) with respect to identifying needed areas of training, and assigning priorities to those areas; and

(c) Identify the target populations for personnel development, including general education and special education instructional and administrative personnel, support personnel, and other personnel (such as paraprofessionals, parents, surrogate parents, and volunteers).

(20 U.S.C. 1413(a)(3))

§ 300.384 Dissemination.

(a) Each annual program plan must include a description of the State's procedures for acquiring, reviewing, and disseminating to general and special educational instructional and support personnel, administrators of programs for handicapped children, and other interested agencies and organizations (including parent, handicapped, and other advocacy organizations) significant information and promising practices derived from educational research, demonstration, and other projects.

(b) Dissemination includes:

(1) Making those personnel, administrators, agencies, and organizations aware of the information and practices;

(2) Training designed to enable the establishment of innovative programs and practices targeted on identified local needs; and

(3) Use of instructional materials and other media for personnel development and instructional programming.

(20 U.S.C. 1413(a)(3))

§ 300.385 Adoption of educational practices.

(a) Each annual program plan must provide for a statewide system designed to adopt, where appropriate, promising educational practices and materials proven effective through research and demonstration.

(b) Each annual program plan must provide for thorough reassessment of educational practices used in the State.

(c) Each annual program plan must provide for the identification of State, local, and regional resources (human and material) which will assist in meeting the State's personnel preparation needs.

(20 U.S.C. 1413(a)(3))

§ 300.386 [Reserved]

§ 300.387 Technical assistance to local educational agencies.

Each annual program plan must include a description of technical assistance that the State educational agency gives to local educational agencies in their implementation of the State's comprehensive system of personnel development.

(20 U.S.C. 1413(a)(3))

SUBPART D—PRIVATE SCHOOLS

Handicapped Children in Private Schools Placed or Referred by Public Agencies

§ 300.400 Applicability of §§ 300.401–300.403.

Sections 300.402–300.403 apply only to

handicapped children who are or have been placed in or referred to a private school or facility by a public agency as a means of providing special education and related services.

(20 U.S.C. 1413(a)(4)(B))

§ 300.401 Responsibility of State educational agency.

Each State educational agency shall insure that a handicapped child who is placed in or referred to a private school or facility by a public agency:

(a) Is provided special education and related services:

(1) In conformance with an individualized education program which meets the requirements under §§ 300.340–300.349 of Subpart C;

(2) At no cost to the parents; and

(3) At a school or facility which meets the standards that apply to State and local educational agencies (including the requirements in this part); and

(b) Has all of the rights of a handicapped child who is served by a public agency.

(20 U.S.C. 1413(a)(4)(B))

§ 300.402 Implementation by State educational agency.

In implementing § 300.401, the State educational agency shall:

(a) Monitor compliance through procedures such as written reports, onsite visits, and parent questionnaires;

(b) Disseminate copies of applicable standards to each private school and facility to which a public agency has referred or placed a handicapped child; and

(c) Provide an opportunity for those private schools and facilities to participate in the development and revision of State standards which apply to them.

(20 U.S.C. 1413(a)(4)(B))

§ 300.403 Placement of children by parents.

(a) If a handicapped child has available a free appropriate public education and the parents choose to place the child in a private school or facility, the public agency is not required by this part to pay for the child's education at the private school or facility. However, the public agency shall make services available to the child as provided under §§ 300.450–300.460.

(b) Disagreements between a parent and a public agency regarding the availability of a program appropriate for the child, and the question of financial responsibility, are subject to the due process procedures under §§ 300.500–300.514 of Subpart E.

(20 U.S.C. 1412(2)(B); 1415)

Handicapped Children in Private Schools Not Placed or Referred by Public Agencies

§300.450 Definition of "private school handicapped children."

As used in §§ 300.451–300.452, "private school handicapped children" means handicapped children enrolled in private schools or facilities other than handicapped children covered under §§ 300.400–300.403.

(20 U.S.C. 1413(a)(4)(A))

[45 FR 22531, Apr. 3, 1980. Redesignated at 45 FR 77368, Nov. 21, 1980]

§ 300.451 State educational agency responsibility

The State educational agency shall insure that—

(a) To the extent consistent with their number and location in the State, provision is made for the participation of private school handicapped children in the program assisted or carried out under this part by providing them with special education and related services; and

(b) The requirements in 34 CFR 76.651–76.663 of EDGAR are met.

(20 U.S.C. 1413(a)(4)(A))

[45 FR 22531, Apr. 3, 1980. Redesignated at 45 FR 77368, Nov. 21, 1980]

§ 300.452 Local educational agency responsibility.

(a) Each local educational agency shall provide special education and related services designed to meet the needs of private school handicapped children residing in the jurisdiction of the agency.

(Sec. 1413(a)(4)(A); 1414(a)(6))

[42 FR 42476, Aug. 23, 1977, as amended at 45 FR 22531, Apr. 3, 1980. Redesignated at 45 FR 77368, Nov. 21, 1980]

SUBPART E—PROCEDURAL SAFEGUARDS

Due Process Procedures for Parents and Children

§ 300.500 Definitions of "consent", "evaluation", and "personally identifiable".

As used in this part: "Consent" means that: (a) The parent has been fully informed of all information relevant to the activity for which consent is sought, in his or her native language, or other mode of communication;

(b) The parent understands and agrees in writing to the carrying out of the activity for which his or her consent is sought, and the consent describes that activity and lists the records (if any) which will be released and to whom; and

(c) The parent understands that the granting of consent is voluntary on the part of the parent and may be revoked at any time.

"Evaluation" means procedures used in accordance with §§ 300.530–300.534 to determine whether a child is handicapped and the nature and extent of the special education and related services that the child needs. The term means procedures used selectively with an individual child and does not include basic tests administered to or procedures used with all children in a school, grade, or class.

"Personally identifiable" means that information includes:

(a) The name of the child, the child's parent, or other family member;

(b) The address of the child;

(c) A personal identifier, such as the child's social security number or student number; or

(d) A list of personal characteristics or other information which would make it possible to identify the child with reasonable certainty.

(20 U.S.C. 1415, 1417(c))

§ 300.501 General responsibility of public agencies.

Each State educational agency shall insure that each public agency establishes and implements procedural safeguards which meet the requirements of §§ 300.500–300.514.

(20 U.S.C. 1415(a))

§ 300.502 Opportunity to examine records.

The parents of a handicapped child shall be afforded, in accordance with the procedures in §§ 300.562–300.569 an opportunity to inspect and review all education records with respect to:

(a) The identification, evaluation, and educational placement of the child, and

(b) The provision of a free appropriate public education to the child.

(20 U.S.C. 1415(b)(1)(A))

§ 300.503 Independent educational evaluation.

(a) *General.* (1) The parents of a handicapped child have the right under this part to obtain an independent educational evaluation of the child, subject to paragraphs (b) through (e) of this section.

(2) Each public agency shall provide to parents, on request, information about where an independent educational evaluation may be obtained.

(3) For the purposes of this part:

(i) "Independent educational evaluation" means an evaluation conducted by a qualified examiner who is not employed by the public agency responsible for the education of the child in question.

(ii) "Public expense" means that the public agency either pays for the full cost of the evaluation or insures that the evaluation is otherwise provided at no cost to the parent, consistent with § 300.301 of Subpart C.

(b) *Parent right to evaluation at public expense.* A parent has the right to an independent educational evaluation at public expense if the parent disagrees with an evaluation obtained by the public agency. However, the public agency may initiate a hearing under § 300.506 of this subpart to show that its evaluation is appropriate. If the final decision is that the evaluation is appropriate, the parent still has the right to an independent educational evaluation, but not at public expense.

(c) *Parent initiated evaluations.* If the parent obtains an independent educational evaluation at private expense, the results of the evaluation:

(1) Must be considered by the public agency in any decision made with respect to the provision of a free appropriate public education to the child, and

(2) May be presented as evidence at a hearing under this subpart regarding that child.

(d) *Requests for evaluations by hearing officers.* If a hearing officer requests an independent educational evaluation as part of a hearing, the cost of the evaluation must be at public expense.

(e) *Agency criteria.* Whenever an independent evaluation is at public expense, the criteria under which the evaluation is obtained, including the location of the evaluation and the qualifications of the examiner, must be the same as the criteria which the public agency uses when it initiates an evaluation.

(20 U.S.C. 1415(b)(1)(A))

§ 300.504 Prior notice; parent consent.

(a) *Notice.* Written notice which meets the requirements under § 300.505 must be

given to the parents of a handicapped child a reasonable time before the public agency:

(1) Proposes to initiate or change the identification, evaluation, or educational placement of the child or the provision of a free appropriate public education to the child, or

(2) Refuses to initiate or change the identification, evaluation, or educational placement of the child or the provision of a free appropriate public education to the child.

(b) *Consent.* (1) Parental consent must be obtained before:

(i) Conducting a preplacement evaluation; and

(ii) Initial placement of a handicapped child in a program providing special education and related services.

(2) Except for preplacement evaluation and initial placement, consent may not be required as a condition of any benefit to the parent or child.

(c) *Procedures where parent refuses consent.* (1) Where State law requires parental consent before a handicapped child is evaluated or initially provided special education and related services, State procedures govern the public agency in overriding a parent's refusal to consent.

(2) (i) Where there is no State law requiring consent before a handicapped child is evaluated or initially provided special education and related services, the public agency may use the hearing procedures in §§ 300.506–300.508 to determine if the child may be evaluated or initially provided special education and related services without parental consent.

(ii) If the hearing officer upholds the agency, the agency may evaluate or initially provide special education and related services to the child without the parent's consent, subject to the parent's rights under §§ 300.510–300.513.

(20 U.S.C. 1415(b)(1)(C), (D))

Comment. 1. Any changes in a child's special education program, after the initial placement, are not subject to parental consent under Part B, but are subject to the prior notice requirement in paragraph (a) and the individualized education program requirements in Subpart C.

2. Paragraph (c) means that where State law requires parental consent before evaluation or before special education and related services are initially provided, and the parent refuses (or otherwise withholds) consent, State procedures, such as obtaining a court order authorizing the public agency to conduct the evaluation or provide the education and related services, must be followed.

If, however, there is no legal requirement for consent outside of these regulations, the public agency may use the due process procedures under this subpart to obtain a decision to allow the evaluation or services without parental consent. The agency must notify the parent of its actions, and the parent has appeal rights as well as rights at the hearing itself.

§ 300.505 Content of notice.

(a) The notice under § 300.504 must include:

(1) A full explanation of all of the procedural safeguards available to the parents under Subpart E;

(2) A description of the action proposed or refused by the agency, an explanation of why the agency proposes or refuses to take the action, and a description of any options the agency considered and the reasons why those options were rejected;

(3) A description of each evaluation procedure, test, record, or report the agency uses as a basis for the proposal or refusal; and

(4) A description of any other factors which are relevant to the agency's proposal or refusal.

(b) The notice must be:

(1) Written in language understandable to the general public, and

(2) Provided in the native language of the parent or other mode of communication used by the parent, unless it is clearly not feasible to do so.

(c) If the native language or other mode of communication of the parent is not a written language, the State or local educational agency shall take steps to insure:

(1) That the notice is translated orally or by other means to the parent in his or her native language or other mode of communication;

(2) That the parent understands the content of the notice, and

(3) That there is written evidence that the requirements in paragraphs (c)(1) and (2) of this section have been met.

(20 U.S.C. 1415(b)(1)(D))

§ 300.506 Impartial due process hearing.

(a) A parent or a public educational agency may initiate a hearing on any of the matters described in § 300.504(a)(1) and (2).

(b) The hearing must be conducted by the State educational agency or the public agency directly responsible for the education of the child, as determined under State statute, State regulation, or a written policy of the State educational agency.

(c) The public agency shall inform the parent of any free or low-cost legal and other relevant services available in the area if:

(1) The parent requests the information; or

(2) The parent or the agency initiates a hearing under this section.

(20 U.S.C. 1416(b)(2))

Comment: Many States have pointed to the success of using mediation as an intervening step prior to conducting a formal due process hearing. Although the process of mediation is not required by the statute or these regulations, an agency may wish to suggest mediation in disputes concerning the identification, evaluation, and educational placement of handicapped children, and the provision of a free appropriate public education to those children. Mediations have been conducted by members of State educational agencies or local educational agency personnel who were not previously involved in the particular case. In many cases, mediation leads to resolution of differences between parents and agencies without the development of an adversarial relationship and with minimal emotional stress. However, mediation may not be used to deny or delay a parent's rights under this subpart.

§ 300.507 Impartial hearing officer.

(a) A hearing may not be conducted:

(1) By a person who is an employee of a public agency which is involved in the education or care of the child, or

(2) By any person having a personal or professional interest which would conflict with his or her objectivity in the hearing.

(b) A person who otherwise qualifies to conduct a hearing under paragraph (a) of this section is not an employee of the agency solely because he or she is paid by the agency to serve as a hearing officer.

(c) Each public agency shall keep a list of the persons who serve as hearing officers. The list must include a statement of the qualifications of each of those persons. (20 U.S.C. 1414(b)(2))

§ 300.508 Hearing rights.

(a) Any party to a hearing has the right to:

(1) Be accompanied and advised by counsel and by individuals with special knowledge or training with respect to the problems of handicapped children;

(2) Present evidence and confront, cross-examine, and compel the attendance of witnesses;

(3) Prohibit the introduction of any evidence at the hearing that has not been disclosed to that party at least five days before the hearing;

(4) Obtain a written or electronic verbatim record of the hearing;

(5) Obtain written findings of fact and decisions. (The public agency shall transmit those findings and decisions, after deleting any personally identifiable information, to the State advisory panel established under Subpart F).

(b) Parents involved in hearings must be given the right to:

(1) Have the child who is the subject of the hearing present; and

(2) Open the hearing to the public. (20 U.S.C. 1415(d))

§ 300.509 Hearing decision: appeal.

A decision made in a hearing conducted under this subpart is final, unless a party to the hearing appeals the decision under § 300.510 or § 300.511. (20 U.S.C. 1415(c))

§ 300.510 Administrative appeal: impartial review.

(a) If the hearing is conducted by a public agency other than the State educational agency, any party aggrieved by the findings and decision in the hearing may appeal to the State educational agency.

(b) If there is an appeal, the State educational agency shall conduct an impartial review of the hearing. The official conducting the review shall:

(1) Examine the entire hearing record;

(2) Insure that the procedures at the hearing were consistent with the requirements of due process;

(3) Seek additional evidence if necessary. If a hearing is held to receive additional evidence, the rights in § 300.508 apply;

(4) Afford the parties an opportunity for oral or written argument, or both, at the discretion of the reviewing official;

(5) Make an independent decision on completion of the review; and

(6) Give a copy of written findings and the decision to the parties.

(c) The decision made by the reviewing official is final, unless a party brings a civil action under § 300.512. (20 U.S.C. 1415 (c), (d); H. Rep. No. 94–664, at p. 49 (1975))

Comment. 1. The State educational agency may conduct its review either directly or through another State agency acting on its behalf. However, the State educational agency remains responsible for the final decision on review.

2. All parties have the right to continue to be represented by counsel at the State administrative review level, whether or not the reviewing official determines that a further hearing is necessary. If the reviewing official decides to hold a hearing to receive additional evidence, the other rights in § 300.508, relating to hearings, also apply.

§ 300.511 Civil action.

Any party aggrieved by the findings and decision made in a hearing who does not have the right to appeal under § 300.510 of this subpart, and any party aggrieved by the decision of a reviewing officer under § 300.510 has the right to bring a civil action under section 615(e)(2) of the Act.
(20 U.S.C. 1415)

§ 300.512 Timeliness and convenience of hearings and reviews.

(a) The public agency shall insure that not later than 45 days after the receipt of a request for a hearing:

(1) A final decision is reached in the hearing; and

(2) A copy of the decision is mailed to each of the parties.

(b) The State educational agency shall insure that not later than 30 days after the receipt of a request for a review:

(1) A final decision is reached in the review; and

(2) A copy of the decision is mailed to each of the parties.

(c) A hearing or reviewing officer may grant specific extensions of time beyond the periods set out in paragraphs (a) and (b) of this section at the request of either party.

(d) Each hearing and each review involving oral arguments must be conducted at a time and place which is reasonably convenient to the parents and child involved.
(20 U.S.C. 1415)

§ 300.513 Child's status during proceedings.

(a) During the pendency of any adminis-

trative or judicial proceeding regarding a complaint, unless the public agency and the parents of the child agree otherwise, the child involved in the complaint must remain in his or her present educational placement.

(b) If the complaint involves an application for initial admission to public school, the child, with the consent of the parents, must be placed in the public school program until the completion of all the proceedings.
(20 U.S.C. 1415(e)(3))

Comment. Section 300.513 does not permit a child's placement to be changed during a complaint proceeding, unless the parents and agency agree otherwise. While the placement may not be changed, this does not preclude the agency from using its normal procedures for dealing with children who are endangering themselves or others.

§ 300.514 Surrogate parents.

(a) *General.* Each public agency shall insure that the rights of a child are protected when:

(1) No parent (as defined in § 300.10) can be identified;

(2) The public agency, after reasonable efforts, cannot discover the whereabouts of a parent; or

(3) The child is a ward of the State under the laws of that State.

(b) *Duty of public agency.* The duty of a public agency under paragraph (a) of this section includes the assignment of an individual to act as a surrogate for the parents. This must include a method (1) for determining whether a child needs a surrogate parent, and (2) for assigning a surrogate parent to the child.

(c) *Criteria for selection of surrogates.* (1) The public agency may select a surrogate parent in any way permitted under State law.

(2) Public agencies shall insure that a person selected as a surrogate:

(i) Has no interest that conflicts with the

interest of the child he or she represents; and

(ii) Has knowledge and skills, that insure adequate representation of the child.

(d) *Non-employee requirement; compensation.* (1) A person assigned as a surrogate may not be an employee of a public agency which is involved in the education or care of the child.

(2) A person who otherwise qualifies to be a surrogate parent under paragraphs (c) and (d)(1) of this section, is not an employee of the agency solely because he or she is paid by the agency to serve as a surrogate parent.

(e) *Responsibilities.* The surrogate parent may represent the child in all matters relating to:

(1) The identification, evaluation, and educational placement of the child, and

(2) The provision of a free appropriate public education to the child.

(20 U.S.C. 1415(b)(1)(B))

Protection in Evaluation Procedures

§ 300.530 General.

(a) Each State educational agency shall insure that each public agency establishes and implements procedures which meet the requirements of §§ 300.530–300.534.

(b) Testing and evaluation materials and procedures used for the purposes of evaluation and placement of handicapped children must be selected and administered so as not to be racially or culturally discriminatory.

(20 U.S.C. 1412(5)(C))

§ 300.531 Preplacement evaluation.

Before any action is taken with respect to the initial placement of a handicapped child in a special education program, a full and individual evaluation of the child's educational needs must be conducted in accordance with the requirements of § 300.532.

(20 U.S.C. 1412(5)(C))

§ 300.532 Evaluation procedures.

State and local educational agencies shall

insure, at a minimum, that:

(a) Tests and other evaluation materials:

(1) Are provided and administered in the child's native language or other mode of communication, unless it is clearly not feasible to do so;

(2) Have been validated for the specific purpose for which they are used; and

(3) Are administered by trained personnel in conformance with the instructions provided by their producer;

(b) Tests and other evaluation materials include those tailored to assess specific areas of educational need and not merely those which are designed to provide a single general intelligence quotient;

(c) Tests are selected and administered so as best to ensure that when a test is administered to a child with impaired sensory, manual, or speaking skills, the test results accurately reflect the child's aptitude or achievement level or whatever other factors the test purports to measure, rather than reflecting the child's impaired sensory, manual, or speaking skills (except where those skills are the factors which the test purports to measure);

(d) No single procedure is used as the sole criterion for determining an appropriate educational program for a child; and

(e) The evaluation is made by a multidisciplinary team or group of persons, including at least one teacher or other specialist with knowledge in the area of suspected disability.

(f) The child is assessed in all areas related to the suspected disability, including, where appropriate, health, vision, hearing, social and emotional status, general intelligence, academic performance, communicative status, and motor abilities.

(20 U.S.C. 1412(5)(C))

Comment. Children who have a speech impairment as their primary handicap may not need a complete battery of assessments (e.g., psychological, physical, or adaptive behavior). However, a qualified speech-language pathologist would (1) evaluate each speech impaired child using procedures that are appropriate for the diagnosis and appraisal of speech and language disorders, and (2) where necessary, make referrals for additional assessments needed to make an appropriate placement decision.

§ 300.533 Placement procedures.

(a) In interpreting evaluation data and in making placement decisions, each public agency shall:

(1) Draw upon information from a variety of sources, including aptitude and achievement tests, teacher recommendations, physical condition, social or cultural background, and adaptive behavior;

(2) Insure that information obtained from all of these sources is documented and carefully considered;

(3) Insure that the placement decision is made by a group of persons, including persons knowledgeable about the child, the meaning of the evaluation data, and the placement options; and

(4) Insure that the placement decision is made in conformity with the least restrictive environment rules in §§ 300.550–300.554.

(b) If a determination is made that a child is handicapped and needs special education and related services, an individualized education program must be developed for the child in accordance with §§ 300.340–300.349 of Subpart C.
(20 U.S.C. 1412(5)(C); 1414(a)(5))

Comment. Paragraph (a)(1) includes a list of examples of sources that may be used by a public agency in making placement decisions. The agency would not have to use all the sources in every instance. The point of the requirement is to insure that more than one source is used in interpreting evaluation data and in making placement decisions. For example, while all of the named sources would have to be used for a child whose suspected disability is mental retardation, they would not be necessary for certain other handicapped children, such as a child who

has a severe articulation disorder as his primary handicap. For such a child, the speech-language pathologist, in complying with the multisource requirement, might use (1) a standardized test of articulation, and (2) observation of the child's articulation behavior in conversational speech.

§ 300.534 Reevaluation.

Each State and local educational agency shall insure:

(a) That each handicapped child's individualized education program is reviewed in accordance with §§ 300.340–300.349 of Subpart C, and

(b) That an evaluation of the child, based on procedures which meet the requirements under § 300.532, is conducted every three years or more frequently if conditions warrant or if the child's parent or teacher requests an evaluation.
(20 U.S.C. 1412(5)(c))

Additional Procedures for Evaluating Specific Learning Disabilities

§ 300.540 Additional team members.

In evaluating a child suspected of having a specific learning disability, in addition to the requirements of § 300.532, each public agency shall include on the multidisciplinary evaluation team:

(a) (1) The child's regular teacher; or

(2) If the child does not have a regular teacher, a regular classroom teacher qualified to teach a child of his or her age; or

(3) For a child of less than school age, an individual qualified by the State educational agency to teach a child of his or her age; and

(b) At least one person qualified to conduct individual diagnostic examinations of children, such as a school psychologist, speech-language pathologist, or remedial reading teacher.
(20 U.S.C. 1411 note)

[42 FR 65083, Dec. 29, 1977. Redesignated at 45 FR 77368, Nov. 21, 1980]

§ 300.541 Criteria for determining the existence of a specific learning disability.

(a) A team may determine that a child has a specific learning disability if:

(1) The child does not achieve commensurate with his or her age and ability levels in one or more of the areas listed in paragraph (a)(2) of this section, when provided with learning experiences appropriate for the child's age and ability levels; and

(2) The team finds that a child has a severe discrepancy between achievement and intellectual ability in one or more of the following areas:

(i) Oral expression;

(ii) Listening comprehension;

(iii) Written expression;

(iv) Basic reading skill;

(v) Reading comprehension;

(vi) Mathematics calculation; or

(vii) Mathematics reasoning.

(b) The team may not identify a child as having a specific learning disability if the severe discrepancy between ability and achievement is primarily the result of:

(1) A visual, hearing, or motor handicap;

(2) Mental retardation;

(3) Emotional disturbance; or

(4) Environmental, cultural or economic disadvantage.

(20 U.S.C. 1411 note)

[42 FR 65083, Dec. 29, 1977. Redesignated at 45 FR 77368, Nov. 21, 1980]

§ 300.542 Observation.

(a) At least one team member other than the child's regular teacher shall observe the child's academic performance in the regular classroom setting.

(b) In the case of a child of less than school age or out of school, a team member shall observe the child in an environment appropriate for a child of that age.

(20 U.S.C. 1411 note)

[42 FR 65083, Dec. 29, 1977. Redesignated at 45 FR 77368, Nov. 21, 1980]

§ 300.543 Written report.

(a) The team shall prepare a written report of the results of the evaluation.

(b) The report must include a statement of:

(1) Whether the child has a specific learning disability;

(2) The basis for making the determination;

(3) The relevant behavior noted during the observation of the child;

(4) The relationship of that behavior to the child's academic functioning;

(5) The educationally relevant medical findings, if any;

(6) Whether there is a severe discrepancy between achievement and ability which is not correctable without special education and related services; and

(7) The determination of the team concerning the effects of environmental, cultural, or economic disadvantage.

(c) Each team member shall certify in writing whether the report reflects his or her conclusion. If it does not reflect his or her conclusion, the team member must submit a separate statement presenting his or her conclusions.

(20 U.S.C. 1411 note)

[42 FR 65083, Dec. 29, 1977. Redesignated at 45 FR 77368, Nov. 21, 1980]

Least Restrictive Environment

§ 300.550 General.

(a) Each State educational agency shall insure that each public agency establishes and implements procedures which meet the requirements of §§ 300.550–300.556.

(b) Each public agency shall insure:

(1) That to the maximum extent appropriate, handicapped children, including children in public or private institutions or other care facilities are educated with children who are not handicapped, and

(2) That special classes, separate schooling or other removal of handicapped children from the regular educational environ-

ment occurs only when the nature or severity of the handicap is such that education in regular classes with the use of supplementary aids and services cannot be achieved satisfactorily.
(20 U.S.C. 1412(5)(B); 1414(a)(1)(C)(iv))

§ 300.551 Continuum of alternative placements.

(a) Each public agency shall insure that a continuum of alternative placements is available to meet the needs of handicapped children for special education and related services.

(b) The continuum required under paragraph (a) of this section must:

(1) Include the alternative placements listed in the definition of special education under § 300.13 of Subpart A (instruction in regular classes, special classes, special schools, home instruction, and instruction in hospitals and institutions), and

(2) Make provision for supplementary services (such as resource room or itinerant instruction) to be provided in conjunction with regular class placement.
(20 U.S.C. 1412(5)(B))

§ 300.552 Placements.

Each public agency shall insure that:

(a) Each handicapped child's educational placement: (1) Is determined at least annually,

(2) Is based on his or her individualized education program, and

(3) Is as close as possible to the child's home;

(b) The various alternative placements included under § 300.551 are available to the extent necessary to implement the individualized education program for each handicapped child;

(c) Unless a handicapped child's individualized education program requires some other arrangement, the child is educated in the school which he or she would attend if not handicapped; and

(d) In selecting the least restrictive environment, consideration is given to any po-

tential harmful effect on the child or on the quality of services which he or she needs.
(20 U.S.C. 1412(5)(B))

Comment. Section 300.552 includes some of the main factors which must be considered in determining the extent to which a handicapped child can be educated with children who are not handicapped. The overriding rule in this section is that placement decisions must be made on an individual basis. The section also requires each agency to have various alternative placements available in order to insure that each handicapped child receives an education which is appropriate to his or her individual needs.

The analysis of the regulations for Section 504 of the Rehabilitation Act of 1973 (34 CFR Part 104—Appendix, Paragraph 24) includes several points regarding educational placements of handicapped children which are pertinent to this section:

1. With respect to determining proper placements, the analysis states: "... it should be stressed that, where a handicapped child is so disruptive in a regular classroom that the education of other students is significantly impaired, the needs of the handicapped child cannot be met in that environment. Therefore regular placement would not be appropriate to his or her needs. . . . "

2. With respect to placing a handicapped child in an alternate setting, the analysis states that among the factors to be considered in placing a child is the need to place the child as close to home as possible. Recipients are required to take this factor into account in making placement decisions. The parent's right to challenge the placement of their child extends not only to placement in special classes or separate schools, but also to placement in a distant school, particularly in a residential program. An equally appropriate education program may exist closer to home; and this issue may be raised by the parent under the due process provisions of this subpart.

§ 300.553 Nonacademic settings.

In providing or arranging for the provision of nonacademic and extracurricular services and activities, including meals, recess periods, and the services and activities set forth in § 300.306 of Subpart C, each public agency shall insure that each handicapped child participates with non-handicapped children in those services and activities to the maximum extent appropriate to the needs of that child.
(20 U.S.C. 1412(5)(B))

Comment. Section 300.553 is taken from a new requirement in the final regulations for Section 504 of the Rehabilitation Act of 1973. With respect to this requirement, the analysis of the Section 504 Regulations includes the following statement: "[A new paragraph] specifies that handicapped children must also be provided nonacademic services in as integrated a setting as possible. This requirement is especially important for children whose educational needs necessitate their being solely with other handicapped children during most of each day. To the maximum extent appropriate, children in residential settings are also to be provided opportunities for participation with other children." (34 CFR Part 104—Appendix, Paragaraph 24.)

§ 300.554 Children in public or private institutions.

Each State educational agency shall make arrangements with public and private institutions (such as a memorandum of agreement or special implementation procedures) as may be necessary to insure that § 300.550 is effectively implemented.
(20 U.S.C. 1412(5)(B))

Comment. Under section 612(5)(B) of the statute, the requirement to educate handicapped children with nonhandicapped children also applies to children in public and private institutions or other care facilities. Each State educational agency

must insure that each applicable agency and institution in the State implements this requirement. Regardless of other reasons for institutional placement, no child in an institution who is capable of education in a regular public school setting may be denied access to an education in that setting.

§ 300.555 Technical assistance and training activities.

Each State educational agency shall carry out activities to insure that teachers and administrators in all public agencies:

(a) Are fully informed about their responsibilities for implementing § 300.550, and

(b) Are provided with technical assistance and training necessary to assist them in this effort.
(20 U.S.C. 1412(5)(B))

§ 300.556 Monitoring activities.

(a) The State educational agency shall carry out activities to insure that § 300.550 is implemented by each public agency.

(b) If there is evidence that a public agency makes placements that are inconsistent with § 300.550 of this subpart, the State educational agency:

(1) Shall review the public agency's justification for its actions, and

(2) Shall assist in planning and implementing any necessary corrective action.
(20 U.S.C. 1412(5)(B))

Confidentiality of Information

§ 300.560 Definitions.

As used in this subpart:

"Destruction" means physical destruction or removal of personal identifiers from information so that the information is no longer personally identifiable.

"Education records" means the type of records covered under the definition of "education records" in Part 99 of this title (the regulations implementing the Family Educational Rights and Privacy Act of 1974).

"Participating agency" means any agency

or institution which collects, maintains, or uses personally identifiable information, or from which information is obtained, under this part.

(20 U.S.C. 1412(2)(D); 1417(c))

§ 300.561 Notice to parents.

(a) The State educational agency shall give notice which is adequate to fully inform parents about the requirements under § 300.128 of Subpart B, including:

(1) A description of the extent to which the notice is given in the native languages of the various population groups in the State;

(2) A description of the children on whom personally identifiable information is maintained, the types of information sought, the methods the State intends to use in gathering the information (including the sources from whom information is gathered), and the uses to be made of the information;

(3) A summary of the policies and procedures which participating agencies must follow regarding storage, disclosure to third parties, retention, and destruction of personally identifiable information; and

(4) A description of all of the rights of parents and children regarding this information, including the rights under section 438 of the General Education Provisions Act and Part 99 of this title (the Family Educational Rights and Privacy Act of 1974, and implementing regulations).

(b) Before any major identification, location, or evaluation activity, the notice must be published or announced in newspapers or other media, or both, with circulation adequate to notify parents throughout the State of the activity.

(20 U.S.C. 1412(2)(D); 1417(c))

§ 300.562 Access rights.

(a) Each participating agency shall permit parents to inspect and review any education records relating to their children which are collected, maintained, or used by the agency under this part. The agency shall comply with a request without unnecessary delay and before any meeting regarding an individualized education program or hearing relating to the identification, evaluation, or placement of the child, and in no case more than 45 days after the request has been made.

(b) The right to inspect and review education records under this section includes:

(1) The right to a response from the participating agency to reasonable requests for explanations and interpretations of the records;

(2) The right to request that the agency provide copies of the records containing the information if failure to provide those copies would effectively prevent the parent from exercising the right to inspect and review the records; and

(3) The right to have a representative of the parent inspect and review the records.

(c) An agency may presume that the parent has authority to inspect and review records relating to his or her child unless the agency has been advised that the parent does not have the authority under applicable State law governing such matters as guardianship, separation, and divorce.

(20 U.S.C. 1412(2)(D); 1417(c))

§ 300.563 Record of access.

Each participating agency shall keep a record of parties obtaining access to education records collected, maintained, or used under this part (except access by parents and authorized employees of the participating agency), including the name of the party, the date access was given, and the purpose for which the party is authorized to use the records.

(20 U.S.C. 1412(2)(D); 1417(c))

§ 300.564 Records on more than one child.

If any education record includes information on more than one child, the parents of those children shall have the right to inspect and review only the information relating to their child or to be informed of that specific information.

(20 U.S.C. 1412(2)(D); 1417(c))

§ 300.565 List of types and locations of information.

Each participating agency shall provide parents on request a list of the types and locations of education records collected, maintained, or used by the agency.
(20 U.S.C. 1412(2)(D); 1417(c))

§ 300.566 Fees.

(a) A participating education agency may charge a fee for copies of records which are made for parents under this part if the fee does not effectively prevent the parents from exercising their right to inspect and review those records.

(b) A participating agency may not charge a fee to search for or to retrieve information under this part.
(20 U.S.C. 1412(2)(D); 1417(c))

§ 300.567 Amendment of records at parent's request.

(a) A parent who believes that information in education records collected, maintained, or used under this part is inaccurate or misleading or violates the privacy or other rights of the child, may request the participating agency which maintains the information to amend the information.

(b) The agency shall decide whether to amend the information in accordance with the request within a reasonable period of time of receipt of the request.

(c) If the agency decides to refuse to amend the information in accordance with the request it shall inform the parent of the refusal, and advise the parent of the right to a hearing under § 300.568.
(20 U.S.C. 1412(2)(D); 1417(c))

§ 300.568 Opportunity for a hearing.

The agency shall, on request, provide an opportunity for a hearing to challenge information in education records to insure that it is not inaccurate, misleading, or otherwise in violation of the privacy or other rights of the child.
(20 U.S.C. 1412(2)(D); 1417(c))

§ 300.569 Result of hearing.

(a) If, as a result of the hearing, the agency decides that the information is inaccurate, misleading or otherwise in violation of the privacy or other rights of the child, it shall amend the information accordingly and so inform the parent in writing.

(b) If, as a result of the hearing, the agency decides that the information is not inaccurate, misleading, or otherwise in violation of the privacy of other rights of the child, it shall inform the parent of the right to place in the records it maintains on the child a statement commenting on the information or setting forth any reasons for disagreeing with the decision of the agency.

(c) Any explanation placed in the records of the child under this section must:

(1) Be maintained by the agency as part of the records of the child as long as the record or contested portion is maintained by the agency; and

(2) If the records of the child or the contested portion is disclosed by the agency to any party, the explanation must also be disclosed to the party.
(20 U.S.C. 1412(2)(D); 1417(c))

§ 300.570 Hearing procedures.

A hearing held under § 300.568 of this subpart must be conducted according to the procedures under § 99.22 of this title.
(20 U.S.C. 1412(2)(D); 1417(c))

§ 300.571 Consent.

(a) Parental consent must be obtained before personally identifiable information is:

(1) Disclosed to anyone other than officials of participating agencies collecting or using the information under this part, subject to paragraph (b) of this section; or

(2) Used for any purpose other than meeting a requirement under this part.

(b) An educational agency or institution subject to Part 99 of this title may not release information from education records to participating agencies without parental consent unless authorized to do so under Part 99 of this title.

(c) The State educational agency shall include policies and procedures in its annual program plan which are used in the event that a parent refuses to provide consent under this section.
(20 U.S.C. 1412(2)(D); 1417(c))

§ 300.572 Safeguards.

(a) Each participating agency shall protect the confidentiality of personally identifiable information at collection, storage, disclosure, and destruction stages.

(b) One official at each participating agency shall assume responsibility for insuring the confidentiality of any personally identifiable information.

(c) All persons collecting or using personally identifiable information must receive training or instruction regarding the State's policies and procedures under § 300.129 of Subpart B and Part 99 of this title.

(d) Each participating agency shall maintain, for public inspection, a current listing of the names and positions of those employees within the agency who may have access to personally identifiable information.
(20 U.S.C. 1412(2)(D); 1417(c))

§ 300.573 Destruction of information.

(a) The public agency shall inform parents when personally identifiable information collected, maintained, or used under this part is no longer needed to provide educational services to the child.

(b) The information must be destroyed at the request of the parents. However, a permanent record of a student's name, address, and phone number, his or her grades, attendance record, classes attended, grade level completed, and year completed may be maintained without time limitation.
(20 U.S.C. 1412(2)(D); 1417(c))

Comment. Under § 300.573, the personally identifiable information on a handicapped child may be retained permanently unless the parents request that it be destroyed. Destruction of records is the best protection against improper and unauthorized disclosure. However, the records may be needed for other purposes. In informing parents about their rights under this section, the agency should remind them that the records may be needed by the child or the parents for social security benefits or other purposes. If the parents request that the information be destroyed, the agency may retain the information in paragraph (b).

§ 300.574 Children's rights.

The State educational agency shall include policies and procedures in its annual program plan regarding the extent to which children are afforded rights of privacy similar to those afforded to parents, taking into consideration the age of the child and type or severity of disability.
(20 U.S.C. 1412(2)(D); 1417(c))

Comment. Note that under the regulations for the Family Educational Rights and Privacy Act (45 CFR 99.4(a)), the rights of parents regarding education records are transferred to the student at age 18.

§ 300.575 Enforcement.

The State educational agency shall describe in its annual program plan the policies and procedures, including sanctions, which the State uses to insure that its policies and procedures are followed and that the requirements of the Act and the regulations in this part are met.
(20 U.S.C. 1412(2)(D); 1417(c))

§ 300.576 Department.

If the Department or its authorized representatives collect any personally identifiable information regarding handicapped children which is not subject to 5 U.S.C. 552a (The Privacy Act of 1974), the Secretary shall apply the requirements of 5 U.S.C. section 552a (b) (1)–(2), (4)–(11); (c); (d); (e)(1); (2); (3)(A), (B), and (D), (5)–(10); (h); (m); and (n), and the regulations implementing those provisions in Part 5b of this title.
(20 U.S.C. 1412(2)(D); 1417(c))

Department Procedures

§ 300.580 Opportunity for a hearing.

The Secretary gives a State educational agency reasonable notice and an opportunity for a hearing before taking any of the following actions:

(a) Disapproval of a State's annual program plan under § 300.113 of Subpart B.

(b) Withholding payments from a State under § 300.590 or under section 434(c) of the General Education Provisions Act.

(c) Waiving the requirement under § 300.589 of this subpart regarding supplementing and supplanting with funds provided under Part B of the Act.

(20 U.S.C. 1232c(c); 1413(a)(9)(B); 1413(c); 1416)

§§ 300.581–300.588. [Reserved]

§ 300.589 Waiver of requirement regarding supplementing and supplanting with Part B funds.

(a) Under sections 613(a)(9)(B) and 614(a)(2)(B)(ii) of the Act, State and local educational agencies must insure that Federal funds provided under Part B of the Act are used to supplement the level of State and local funds expended for the education of handicapped children, and in no case to supplant those State and local funds. Beginning with funds appropriated for fiscal year 1979 and for each following fiscal year, the nonsupplanting requirement only applies to funds allocated to local educational agencies. (See § 300.372.)

(b) If the State provides clear and convincing evidence that all handicapped children have available to them a free appropriate public education, the Secretary may waive in part the requirement under sections 613(a)(9)(B) and 614(a)(2)(B)(ii) of the Act if the Secretary concurs with the evidence provided by the State.

(c) If a State wishes to request a waiver, it must inform the Secretary in writing. The Secretary then provides the State with a finance and membership report form which provides the basis for the request.

(d) In its request for a waiver, the State shall include the results of a special study made by the State to obtain evidence of the availability of a free appropriate public education to all handicapped children. The special study must include statements by a representative sample of organizations which deal with handicapped children, and parents and teachers of handicapped children, relating to the following areas:

(1) The adequacy and comprehensiveness of the State's system for locating, identifying, and evaluating handicapped children, and

(2) The cost to parents, if any, for education for children enrolled in public and private day schools, and in public and private residential schools and institutions, and

(3) The adequacy of the State's due process procedures.

(e) In its request for a waiver, the State shall include finance data relating to the availability of a free appropriate public education for all handicapped children, including:

(1) The total current expenditures for regular education programs and special education programs by function and by source of funds (State, local, and Federal) for the previous school year, and

(2) The full-time equivalent membership of students enrolled in regular programs and in special programs in the previous school year.

(f) The Secretary considers the information which the State provides under paragraphs (d) and (e) of this section, along with any additional information he may request, or obtain through on-site reviews of the State's education programs and records, to determine if all children have available to them a free appropriate public education, and if so, the extent of the waiver.

(g) The State may request a hearing under §§ 300.580–300.583 with regard to any final action by the Secretary under this section. (20 U.S.C. 1411(c)(3); 1413(a)(9)(B))

SUBPART F—STATE ADMINISTRATION

Education of the Handicapped Act Amendments of 1986 P.L. 99–457

TITLE I—HANDICAPPED INFANTS AND TODDLERS

SEC. 101. ADDITION OF A NEW PART RELATING TO HANDICAPPED INFANTS AND TODDLERS.

(a) AMENDMENT—The Act is amended by inserting after the part added by section 316 the following new part:

PART H—HANDICAPPED INFANTS AND TODDLERS
Findings and Policy

SEC. 671. (a) FINDINGS.—The Congress finds that there is an urgent and substantial need—*(20 USC 1471)*

(1) to enhance the development of handicapped infants and toddlers and to minimize their potential for developmental delay,

(2) to reduce the educational costs to our society, including our Nation's schools, by minimizing the need for special education and related services after handicapped infants and toddlers reach school age,

(3) to minimize the likelihood of institutionalization of handicapped individuals and maximize the potential for their independent living in society, and

(4) to enhance the capacity of families to meet the special needs of their infants and toddlers with handicaps,

(b) POLICY—It is therefore the policy of the United States to provide financial assistance to States—

(1) to develop and implement a statewide, comprehensive, coordinated, multidisciplinary, interagency program of early intervention services for handicapped infants and toddlers and their families,

(2) to facilitate the coordination of payment for early intervention services from Federal, State, local, and private sources (including public and private insurance coverage), and

(3) to enhance its capacity to provide quality early intervention services and expand and improve existing early intervention services being provided to handicapped infants, toddlers, and their families.

Definitions

SEC. 672. As used in this part—*(20 USC 1472)*

(1) The term "handicapped infants and toddlers" means individuals from birth to age 2, inclusive, who need early intervention services because they—

(A) are experiencing developmental delays, as measured by appropriate diagnostic instruments and procedures in one or more of the following areas: Cognitive development, physical development, language and speech development, psychosocial development, or self-help skills, or

(B) have a diagnosed physical or mental condition which has a high probability of resulting in developmental delay.

Such term may also include, at a State's discretion, individuals from birth to age 2, inclusive, who are at risk of having substantial developmental delays if early intervention services are not provided.

(2) "Early intervention services" are developmental services which—

(A) are provided under public supervision,

(B) are provided at no cost except where Federal or State law provides for a system of payments by families, including a schedule of sliding fees,

(C) are designed to meet a handicapped infant's or toddler's developmental needs in any one or more of the following areas:

(i) physical development,

(ii) cognitive development,

(iii) language and speech development,

(iv) psycho-social development, or

(v) self-help skills,

(D) meet the standards of the State, including the requirements of this part,

(E) include—

(i) family training, counseling, and home visits,

(ii) special instruction,

(iii) speech pathology and audiology,

(iv) occupational therapy,

(v) physical therapy,

(vi) psychological services,

(vii) case management services,

(viii) medical services only for diagnostic or evaluation purposes,

(ix) early identification, screening, and assessment services, and

(x) health services necessary to enable the infant or toddler to benefit from the other early intervention services,

(F) are provided by qualified personnel, including—

(i) special educators,

(ii) speech and language pathologists and audiologists,

(iii) occupational therapists,

(iv) physical therapists,

(v) psychologists,

(vi) social workers,

(vii) nurses, and

(viii) nutritionists, and

(G) are provided in conformity with an individualized family service plan adopted by accordance with section 677.

(3) The term "developmental delay" has the meaning given such term by a State under section 676(b)(1).

(4) The term "Council" means the State Interagency Coordinating Council established under section 682.

General Authority

SEC. 673. The Secretary shall, in accordance with this part, make grants to States (from their allocations under section 684) to assist each State to develop a statewide, comprehensive, coordinated, multidisciplinary, interagency system to provide early intervention services for handicapped infants and toddlers and their families. *(20 USC 1473)*

General Eligibility

SEC. 674. In order to be eligible for a grant under section 673 for any fiscal year, a State shall demonstrate to the Secretary (in its application under section 678) that the State has established a State Interagency Coordinating Council which meets the requirements of section 682. *(20 USC 1474)*

Continuing Eligibility

[Five-year phase-in plan omitted]

Requirements For Statewide System

SEC. 676. (a) IN GENERAL.—A statewide system of coordinated, comprehensive, multidisciplinary, interagency programs providing appropriate early intervention services to all handicapped infants and toddlers and their families shall include the minimum components under subsection (b). *(20 USC 1476)*

(b) MINIMUM COMPONENTS.—The statewide system required by subsection (a) shall include, at a minimum—

(1) a definition of the term "developmentally delayed" that will be used by the State in carrying out programs under this part,

(2) timetables for ensuring that appropriate early intervention services will be available to all handicapped infants and toddlers in the State before the beginning of the fifth year of a State's participation under this part,

(3) a timely, comprehensive, multidisciplinary evaluation of the functioning of each handicapped infant and toddler in the State and the needs of the families to appropriately assist in the development of the handicapped infant or toddler,

(4) for each handicapped infant and toddler in the State, an individualized family service plan in accordance with section 677, including case management services in accordance with such service plan,

(5) a comprehensive child find system, consistent with part B, including a system for making referrals to service providers that includes timelines and provides for the participation by primary referral sources,

(6) a public awareness program focusing on early identification of handicapped infants and toddlers,

(7) a central directory which includes early intervention services, resources, and experts available in the State and research and demonstration projects being conducted in the State,

(8) a comprehensive system of personnel development,

(9) a single line of responsibility in a lead agency designated or established by the Governor for carrying out—

(A) the general administration, supervision, and monitoring of programs and activities receiving assistance under section 673 to ensure compliance with this part,

(B) the identification and coordination of all available resources within the State from Federal, State, local and private sources,

(C) the assignment of financial responsibility to the appropriate agency,

(D) the development of procedures to ensure that services are provided to handicapped infants and toddlers and their families in a timely manner pending the resolution of any disputes among public agencies or service providers,

(E) the resolution of intra- and interagency disputes, and

(F) the entry into formal interagency agreements that define the financial responsibility of each agency for paying for early intervention services (consistent with State law) and procedures for resolving disputes and that include all additional components necessary to ensure meaningful cooperation and coordination,

(10) a policy pertaining to the contracting or making of other arrangements with service providers to provide early intervention services in the State, consistent with the provisions of this part, including the contents of the application used and the conditions of the contract or other arrangements,

(11) a procedure for securing timely reimbursement of funds used under this part in accordance with section 681(a),

(12) procedural safeguards with respect to programs under this part as required by section 680, and procedures relating to the establishment and maintenance of standards to ensure that personnel necessary to carry out this part are appropriately and adequately prepared and trained, including—

(A) the establishment and maintenance of standards which are consistent with any State approved or recognized certification, licensing, registration, or other comparable requirements which apply to the area in which such personnel are providing early intervention services, and

(B) to the extent such standards are not based on the highest requirements in the State applicable to a specific profession or discipline, the steps the State is taking to require the retraining or hiring of personnel that meet appropriate professional requirements in the State, and

(14) a system for compiling data on the numbers of handicapped infants and toddlers and their families in the State in need of appropriate early intervention services (which may be based on a sampling of data), the numbers of such infants and toddlers and their families served, the types of services provided (which may be based on a sampling of data), and other information required by the Secretary.

Individualized Family Service Plan

SEC. 677. (a) ASSESSMENT AND PROGRAM DEVELOPMENT.—Each handicapped infant or toddler and the infant or toddler's family will receive — *(20 USC 1477)*

(1) a multidisciplinary assessment to unique needs and the identification of services appropriate to meet such needs, and

(2) a written individualized family service plan developed by a multidisciplinary team, including the parent or guardian, as required by subsection (d).

(b) PERIODIC REVIEW.—The individualized family service plan shall be evaluated once a year and the family shall be provided a review of the plan at 6 month-intervals (or more often where appropriate based on infant and toddler and family needs).

(c) PROMPTNESS AFTER ASSESSMENT.—The individualized family service plan shall be developed within a reasonable time after the assessment required by subsection (a)(1) is completed. With the parent's consent, early intervention services may commence prior to the completion of such assessment.

(d) CONTENT OF PLAN.—The individualized family service plan shall be in writing and contain—

(1) a statement of the infant's or toddler's present levels of physical development, cognitive development, language and speech development, psycho-social development, and self-help skills, based on acceptable objective criteria,

(2) a statement of the family's strengths and needs relating to enhancing the development of the family's handicapped infant or toddler,

(3) a statement of the major outcomes expected to be achieved for the infant and toddler and the family, and the criteria, procedures, and timelines used to determine the degree to which progress toward achieving the outcomes are being made and whether modifications or revisions of the outcomes or services are necessary,

(4) a statement of specific early intervention services necessary to meet the unique needs of the infant or toddler and the family, including the frequency, intensity, and the method of delivering services,

(5) the projected dates for initiation of services and the anticipated duration of such services,

(6) the name of the case manager from the profession most immediately relevant to the infant's and toddler's or family's needs who will be responsible for the implementation of the plan and coordination with other agencies and persons, and

(7) the steps to be taken supporting the transition of the handicapped toddler to services provided under part B to the extent such services are considered appropriate. *(20 USC 1411)*

Procedural Safeguards

SEC. 680. The procedural safeguards required to be included in a statewide system under section 676(b)(12) shall provide, at a minimum, the following: *(20 USC 1480)*

(1) The timely administrative resolution of complaints by parents. Any party aggrieved by the findings and decision regarding an administrative complaint shall have the right to bring a civil action with respect to the complaint, which action may be brought in any State court of competent jurisdiction or in a district court of the United States without regard to the amount in controversy. In any action brought under this paragraph, the court shall receive the records of the administrative proceedings, shall hear additional evidence at the request of a party, and, basing its decision on the preponderance of the evidence, grant such relief as the court determines is appropriate.

(2) The right to confidentiality of personally identifiable information.

(3) The opportunity for parents and a guardian to examine records relating to assessment, screening, eligibility determinations, and the development and implementation of the individualized family service plan.

(4) Procedures to protect the rights of the handicapped infant and toddlers whenever the parents or guardian of the child are not known or unavailable or the child is a ward of the State, including the assignment of an individual (who shall not be an employee of the State agency providing services) to act as a surrogate for the parents or guardian.

(5) Written prior notice to the parents or guardian of the handicapped infant or toddler whenever the State agency or service provider proposes to initiate or change or refuses to initiate or change the identification, evaluation, placement, or the provision of appropriate early intervention services to the handicapped infant or toddler.

(6) Procedures designed to assure that the notice required by paragraph (5) fully informs the parents or guardian, in the parents' or guardian's native language, unless it clearly is not feasible to do so, of all procedures available pursuant to this section.

(7) During the pendency of any proceeding or action involving a complaint, unless the State agency and the parents or guardian otherwise agree, the child shall

continue to receive the appropriate early intervention services currently being provided or if applying for initial services shall receive the services not in dispute.

TITLE II—HANDICAPPED CHILDREN AGED 3 TO 5

SEC. 201. PRE-SCHOOL GRANTS.

(a) AMENDMENT.—Section 619 of the Act (20 U.S.C. 1419) is amended to read as follows:

Pre-school Grants

SEC. 619. (a)(1) For fiscal years 1987 through 1989 (or fiscal year 1990 if the Secretary makes a grant under this paragraph for such fiscal year) the Secretary shall make a grant to any State which—

(A) has met the eligibility requirements of section 612, *(20 USC 1412)*

(B) has a State plan approved under section 613, and *(20 USC 1413)*

(C) provides special education and related services to handicapped children ages three to five inclusive.

[Funding formula—phase-in omitted]

Index